D1422495

MOTOR and SENSORY PROCESSES of LANGUAGE

NEUROPSYCHOLOGY AND NEUROLINGUISTICS

a series of books edited by **Harry A. Whitaker**

MOTOR and SENSORY PROCESSES of LANGUAGE

Edited by

Eric Keller
Centre de recherche, Centre Hospitalier Côte-des-Neiges, Montreal, Canada

Myrna Gopnik
McGill University

LEA LAWRENCE ERLBAUM ASSOCIATES, PUBLISHERS
1987 Hillsdale, New Jersey   London

Lawrence Erlbaum Associates, Inc., Publishers
365 Broadway
Hillsdale, New Jersey 07642

Library of Congress Cataloging-in-Publication Data

Main entry under title:

Motor and sensory processes of language.

  Includes indexes.
  1. Language disorders. 2. Neuropsychology.
I. Keller, Eric. II. Gopnik, Myrna.
RC423.M617 1986   612′.78   85-20657
ISBN 0-89859-631-9

Printed in the United States of America
10 9 8 7 6 5 4 3 2 1

Contents

List of Contributors

JAMES H. ABBS • *Speech Motor Control Laboratories, Waisman Center, Madison, WI, 53706*

SANDRA BLACK • *Room A4034, Sunnybrooke Medical Center, 2075 Bayview Avenue, Toronto, ON M4N 3M5, Canada*

SHEILA E. BLUMSTEIN • *Department of Linguistics, Brown University, Box 1978, Providence, RI 02912*

DANIEL BUB • *Department of Neurology, Montreal Neurological Institute, 3801 University Street, Montreal, QC H3A 2B4, Canada*

J. DAVID CAPLAN • *Department of Neurology, Montreal Neurological Institute, 3801 University Street, Montreal, QC H3A 2B4, Canada*

DAVID COOKE • *Department of Physiology, University of Western Ontario, Medical Sciences Bldg., London, ON N6A 5C2, Canada*

MYRNA GOPNIK • *Department of Linguistics, McGill University, 1001 Sherbrooke St. West, Montreal, QC H3A 1G5, Canada*

VINCENT L. GRACCO • *Speech Motor Control Laboratories, Waisman Center, Madison, WI 53706*

JANICE HOWELL • *Department of Clinical Neurological Sciences, St. Joseph's Hospital, London, ON N6A 4V2, Canada*

YVES JOANETTE • *Centre de recherche, Centre Hospitalier Côte-des-Neiges, 4565 Queen Mary, Montreal, QC H3W 1W5, Canada*

ERIC KELLER • *Centre de recherche, Centre Hospitalier Côte-des-Neiges, 4565 Queen Mary, Montreal, QC H3W 1W5, Canada*

J. A. SCOTT KELSO • *Department of Psychology, Florida Atlantic University, Boca Raton, FL 34431*

ANDREW KERTESZ • *Department of Clinical Neurological Sciences, St. Joseph's Hospital, London, ON N6A 4V2, Canada*

ANDRÉ ROCH LECOURS • *Centre de recherche, Centre Hospitalier Côte-des-Neiges, 4565 Queen Mary, Montreal, QC H3W 1W5, Canada*

JOHN C. MARSHALL • *Neuropsychology Unit, The Radcliffe Infirmary, Woodstock Rd., Oxford, OX2 6HE, Great Britain*

JEAN-LUC NESPOULOUS • *Centre de recherche, Centre Hospitalier Côte-des-Neiges, 4656 Queen Mary, Montreal, QC H3W 1W5, Canada*

DAVID J. OSTRY • *Department of Psychology, McGill University, 1204 Ave. Dr. Penfield, Montreal, QC H3A 1B1, Canada*

MICHEL PARADIS • *Department of Linguistics, McGill University, 1001 Sherbrooke St. West, Montreal, QC H3A 1G5, Canada*

DOMINIQUE PIOGER • *Centre de recherche, Centre Hospitalier Côte-des-Neiges, 4565 Queen Mary, Montreal, QC H3W 1W5, Canada*

STEFANIE SHATTUCK-HUFNAGEL • *Research Laboratory of Electronics, Massachusetts Institute of Technology, Cambridge, MA 02139*

BERNADETTE SKA • *Centre de recherche, Centre Hospitalier Côte-des-Neiges, 4656 Queen Mary, Montreal, QC H3W 1W5, Canada*

BETTY TULLER • *Department of Psychology, Florida Atlantic University, Boca Raton, FL 34431*

Introduction:
The Neuropsychology of
Motor and Sensory
Processes of Language

Eric Keller
*Centre de recherche, Center Hospitalier Côte-des-Neiges and
Université du Québec à Montréal*

Myrna Gopnik
McGill University

Until about 1970, neuropsychological and neurolinguistic research remained largely rooted in its medical origins and pursued a tradition of taxonomic distinction of language behaviors.

This approach to language had evolved from the diagnosis of neurological dysfunctions, and it defined classes of behaviors primarily by their degree of impairment through insults to various parts of the brain. For example, articulation behaviors were systematically distinguished from comprehension behaviors in this tradition, because one type of patient (the Broca's aphasic) regularly showed disturbed articulation in the presence of essentially intact auditory comprehension, whereas another type of patient (the Wernicke's aphasic) had a relatively greater comprehension disturbance, accompanied by a lesser articulation impairment. During a century and a half, this approach proved to be invaluable for patient classification and for distinguishing those cognitive and linguistic functions that can be selectively impaired through a neurological lesion.

However, as neuropsychological and neurolinguistic concerns expanded into a search for larger models of real-time language functions in the brain, the taxonomic tradition began to give way to the information-processing approach. In this perspective, various subsystems of human functioning are proposed on the basis of both, normal and neurally impaired behavior, and an attempt is made to understand the effects of a neurological lesion as the interaction of normal, pathological, and compensatory processes. A disorder such as Broca's aphasia might thus be seen as a partially compensated impairment of the articulatory programming process, a language function that can be defined on the independent basis of slips of the tongue of normal speakers and experiments in articulatory phonetics.

MOTOR AND SENSORY PROCESSES OF LANGUAGE

In the forefront of this change in research emphasis has been the study of motor and sensory language processes. These processes are easier to represent symbolically than are most other higher functions, and thus admit more readily of experimental verification, statistical analysis, and theoretical manipulation. Further, the study of these processes often provides insights into the functioning of associated, more central processes, and because they show considerable complexity, they are excellent representatives of higher mental processes in general.

A variety of empirical approaches and theoretical presuppositions are typically brought to bear on these questions. Empirically, error frequencies on specific tasks in normal and neurologically impaired populations, reaction times, kinematic and perceptual measures, as well as neurophysiological and neuroanatomical evidence, forms the rich source of data considered in connection with these issues. Theoretically, the research has been guided by notions originating in linguistics, psycholinguistics, cognitive psychology, phonetics, neurology, and neurophysiology. Yet despite the sometimes bewildering variety of empirical and theoretical arguments, some lines of general agreement are beginning to emerge concerning how neuropsychological phenomena should be understood.

First of all, real-time language processes are clearly modular in nature. This has been demonstrated not only through differential neural impairment, but also by means of detailed analyses of normal speech and perception errors. This is not surprising, because physiological and anatomical evidence bearing on linguistic as well as non-linguistic functions in humans and animals leads us to fully expect modular functioning in language. Today, the question is no longer whether language processes are modular, but which components are to be distinguished, how sharply the components are demarcated from each other, how they operate internally, and how they communicate among themselves.

Secondly, and even more fundamentally, there is general agreement concerning the desirability of understanding language processes in terms of their real-time, or "on-line," functioning. Researchers in this domain specifically address questions of how real-time language processes should be conceived when constrained by time and when interacting with learning and memory processes. This work is a natural complement to the work being done in theoretical linguistics, where the aim is to discover the universal properties that underlie all grammars of natural languages, irrespective of time and memory constraints.

Finally, there is wide agreement in this field that theories of language processing must ultimately link up with theories of brain function. Although points of view differ as to the degree of correspondence that can presently be documented for a given language process, there is little dispute about the desirability of this conceptual link, about the pertinence of information from lesions to circumscribed portions of the brain, and about the relevance of neurophysiological and behavioral experiments on motor and sensory processes similar to those used in language. Gone are the days, one may hope, where noted psychologists publicly insisted that it did not matter whether language was processed by the brain or by the big toe.

THE HISTORICAL CONTEXT

Present-day concerns in this domain can thus be seen to be coalescing around a perspective of real-time, modular language processes mediated by the brain. It is useful to consider the development of this view in the context of the large-scale conceptual changes that have permeated the behavioral sciences during the past 20 years.

Prior to 1960, all human and animal behavior, no matter whether motoric, sensory, or cognitive, tended to be interpreted in terms of real-time processes of very great generality. In this, the so-called behaviorist or associative chain view, stimulus A was seen as giving rise to a learned response B, which in turn could evoke learned response C. For A to occur, it did not matter whether B or C was meaningfully or physiologically related to A, just that it had been learned as a regular contingency of A; further, any action was thought to be motivated by the animal's immediate "need" to reduce a fundamental drive, such as hunger, thirst, or sexual desire.

It was in their application to language that these notions were most clearly shown to be inadequate. One of the first major critiques came from the noted physiological psychologist Lashley (1951), who pointed out that an associative chain notion of motor action could not explain spoonerisms (because associative chain theories make no provision for speech plannning), and that associative chain control would be too slow to account for measured delay times in limb movements. In another celebrated critique, Chomsky (1957) took exception to a number of aspects of behaviorist theory, such as the notion that language learning should be contingent on the need to reduce a given drive. He reflected a growing sentiment in the behavioral sciences; in

1953, Harlow had summarized a large number of observations showing that contrary to behaviorist expectations, simians do worse at learning various cognitive tasks when in physiological need than when not obviously affected by a primary drive. Other authors, such as the European ethologists, pointed out that responses differed from species to species and depended on the existence of predispositions toward such behaviors. Although not directly concerned with language, they prepared the terrain for Lenneberg (1967) and Chomsky (1968), who argued convincingly that language, too, depends on a special predisposition for its development.

From the profound reevaluation of the understanding of human and animal behavior that ensued, two divergent, yet ultimately compatible lines of research have emerged. One of these research endeavors is to identify the extent, the internal structure and the content of these predispositions toward the development of given behaviors in various specific domains. In the domain of language, this approach has been pursued within the Chomskyan framework, which examines in detail the species-specific innate constraints on constructing grammars, constraints that are claimed to be autonomous and not derivable from general cognitive functions. In the domain of social behavior, there has been a similar attempt by sociobiologists to account for specific behavior patterns toward which organisms might be predisposed. Although the existence of predisposition in one domain does not necessarily argue for the existence of predispositions in another, these two research endeavors are inspired by the same fundamental question.

The other major research trend is to examine the real-time processes of behavioral functioning. As exemplified primarily by research in physiological psychology, perception and motor control, this trend is concerned with establishing the real-time functional and neurophysiological events associated with a given process. In language, this means attempting to pursue the path of perceived linguistic events through its functional sequence of sensation, perception, and comprehension (mediated by cranial nerve, brain stem, thalamic, and cortical structures), and to chart out the path of produced linguistic events from intention through planning to motor processing (involving the cortex, the central gray structures, the cerebellum, and the brain stem).

Although the two research traditions presently tend to involve separate practitioners, different research tools and heterogeneous conceptual presuppositions, it is inevitable that the two manners of understanding language will ultimately have to converge. This is because language can only be manifested through the interaction between predisposition and real-time processing: language develops spontaneously through predisposition, and the predisposition only becomes evident through real-time language use. A full understanding of language can thus only emerge from an appreciation of research results of both approaches to this question.

THE PRESENT VOLUME

The chapters in this volume were contributed by a group of dynamic and resourceful representatives of the neuropsychological process approach to language research. The purpose of this volume is to collect chapters that represent the state of the art in this domain both theoretically and empirically, and that bring together researchers who, despite their different backgrounds, present a coherent and contemporary view of the motor and sensory processes of language.

Two major concerns characterize these chapters. Some authors, particularly those focusing on motor processes, are concerned with how to describe the details of language processing. Novel conceptions of processing mechanics are presented in chapters by Shattuck-Hufnagel, Bub, Keller, and Kelso and Tuller, and established processing hypotheses are examined by Nespoulous, Joanette, Ska, Caplan and Lecours, Caplan, Gracco and Abbs, and Ostry and Cooke. Some other contributors, especially those working in the domain of sensory processes, have focused on the issue of modularity: chapters by Bub, Marshall, Blumstein, and Paradis provide further details on the functional independence (as well as the interdependence) of various subcategories of the motor and sensory processes of language.

The book opens with a report by Lecours, Nespoulous, and Pioger on Jacques Lordat (chapter 1), a hitherto practically unknown early aphasiologist. Lordat was an insightful observer of neuropsychological phenomena (the authors call him "the first cognitive neuropsychologist"), who lived in southern France in the middle of the 19th century and probably published his first aphasiological treatise some 40 years before Broca's celebrated report of 1865. All but ignored by the Parisian neurological establishment, it appears that Lordat was instrumental in launching the modern aphasiological tradition.

The section on motor processes begins with chapter 2 by Stefanie Shattuck-Hufnagel; she summarizes her previous theoretical contributions to a speech production model, derived from spontaneous speech errors in normal speech (spoonerisms, etc.). In her present contribution, she argues that errors that exchange a single phoneme provide powerful evidence in favor of word-onset consonants forming a separate processing class. Shattuck-Hufnagel integrates these results into a "slot-and-filler" model of speech production, whereby word-onset consonants form one type of slot in the motoric matrix into which words are copied as they are transferred from planning to motor processes during speech production.

The study by Nespoulous, Joanette, Ska, Caplan, and Lecours (chapter 3) examines phonological errors on repetition and oral reading tasks for conduction and Broca's aphasics. This comparison is of importance to our understanding of speech production because it confirms previous analyses that suggested that errors of conduction aphasics probably occur at the interface between planning and motor processes, whereas errors of Broca's aphasics are more indicative of motoric impairments. In a detailed statistical analysis, the authors show that the errors of conduction aphasics are essentially unpatterned, whereas those of Broca's aphasics show systematic tendencies likely to be related to motoric difficulties (devoicing and changes in place of articulation). These results lend credence to what seemed at the time to be a somewhat risky hypothesis that suggested that vowel errors of Broca's aphasics (which show a lowering tendency) are primarily indicative of motoric execution difficulties (Keller, 1975, 1978).

Chapter 4 by Bub, Black, Howell, and Kertesz investigates the question of the relative independence of language modules with respect to two specific processes, a central process specifying lexical information to be used in speaking and writing, and a more peripheral planning process charged with cumulating, or buffering, this information prior to motor outputting. By comparing meaningful and nonsense word production by three neurologically impaired patients, and by eliminating alternative hypotheses, the authors arrive at a very specific hypothesis of the impairment. They show on the one hand, that the patients' difficulties are best explained by assuming a decaying output trace in the planning buffer, and on the other hand, that these impairments are partially compensated (or even overcompensated) by information furnished to the planning buffer by the lexical process.

Caplan's contribution (chapter 5) is concerned with developing a model for word production that accounts for the data and is consistent with current linguistic theory. In order to test several proposed models, he uses data from a conduction aphasic. Caplan shows that this data is inconsistent with several of the proposed models. However, it is consistent with a model that includes a level of representation of the underlying phonological form of the word. Such a representation is necessary for the construction of adequate phonological theories of normal language. The patient's disturbance can therefore best be accounted for within the framework of a linguistically rich model. Caplan claims that this model has further implications, for example in accounting for dyslexia. The existence of an abstract, underlying phonological representation is justified both at the theoretical and the empirical level.

Keller's chapter (6) provides a transition between the immediately preceding contributions, which are primarily of relevance to neurological speech impairments, and the directly succeeding chapters that treat normal speech production. An integrated hypothesis for speech motor control is outlined on the basis of a review of the main currents of recent research on normal speech processes, as well as by considering some relevant neurophysiological data; neurological speech impairments are then related to the proposed speech processes. In this manner, the chapter attempts to relate information from a large variety of sources to the question of what specific operations are pre-

formed by the various planning and motor processes in real-time speech production, and tries to characterize neurological impairments in the light of the
proposed operations.

Gracco and Abbs (chapter 7) contribute a chapter that takes this approach
yet one step further. By concentrating on processes concerned with the integration of sensory and motor information in speech, the authors painstak-
ingly review literature indicating likely neuroanatomical pathways mediating
these processes. The combined effect of the reviewed information is overwhelming; with respect to strongly motoric or strongly sensory language
functions, progress is clearly being made in charting out the likely neuronal
structures subserving those functions.

Kelso and Tuller's chapter (8) takes us into another major current of contemporary thinking in speech motor control, a conception of speech in terms
of the kinetic interactions of the participating neuromuscular structures. In
previous papers (Kelso & Tuller, 1981; Kelso, Tuller, & Harris, 1983), these
authors presented arguments and experimental evidence in favor of a strong
interaction between central and peripheral components of speech. In contradistinction to the common assumption that the speech event is fully specified
at central processing levels, these authors have argued that several aspects of
speech production, such as control over speech rate and over the coordination between various articulatory organs, are in fact achieved by biasing a set
of fairly peripheral neuromuscular programs. In the present chapter, they ex-
pand on these concepts by arguing that the timing of all articulatory events
(not merely the general speech rate) can be explained in terms of processes intrinsic to the articulatory system's kinetic behavior.

A similar theoretical position emerges from chapter 9 by Ostry and Cooke.
Although more central events may be usefully characterized in terms of phonemic or syllabic events, the specification of articulatory events will bring
into play such kinematic variables as duration, displacement, and velocity.
Because the interaction between these variables is likely to be specified in
manners that are not unique to speech, but that can be observed for all motor
actions, it is of interest to examine whether speech and limb movements share
systematic properties of motor control. Indeed, the contribution by Ostry
and Cooke is most revealing in this respect; the authors show that the tongue
and arm movements of the same subject can be described by a single function
relating velocity, duration, and extent of displacement ("movement amplitude") to all speech or arm movement variables, such as variations of rate,
stress, and phonemes in speech, or variations in the duration of arm movements. The existence of such "grand" functions poses a provocative challenge
to the researcher seeking to relate planning events at the phonemic level to
motor events at the kinematic level.

The last three chapters in this volume are most directly concerned with the
question of modularity. Marshall (chapter 10) addresses the question of the

modularity of various motorsensory language processes with respect to reading and writing. He shows that the acquired (adult) dyslexias and dysgraphias can impair distinctive processing routes in writing from written text, and that phonological and graphemic processes in speech and writing are probably largely independent from each other.

Blumstein (chapter 11) is also concerned with sensory processes and she addresses similar questions, though from a different perspective. With respect to her own extensive studies in phonemic perception and its breakdown, she demonstrates that linguistic auditory perception is clearly different from general auditory performance. Aphasics, for instance, have no problem distinguishing non-speech sounds, whereas patients with auditory agnosia do, and peformance on speech stimuli is not necessarily correlated with performance on similar non-speech, or synthesized stimuli. Yet just as in speech production processing, auditory processing for language is subject to interaction with more central processes; whereas aphasic reaction times on a lexical decision task were shorter for meaningful than for nonsense words (as in normal performance), it showed additional traits reflective of the phonetic impairment typical of these patients.

Finally, chapter 12 by Paradis summarizes some of the most surprising aspects of the modularity of language processes. In Japanese patients with neurological impairments of language, the disorder can affect *kanji* (ideographic) reading and writing independently from *kana* (syllabic) reading and writing. Also, aphasia can impair one language nearly independently of another language, sometimes in alternating fashion. As Paradis maintains, this is indicative of fairly independent processing for different language systems in at least some polyglots. Moreover, relatively independent processing may exist for each orthographic system within each language system.

THE FUTURE

In view of the considerable progress that has been made over the last 15 years in the domain of the neuropsychology of language, it may be of interest to consider some potential future developments in this field.

Just as some of the most important recent gains have been due to the advent of novel techniques of relating mental processes to brain function (dichotic listening, CT-scans, event-related EEG potential, etc.), certain of the future developments in this domain will no doubt be related to further technical improvements in observational techniques. PET scans, nuclear magnetic raditation (NMR), blood flow measurements, intracranial neural recordings and magnetoencephalography (and likely others as well), will be certain to extend and deepen our understanding of the relation between brain function and language processing and its impairments. To take just one of these techniques in some more detail, consider the measurement of magneto-encapholagraphic potentials, which is of particular interest to students of the relationship between brain and language functioning. In contrast to EEG event-related potentials, which represent the summation of electric activity over large portions of the cranium, magnetic currents result from the electric activity of relatively small neuronal pools; as a result, it becomes possible to localize more precisely the activity of neuron pools involved in specific language processes than it has been through EEG. It is evident already that this technique is capable of identifying fairly specific and localizable neuron pools related to various aspects of language processing (see Beatty, Richer, & Barth, in press).

Another probable development is the emergence of a coherent theoretical statement, which will characterize the functions of motor and sensory language processes in considerable detail. Skeletal hypotheses of speech production first emerged a few years ago from the analysis of spontaneous speech errors; more recently, we have witnessed the integration of findings from neurologically impaired populations. If this volume is any indication, we will soon witness an even grander integration of observations, coalescing notions bearing upon central and peripheral processing into a single hypothesis, and predictive of events observed in normal, aphasic, dysarthric and acquisitional language behaviors. One important area of present imprecision that such a hypothesis will have to deal with is the relative distribution of "intelligence" in the system. What processing is possible in the more peripheral modules of speech production and perception, and what aspects must be reserved for more central processes? How, and to what degree are these responsibilities shared? And how much information is conveyed from one module to another?

Also, there is no doubt that more work will be devoted to an exploration of the relation between language processing, memory, and learning. As psychology has broken away from the shackles of the rat learning model, and has begun to examine more systematically memory loss through neurological impairment, avenues of commonality have developed that permit a productive interplay of hypotheses concerning memory functions and language processes. To which degree, for instance, is the difference between procedural and declarative memory reflected in differential impairments of function and content words (agrammatism vs. anomia)? To which extent is the difference between procedural and declarative memory types conditioned by their strong or weak association with motor processes, and ultimately, temporal constraints acting upon processing speed? It seems evident that questions of this nature can be usefully addressed with existing observational techniques, and that they provide a promising avenue of further exploration.

And finally, computer modeling of language processes will be certain to come into its own right. Hampered by the difficulties of representing a large set of complex, parallel language processing functions on machines that are still largely built around single, serial processors, computer modelling of natural language production processes has to date been of little theoretical impact in psycho- and neurolinguistics. But toward the end of the decade, when large-scale parallel processors (100 or more) are likely to become available, it will be possible to experiment with the simulation of real-time interactions between several language processing modules. In a relatively short time, in fact, there may not be much choice in the matter. Theories will attain such complexity that the only way of predicting a pattern of interaction between processing functions, or their impairment, may be by means of an astute simulation of language production or language reception processes.

To sum up, it is evident that the study of real-time language processes has now attained vigorous maturity. Kuhn (1970) argued that a given scientific domain comes into its own when it develops a set of reliable demonstrations of empirical fact, what can be called its own "paradigmatic demonstrations." Just such demonstrations are beginning to emerge in this domain, such as the distinction of planning and motor processes on the basis of spontaneous speech errors, or the demonstration of continuous articulatory feedback by means of the perturbation paradigm.

But perhaps even more significantly, it appears that a group of researchers are presently developing various aspects of what is very much beginning to look like a coherent framework of language processing notions. Upon careful reading of the contributions to this volume, it will be found that whether authors state their theoretical presuppositions explicitly or not, they tend to work within a set of overlapping hypotheses. No longer concerned with testing hypotheses derived from a sister science, these researchers are pursuing a theoretical and empirical purpose of their own.

The solid achievements that are reflected in these pages, and the excellent promise of further developments, bode well for the future of the neuropsychology of language.

REFERENCES

Beatty, J., Richer, F., & Barth, D. S. (in press). Magnetoencephalography. In M. G. H. Colse, S. W. Porges, & E. Donchin (Eds.), *Psychophysiology: Systems, processes, and applications. Vol. I: Systems.* New York: Guilford Press.

Chomsky, N. (1957). Review of Skinner's Verbal Behavior. *Language, 35,* 26–58.

Chomsky, N. (1968). *Language and mind.* New York: Harcourt, Brace & World.

Harlow, H. F. (1953). Mice, monkeys, men, and motives. *Psychological Review, 60,* 23–32.

Keller, E. (1975). *Vowel errors in aphasia.* Unpublished Ph.D. thesis, University of Toronto.

Keller, E. (1978). Parameters for vowel substitutions in aphasia. *Brain and Language, 5,* 265–285.

Kelso, J. A. S., & Tuller, B. (1981). Toward a theory of apractic syndromes. *Brain and Language, 12,* 224–245.

Kelso, J. A. S., Tuller, B., & Harris, K. (1983). A "dynamic pattern" perspective on the control and coordination of movement. In P. F. MacNeilage (Ed.), *The production of speech.* (pp. 137-173). New York: Springer-Verlag.

Kertesz, A. (1983). Issues in localization. In A. Kertesz (Ed.), *Localization in neuropsychology* (pp. 1-20). London: Academic Press.

Kuhn, T. S. (1970). *The structures of scientific revolutions.* (2nd edition, enlarged). Chicago: The University of Chicago Press.

Lashley, K. S. (1951). The problem of serial order in behavior. In L. A. Jeffress (Ed.), *Cerebral mechanisms in behavior* (pp. 112-136). New York: Wiley.

Lenneberg, E. H. (1967). *Biological foundations of language.* New York: Wiley.

1 Jacques Lordat or the Birth of Cognitive Neuropsychology

André Roch Lecours
Jean-Luc Nespoulous
Dominique Pioger
Laboratoire Théophile–Alajouanine
Centre de recherche du Centre hospitalier Côte–des–Neiges
Université de Montréal

ABSTRACT

A few aspects of Jacques Lordat's life, personal experience of aphasia, interactions with his contemporaries, teachings, and scientific influence are outlined. Lordat is presented as a (if not the) founder of aphasiology. It is underlined that his approach to aphasia was very much akin to that of modern cognitive neuropsychology.

Jacques Lordat (Fig. 1.1) was born in Tournay, near Tarbes, in the Hautes-Pyrénées, on February 11th, 1773. In 1793 he became a military hospital student in surgery ("admis dans les hôpitaux militaires comme élève en chirurgie") (Larousse, 1878); thus, part or all of the training which led to his title of military surgeon ("chirurgien militaire") took place in Plaisance, Gers, where, according to Bayle (1939), Lordat was the disciple of a Doctor Broca.

Now, Schiller (1979) points out that "Broca" is not a common name and that the Broca family (which included a number of soldiers and doctors) was a tightly knit group. However, one only has to glance at a map of France (Fig. 1.2) to see that Plaisance is less than 150 kilometers south of Sainte-Foy–la–Grande, Gironde, where Pierre Paul Broca was born in 1824 and where his family had in all likelihood dwelt since the second half of the 16th century (Schiller, 1979). One wonders if young Lordat's first mentor, Doctor Broca of Plaisance, lived long enough to keep an eye on the earlier phases of

FIG. 1.1   Jacques Lordat teaching at the Faculty of Montpellier (circa 1860).

his disciple's medical career. One also wonders when, and in what circumstances, Pierre Paul Broca—whose father, Jean-Pierre dit Benjamin, was also a medical doctor—first heard about speech disorders resulting from brain lesions.

Lordat soon left Plaisance to study medicine at the famous Faculty of Montpellier, which in those days was considered by many scholars to outrank the faculty of Paris. Lordat's link to the Montpellier School of Medicine was a long lasting one. In 1797, at the age of 24, he received his diploma of Doctor in Medicine. Two years later, after having served as a prosector, he was teaching at the Faculty as a "Professeur libre." Tenure came in 1811 when, then aged 38, Lordat was appointed "Professeur agrégé de médicine opératoire." In 1813, when Dumas died, Lordat succeeded him as "Professeur titulaire de la chaire de physiologie," an appointment that he retained for half a century (including the period when he served as Dean of the Faculty; Bayle, 1939), that is, until a little before his 90th birthday. It was Lordat's overt opinion that, just like the cardinals of the Roman church, the professors of great medical schools should never retire (Lhermitte, personal communication, 1984).

Lordat died in Montpellier, on April 25th, 1870, at the age of 97 (Bayle, 1939). By then, Paul Broca had lost his interest in aphasia, or rather

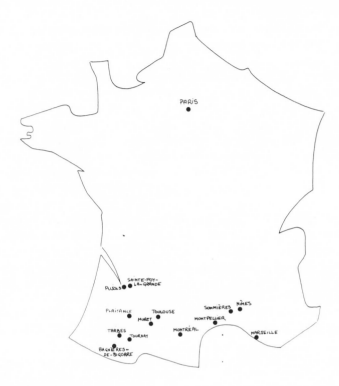

FIG. 1.2 The Hexagon.

aphemia, and, before becoming a Republican senator (Schiller, 1979), he had turned his attention and energy to worthier causes such as demonstrating that, although German big-brainedness became an obvious artifact once one's data were cleaned with great scientific care, women did indeed have smaller brains than men, and that Negroes did indeed have smaller brains than white men, and therefore that " 'inferior' groups are interchangeable in the general theory of biological determinism," and therefore that "social rank reflects inner worth," and so forth (Gould, 1981).

Schiller (1979) wrote that "the subject of loss of speech is in several ways tied to Montpellier, where Lallemand had been interested in it and where Lordat had given in 1820 (sic) a classical account of the mechanism and psychology of speech and its clinical disorders" (p. 193). Schiller's bibliography indicates that he found this information on Lordat's 1820 contribution in Ombredane's "L'aphasie et l'élaboration de la pensée explicite" (1951). Now, if one goes to pages 47 and 48 of Ombredane's most remarkable monograph, one can read interesting comments on Lordat's teachings as published in 1843, not 1820.

Before Schiller, Moutier, a few weeks before he was dismissed by Pierre Marie in 1908 (Lecours & Caplan, 1984; Lecours & Joanette, 1984), published his inaugural dissertation entitled "L'aphasie de Broca." The first section of this monumental book deals with the evolution of ideas concerning the mutual relationships of brain and language. Moutier (1908, p. 16) mentions three publications by Lordat: a paper printed in 1820, a book entitled *analyse de la parole* and published in 1823, and the well known Montpellier lessons of the 1804s, published in two consecutive issues of the *Journal de la Société de médecine pratique de Montpellier* (1843). Moutier raises several points in relation to the 1823 book, and he claims that this publication and the earlier one are much clearer and far more enlightening than the lessons published in 1843.[1] But then, when one consults the astonishingly exhaustive bibliographical index of Moutier's dissertation, in which are listed nearly 1,500 references on aphasia and related topics, one finds (p. 689) an 1820 reference to a paper written by Lordat in a journal identified by Moutier as *Revue périodique de la Société de médecine de Paris,* and also (p. 690) an 1843 reference to the Lordat lessons published in Montpellier. No reference is provided in relation to the 1823 "enlightening" monograph.

Likewise, before François Moutier (1908), Armand Trousseau (1877) had alluded to Lordat's early publications on aphasia (cf. infra), and before Trousseau the Daxes, father and son, Marc and Gustave, both of whom were of strict Montpellieran obedience. In brief, this latter story is the following:

Act I

In July, 1836, Marc Dax, who was then practicing medicine in Sommières, a small town in the vicinity of Nîmes (Fig. 1.2), submits and probably reads a paper at the "Coñgrès méridional de Montpellier" (Hécaen & Dubois, 1969). In this paper, Dax, the father tells about his own clinical and anatomical observations as well as those of others, and he concludes that acquired disorders of "verbal memory" are the result of lesions of the left but not of the right cerebral hemisphere. This communication is not published in Montpellier, as it might have been—although it seems to be a recognized fact that, contrary to the Faculty of Paris, the Faculty of Montpellier traditionally gave credit to oral transmission of knowledge at least as much as, and conceivably more than, to written documents (Bayle, 1939; Guedje, personal communication, 1984). The original manuscript is lost but Dax has a copy. Marc Dax dies in 1837 and his son inherits the copy as well as

---

[1] Of course, Moutier knew, in 1908, that Lordat had himself been struck by aphasia in 1825, but little did he know that the same would happen to him 53 years later.

his father's practice and, apparently, his preoccupation concerning the lateralization of the brain lesions responsible for acquired disorders of "verbal memory".

Act II

According to Quercy (1943), whom we believe to be a particularly reliable historian of early French aphasiology, the sequence of events is thereafter the following: **Scene I:** On March 24th, 1863, Gustave Dax officially deposits his copy of the paternal manuscript at the "Académie de médecine," in Paris, together with a paper of his own on the same topic; Joynt and Benton (1964) might be right when they suggest that Marc Dax was not ready to claim priority in 1836, but it is quite clear that Gustave was in 1863. An editorial committee is then appointed by the Academy, which decides not to publish the Meridional manuscripts for the time being (Hécaen & Dubois, 1969). Bouillaud is a member of this committee (Bayle, 1939). **Scene II:** Hardly a month later, in April of 1863, Broca publishes an updated version of his *Exposé de titres et travaux,* in which he raises the possibility of left hemisphere specialization for language. When the *Exposé* comes out in printed form, it is dated 1862 rather than 1863 (Quercy, 1943). As Bogen and Bogen (1976) wrote about Wernicke's 1874 representation of the speech area at the surface of a right hemisphere, this was probably "more in the nature of a printer's error than anything else". **Scene III:** Broca (1863) strikes again in May, this time through a note entitled "Siège du langage articulé" and published in the *Bulletin de la Société d'anthropologie* (Bayle, 1939). This is not yet the 1865 paper but Broca is explicit enough and, according to Quercy (1943), this note is the document that led Bouillaud, and Paris after him, to attribute priority to Broca rather than Dax: "Broca avait précisé en 63 et Bouillaud lui accorda l'honneur de la découverte'." Interestingly enough, in his May note to the "Société d'anthropologie" (of which he was the most influential founding member), Broca refers to a January note to the "Socité de biologie" that preceded the Gustave Dax move at the Academy. Of this January note, Quercy (1943) devastatingly writes, as it were *en passant:* "Je ne l'ai pas trouvée (I did not find it)".

Act III

The Dax papers are finally exhumed and published in 1865, Marc's first and Gustave's immediately following, in the April

25 issue of the *Gazette hebdomadaire de médecine et de chirurgie*. Broca's best and most famous aphasia paper (the one everyone has heard of and the one one quotes, whether or not one has read it, whenever the question of priority is raised) is published a little less than 2 months later, in the June 15 issue of the *Bulletin de la Société d'anthropologie*.

Act IV

In 1879, a Doctor R. Caizergues, of Montpellier, reports in the *Montpellier médical* that he has found the original manuscript of Marc Dax while classifying the papers of his grandfather, Professor F.C. Caizergues, who was the Dean of the Faculty of Montpellier in 1836, at the time of the "Congrès méridional." This fact is mentioned by Bayle, in 1939, by Joynt and Benton in 1964, and by Hécaen and Dubois, in 1969.

Now, this was a longish digression, although not without interest nor without purpose. What we were in fact driving at, on the one hand, is that the post-mortem 1865 paper by Marc Dax includes references to four researchers: The first is Gall, of course, and the second, Bouillaud, of course. The third is a German physician, whose mangificient name is Atheus although he wrote in Latin: "Observatum a me est plurimos, post apoplexiam, aut lethargum, aut similes magnos capitis morbos, etiam non praesente linguae paralysi, loqui non posse quod memoriae facultate extincta verba proferanda non succurant." Marc Dax writes that he has excerpted this passage from a book edited (?) by Schenkius in 1585, that is, 280 years before the nearly joint publication of his own and Broca's manuscripts. The fourth researcher quoted by Marc Dax in 1865, or rather in 1836 if Gustave did not alter his father's manuscript, is Jacques Lordat. Marc Dax writes that Lordat's ideas on *verbal amnesia* are more in line with his own than are Bouillaud's (Dax senior could not know that Bouillaud would be there to chair the 1863 committee), and he quotes two early papers by Lordat: one in the September 1820 issue of the *Recueil périodique de la Société de médecine de Paris,* probably the same that Moutier quoted in 1908 as published in the *Revue périodique de médecine de Paris* (cf. supra), and the other in the September 1821 issue of the *Revue médicale* (p. 25).

And what we were driving at, on the other hand, is that there exists a problem with Lordat's early publications (1820, 1821, 1823): We tried to find them, but without success. Bayle (1939), who was much closer to the sources than we are in Montréal, tried before us, also without success. Nonetheless, Bayle (1939) found a paper by Bousquet in which he sees proof that Lordat's teachings were known in Paris before Bouillaud's initial paper on aphasia:

As you know, Gentlemen, the musculary movements of speech production succeed to one another as a result of habit, so that one movement calls the next without the intervention of will power. These chains of movements correspond, and I borrow this expression from Monsieur Lordat, to a form of bodily memory ("mémoire corporelle"), which is sometimes mistaken for a mental memory although these two forms of memory represent phenomena that are quite different. (Bousquet, 1820)

Be this as it may, Bayle's (1939) conclusion concerning Lordat's "early publications" is that they never existed, a point of view that we find difficult to share if only because it is somehow disquieting to ignore bibliographies that were constituted by Marc Dax (1865), Adolf Kussmaul (1876), Armand Trousseau (1877), François Moutier (1908), and Francis Schiller (1979). And the whole affair is of some interest because, if Bayle (1939) is right, it follows that the Marc Dax publication of 1865 was at least in part a fraud: Given that he died in 1837, how could he have quoted papers by Lordat if Lordat did not write on aphasia before 1843? But if Bayle (1939) is wrong, Lordat (1820, 1821, 1823) rather than Bouillaud (1825) deserves the credit of having been the founder of French aphasiology.

For the time being, given our subject matter, we will have to rely exclusively on Lordat's 1843 Montpellier publication. The first thing one might say about it is that, although Lordat's and only Lordat's in all likelihood, and signed by Lordat alone, it was not actually "written" by Lordat but by one of the students who attended his lessons in the course of the academical year 1842–1843. The name of the student was Kuhnholtz (Quercy & Bayle, 1940) and he was probably not the first and certainly not the last student in medicine to write for a French professor of medicine.

Now, if one chooses to consider Lordat as the founder of French aphasiology, as we would be inclined to do after pondering available documents, it should then be said that French aphasiology was founded by one who believed that students in medicine should first learn about normal language production and, from there, learn, as it were by deduction, to recognize the nature of the various types of communication disorders that can result of various types of diseases.

Lordat (1843) teaches his students that "from one's decision to communicate one's thought, to the embodiment of this thought into conventional sounds, one has to accomplish a succession of various acts, (some of them exclusively mental), each of which should be studied separately" (p. 130). We found it reasonably easy to translate Lordat's formulation of his ideas into contemporary terms and to represent them following the requirements of contemporary boxology (Fig. 1.3).

The first act, isolating the "topic" or "thought" to be transmitted, is purely intellectual according to Lordat—or perhaps one might say "purely

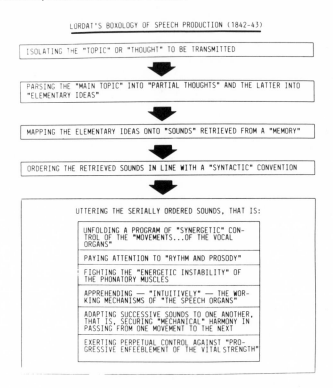

FIG. 1.3 Lordat's boxology of speech production (1842–1843).

cognitive." At all events, it is prelinguistic: It occurs without language and can persist when language is no longer possible or is grossly impaired. Nonetheless, a dysfunction of this initial act will have manifestations in language behavior: *Incoherence* is then the characteristic feature. Alcoholic intoxication, typhus, and somniloquia are the main clinical entities that Lordat presents as typical in this respect: The subject's mental state, in any of these conditions, is such that thoughts can no longer be properly circumscribed; they are disordered, hence the incoherence in discourse, and this incoherence, discreet or gross, is proportional to the intensity of the intellectual (prelinguistic) impairment. This conception, as developed by Lordat, is perhaps at the origin of the notion of "alogia" as it was 50 years later redefined by Jules Ernest Séglas (1892), one of the early mentors of Théophile Alajouanine (Lecours, Lhermitte, & Signoret, 1981).

Lordat's second act, parsing the "main topic" into "partial thoughts" and the latter into "elementary ideas", is also purely intellectual and prelinguistic. Disorders of this particular act, according to Lordat, do not occur in organic pathology but, rather, as an effect of strong emotions such as surprise, wrath and indignation. It is because the parsing mechanism is momentarily disturbed by such emotions that the individual in whom they are suddenly aroused cannot talk or, more typically, will attempt uttering "five or six sentences in a row without being capable of finishing a single one."

After having told his students about these two prelinguistic steps, Lordat turns to the "admirable mental operation;" that constitutes the psychological foundation of human language. His third and fourth acts deal with internal language, and the subsequent ones with overt articulated speech.

The third act is defined as mapping the elementary ideas onto "sounds" retrieved from a memory. Here, the key words are "sounds" and "memory"; Lordat clearly thinks in terms of mental representations of sounds that must be accessed from a specialized memory. What this particular memory has in stock, specifically, has been acquired through associative learning. Sounds have been matched to sharable meanings (sharable insofar as one belongs to a given lingusitic community): What others will soon designate as *images,* he labels as *correlative modes* ("les modes corrélatifs du souvenir"), and he apparently conceives of them as plurimodal nets rather than modality specific entities. In order to speak, or else to understand what the interlocutor says, one has to retrieve sets of correlative modes from a specific memory. What would happen, asks Lordat of his students, if one could no longer access this particular memory, or could access it only in a fragmentary or intermittent manner? Well, one would find oneself facing the double drama of impossible or imperfect speech production and impossible or imperfect speech comprehension; although one's intellectual ability (one's "sens intime") would not be impaired, one would be cut from intellectual links with one's kins. Does such a condition occur in nature? Yes, teaches Lordat; certain diseases, such as apoplexy, can interfere with the retrieving-mapping act, which will perforce interfere with certain aspects of the accomplishment of further acts but not with that of the two preceding ones, the exclusively mental ones (Lordat does not like at all the teachings of Condillac and disciples, especially since 1825: thought is not language nor vice versa, Lordat assures his students). This condition, continues the Professor, is known as "alalia". This term is not precise enough for him, however, and he says that he has coined another to qualify this particular form of alalia: "verbal amnesia" (Lordat, 1843) or "alalia by verbal amnesia" (Quercy & Bayle, 1940). Here, Lordat takes time to tell about observations that he has made or read about, some of them well before 1820. For instance, he bears in mind this rainy day, many years before the disease that has led him to experience alalia in his own flesh, when he saddled his horse and went to visit the parish priest of Saint-Guillen-le-Désert (Fig. 1.4), the very first alalic patient that he has observed. The priest had been struck by apoplexia, which had resulted in complete verbal amnesia. His actions were appropriate to the situation, notes Lordat; for instance, he made it clear through gestures that his host should,

FIG. 1.4   Lordat on his way to Saint-Guillen-le-Désert. It rains.

before any medical issues were raised, sit near the fireplace, dry himself and have something to drink and eat; but all he could then utter were "two vigorous words," one of which was "i" and the other "the most forcible oath of our tongue, which beings with an 'f' and which our Dictionaries have never dared to print." The Professor also takes time to tell about his own agonizing experience with verbal amnesia, in 1825. He insists that impairment of the retrieving-mapping act will lead to disorders in both production and comprehension. He says that this impairment need not be absolute. When it is not, as was his case, familiar words are more available than less familiar ones, and very infrequent words are not available at all. Moreover, retrieval is sometimes achieved but faulty; Lordat the word coiner enters into action anew. This phenomenon he calls *paramnesia* for its mental part (and he retains *paralalia* to designate the faulty production if it occurs); he very explicitly recognizes two forms of paramnesia. In the first, the idea is mapped onto an existing word but not the target one, and the resulting paralalia is a word substitution. In the second, the target is retrieved but, in production, "the letters and syllables are interverted" (from his auto-observation, Lordat provides his students with examples that would today be labeled as verbal and phonemic paraphasias: for instance, he wished to be handed a book and asked for a "handkerchief", he uttered "sairin" and

"Sumulman" when his targets were "raisin" and "Musulman"). There are also cases in which faulty retrieval dominates the clinical picture. Thus, Monsieur Auguste Broussonnet, another patient whom the Professor has observed when he was a young practitioner, presented "incorrigible and unconscious paralalia" (an obvious equivalent of our anosognosic jargonaphasia). Regarding comprehension, Lordat insists that the speed of elocution of the interlocutor is primordial; shorter messages, uttered a bit slower, are better understood.

Then, again and again, Lordat says that intelligence remains intact if brain disease is such that it causes only verbal amnesia, as was the fact in his own case:

> Car, ne croyez pas qu'il y ait le moindre changement dans les fonctions du sens intime. Je me sentais toujours le même intérieurement. L'isolement mental dont je parle, la tristesse, l'embarras, l'air stupide qui en provenait, faisaient croire à plusieurs qu'il existait en moi un affaiblissement des facultés intellectuelles. Cette erreur, qui causa du chagrin à quelques-uns, de la satisfaction à quelques autres, ne fut partagée ni par M. Caizergues, ni par M. Anglada.

Guardia (1870), quoted by Bayle (1939), reports in this respect an interesting anecdote: In 1825, during the worst period of his aphasia, Lordat was visited by Lallemand and Dubreuil, two of his colleagues at the Faculty. At one point, Lallemand, who had himself observed a number of aphasics (Schiller, 1979) and was very much aware of Lordat's comprehension difficulties, turned to Dubreuil and told him: "Pour le coup, le principe vital est bien foutu!" which, not taking into account the cruel play on Lordat's most sacred words, would now translate as "Well, this time, he has become a real vegetable!". Now, university professors will be university professors and Lordat kept his "air stupide," for the time being. But months later, after Lordat came back to his work at the Faculty, he one day had and did not miss the occasion to return Lallemand's energetic prognosis to the offender, word for word, and no doubt to add a few comments. (Perhaps Lallemand had talked just at the right speed and, after all, Lordat's verbal amnesia was not complete.)

Lordat's fourth act is "ordering the retrieved sounds in line with a 'syntactic' convention". From the point of view of normal (mental and overt) exercise of linguistic abilities, Lordat establishes a strict distinction between this act and the preceding one: each depends on a special memory, that is, both are founded on having learned an arbitrary convention. But these acts and subserving conventions are clearly of a different order: matching ideas to sounds in the former case, ordering these sounds in the latter. Things are not as clearly separated from the pathological point of view and Lordat teaches that verbal amnesia, as a clinical entity, usually interferes with both the third and the fourth acts. As a matter of fact, in the context of his 1842-1843 lessons of "physiology", his clinical comments concerning verbal amnesia come only after he has told his students about the serial ordering act. Lordat does not quote patients showing the conversational behavior that would now be referred to as agrammatism. Maybe he had not observed any such patient. But that need be no obstacle and the Professor will invent a case for his students: there comes a point in his exposé when he teaches that an individual with an isolated disorder of the fourth act might, for instance, say: "Moi aimer vous, désirer beaucoup vous être utile." And Lordat adds that the interlocutor would understand a faulty sentence of this sort and, of course, would recognize that the speaker's "sens intime" is intact.

As we have indicated in our boxes-and-arrows representation of Lordat's teachings (see Fig. 1.3), our reading of his psycholinguistic model, unlike the reading of Bayle (1939) and of Quercy and Bayle (1940), has led us to conclude that the Montpellieran conceived of his last six acts as being concomitant although he numbered them from five to ten in the introductory part of his lessons. At all events, he actually stops at five in the available published version (Lordat, 1843): somewhat abruptly, it is true (Quercy & Bayle, 1940).

Lordat's discussion of articulated speech begins with an astounding lecture on elementary phonetics: to him, this is basic "physiology" and it is consequently a form of knowledge that students in medicine should master. He therefore teaches about the participation of respiratory and laryngeal muscles in phonation. He goes on to tell his students that vowel sounds are determined by various configurations of the oral cavity. He shows how the *velum palati* moves in a manner such that it will either direct laryngeal air to both nose and mouth, or to mouth only, and he then explains the difference between buccal sounds and nasal sounds ("Le voile du palais est une écluse qui dirige le vent du larynx à volonté, soit pour le faire sortir entièrement par la bouche, soit pour le diviser en partie par la bouche et en partie par le nez: d'où des sons buccaux et des sons nasaux dont tous les bruits vocaux sont susceptibles."). He tells about the various muscles and movements of the tongue, and of the interactions between tongue, teeth, palate, and lips, and he goes on explaining the differences between "lingual, dental, palatal and labial letters". He then tackles the description of the liquids (he has doubts about the status of 'L' as a liquid: "il est douteux que l'L soit réellement liquide"); of the sibilants as opposed to the "éruptives"; of the aspirated 'H'; and what not. All of this, says Lordat, is "matière d'examen" at the Faculty of Montpellier and, in order to acquire proper knowledge in this respect, students should read, by their fireside ("sans vous éloigner de votre feu"), "physiology" textbooks such as those of Muller, of Amman, of Haller (Lordat, 1843).

Then Lordat turns back to pathology. Now he is no longer teaching about diseases of language as a system of sounds, but about diseases of speech as a system of movements. In order to produce speech, all of these movements of the "loquèle" that the Professor has just described have to be produced in synergy. Such a synergetic production depends on yet another specialized memory, which Lordat calls a "vital instinct", or an "instinctive memory", or a "vital memory." Bousquet (1820) notes that Lordat also used the expression 'bodily memory' ("mémoire corporelle") to designate this particular module, which clearly shows that the Montpellieran's psycholinguistic preoccupations were quite close to those of researchers to come, such as Wernicke (1874), who had yet to write about "Bewegungsvorstellungen" ("bodily movements and changes in the state of the musculature, give rise to sensations, memory of which also remain in the cerebral cortex"); and also such as Luria (1964) who had yet to write about "articulemes" after saying that Wernicke was all wrong (Lecours & Lhermitte, 1979). Of this "bodily memory," Lordat says that "intelligence" governs it only in a general manner, only insofar as "intelligence" is needed to initiate speech production—one inescapably thinks of Lashley's (1951) "determining tendency"—: the synergetic movements thereafter attract one another and are serially ordered, as it were, spontaneously; such are the ways of "vital instinct". If disease interferes with this particular memory, nonlinguistic movements of the tongue, lips, etc., remain possible as Atheus taught (cf. supra) but movements of the same muscles will be impossible or impaired when it comes to speech production. A patient with such a disease can no longer unfold a program of synergetic control of the movements of his peripheral speech organs; he cannot harmoniously adapt successive sounds to each other: in brief, he shows "asynergetic alalia."

The road is paved for Gilbert Ballet (1853-1916), another forgotten Meridional, to tell his colleagues about "apraxic aphasia" in the context of the 1908 meetings of the Paris Society of Neurology (Klippel, 1908), of course without being aware that this notion would later know a certain popularity in the United States of America (outside of Boston). And the road is also paved for Alajouanine and his collaborators, André Ombredane, the psychologist, and Marguerite Durand, the linguist, to inaugurate formal neurolingustics with their 1939 description of the phonetic disintegration syndrome ("Le syndrome de désintégration phonétique dans l'aphasie").

Meanwhile, Professor Jacques Lordat has done his trick again: from theoretical considerations on normal function, he has deduced for his students what dysfunction should be; he has then coined a term to designate this dysfunction; and now, he will turn back to his clinical experience and tell his students about a few patients. At this point, his case reports are not all equally convincing (at least to us). One wonders, for instance, as Lordat himself did, about the etiology of the alalia of this student in medicine who became deaf and dumb after receiving a troublesome letter ("une lettre qui l'affligea"). But Lordat also tells about other patients with "asynergetic alalia," most of whom would nowadays be considered as presenting either pure anarthria or Broca's aphasia. He says, among other things, that some of these patients could sing perfectly in spite of their speech disorder; this fact, says the Professor, is physiologically of such great importance that it will by itself constitute the object of another lesson (Quercy & Bayle, 1940).

At the end of his 1843 lessons, Lordat tells his students that alalia by verbal amnesia and asynergetic alalia can coexist in certain patients. In this respect, he quotes a document that has been sent to him by a colleague from Bordeaux who sought his advice. This patient, says Lordat, showed asynergia since she failed or had difficulty uttering words that she knew, but she also showed amnesia because copying was the single residual capacity of written expression ("elle ne peut que copier, ce qui prouve que la mémoire est courte, et qu'elle a besoin d'avoir vu très récemment les traits graphiques qui expriment le mot").

After Lordat's death, a chronicler who hated him, according to Quercy and Bayle (1940)—and whose papers Broca and Trousseau were likely to read—(nevertheless) wrote: "Cette aphasie dont on parle tant, et sous une terminologie si ridicule, il n'y a pas un élève de médecine [de la Faculté de Montpellier] qui ne l'ait étudiée en suivant les leçons de M. Lordat."

Lordat, the Montpellieran among Montpellierans, refused to localize (Quercy, 1943). He certainly was aware of the presence of Gall in Paris, and of the new theories; he no doubt recognized that the cerebral cortex is essential to intellectual and voluntary activities in the human species but, as to localizations, struck by the apparent homogeneity of the cortical mantle, he thought that they were contingent and "quodlibetical" (Quercy & Bayle, 1940). But, as early as 1843, and in all likelihood as early as 1820, Jacques Lordat had elaborated an original and coherent theory of aphasia, a theory grounded on an attempt at introspective analysis of the mental mechanisms behind normal language production and comprehension. This approach was all but forgotten for a long period after the anatomoclinical works of Bouillaud and Broca but, in 1986, in view of the ways and claims of "cognitive neuropsychology," one must recognize that Lordat's approach reassumes a rather fashionable look even if, as underlined by Hécaen and Dubois (1969), his vocabulary is at times disheartening with its "vital strength," its "intimate sense," its "pananthropic functions," and so forth (but is it not the case that, once in a while, readers of modern texts also have to figure out the meanings of strange words and notations?).

With the obvious exception of Bouillaud, who ignored mental processes just as his Montpellieran colleague ignored localizations, we cannot think of a single French aphasiologist of the nineteenth century who was not influenced by Lordat's teachings. This includes Dax (1836), admittedly; and Baillarger (1890), the gentleman; and Trousseau, who coined the word "aphasia" in 1865 (Hécaen & Dubois, 1969) and treated what he had named with leeches around the anus (Trousseau, 1877), a trick he had learned from Bouillaud (1824), and who agreed with Condillac to the point of suggesting, in the context of his lessons at the Hôtel-Dieu de Paris, that Lordat's intelligence had been permanently damaged since 1825 ("Que l'illustre Professeur de Montpellier me permette de le lui dire: ne se fait-il pas illusion?" etc.; Trousseau (1877); and Broca who, as we have seen, regularly updated his "Exposé de titres et travaux" and who, in the 1868 version, writes about the four types of language impairments that he recognizes: alogia, amnesia, aphemia, and alalia (Quercy, 1943), and Charcot, and Dejerine, and Pierre Marie, and others. Some were conscious of this influence and others perhaps not. Few acknowledged it: indeed, Montpellier remained quite far from Paris (see Fig. 1.2).

ACKNOWLEDGMENTS

The authors are indebted to Doctors Max and Gérard Dordain and to Doctor Michèle Puel for providing copies of historical publications that were not available in Montréal.

REFERENCES

Alajouanine, Th., Ombredane, A., & Durand, M. (1939). *Le syndrome de désintégration phonétique dans l'aphasie*. Paris: Masson.

Baillarger, J. G. F. (1890). *Recherches sur les maladies mentales*. Paris: Masson.

Bayle, J. M. J. (1939). *Les fondateurs de la doctrine française de l'aphasie*. Bordeaux: Biere.

Bogen, J. E. & Bogen, G. M. (1976). Wernicke's region: where is it? *Annals of the New York Academy of Sciences, 280*, 834–843.

Bouillaud, J.-B. (1865). Recherches cliniques propres a démontrer que la perte de la parole correspond à la lésion des lobules antérieurs du cerveau et à confirmer l'opinion de M. Gall sur le siège de l'organe du langage articulé. *Archives Générales de Médecine, 3*, 25–45.

Bousquet (1820). Rapport sur une observation. *Recueil périodique de la Société de médecine de Paris*, p. 317. (quoted by Bayle, 1939).

Broca, P. (1863). *Exposé des titres et travaux scientifiques de M. Paul Broca*. Paris, (quoted by Quercy, 1943).

Broca, P. (1863a). Siège du langage articulé. *Bulletin de la Société d'anthropologie, 4*, 200–203. (quoted by Bayle, 1939).

Broca, P. (1868). Sur le siège de la faculté du langage articulé. *Exposé des titres et travaux scientifiques de Paul Broca*, Paris.

Caizergues, R. (1879). Notes pour servir a l'histoire de l'aphasie. *Montpellier médical, 42*, 178–180.

Dax, G. (1865). Sur le même sujet. *Gazette hebdomadaire de médecine et de chirurgie, 2*, 260–262.

Dax, M. (1865). Lésions de la moitié gauche de l'encéphale coïncidant avec l'oubli des signes de la pensée: Lu au Congrès méridional tenu à Montpellier en 1836. *Gazette hebdomadaire de médecine et chirurgie, 2*, 259–260.

Gould, S. J. (1981). The mismeasure of man. New York: Norton.

Guardia (1870). Le Professeur Jacques Lordat. Gazette médicale de Paris, XXV, (quoted by Bayle, 1939).

Hécaen, H., & Dubois, J. (1969). La naissance de la neuropsychologie du langage (1825-1865). Paris: Flammarion.

Joynt, R. J., & Benton, A. (1964). The memoir of Marc Dax on aphasia. Neurology, 14, 851-854.

Klippel, M. (1908). Société de neurologie de Paris: Séance du ll juin 1908: Discussion sur l'aphasie. Revue neurologique, 16, 611-636.

Kussmaul, A. (1876). Die Störungen der Sprache. Handbuch von Pathologie und Therapie von Ziemssen's, 12, 168. (quoted by Moutier, 1908).

Larousse, P. (1878). Grand dictionnaire. Paris: Larousse.

Lashley, K. S. (1951). The problem of serial order in behavior. In L. A. Jeffress (Ed.), Cerebral mechanisms in behavior (pp. 112-136). New York: Wiley.

Lecours, A. R., & Caplan, D. (1984). Augusta Dejerine-Klumpke or "The lesson in anatomy." Brain and Cognition, 3, 166-197.

Lecours, A. R., & Joanette, Y. (1984). François Moutier or "From folds to folds". Brain and Cognition, 3, 198-230.

Lecours, A. R., & Lhermitte, F. (1979). L'aphasie. Paris: Flammarion. (English translation: Lecours, A. R., Lhermitte, F. & Bryans, B. Aphasiology. London: Baillière Tindall, 1983.).

Lecours, A. R., Lhermitte, F., & Signoret, J.-L. (1981). Théophile Alajouanine (1890-1980). Brain and Language, 13, 191-196.

Lordat, J. (1820, December). Recueil périodique de la Société de médecine de Paris (p. 317). (quoted by M. Dax, 1865).

Lordat, J. (1820, December). Revue périodique de la Sociéte de médecine de Paris (p. 317). (quoted by Moutier, 1908).

Lordat, J. (1821, September). Revue médicale (p. 25). (quoted by M. Dax, 1865).

Lordat, J. (1823). Analyse de la parole, (quoted by Moutier, 1908).

Lordat, J. (1843). Lecons tirées du cours de physiologie de l'année scolaire 1842-1843: Analyse de la parole pour servir à la théorie de divers cas d'alalie et de paralalie que les nosologistes ont mal connus (publiées, avec l'autorisation de Lordat, par son élève Kuhnholtz). Journal de la Société de médecine pratique de Montpellier, 7, 333-353, 417-433, and 8, 1-17. (Reprinted in: Lordat, J. Analyse de la parole pour servir à la théorie de divers cas d'alalie et de paralalie que les nosologistes ont mal connus. Paris: Baillière, 1843-44.) Reprinted in, H. Hécaen and J. Dubois, eds., La naissance de la neuropsychologie du langage, pp. 129-167, Flammarion, Paris, 1969.

Luria, A. R. (1964). Factors and forms of aphasia. In A. V. S. de Reuck & M. O'Connor (Eds.), Disorders of language (pp. 143-167). London: Churchill.

Moutier, F. (1908). L'aphasie de Broca. Paris: Steinheil.

Ombredane, A. (1951). L'aphasie et l'élaboration de la pensée explicite. Paris: Preseses Universitaires de France.

Quercy, M. (1943). Les fondateurs de la doctrine française de l'aphasie: Broca. Annales médico-psychologiques, 101, 161-188.

Quercy, M., & Bayle, J. M. J. (1940). Les fondateurs de la doctrine française de l'aphasie. Annales médico-psychologiques, 98, 297-310.

Schiller, F. (1979). Paul Broca: Founder of French anthropology, explorer of the brain. Berkeley: University of California Press.

Séglas, J. E. (1892). Troubles du langage chez les aliénés. Paris: Rueff.

Trousseau, A. (1877). Clinique médicale de l'Hôtel-Dieu de Paris (Vol. 2). Paris: Baillière.

Wernicke, C. (1874). Der Aphasische Symptomenkomplex. Breslau: Cohn & Weigert. (English translation: Wernicke, C. The Symptom Complex of Aphasia. In R. S. Cohen & M. W. Watofsky (Eds.), Boston Studies in the Philosophy of Science (Vol. 4). Boston: Riedel.

2

The Role of Word-Onset Consonants in Speech Production Planning: New Evidence From Speech Error Patterns

Stefanie Shattuck-Hufnagel
Research Laboratory of Electronics
Massachusetts Institute of Technology

ABSTRACT

A slots-and-fillers model of the speech production planning process, based on patterns and constraints in sublexical speech error data, proposed the separate representation of (a) single phonemic segments and (b) the utterance-specific framework that guides their processing, as well as (c) a segment-by-segment process to associate segments with their target locations in the framework. In this model, all sublexical errors occur during the operation of this serial ordering mechanism. Further analysis of sublexical errors, however, shows that the error data are concentrated largely in word-onset consonants. Evidence from both spontaneous and experimentally elicited speech supports the claim that word-onset consonants in particular (rather than syllable onsets or prestressed consonants in general) undergo separate processing that renders them particularly liable to confusions. An expanded slots-and-fillers model is proposed to take account of these findings; it includes a processing mechanism that deals with word-onset consonant information separately during the elaboration of metrical structure.

Most models of the speech production planning process assume that the word or lexical item is a processing unit; i.e., that the word is a language element that is manipulated during the planning of an utterance. Speech error data support this view, showing that individual words and morphemes are sometimes reshuffled during processing, to create errors like "the shirts fall off his buttons" for "the buttons fall off his shirts." Similar kinds of error evidence at the phonological level suggests that individual phonemic segments also are processing units. For example, segment exchanges like the ones in Table 2.1 support the claim that the planning of an utterance involves some steps in

TABLE 2.1
Examples of single-segment errors

1.	The *r*icious *v*at (vicious rat)
2.	A *c*url *g*alled her up (girl called)
3.	. . . *s*issle *th*eeds . . . (thistle seeds)
4.	My *j*ears are *g*ammed (gears are jammed)
5.	. . . differ by the *s*erry *v*ame—very ame features . . .
6.	This is the most *l*eesent *r*isting (recent listing)
7.	Did the g*r*ass c*l*ack? (glass crack)
8.	. . . *th*eep *d*roat . . . (deep throat)
9.	I have a sti*ck* ne*ff* (stiff neck)
10.	. . . is no*th* wor*t* knowing . . . (not worth)

which individual phonemic segments, both consonants and vowels, are represented and manipulated in such a way that they can separate from their target locations and interact with each other in a speech error. Errors that move or change pieces of morphemes have been called *sublexical errors.*

Given the error evidence that strongly favors words and morphemes as processing units on one hand, and individual phonemic segments on the other, what support is there for other suprasegmental structural units like the syllable? Although a few errors involving the syllable as an error unit are found (Fromkin, 1971), in general very little evidence from spontaneous error corpora favors the syllable as a moveable processing unit (Shattuck-Hufnagel, 1979). In contrast, some of the structural subunits of the syllable do find support in error data, in the form of errors that involve the movement or replacement of whole onsets, rhymes, nuclei, and codas (MacKay, 1972; Shattuck-Hufnagel, 1983).

On the basis of these and other error data, some investigators have postulated that syllable structure plays a significant role in production planning (Dell, 1984; MacKay, 1972). Interest in the syllable and its constituent structure has been growing in the past decade, partly because of a new emphasis on the role of syllabic affiliation in determining the allophonic shape of a segment (Kahn, 1976), and partly because of concurrent developments in autosegmental phonology, metrical phonology, tiered phonology, lexical phonology, and nonconcatenative morphology (Clements & Keyser, 1981; Halle & Vergnaud, 1981; Harris, 1983; Hayes, 1981; Kiparsky, 1979, 1982; Liberman & Prince, 1977; McCarthy, 1979, 1981; Mohanan, 1981; Prince, 1982, Selkirk, 1980). Because syllabic structure is now playing a more significant role in generative phonological theory, it is appropriate to re-examine the sublexical error evidence that seems to motivate a processing role for syllabic subconstituents, with two questions in mind: (a) What aspects of suprasegmental structure do the error data support, and (b) What role does this structure play in the elaboration of an utterance during speech production planning?

This chapter is divided into six sections. The first section reviews the slots-and-fillers model of sublexical planning that was proposed in Shattuck (1975), a model that emphasizes the role of the individual phonemic segment as a planning unit, but does not explicitly define the role of other aspects of sublexical structure. The second through fifth sections examine a range of speech error evidence that bears on the question of sublexical structure, concluding that the weight of the evidence favors word-onset consonants as a special processing class, but that currently available error data do not motivate a representation of the full syllabic substructure of the utterance during planning. In the final section, we explore the implications of this finding for the model, suggesting one way in which a word-onset processing mechanism can be integrated into the slots-and-fillers model.

1. THE SLOTS-AND-FILLERS MODEL

The sublexical serial ordering model described in Shattuck (1975) and elaborated in Shattuck-Hufnagel (1979, 1983) was influenced by several surprising aspects of a corpus of errors collected from spontaneous speech. The corpus has been accumulating at the Massachusetts Institute of Technology since the late 1960s (Garrett, 1975). One of the most striking facts about this corpus is that single segment errors are very common; for example, errors involving a single phonemic segment made up about 40% of the 1974 count of the corpus. Shattuck-Hufnagel and Klatt (1979) have shown that even errors that appear to involve a change in just a single distinctive feature are whole-segment errors rather than feature errors (see that paper for the details of the argument).

While the substitution or movement of single phonemic segments is common in the corpus, there are only a few errors that move syllable-sized units. This contrast points to two hypotheses:

1. The processing of sublexical information in speech production planning makes use of representational units that correspond to single phonemic segments, as suggested by Fromkin (1971) and others, and

2. This planning process includes a mechanism for the serial ordering of individual phonemic segments, during whose operation ordering errors can occur. The mechanism is referred to here as the sublexical serial ordering mechanism.

An examination of the patterns in single segment errors suggests a more detailed characterization of this sublexical serial ordering mechanism, which can be summarized in the following four points:

1. Segments and their slots are represented independently.
2. An association process links segments to their slots.
3. Errors in this process occur by misselection between similar target segments during the association process.
4. The ordering mechanism operates during a pre-execution planning process.

Independent Representation of Segments and Slots

In this model, serial ordering of sublexical elements operates on a two part representation of the planned utterance, consisting of: (a) The segments that make up the candidate lexical items selected for the utterance, and (b) A separate framework of sequentially ordered locations or slots with which the segments are to be associated.

Two major arguments support the separate representation of segments and their locations. The first derives from a line of reasoning pointed out by Lashley (1951). He noted that, in anticipation errors, planning elements occur earlier than they would in an error-free rendition of the utterance. In other words, these elements are available to the processor at moments that are substantially removed in time from their target locations in the utterance, often by several syllables or even words. Lashley used this observation to argue against a simple association model of speech production, in which each word serves as the stimulus to evoke the next word as a response. Instead, anticipatory speech errors show that speech is planned in some detail over spans longer than the single word, and that the elements in that planning span are being processed well before the speaker reaches their target location in the utterance.

One way of instantiating this claim in a model is to postulate that all of the planning elements in the planning span are available concurrently, in a storage buffer separate from the overall framework of the utterance. This formulation also satisfies the requirement that candidate segments be available later than one might expect, as is suggested by perseveratory errors.

The second argument in support of the separate representation of segments and their slots comes from the observation that if a displaced target segment is inserted somewhere else in the utterance, it does not appear at a random location. Instead, a displaced target segment can appear only in the slot that was left empty by the target segment that displaced it. For example, in the exchange error "*t*ame *s*ime" for "same time", the target /s/ that is displaced from the first slot by the intrusion /t/ reappears at the precise location that would have been filled by the displacing segment /t/ if an error had not occurred. The displaced target /s/ does not appear at some other location unrelated to the source of the intruding /t/. This constraint suggests that the information specifying the existence and location of a slot for the initial /t/ in "time" is represented independent of its contents, and that this slot specification persists even if its target segment, in this case /t/, has already appeared earlier in the utterance.

To summarize the argument for the separate representation of segments and the framework that specifies their location: Segments can appear in locations other than their target slots, and slots can be filled by other than their target segments. Combined with the powerful constraint on where displaced target segments can appear, these facts suggest an independent representation of (a) a framework of slots, and (b) the segmental elements that will fill them.

This claim raises questions about the form of the two representations; for example, what information is specified about each slot in the serial framework, and what information is specified about each segment in the candidate set. In the original model, we noted that the two representations must contain enough information to permit the right match to be made between them most of the time, and hypothesized that syllable structure plays a role in the framework representation, but otherwise had little to say about this issue.

A Segment-to-Slot Association Process

A second claim in the model is that a serial ordering process normally operates to associate each segment in the candidate set with a slot in the structural framework, in a left to right manner, over the length of some processing chunk of the utterance, perhaps the phrase. We described this association process as one of *copying* segmental information into each slot, and proposed that as each segment becomes associated with a slot, it is deleted from the set of candidate segments, so that it becomes unavailable for copying into later slots.

The major argument in support of this serial ordering mechanism is the observation that sublexical elements can become misordered. That is, the retrieved lexical entry alone does not determine the serial ordering of its segments, because that would leave no room for single-segment misorderings. There must be some further process that involves individual target segments; when this process malfunctions, interaction errors between such segments can occur.

The constraints on these misorderings provide more information about the nature of the structures and principles that govern the normal operation of the ordering or association mechanism. For example, interacting segments usually appear in parallel positions, share distinctive features and are equivalent sized elements at some level of description (Shattuck-Hufnagel, 1979). These constraints suggest that segmental interaction errors result from malfunctions in a system that is sensitive to structure, rather than from random misactivation of language elements at the wrong point in time. Furthermore, the error constraints support the claim that such dimensions as suprasegmental structure, lexical stress, and distinctive features are reflected in the processing representation.

The original model also postulated a monitor mechanism, responsible for deleting already-used segments from the candidate set. Different combinations of malfunctions in the monitor and in the association mechanism account for differences among various error types. Several of these are illustrated here with respect to the target phase "same time."

1. Exchanges (e.g., "*t*ame *s*ime"): In this error, the association mechanism mistakenly matches the /t/ to the first slot, and the monitor correctly eliminates the /t/ from the set of candidate segments. Since the /t/ is now unavailable to be selected for its own target slot in the second word, the still-available (and phonemically similar) segment /s/ is selected for that slot, completing the exchange error.

2. Anticipatory substitutions (e.g., "*t*ame time"): Here, the monitor fails to check off the segment /t/ after it has been mistakenly associated with the first slot. As a result, the /t/ is available to be copied again into its correct target slot in the second word.

3. Perseveratory substitutions (e.g., "same *s*ime"): In this error, the monitor fails to check off the segment /s/ after it has been correctly associated with the initial target slot in the first word. This malfunction leaves the /s/ available for association with the initial slot in the second word. The likelihood of this mis-selection is presumably enhanced by the phonological similarity between /s/ and /t/.

The slot-and-filler model predicts an equal likelihood for anticipatory and perseveratory substitutions, because each requires two malfunctions, one during selection and one by the monitor. Earlier reports have suggested that anticipatory substitutions are far more common than perseveratory (Nooteboom, 1967). Our analysis of the 1979 count of the MIT corpus shows that the apparent predominance of anticipatory substitutions is misleading. It arises from the fact that an incomplete error (like "*t*ame—same time") looks like an anticipatory substitution, but might easily be the first half of an exchange. Because the utterance was interrupted in midstream, the error can't be classified as either type. When the incomplete consonant errors in the MIT corpus are set aside, completed anticipatory substitutions of consonants are actually less numerous than completed perseveratory substitutions (95 vs. 182). If most of the incomplete errors are incomplete exchanges but some are incomplete anticipatory substitutions, as seems likely, the data are compatible with the model's prediction that the anticipatory and perseveratory mis-selections occur with approximately equal frequency.

Three other single segment error types—additions, omissions, and shifts—can also be accounted for by breakdowns in the slot-to-segment association mechanism, the checkoff monitor, or both. Thus, the model that accounts for sublexical errors as malfunctions in a serial ordering process involving separate representations of the segments and their organizing framework can account for five major sublexical error types: exchanges, substitutions, additions, omissions, and shifts. A sixth type of sublexical error, word blends like "symblem" for "symbol" + "emblem", can also be accounted for, on the assumption that more than one lexical candidate is sometimes retrieved for a particular word slot in the phrasal frame, making the candidate phonemic segments of both words available to the processer. When the association mechanism reaches a point where the two candidates are phonemically similar, it jumps to the alternate item and finishes it.

A few of these word blend errors show a pattern that provides further evidence for the activity of a checkoff or deletion monitor. When word or phrase blends are corrected by the speaker, the result is sometimes a second blend made up of the unused pieces left over from the first blend. For example, "pack" and "batch" combined to form the blend error "back", and the speaker's correction of the error was "patch", using the still-available word portions "p–" and "–atch". Error corrections like this support the claim that the monitor deletes the used segments of candidate words, leaving the unused elements to be gathered into a second attempt.

The major question raised by the proposed serial ordering mechanism is, why is it necessary to re-order the segments of words and morphemes, when information about their order is already available as part of their definition in the lexicon? We hypothesized that serial ordering errors are a byproduct of the normal steps in speech planning, which requires the transfer or copying of individual phonemic segments from one processor to another (see Keller, this volume, for a more detailed discussion of why resequentialization might be necessary.) During the transfer, information is sometimes copied into the wrong slot in the new processer. We had little to say about the nature of the slot representation in the new processer, or how it might have been derived.

Errors Occur by Mis-Selection between Similar Target Segments

A third claim in the model is that interaction errors between target segments in an utterance occur by a process of mis-selection between similar candidate segments, rather than by a process one might characterize as a stronger element replacing a weaker one. In other words, we postulated that for a given pair of target segments, each has an equal chance of displacing the other in an error, without respect to their relative frequency, degree of markedness, degree of stress, etc. In this model, some pairs of segments are more likely to interact in errors than other pairs, but for any given pair, both directions of substitution are equally likely; nothing hinges on the relative strength of one segment versus another.

Evidence for mis-selection under similarity as a source of error is of two types: (a) target and intrusion segments are similar, both intrinsically and in their utterance-specific roles, and (b) most phonemic segments serve as error targets (i.e., are displace in an error) just about as often as they serve as error intrusions (i.e., displace another segment in an error).

Target-Intrusion Similarity. Many investigators have reported that interacting pairs of segments tend to share distinctive features more often than chance would predict (MacKay, 1970; Nooteboom, 1967; Shattuck-Hufnagel & Klatt, 1979). In addition, a powerful position similarity constraint has been observed to govern interacting segments (Boomer & Laver, 1968; Nooteboom, 1967; Shattuck-Hufnagel, 1983). The position similarity constraint is discussed later in this chapter.

Another finding in the MIT corpus lends further support to the general principle of mis-selection under similarity: Two words that are blended together in an error (like "symblem" for 'symbol' and 'emblem') tend to share one or more segments at the blend point. More than 40% of the 190 word blends in the 1984 count of the corpus show this pattern. Apparently, the processing that results in word blends is sensitive to phonological similarity between the segments of the candidate words involved.

Similar Target and Intrusion Rates. Most pairs of segments exhibit symmetry in the direction of error substitution between them, even when there is wide variation in their respective frequencies. In both the MIT corpus and Fromkin's UCLA corpus as summarized by Goldstein (1977), the frequency with which a segment serves as an error target (i.e., is displaced) is indistinguishable from the frequency with which it serves as an intrusion (Shattuck-Hufnagel & Klatt, 1979). The striking exception to this general rule of symmetry is a set of palatalizing errors, like /s/ $\longrightarrow$ /š/, /t/ $\longrightarrow$ /č/ and /s/ $\longrightarrow$ /ĉ/. For these pairs, surprisingly, the substitution of the less frequent palatal for the more frequent coronal was much more common than the reverse. We hypothesized that these excess palatalizing errors occur at a different point in the planning process from the errors that fill the rest of the confusion matrix. Overall, the symmetry between target and intrusion rates in the matrix supports the view that interaction errors occur by mis-selection between similar alternatives, rather than by selection of an intrusion segment that is more frequent than the target, or stronger in some other sense.

Pre-Execution Planning

The final claim embodied in the original model is that the serial ordering process for sublexical elements operates on a representation made up of abstract phonemic segments, rather than of contextually adjusted segments or even motor commands. The model proposed that all sublexical errors occur during this same process, that the elements being manipulated during this process have not yet been shaped to fit their phonemic contexts, and that detailed phonetic specifications are computed at a later processing stage.

Evidence for the claim that sublexical errors precede phonetic adjustment is found in the observation, as yet informal, that error segments themselves undergo this shaping to fit their new contexts. The anecdotal evidence supporting this view is the listener's perception of that intrusion segments sound appropriate in their new locations. For example, a /t/ moved out of an /st/ cluster, where it would normally not be aspirated, and into initial position, does not strike the listener as lacking in the aspiration appropriate to its new position (as in "s*k*op the *t*ar" for "stop the car"). This suggests that the segment was moved before it took on its surface phonetic shape, or at the very least that the phonetics can be readjusted after the error occurs. Other examples include the adjustment of plural, past, and person morphemes to fit an intrusion segment that changes the voicing value of the last segment of the root morpheme, and adjustment of the articles "the" and "a" when an error introduces a consonant at the onset of a vowel-initial word.

These kinds of intuitions are only beginning to be tested by careful measurement of recorded errors. For example, when two final consonants that differ in voicing value participate in an exchange error (as in "fa*t* f[v]*d*" for "fad foot"), the durations of the two vocalic nuclei are adjusted to fit the voicing value of new final segments: longer for voiced stops, shorter for voiceless (Shattuck-Hufnagel, 1985a). Thus, the specification of duration must have been made after the error occurred. This fits with the claim that segmental errors involve abstract segments, which only later receive their phonetic specifications. The implication of this claim for a model of normal speech planning is that the segments of an utterance are first represented as abstract elements; that sublexical errors occur during this stage of processing; and that both correct segments and error segments are later shaped to fit their contexts in the same way.

In summary, the proposed phonological planning model includes:

1. a two part representation of the utterance, consisting of the abstract segments specified by the candidate lexical items, and a structural framework of serially ordered slots;

2. an association mechanism to relate the two parts of the representation; and

3. a monitor to eliminate target segments as they become associated with their target slots.

The segment-to-slot matching process operates on representations that have not yet received their detailed phonetic specifications. When an interaction error occurs, by mis-selection among similar target elements, the normal processes of phonetic adjustment to context operate as usual, fitting the intruding segment into its new environment.

As we have seen, a number of lines of evidence from sublexical speech error patterns support the basic tenets of this formulation. At the same time, many questions about both the process and the error data remain unanswered. One observation in particular remains unaccounted for: the substantial proportion of sublexical errors that involve consonants located in the word onset. In the following sections we turn to an analysis of these word-onset consonant errors, and a discussion of their implications for the model.

2. ERROR EVIDENCE FOR SUPRASEGMENTAL STRUCTURE

Although error units of the size of the syllable are extremely rare, there is some evidence for the syllabic constituents of onset and rhyme. This speech error evidence has highlighted the possibility that syllabic structure, which is playing an increasingly significant role in phonological theory, is represented during utterance planning (Dell, 1984; MacKay, 1972; Shattuck-Hufnagel, 1983). However, evidence that has recently emerged, both from further analyses of spontaneously occurring speech errors and from elicitation experiments, suggests that the bulk of the error evidence for suprasegmental structure supports the morpheme rather than the syllable. That is, the error data can be accounted for on the assumption that one particular subset of syllable onsets, i.e., word-onset consonants, form a special processing class. Evidence for other aspects of syllabic structure is considerably weaker. This raises the question of whether or not it is necessary to postulate a full syllabic representation in order to account for constraints on speech error patterns. In this section we reexamine the error evidence in light of both candidates for suprasegmental processing structure: the morpheme and the syllable.

Syllable-Based Structure

An obvious candidate for suprasegmental structure is the syllable, along with its constituents. Several formulations of this structure have been suggested in the phonological literature, ranging from the simple division into onset and rhyme, to a more complex structure in which the rhyme is further subdivided into nucleus and coda, with coronal affixes tacked on at the end (Clements & Keyser, 1983).

Syllable structure played no role in generative phonology in its first decade, but has recently reemerged as a significant concept. For example, the syllable affiliation of a segment partially determines its surface phonetic shape (Kahn, 1976; Kiparsky, 1979 and others). Similarly, recent formulations of prosodic structure, beginning with the work of Liberman and Prince (1979), refer crucially to the relative prominence of syllable rhymes. In fact, a broad range of recent advances in generative phonology make reference to syllable structure.

Given the breadth of theoretical support for the constituent structure of syllables, it seems reasonable to hypothesize that syllables, onsets and rhymes play a role in the representations that underlie speech production planning. The speaker's output must have the appropriate phonetic characteristics and prosodic shape; to the extent that syllabic structure has proven useful in formulating rules that capture these regularities, we can argue that either speakers must refer to syllable-structure representations in making these decisions, or else they must determine the appropriate phonetics and prosody in some other way that produces the same results. Given this choice, it makes sense to examine the sublexical error evidence for indications of syllabic structure.

Word-Based Structure

The alternate possibility that suprasegmental representations are structured in terms of constituents of the word or morpheme was proposed by Hockett (1968), who suggested that monosyllabic morphemes like "scat" are represented in terms of two units: the onset, made up of the initial consonants, and the rest of the word. There is also a considerable body of relevant theory and experimentation in the psychological literature, focused on the size and structural nature of the access unit for lexical items in perception (Forster, 1976). The evidence suggests, not surprisingly, that the early portions of words play an important role in lexical access during the recognition process, although a precise definition of "the early portion" has remained elusive. Even if we had such a definition, the evidence from word recognition would provide only a hint about which suprasegmental structures might play a role in the presumably very different process of production planning. But this line of investigation does provide some motivation for a morpheme-based view of processing. The proposal we will evaluate here is that at some level of production processing, all lexical items (whether monosyllables or polysyllables) are represented in terms of two constituents: the onset consonant sequence, and the rest of the word.

The Error Evidence

Speech error evidence for suprasegmental sublexical structure is of three major kinds:

1. Susceptibility: certain structurally defined classes of segments are differentially susceptible to errors,
2. Error Units: certain structurally motivated sequences of adjacent segments appear as discrete error units more often than unmotivated sequences do, and
3. Position-Similarity Constraints: pairs of segments that occur in structurally similar locations often interact in an error, whereas pairs of segments in structurally different slots rarely do.

In the sections that follow, we examine each of these kinds of evidence from the point of view of both word structure and syllable structure.

3. ERROR EVIDENCE FOR SUPRASEGMENTAL STRUCTURE: SUSCEPTIBILITY

The fact that consonants in word onsets are particularly likely to participate in errors is clear from even a cursory examination of the errors in a corpus collected from spontaneous speech. In the 1984 count of the MIT corpus, 66% of the 1520 consonantal errors occurred in word onsets. This is twice the 33% rate at which consonants occur in word onsets in running speech, as estimated from a sample (Carterette & Jones, 1974) of adult speech from three speakers.

By itself this finding does not distinguish between a word-based and a syllable-based definition of the set of susceptible consonants, because so many of the errors occur in monosyllabic words, like "*ch*ung in *t*eek" for "tongue in cheek." These consonants are located both in the word onset and in the syllable onset, and so satisfy both of these formulations of the position constraint. Polysyllabic target words provide the critical cases; if at least one of the two target words is polysyllabic, there is the potential for errors between pairs of segments which share syllable onset position but do not share word onset position. A separate analysis for errors in polysyllabic words is shown in Table 2.2. Even here, where there are opportunities for onset errors in other word positions, word-onset consonants are particularly error-prone. That is, about half of the consonant errors in polysyllabic words (56%) involve segments in the word onset. This is more than expected, based on the observation that word-onset consonants make up only 19% of the consonants in polysyllabic words, as estimated from the same sample (Carterette & Jones, 1974) of running speech from three adult speakers. Consonants out-

TABLE 2.2
Susceptibility of consonants to errors in onset vs. non-onset position

	Word-onset position	Other word positions	Total
Monosyllabic words			
Sample of spontaneous speech	129 (50%)	130 (50%)	259 (100%)
Errors (all types)	566 (78%)	161 (22%)	727 (100%)
Polysyllabic words			
Sample of spontaneous speech	62 (19%)	265 (81%)	327 (100%)
Errors (all types)	442 (56%)	351 (44%)	793 (100%)

side the word onset, which make up 81% of the polysyllabic sample, account for only 44% of the consonant errors in polysyllabic words.

The striking error susceptibility of word-onset consonants raises the possibility that they are processed differently from other consonants during speech production planning, and suggests that this special processing makes them particularly prone to disruption.

Three aspects of this claim need clarification. First, it concerns all of the consonants at the beginning of the word, not just the one in absolute initial position. Second, it does not postulate that the word onset forms a processing unit, but rather that onset consonants as a class are subject to different processing. (The question of the onset as a unit is addressed later, in the discussion of error units.) Third, it is not claimed that there is an absolute processing segregation between word onset consonants and other segments throughout the phonological planning process, but only that at some point, these consonants play a special role that makes them particularly susceptible to confusions with each other.

There are several constraints on the conditions under which this susceptibility appears. First, it shows up particularly clearly in errors that involve an interaction between two target segments in the utterance. Second, it appears for errors elicited by utterances that have grammatical structure, but not for utterances structured as lists of words.

Susceptibility of Word-Onset Consonants to Interaction Errors

Segmental errors can be divided into two groups, those that involve an interaction between two target segments of the utterance (like an exchange or an anticipatory substitution), and those that do not involve an interaction (i.e. a substitution with no identifiable source in the utterance). Several examples

TABLE 2.3
Interactions vs. noninteraction errors

	Interactions
1.	. . . a *bee wit* . . . (wee bit)
2.	. . . a *lung*—a *young lady* . . .
3.	. . . my *riving room* . . . (living room)
4.	. . . *stoff* at the *Gulf* station (stop at the Gulf)
5.	. . . *verb vias*—bias . . .

	Non-Interactions
1.	. . . modes of vocal *pold*—vocal fold vibration . . .
2.	. . . the inflation *wate* . . . (rate)
3.	. . . that *yeed* one to . . . (lead)
4.	. . . the Ar*mold*—Arnold Aboretum . . .
5.	. . . *wiz* Max Morant—with Max Morant . . .

of each type of error are shown in Table 2.3. If the predominance of word-onset consonant errors is compared for these two types of errors (Table 2.4), we find that it is more pronounced for interaction errors, where 82% of the consonant errors involve onset consonants, and less pronounced for noninteractions, where only 43% are located in the onset.

To determine whether this susceptibility to a particular type of error, i.e., interactions, affects syllable onsets in general or the more limited set of word onsets, we must again compare the distribution for monosyllabic words with that for polysyllables. The analysis here is limited to those errors where the two interacting segments have target locations in the same positions, so that the categorization of the position of the error is straightforward. Interaction errors between segments in different positions are dealt with below in the discussion of position similarity constraints.

Table 2.5 shows that, even for the polysyllabic target words analysed separately, word onset consonants are particularly susceptible to interactions.

TABLE 2.4
Susceptibility of consonants to interaction vs.
noninteraction errors, across word position

	Word-onset position	*Other word positions*	*Total*
Interaction Errors	744 (82%)	160 (18%)	904 (100%)
Non-Interaction Errors	264 (43%)	352 (57%)	616 (100%)
Sample of Spontaneous Speech	191 (33%)	395 (67%)	586 (100%)

TABLE 2.5

Susceptibility of consonants to interaction vs. noninteraction errors, across word position in monosyllables vs. polysyllables

	Monosyllabic Target Words			Polysyllabic Target Words		
	Word-Onset Consonants	*Other Consonants*	*Total Consonants*	*Word-Onset Consonants*	*Other Consonants*	*Total Consonants*
Interaction Errors	401 (87%)	60 (13%)	461 (100%)	343 (77%)	100 (23%)	443 (100%)
Noninteraction Errors	165 (62%)	101 (38%)	266 (100%)	99 (28%)	251 (72%)	350 (100%)
Distribution in a Sample of Sponaneous Speech	129 (50%)	130 (50%)	259 (100%)	62 (19%)	265 (81%)	327 (100%)

In fact, 77% of the interaction errors involve word onset consonants, compared with the 19% of consonants that occur in that position in polysyllabic words in running speech. The significance of this finding is highlighted by a comparison with non-interaction errors in polysyllables. For noninteraction errors in polysyllabic words, only 28% occur in word onsets, far fewer than the 77% for interaction errors.

This close association between word-onset consonants and interaction errors suggests that the special processing of word onset segments, whatever its nature, renders them susceptible to errors involving an interaction between two target segments, but has less effect on their tendency to participate in non-interaction errors.

A more detailed analysis of the same data broken down further by error type offers additional support for the association between word onsets and interaction errors. When different types of interaction errors are compared, we find that the proportion of word-onset involvement is larger for errors where we can be sure that an interaction between two target segments occurred, and smaller for errors where we are less sure that there was an interaction. To illustrate this point, we must distinguish among two different types of interaction errors, exchanges and directional substitutions, shown in Table 2.6.

TABLE 2.6
Two Different Types of Interaction Errors

Exchanges

1.   . . . a *j*ee in *d*eometry . . . (D in geometry)
2.   They cut their *s*hair *h*ort . . . (hair short)
3.   He had a *n*ot of *l*ice . . . (lot of nice . . .)
4.   . . . *g*lue-*b*reen . . . (blue-green)
5.   . . . gree*p*-gra*n*e season . . . (green grape)

Directional Substitutions

Anticipatory

1.   McNeill *t*ays to *t*ell you (says to tell)
2.   . . . the *w*arch on *W*ashington . . . (march on Washington)
3.   You don't *l*eed *l*exical stuff . . . (need lexical)
4.   . . . *w*ight a*w*ay . . . (right away)
5.   . . . Panca*s*e House . . . (Pancake House)

Perseveratory

1.   . . . ricotta *ch*eese *ch*auce . . . (cheese sauce)
2.   . . . the *p*ast *p*aive—five years
3.   . . . *sh*oes and *sh*ocks . . . (shoes and socks)
4.   . . . or the *b*oys a*b*ung themselves . . . (boys among)
5.   . . . the Ara*b* ro*b*e—road

In the case of exchanges, the symmetrical nature of the double error makes it almost certain that an interaction between two target segments has occurred; it is unlikely that the two parts of the error could have occurred by chance. However, in the case of anticipatory or perseveratory substitutions, it is possible that the substitution of the intrusion segment for the target segment occurred independently of the fact that an identical segment appears nearby in the utterance. Although we classify these errors as directional substitution errors and therefore as interactions, because there is a putative source segment present, it is possible that for some percentage of them the apparent source segment is unrelated to the error, which actually occurred by simple substitution. Thus, for exchanges we can be confident that our operational definition of an interaction (i.e., the utterance contains a source for the error segment) correctly labels the error as an interaction, but there are some doubts about the labelling for directional substitutions.

When we compare the prevalence of word-initial consonant errors in exchanges versus directional substitutions (Table 2.7), we find that it is stronger where we can be sure that an interaction occurred (i.e., 91% for exchanges), and less strong where some of the errors may not involve interactions between target segments (only 67% for directional substitutions). This finding again supports the claim that it is a particular kind of error, that is, interaction errors between two target segments, that is associated with special processing of word-onset consonants.

The distribution across error types in Table 2.7 also supports the claim made in an earlier paper (Shattuck-Hufnagel, 1979), that incomplete errors like "Where is the *m*uss—bus to Monticello?" are usually incomplete exchanges (i.e., *m*uss to *B*onticello) rather than incomplete anticipatory substitutions (i.e., *m*uss to *M*onticello). The proportion of word-onset involvement for incomplete errors is close to that for exchange errors (88% vs. 91%), and substantially higher than that for directional substitutions (67%), suggesting that incompletes and exchanges occur in the same contexts. This fact is important, because incomplete errors are so numerous; they make up about half the sublexical interaction errors. If they are incipient exchanges, and follow the same constraints shown by exchange errors, then the arguments based on those constraints rest on a much larger data base.

TABLE 2.7
Susceptibility of consonants to different types
of interaction errors across word position

	Errors in Word Onset Consonants	Other Consonant Errors	Total Consonant Errors
Exchanges	165 (91%)	16 (9%)	181 (100%)
Incomplete Errors	393 (88%)	53 (12%)	446 (100%)
Directional Substitutions (anticipatory and perseveratory)	186 (67%)	91 (33%)	277 (100%)

Association of Susceptibility with Phrasal Planning

The proclivity toward word-onset errors appears to vary not only with the type of error, but also with the grammatical shape of the utterance being planned. To see this, we must compare the error distribution across word position in spontaneous speech with the distribution in two experimental conditions: (a) the utterance of words in lists, and (b) the utterance of those same words in grammatically well-formed phrases.

We saw in Table 2.4 that 82% of the consonant interaction errors in the MIT corpus occur in word onsets. Similar results are found for utterances elicited with a set of tongue twisters like "From the leap of the note to the nap of the lute", and "It's the pan of the tool that can peel to the tone." These jabberwocky-like stimuli are made up of individual phrases that are well formed, and on average 80% of the consonant interaction errors they elicit involve word-onset consonants (Shattuck-Hufnagel, 1982).

In contrast, when these same words were produced in lists, like "leap note nap lute" and "peal tone pan tool", the distribution across word position changed dramatically (Table 2.8). The number of errors in word onsets rose slightly, but the number of errors in word-final consonants rose sharply, to equal or surpass the number of onset errors. This result is compatible with the view that the planning of grammatically well-formed phrases requires the computation of a structure that protects final consonants from interaction errors. Like the spontaneous speech from which the error corpus was collected, the phrasal tongue twisters require phrasal planning, and this apparently protects non-word-onset consonants. Lists, which undergo a different kind of planning, offer no such protection. This contrast is discussed further in Section 6.

The susceptibility evidence for suprasegmental structure can be summed up in the following claims. Segmental errors occur at all word positions, but

TABLE 2.8
Susceptibility of consonants to errors in lists and phrases:
Word onsets vs. other consonants

	Interaction Errors in Word Onset Consonants	Interaction Errors in Non-Onset Consonants	Total Consonant Interaction Errors
Eliciting Stimuli			
4 CVC words in phrases	64 (77%)	19 (23%)	83 (100%)
4 CVC words in a list	76 (44%)	96 (56%)	172 (100%)

interaction errors have a special affinity for word-onset consonants. This is true even in polysyllabic words, where opportunities for syllable onset errors in other word positions abound. The fact that this effect disappears for list utterances suggests that, in phrasal planning, word-onset consonants are processed in a way that leaves them open to confusions, while consonants in other positions are somewhat protected against confusion errors. When the protective representation imposed by phrasal planning is withdrawn, final consonants are at least as likely as initial consonants to participate in interaction errors. One hypothesis about the nature of this protective mechanism is discussed in the last section of this chapter.

4. ERROR EVIDENCE FOR SUPRASEGMENTAL STRUCTURE: UNITS

Sublexical error unit evidence bears on the suprasegmental planning framework in two separate ways. First, such evidence as there is provides strong support for the word onset as a planning unit, and much less substantial support for syllable onsets in other locations. Second, the weakness of the remaining scattered evidence for suprasegmental units suggests that other aspects of syllable structure play a very different role in production planning from that assigned to single phonemic segments or to word onsets. We look first at the word onset evidence, and then at the evidence for other constituents.

Onset units

Sublexical errors sometimes break words and morphemes into sequences that contain more than one phonemic segment and thus provide a prime source of data about suprasegmental structure. For example, error units that correspond to syllable onsets and rhymes have been interpreted as support for a representation in terms of syllabic constituents (MacKay, 1972, Shattuck-Hufnagel, 1983). However, this evidence is almost entirely concentrated in word-onset units. The evidence comes from two sources:

1. errors that move or change several adjacent segments as a unit, and
2. errors that blend two words, combining the initial portion from one word with the final portion of the other.

Movement Error Evidence. Most of the errors that move or change polysegmental onsets as units involve word onsets, rather than syllable onsets in other positions in the word. For example, there are 36 exchanges in the MIT corpus that indisputably involve a whole consonant cluster, and all 36 occur at the beginnings of words. In these errors, the exchange involves either (a) two word-onset clusters, as in "*sm*eething and *br*oking" for "breathing and smoking", and "*tr*ump *pl*out" for "plump trout", or (b) one word-onset cluster and one single-segment word onset, as in "*cr*ousing *h*unch" for "housing crunch", and "*H*atler-*St*ilton" for "Statler-Hilton."

A similar pattern is found for the incomplete errors previously mentioned. In this set there are 73 errors that move an entire consonant cluster as a unit, and 90% of them are word onsets.

The significance of the fact that most cluster error units are word onsets depends on the number of syllables in the words. If the cluster is a word onset in a monosyllable, as in "*tr*ump *pl*out", then the error does not distinguish between a word-based and a syllable-based onset unit. If the cluster is a word onset in a polysyllabic word, however, where syllable onsets in other word positions are also available, the evidence is more suggestive of a word-based onset category. In the MIT corpus, most of the cluster errors are in word onsets even for polysyllables: 100% of the 23 exchanges that involve polysyllabic words, and 86% of the 37 incomplete errors.

Because most of the cluster errors in polysyllables are in word onset position, we can infer that when a cluster error occurs at the beginning of a monosyllabic word, it is also usually by virtue of its word-onset (rather than its syllable-onset) position. These results provide support for the claim that syllable onsets in word onset position, rather than syllable onsets in general, are particularly likely to serve as error units.

Blend Error Evidence. Another kind of error that breaks lexical items into smaller sequences of segments is the word blend. For example, the MIT corpus (1984 count) contains 190 blends between pairs of quasi-synonymous words, like "k-ort" for "kind" plus "sort," and "st-annel" for "station" plus "channel." Many of these errors do not help to resolve the word-onset/ syllable-onset dilemma, because they do not clearly separate an onset from its rhyme. For example, almost half occurred at a point where the two target words shared a segment (like "prubble" for "problem" and "trouble"), so that it was not possible to determine the nature of the units before and after the blend point. Of the remainder, many divided the two words either within the onset or rhyme, or at a syllable boundary. However, 64 of the blends occurred clearly and unambiguously between a syllable onset and a rhyme, and thus defined an onset unit. In 56 of these onset-rhyme blends, or 88%, the syllable onset was in word-onset position; only 8 (12%) separated a syllable onset from its rhyme in some other position in the word. Again the evidence, although limited, favors a word-based onset unit.

The error unit evidence presented so far shows that multisegment error units sometimes correspond to syllable onsets, but this occurs almost entirely in word-onset position. This finding offers some support for the view that word onset consonant clusters form integrated planning units. But this is not always the case; a word onset can also come apart into its individual segments in a speech error. The MIT corpus includes 62 incomplete errors that break up a word-onset cluster (e.g., "twicky—tricky question"), and 4 complete exchanges that do (e.g., "Did the *gr*ass *cl*ack?" for "Did the glass crack?") This compares with the 73 incompletes and 36 exchanges that treat word onset clusters as units.

The observation that speech errors both preserve word onsets as units and break them up into individual segments makes it difficult to interpret the ambiguous evidence of single consonant onset errors like "*t*op *s*halk" for "shop talk". What is the appropriate description for these single-consonant errors? Is the error unit a single phonemic segment that happens to make up the entire onset of the word, or is it a word onset that happens to be made up of a single segment? It would be particularly useful to know which is the appropriate level of description, because this kind of error is so common in the MIT corpus; single word-onset consonants make up two thirds of the interactions that involve consonantal elements (e.g., 69% of the 181 exchanges and 64% of the 446 incompletes.) Later we argue that when a single consonant at the beginning of a word participates in an error, it usually does so by virtue of the fact that it is a word onset, but the ambiguity of the single consonant evidence is a forerunner of the difficulties that confront us as we turn to the error unit evidence for non-onset constituents.

Difficult Aspects of the Evidence for Polysegmental Units Outside the Word Onset

Error unit evidence for other suprasegmental constituents is difficult to interpret, because of the rarity of the examples, the unit ambiguity of hierarchical structures, and the fact that there are numerous counterexamples to both the word-based and the syllable-based accounts. We look briefly at each of these difficulties in turn.

Rarity. Polysegmental error units are rare among sublexical errors. For example, in the set of incomplete sublexical errors in the MIT corpus (which includes error units that range from the distinctive feature to strings of segments longer than the syllable), 66% involve word onset consonants, either single segments or clusters. A further 25% are single phonemic segments in other locations in the word. Only 9% involve sequences of segments outside the word onset. For exchanges and directional substitutions, the proportion of errors that involve polysegmental sequences outside the word onset is similarly small. This makes the influence of suprasegmental structure on errors outside the word onset difficult to discern in detail.

Counterexamples. A second difficulty arises because, even within this small set, there are some error units that do not correspond to either word-based or syllable-based structural constituents. Some are puzzling on any view of suprasegmental structure, like those that move a CV- unit in a CVC (as in "*ca*ssy p*u*t" for "pussy cat," and "*Bla*xie *De*ff" for "Dexie Blaff").

Ambiguity. A third difficulty arises from the unit ambiguity that is pervasive in hierarchical structure. The difficulty described earlier for categorizing single segment onset errors as either onset units or single segments arises for non-onset units as well. For example, if an error involves the -VC of a monosyllable, as in "*Sa*ke *La*lt City" for "Salt Lake City", is it evidence for a word-based or a syllable-based representation?

Despite these difficulties, several lines of evidence in the error unit data hint at the influence of suprasegmental structure beyond the word onset. This evidence is found in the distribution of polysegmental sequences that do and do not appear as error units. Sequences of segments that correspond to non-onset constituents do occasionally appear as error units, while certain others that are incompatible with suprasegmental structure have not been observed.

Non-Onset Units

Word- Versus Syllable-Based Non-Onset Constituents. One possible non-onset unit is the rest of the word minus the onset, like the -alt in "Salt" or the -inal in "final." Another candidate is the syllable rhyme. Evidence that might distinguish between these two possible representations comes from polysegmental error units that contain at least one C and one V. If any unit stands out in this set of errors in the MIT corpus, it is the -VC. For example, the corpus includes 28 polysegmental errors where both the error type and the extent of the error unit are unambiguous, and where the error unit includes at least one C and one V. In half of them (14), the error unit is a -VC. This distribution would seem to favor a description in terms of the syllabic rhyme. However, 10 of the -VC errors occur in monosyllabic words, where the -VC rhyme is also equivalent to the alternative non-onset unit, the rest of the word minus the onset. The other 14 errors do not resolve the problem; their error units are evenly divided among strings that correspond to full syllables, polysyllabic rest-of-word units, units that leave behind what Garrett (1976) has called pseudomorphs, and #CV- units that are not well-motivated on either a word-based or a syllable-based hypothesis about suprasegmental structure.

The unclear picture in the exchange errors is not resolved by the incomplete errors. Of the 14 incompletes where the error unit contains at least one C and one V and the extent of the unit is clear, 4 isolate a -VC, 4 a #CV-, 2 a rest-of-word unit, 2 a full syllable and 2 an apparently unmotivated string of segments. Clearly, although both syllable-based and word-based units occur, the number of examples is so small, and the proportion of counterexamples and ambiguities is so great, that we are unable to determine from the spontaneous error unit data the extent to which either of these two kinds of suprasegmental structure has an influence on sublexical errors.

Single Segments Versus Syllable-Based Nononset Constituents. Interpretation of the evidence for nononset constituents is made difficult by a second problem, and that is the difficulty of distinguishing between the single segment and the syllabic constituents of nucleus and coda, in cases where the syllabic constituent contains only one segment. Here again the bulk of the evidence is ambiguous. A single vowel exchanging with another single vowel could be an individual segment or could be a syllabic nucleus (e.g., "monos*u*dium gl*o*tamate" for "monosodium glutamate"). A single final consonant exchanging with another final consonant could be an individual segment or it could be a syllabic coda (e.g., "no*th* wo*rt*" for "not worth.") The critical data are found in the behavior of complex nuclei and codas. Do they come apart into their individual segments, or do they behave as integrated units, at least now and then?

In the MIT corpus we see some evidence that a complex nucleus can serve as an error unit. For example, there are four errors in which a tense vowel exchanges with a (V + /r/) sequence, and one exchange between a (V + /l/) sequence and a (V + /r/) sequence, in CVCC contexts (e.g., "m*er*k bi*l*ning") for "milk burning"). Linguistic analysis suggests that these sequences may correspond to complex nuclei.

In general, in the set of errors outside the word onset where the extent of the error unit is clear and where the identity of the hierarchical unit can be unambiguously determined, there are not enough data in the spontaneous error corpus to establish that either syllabic constituent structure or rest-of-the-word structure is more than a marginal factor in determining the shape of sublexical error units. However, we shall see that certain sequences of segments that would violate syllabic structure have not been found as error units, which lends some support to the syllabic view.

Non-Occurring Sequences. The equivocal pattern of evidence just presented might lead one to infer that any sequence of segments within the word or morpheme can serve, albeit rarely, as an error unit. There are, however, several interesting gaps in the distribution (Shattuck-Hufnagel, 1983). These gaps correspond to combinations of adjacent segments that would do severe violence to syllable structure. For example, a unit made up of the sequence -CV- in a word consisting of CCVC, like "clip", would break both the onset and the rhyme; error units of this nature (like "g*lit* cr*ape*" for "great clip") do not appear in the MIT corpus.

The converse pattern appears for (V + /s/) sequences. Analyses of syllable structure suggest that the sequence (V + /s/) in a word like "list" does not correspond to a complex nucleus. Instead, the /s/ is grouped with the final -C to form a complex coda, and (V + /s/) error units do not arise in these contexts. This pattern complements the errors just described, that treat the complex nucleus (V + liquid) as a unit in words like "court". That is, -VC- sequences that correspond to complex nuclei and -CC sequences that correspond to complex codas can serve as error units, but -VC- and -CC sequences are not found as error units in contexts where they would break up a complex coda or nucleus.

In sum, the error unit evidence offers some support for the word onset as a representational unit, even though counterexamples to this claim occur in both directions: onsets break apart into their constituent segments, and onset segments also combine with the following vowel to form C(C)V- units like the /pʊ/ and /frI/ in ". . . /pʊk/—Frick put . . .") Evidence for word-based or syllable-based suprasegmental units other than the word onset is equivocal, although -VC error units occur fairly regularly, and certain segment sequences which would violate syllable structure are not found at all as error units.

If suprasegmental structure beyond the word onset plays a role in constraining errors, it appears that it is a different role from that of defining the independently represented and moveable planning units, i.e., the individual phonemic elements that commonly become misordered in sublexical errors. If that different role consists of providing the integrated organizational framework that guides the sequential processing of the individually represented units, perhaps its effects can be seen more clearly in the next section on the position similarity between pairs of interacting error segments.

5. ERROR EVIDENCE FOR SUPRASEGMENTAL STRUCTURE: POSITION SIMILARITY

When two target segments of an utterance interact in an error, the similarity of their target positions in the larger structure of the utterance provides information about the representation of that structure. It is commonplace to note the similarity between the target locations of two interacting segments: initial segments interact with other initial segments, final segments with final segments, etc. The position similarity constraint has been interpreted as support for a syllable-based structural representation (MacKay, 1972), and has been incorporated into models by postulating that syllable onset segments, nuclei and syllable coda segments belong to separate processing classes (Dell, 1984).

However, the position similarity evidence is subject to the same caveat as the evidence from error susceptibility and error units already discussed: almost all of it supports the word onset position, and very little supports the representation of other aspects of suprasegmental structure. Moreover, the position similarity constraint is not absolute; some errors occur between pairs of target consonants in different positions. To see the nature of the position constraint more clearly, we need to compare (a) errors where the pairs of interacting target segments share a common position, with (b) errors where each member of the pair of target segments occupies a different position. The data for this set of errors are shown in Table 2.9. The analysis is limited to exchanges and incomplete errors, since we are testing constraints on interaction errors, and these error types provide the greatest degree of confidence that two target segments of each pair have actually interacted in the error.

Table 2.9 indicates not only the susceptibility of word-onset consonants to interaction errors, which was discussed earlier, but also the fact that word-onset segments interact mainly with each other. The fact that this is true even for polysyllabic target words is evidence for a word-based rather than a syllable-based effect (since a syllable-based constraint would permit word-onset consonants to interact freely with syllable-onset consonants in other positions). Some evidence for an additional final position similarity constraint is found in the data, but because it is strongest for monosyllabic words (column 3 of Table 2.9), it is ambiguous between a syllable-final and word-final constraint.

The position similarity constraint in these data points most directly to the word onset, but interpretation of this finding is clouded by still another ambiguity: is the constraint based on word structure, or on lexical stress? This ambiguity arises because so many of the spontaneous errors occur in words that carry main stress on the first syllable, so that the word onset consonants are also in prestressed position.

Position Similarity Ambiguity: Word Position or Stress?

The first column of Table 2.9 shows that in the MIT corpus 55% of the consonant exchanges and incomplete errors occur between pairs of word onset consonants. (Anticipatory and perseveratory substitutions have been omitted from this tabulation for reasons previously discussed.) What proportion of these interacting word-onset consonant pairs are also in prestressed position?

Table 2.10 shows that the proportion is very high: 94% of the pairs of interacting word onset consonants occur before a primary stressed vowel. Because onset consonants in monosyllabic target words are by definition prestressed, the 267 errors in monosyllabic words (rows 1 & 2) do not distinguish between a similarity constraint based on word position and one

TABLE 2.9
The position similarity constraint for consonant interaction errors in three different word positions

	Onset consonant × Onset consonant	Medial consonant × Medial consonant	Final consonant × Final consonant	Mixed Word Position	Total
Monosyllabic words					
Exchanges	89 (86%)	*	14 (14%)	—	103 (100%)
Incompletes	178 (91%)	*	17 (8%)	1 (1%)	196 (100%)
Total	267 (89%)	*	31 (10%)	1 (1%)	299 (100%)
Polysyllabic words					
Exchanges	76 (91%)	2 (2%)	—	6 (7%)	84 (100%)
Incompletes	215 (65%)	31 (9%)	5 (2%)	81 (24%)	332 (100%)
Total	291 (70%)	33 (8%)	5 (1%)	87 (21%)	416 (100%)
All Words	558 (78%)	33 (5%)	36 (5%)	88 (12%)	715 (100%)

TABLE 2.10
Word onset consonant errors in prestressed vs. nonprestressed position

	Both word-onset consonants prestressed	One or both word-onset consonants not prestressed	Total errors
Both target words monosyllabic			
Exchanges	89 (100%)	*	89 (100%)
Incompletes	178 (100%)	*	178 (100%)
One or both of the two target words polysyllabic			
Exchanges	69 (91%)	7 (9%)	76 (100%)
Incompletes	190 (88%)	25 (12%)	215 (100%)
Total errors, monosyllabic and polysyllabic target words	526 (94%)	32 (6%)	558 (100%)

based on stress position. The critical cases are the 291 word-onset errors that involve at least one polysyllabic target word. Even for these errors (rows 3 & 4), 89% of the word onset errors occur before prestress consonants, because the polysyllabic words have stress on the first syllable.

These proportions are similar to the 92% stress initial words in a sample of spontaneous speech taken from Carterette and Jones (1974). Does this indicate that lexical stress similarity has no additional effect on sublexical error patterns, i.e., is the apparent association between consonant errors and lexical stress an accidental result of the fact that most words carry lexical stress on their first vowel? Or, is shared prestress position another of the kinds of similarity that predisposes pairs of consonants to interact in errors?

To distinguish the effects of the two possible position constraints, one based on word structure and one on lexical stress, we need to look at errors in words where the word-onset consonants differ from the prestressed consonants. That is, we need errors in words where main lexical stress does not fall on the first syllable, like "repeat" and "parade". The corpus provides a few examples, shown in Table 2.11, which suggest that it is word position rather than prestress position that is constraining the interaction errors. But these errors are too few in number to decide the question. To resolve the ambiguity, we designed an error elicitation experiment using iambs like "repeat" and "parade" (Shattuck-Hufnagel, 1985b).

TABLE 2.11
Errors That Separate Word-onset Position Similarity
From Stress Simarility

1.	. . . *r*ath *m*eview . . . (math review)
2.	. . . *s*oulder *sh*eparation (shoulder separation)
3.	. . . *p*ult of *cc*uronality . . . (*cult of personality*)
4.	. . . *p*orm-*f*ersuasive . . . (form-persuasive)
5.	. . . *r*ode of *N*anview . . . (node of Ranvier)

Word-Position Vs. Stress-Position Experiment

The experiment was designed to test the prediction that the prevalence of word-onset consonant errors would persist even when the target words did not carry main lexical stress on their initial syllables. This is what would be expected if the position similarity constraint is based on word-position. The alternative is that interaction errors occur between the prestressed consonants even when they are not part of the word onset; this is what would be predicted if the constraint is stress-based. We used four-word stimuli like the following:

1. a) parade fad foot parole
   b) repeat load lot repaid,

where highly confusable pairs of target consonants (like p/f and r/l) shared word-onset position, but did not share position with respect to main stress.

2. a) repeat fad foot repaid
   b) parade load lot parole,

where p/f and r/l share prestress position, but not position in their respective word onsets.

Results for 24 pairs of target consonants and 20 speakers showed that the shared word position of Type 1 stimuli provokes twice as many errors as the shared stress position of Type 2 stimuli, for the same pairs of target consonants. Pilot results indicate a similar pattern when the four words of these lists are uttered in phrasal contexts (e.g., You repeat from the fad though the foot is repaid). Thus, although spontaneous errors confound the two factors of word position and stress position, experimental dissection suggests that word-onset position similarity has a more powerful effect on sublexical errors than does one based on stress.

The elicitation experiment also included two further types of stimuli:

3. a) peril fad foot parrot
   b) ripple load lot rapid,

where the p/f and l/r pairs shared both word-onset position and stress position, and

4. a) ripple fad foot rapid
   b) peril load lot parrot,

where the target pairs shared neither word-onset nor stress position.

Results for these additional stimuli suggest two further conclusions. First, the number of errors for Type 3 stimuli (where both word position and stress are shared) was equal to what would be expected from results for Type 1 (shared word onset position) and Type 2 (shared stress position). Statistically, there is no evidence of an interaction between the two kinds of position similarity. This lack of interaction is consistent with a two-stage model of sublexical processing, in which (a) there are two separate processing mechanisms which produce sublexical errors, and (b) each is governed by a separate position similarity constraint, one based on word onset position and the other on lexical stress.

The second result was that very few errors occurred for Type 4 stimuli (where neither word position nor stress position were shared by the two target segments). Apparently, the simple occurrence of two confusable target segments in the utterance is not sufficient to open the way to an interaction error between them. Instead, some further degree of similarity between the two consonants is required, and this further similarity is based on extrinsic factors which include the lexical stress and word position associated with each segment in the utterance that is being processed.

We turn now to a discussion of what the word onset findings imply for the original slot-and-fillers model described earlier in this chapter.

6. IMPLICATIONS FOR THE MODEL

The evidence reviewed in this chapter shows that the majority of consonant interaction errors occur in word-onset consonants. This is true even when the target words are polysyllabic (and thus provide numerous target consonants in other positions), and it is true even for word-onset consonants that are not prestressed. This pattern of results suggests that word onsets are represented and processed separately from other aspects of words, at some point during production planning.

Not only do the error patterns implicate word-onset consonants as generally error-prone; the data also suggest that the word-onset consonants are subject to a particular type of error, i.e., interactions like exchanges, anticipations, and perseverations. How can the slots-and-fillers model be expanded to account for these findings?

Preliminaries to an Expanded Model

One way to adjust the model to account for the error-prone processing of word-onset consonants is to propose that there are two separate processes during which sublexical errors can occur, rather than the single processing stage suggested in the original model. For one of these processes, the sublexical representation consists of two parts: the onset consonants of the word, and some representation (still unclear) of its remainder. The second processor has access to all of the individual segments of each word. During the time when the words are represented in terms of the onset plus the rest of the word, most of the errors that occur involve word-onset consonants. In contrast, during the processing that takes place while words are represented in terms of all their individual segments, errors are distributed more evenly across positions in the word. How might such a two-stage process be instantiated in the slots-plus-fillers model?

Our proposal for an expansion of the model is based in part on the finding that phrasal processing apparently protects non-word-onset consonants against interaction errors (Shattuck-Hufnagel, 1982). How is the processing of phrases different from the processing of words in lists, and how might this difference account for the lower error rate among final consonants in phrases? One obvious difference between the planning of lists and the planning of phrases is that, for a phrase, the speaker must integrate phonological information from the lexicon with the syntactic structure of the utterance. Selkirk (1984) and others have suggested that the integration of these two kinds of information is accomplished by the building of metrical structures which determine the prosodic shape of the utterance. We propose that one step during this integration involves the separate transfer of phonological information about word onset consonants. The theoretical motivation for the separate representation of word-onset consonants during this aspect of production planning is very simple: they play no role in the determination of the relative prominence of syllables or of any other metrical elements, so it is possible to delay their integration into larger metrical structures until a later processing stage. After onset consonants have been re-integrated into the phrasal structure, segments in all word positions will be more equally likely to participate in any sublexical errors that occur in subsequent processing. Only during the earlier step, while words are represented as the onset plus the rest, will the interaction errors that occur be concentrated in word-onset consonants.

The available data severely underdetermine the details of any production planning model, but we can describe in a very general way how this proposed expansion of the model might work. We assume that the construction of the phrasal geometry of the utterance described in Garrett (1975, 1984) is already well under way when the process we are describing begins. Moreover, we assume that this process operates initially on open class or content items (nouns, verbs, adjectives and adverbs), separately from closed class or function items (like grammatical morphemes). See Garrett (1984) for a discussion of the motivation for these assumptions. The operation of the expanded slots-and-fillers model can be summarized in the following five steps.

Step 1. Selection of a set of candidate open class or content words from the lexicon. Selection can be accomplished by transferring lexical items to a short-term processing store, or by marking their lexical representations temporarily. These candidate lexical items provide the set of phonemic segments among which final selection for the utterance will be made, and among which interaction errors can occur. The form of each lexical item specifies its segments and their serial order.

Step 2. Construction of syllabic structure and other apparatus for assigning main lexical stress to the open class lexical items. These processes incorporate the rest of the word minus the onset; word onset consonants are ignored until later.

Step 3. Transfer or association of the non-onset portions of content morphemes, now organized into the metrical structures that govern lexical stress, to the emerging phrasal framework. While the hierarchical structure of the phrasal frames that receive the non-onset portions of the content words is not fully specified in this model, we propose that among other things they define two classes of components for open class items: word onset locations (which at this point in the processing remain empty), and locations for the rest of each word (which have now been filled). These two structural components are present for every content word in the phrasal frame, even for vowel-initial words whose word-onset consonant component will not be filled.

Step 4. Eventual transfer or association of word-onset consonants into the word-onset locations for content words in the phrasal frame. All segments of the content words of the phrase are now in place.

Step 5. Transformation of this representation with its accompanying hierarchical organization into a complete string of discrete fully specified segmental elements, including those of grammatical morphemes, and subsequently into a pattern of motor commands characterized by substantial temporal overlap in the effects of adjacent segments. This process presumably involves many steps, among them one that is subject to single-segment errors at any position in the word. The influence of suprasegmental structure on interaction errors at this point in the processing is not clear, but non-interaction errors, which are distributed more evenly across word positions, may occur here.

This expansion of the model does not weaken the claim that individual phonemic segments are represented and manipulated during sublexical planning. It does, however, supplement that claim with the recognition that most of the consonant interaction errors involve segments located in word onsets. Single segment errors also occur in other word positions, and the weight of the error unit evidence clearly implicates individual segments in all word positions as representational units.

The expanded model offers several advantages over the original formulation. First, it motivates the transfer of information from one processing mechanism to another, during which sublexical interaction errors are presumed to occur. Instead of a seemingly unnecessary reordering of already-ordered segments, we postulate a transfer from the lexical processor to the phrasal processor Steps 3 & 4, and from the phrasal processer to the motor command processor Step 5. Second, it accounts for the predominance of interaction errors that involve word onset consonants.

A third advantage of the expanded model is its account of a pervasive aspect of the error corpus: pairs of exchanged segments often occur in identical vowel contexts, as in "Dack Janiels" for "Jack Daniels", or "Livil Sih— Civil Liberties Union". These errors were not analysed above, because the size of their error unit is ambiguous. That is, the error unit might be either the onset C-, or the initial CV-. In the errors we considered earlier, where the error unit was clear, CV- error units were very rare. The combination of two facts about the clear cases, i.e., the rarity of CV error units and the common occurrence of single onset C errors, suggests that most of the errors like "Dack Janiels" involve the exchange of two target consonants that occur before identical vowels, rather than the exchange of two CV units that contain identical vowels. Such interaction errors between word-onset consonants with identical following vowels is a natural result for the new model, because in Step 4 the word-onset consonants are transferred to a phrasal frame that already contains the non-onset portions of each word; similarities of phonological context might easily confuse the transfer mechanism, causing interaction errors of the types observed.

A fourth advantage is the account this model offers for the fact that errors sometimes move an onset consonant into a vowel-initial word, as in "feed Handrew __ot dogs" for "feed Andrew hot dogs". The canonical representation of word-onset slots in the phrasal framework makes it natural for this kind of error to occur during Step 4, because every content word location in the frame has a word-onset component, and this component is available to receive the error segment. Other types of errors that change the number of segments in either the onset or the rest of the word can be similarly accommodated, because the framework specifies only the two structural components for each word, without specifying the number of segments in either one. Other examples include word blends like "symblem" for "symbol" and "emblem", or interactions between a C- and a CC-, like "Hatler-Stilton for Statler-Hilton.

A fifth advantage is that we can now explain the lack of interaction between word-onset position similarity and prestress similarity, in the tongue-twister experiment described earlier. If these two factors operate during separate processing steps, they should not interact.

Finally, this model can account for the protective effect of phrasal processing on non-word-onset consonants, in the following way. Steps 1 and 2 occur similarly for the planning of word lists and grammatically well-formed phrases. Steps 3 and 4, however, are not relevant for lists, because the word stress pattern will not need to be integrated into the complex prosody of a syntactic structure. During the planning for a list, the processor goes directly from Step 2 to Step 5. As a result, the hierarchical structure imposed on the string of segments in each word is shallower for a list than the structure that would be constructed for a phrase, and the individual segments at all positions in the word are more free to participate in an error at Step 5. Thus, sublexical errors in word lists will affect consonants at all word locations, just as the experimental findings suggest.

In contrast, in the planning of a phrase, the processor must go through Steps 3 and 4. The transfer of rest-of-word strings as entire units, and the subsequent construction of deeper metrical trees over the phrase, give non-word-onset segments some protection against interaction errors later. In other words, the syntactic difference between phrases and lists results in a metrical difference, and the error difference between phrases and lists arises from the processing consequences of the need to elaborate a complex metrical structure.

This reformulation of the model represents only one possible approach to the problem of accounting for the predominance of word onset errors. In addition, many questions remain to be answered about the processing of segments (and the representation of suprasegmental structure) at other word positions. For example, does the processing of vowels differ from that of consonants? Do position constraints on interacting word-medial consonants suggest the influence of syllabic structure? Are all of the segments of a phrase, including those of function words and affixes, subject to sublexical errors at Step 5? Further analyses of spontaneous errors in the non-onset portions of words, as well as elicitation experiments that test specific predictions about the effects of non-onset structure, will help to resolve these questions.

ACKNOWLEDGMENTS

For valuable comments on an earlier draft of this chapter, thanks are due to Merrill Garrett, Pim Levelt, Dennis Klatt, and Ann Stuart Laubstein. This work was supported by a grant from the National Institutes of Health.

REFERENCES

Boomer, D. S., & Laver, J. D. M. (1968). Slips of the tongue. *British Journal of Disorders of Communication, 3,* 1–12.

Carterette, E. C., & Jones, M. H. (1974). *Informal speech.* Berkeley: University of California Press.

Clements, G. N., & Keyser, J. (1981). *A three-tiered theory of the syllable.* Center for Cognitive Science Occasional Papers No. 19. Cambridge, MA: Massachusetts Institute of Technology.

Dell, G. S. (1984). *A spreading activation theory of retrieval in sentence production. (Cognitive Science Tech. Rep. No. 21).* Rochester, NY: University of Rochester.

Forster, K. I. (1976) Accessing the mental lexicon. In E. C. T. Walker & R. Wales (Eds.) New approaches to language mechanisms. Amsterdam: North Holland.

Fromkin, V. A. (1971). The nonanomalous nature of anomalous utterances. *Language, 47,* 27–52.

Garrett, M. F. (1975). The analysis of sentence production. In G. H. Bower (Ed.), *The psychology of learning and motivation* (pp. 133–177). New York: Academic Press.

Garrett, M. F. (1976). Syntactic process in sentence production. In R. J. Wales & E. Walker (Eds.), *New approach to language mechanisms* (pp. 231–256). New York: North-Holland.

Garrett, M. F. (1984). The organization of processing structure for language production: Applications to aphasic speech. In D. Caplan & A. R. Lecours (Eds.), *Biological perspectives on language* (pp. 172–193). Cambridge: MIT Press.

Goldstein, L. (1977). Features, salience and bias. *UCLA Working papers in phonetics, 39.*

Halle, M., & Vergnaud, J. R. (1981). Three dimensional phonology. *Journal of Linguistic Research, 1,* 83–105.

Harris, J. (1983). Syllable structure and stress in Spanish (Linguistic Inquiry Monograph No. 8). Cambridge, MA: MIT Press.

Hayes, B. (1981). *A metrical theory of stress rules.* Unpublished doctoral dissertation, MIT, Cambridge, MA.

Hockett, C. F. (1967). Where the tongue slips, there slip I. In *To honor Roman Jakobson,* (Janua Linguarum Series Major No. 32) The Hague: Mouton.

Kahn, D. (1976). *Syllable-based generalizations in English Phonology.* Doctoral dissertation, Massachusetts Institute of Technology.

Kiparsky, P. (1979). Metrical structure assignment is cyclic. *Linguistic Inquiry, 10,* 421–442.

Kiparsky, P. (1982). From cyclic phonology to lexical phonology. In H. van der Hulst & N. Smith (Eds.), *The structure of phonological representations (Part I),* (pp. 131–175). Dordrecht, Holland: Foris.

Lashley, K. S. (1951). The problem of serial order in behavior. In L. A. Jefress (Ed.), *Cerebral mechanisms in behavior* (pp. 112–136). New York: Wiley.

Liberman, M., & Prince, A. (1977). On stress and linguistic rhythm. *Linguistic Inquiry, 8,* 249–336.

MacKay, D. G. (1970). Spoonerisms: The structure of errors in the serial order of speech. *Neuropsychologia, 8,* 323–350.

MacKay, D. G. (1972). The structure of words and syllables: Evidence from errors in speech. *Cognitive Psychology, 3,* 210–227.

McCarthy, J. (1979). On stress and syllabification. *Linguistic Inquiry, 10,* 443–465.

McCarthy, J. (1981). A prosodic theory of nonconcatenative morphology. *Linguistic Inquiry, 12,* 373–418.

Mohanan, K. P. (1981). *Lexical phonology.* Doctoral dissertation, Massachusetts Institute of Technology, Cambridge, MA.

Nooteboom, S. G. (1967). Some regularities in phonemic speech errors, Instituut voor Perceptie Onderzoek. *Annual Progress Report, 2,* 65–70.

Prince, A. S. (1982). *Relating to the grid.* Unpublished manuscript, University of Massachusetts at Amherst.

Selkirk, E. O. (1980). The role of prosodic categories in English word stress. *Linguistic Inquiry, 11,* 563–605.

Selkirk, E. O. (1984). *Phonology and syntax: The relation between sound and structure.* Cambridge, MA: MIT Press.

Shattuck, S. R. (1975). *Speech errors and sentence production.* Unpublished doctoral dissertation, Massachusetts Institute of Technology.

Shattuck-Hufnagel, S. (1979). Speech errors as evidence for a serial ordering mechanism in sentence production. In W. E. Cooper & E. C. T. Walker (Eds.), *Sentence processing* (pp. 295–342). Hillsdale, NJ: Lawrence Erlbaum Associates.

Shattuck-Hufnagel, S. (1982). Position errors in tongue twisters and spontaneous speech: Evidence for two processing mechanisms? *Speech Group Working Papers, Research Laboratory of Electronics, Massachusetts Institute of Technology.*

Shattuck-Hufnagel, S. (1983). Sublexical units and suprasegmental structure in speech production planning. In P. F. MacNeilage (Ed.), *The production of speech* (pp. 109–136). New York: Springer-Verlag.

Shattuck-Hufnagel, S. (1985a). Segmental speech errors occur earlier in utterance planning than certain phonetic processes. *Journal of the Acoustical Society of America, 77,* S1, 84.

Shattuck-Hufnagel, S. (1985b). Context similarity constraints on segmental speech errors: An experimental investigation of the role of word position and lexical stress. In J. Lauter (Ed.), *On the planning and production of speech in normal and hearing-impaired individuals: A seminar in honor of S. Richard Silverman* (pp. 43–49). ASHA Reports 15 (ISSN 0569-8553).

Shattuck-Hufnagel, S., & Klatt, D. H. (1979). Minimal use of features and markedness in speech production. *Journal of Verbal Learning and Verbal Behavior, 18,* 41–55.

3 Production Deficits in Broca's and Conduction Aphasia: Repetition Versus Reading

J.-L. Nespoulous* **, Y. Joanette* **,
B. Ska*, D. Caplan* *** & A.R. Lecours* **
* Laboratoire Théophile-Alajouanine,
** Université de Montréal, Montréal, Québec, Canada.
*** Montreal Neurological Institute, Montréal, Canada.

ABSTRACT

Former studies from our research group have shown a discrepancy between the errors produced by Broca's aphasics and those produced by conduction aphasics in repetition tasks. This discrepancy was interpreted as the manifestation of (a) a "phonetic" deficit in the patients belonging to the former group and (b) a processing deficit affecting, possibly among other things, the serial ordering of the phonemic units in the latter group.

Within the context of this chapter, we compare the patterns of errors observed in repetition tasks to errors produced by the same patients in oral reading of the same lexical items as those which constituted the repetition test. Results suggest that (a) there is indeed a *qualitative discrepancy* between Broca's aphasics and conduction aphasics in *both* tasks under question, (b) such a difference implies the existence of *different pathogenetic causal factors* in the two clinical patient groups. A tentative synthetic psycholinguistic model is proposed (derived from Garrett's, Shattuck-Hufnagel's, and MacNeilage's models of speech production) in an attempt to account for the pathogenesis of all phenomena (and discrepancies) observed in both groups of patients and in both tasks.

In the great majority of studies dealing with phonological disturbances in aphasia, subjects' deviations have been viewed as resulting from the disruption of one (or several) of the processes underlying oral production. The explicit or implicit goal was to determine whether phonemic errors (additions, omissions, displacements, and substitutions) were randomly produced or generated in a (psycho)-linguistically "principled" way. In order to account for such errors, both formal models of linguistic structure (i.e., phonological models) and psycholinguistic models of speech production have been resorted to. In most of these studies, however, the specificity of the tasks (spontaneous speech vs. naming vs. repetition vs. oral reading . . .) by means of which pathological data were gathered has not always been systematically taken into account.

In many respects, the present contribution can be said to follow the same trend in that, when launched in 1969 by Lecours and Lhermitte, the authors' intention was clearly to substantiate Alajouanine's hypothetical distinction between errors shown by Broca's aphasics and those shown by conduction aphasics, a distinction according to which: (a) subjects with Broca's aphasia or pure anarthria would show "phonetic" disturbances or "troubles de l'articulation verbale résultant d'une altération des mécanismes sensori-moteurs de l'élocution, lesquels mettent en jeu les muscles du larynx, du pharynx, du voile du palais et les muscles faciaux péri-buccaux[1]" (Alajouanine, Ombredane, & Durand, 1939); and (b) subjects with conduction aphasia would evidence "phonemic" paraphasias, "une variété de paraphasies qui viennent modifier la structure phonémique du mot en l'absence de toute perturbation articulatoire stricto sensu" (Alajouanine, 1968).[2]

Nevertheless, it has always been very clear, in both Alajouanine's and Lhermitte's teachings (Alajouanine et al., 1964), that there was another worthwhile hypothesis to test, an hypothesis according to which conduction aphasics, who produce frequent phonemic paraphasias in verbal repetition, would not behave in the same manner in oral reading. They did not offer any specific interpretation at the time for the potential divergence between the two tasks, limiting themselves to an account of the presence of phonemic paraphasias *in repetition* in terms of an "incapacity to build up the phonemic structure of words from a purely auditory stimulus." It is basically because of the clinical observation of such a discrepancy that Lecours and Lhermitte (1969) decided to test both repetition and oral reading within the context of their protocol, the very same protocol as the one which has been used for the present study.

Within such a context, set up by La Salpetrière's neurolinguists, the basic aim of our presentation—to compare oral performances from Broca's and conduction aphasics in repetition and oral reading of words—can be summarized as follows:

---

[1] "Disturbances of oral articulation resulting from the disruption of sensory-motor speech mechanisms involving laryngeal, pharyngeal, velar and peri-buccal muscles" (translated by the authors).

[2] "A subtype of paraphasias which alter the phonemic structure of words in the absence of any arthric disorder proper" (translated by the authors).

1. To substantiate, on a number of specific parameters, the existence of a quantitative and/or qualitative discrepancy between the error patterns shown by the two groups of subjects, as suggested by many former studies (Burns & Canter, 1977; Keller, 1984; Lecours & Lhermitte, 1969; MacNeilage, 1982; Martory & Messerli, 1983; Monoi, Fukusako, Itoh, & Sasanuma, 1983; Nespoulous, Lecours, & Joanette, 1982, 1983a, Trost & Canter, 1974), with the exception of that of Blumstein (1973).

2. To determine whether these patterns are consistently observed across tasks for each group of subjects, with the prediction, based on Alajouanine's preliminary observations, that Broca's aphasics would show a similar pattern of errors in both tasks whereas conduction aphasics might behave "differently" in both tasks.

3. To put forward tentative interpretations on the pathogenesis of all phonological disturbances observed in both groups of subjects and in both tasks.

SUBJECTS

Subjects were eight aphasics showing evidence of phonetic (arthric) and/or phonemic disturbances. Four of them were clinically labelled as Broca's aphasics, that is to say, according to Lecours & Lhermitte (1979), nonfluent aphasics with (a) no, or minimal, comprehension deficits; (b) word-finding difficulties; (c) arthric disturbances (*phonetic disintegration* in Alajouanine's terms); and (d) agrammatism (although non constantly[3]). The other four subjects were clinically labelled as conduction aphasics, that is to say, according to Lecours et al. (1979), fluent aphasics with (a) no, or minimal, comprehension deficits; (b) word-finding difficulties; (c) no arthric disorder; and (d) numerous phonemic paraphasias (most typically in repetition tasks) as well as some verbal paraphasias (usually of the "formal" type).

METHODOLOGY

Subjects were submitted to a repetition and oral reading test comprising 300 words (the same in both tasks) differing as to (a) length (from one to four syllables), and (b) phonemic structure (words, with, or without, consonantal clusters). All selected items were presented in a randomized fashion at time of testing. All subjects' responses and attempts at producing the correct target words were tape recorded and broadly transcribed using the International Phonetic Alphabet. Data were computerized in view of statistical analyses. Given the small number of subjects, statistical procedures chosen were of the

---

[3] And, in fact, none of our four Broca's aphasics was agrammatic.

non-parametric type. Tests used were either a Mann-Whitney test, a Friedman test, Kendall Tau and "W" coefficients (Siegel, 1956), or a Spitz "L" test (Delvaux, 1970).

RESULTS

1. Total Number of Errors

Deviant phonemes totaling 2,858 were gathered in *repetition:* 974 produced by Broca's aphasics and 1,884 produced by conduction aphasics. In spite of the important quantitative difference between the two groups of subjects, a Mann-Whitney test did not yield any statistically significant difference ($p = $ .248), this mainly due to the important dispersion (related to variance in the degree of severity of the illness) observed in our population of conduction aphasics (from 185 to 737 errors).

In *oral reading,* 1,818 deviant phonemes were gathered: 1,248 produced by Broca's aphasics and 570 produced by conduction aphasics, and a Mann-Whitney test reveals that such a difference is significant at the .06 level ($p < $ 0.06). This observation gives some credit to Alajouanine's and Lhermitte's intuition about the existence of a clearcut discrepancy between repetition and oral reading among conduction aphasics (Alajouanine & Lhermitte, 1964). Nevertheless, as can be seen on Table 3.1, these subjects are far from producing *no* error at all in the latter task.[4]

TABLE 3.1
Total Number of Errors, in Repetition and Reading,
in Broca's vs. Conduction Aphasics

	REPETITION N = 2,858		ORAL READING N = 1,818	
BROCA	974	44%*	1,248	56%
N = 2,222	34%		69%	
CONDUCTION	1,884	77%	570	23%
N = 2,454	66%		31%	

*In all tables, percentages to the right of the horizontal line are by reference to rows whereas percentages under the vertical lines are by reference to columns.

---

[4] On all tables presented in this chapter, percentages at the right of the small horizontal line refer to "row" totals and the other percentages refer to column totals.

When comparing the distribution of errors in both tasks within each group of subjects, Broca's aphasics appear to produce a slightly greater proportion of deviations in oral reading than in repetition whereas conduction aphasics show the opposite tendency.

2. Error Types

Four types of errors were systematically analyzed: additions, omissions, displacements, and substitutions.

2.1. Repetition.   No significant difference was found between Broca's and conduction aphasics with respect to additions, omissions and substitutions (cf. Table 3.2a). On the contrary, a Mann–Whitney test revealed that conduction aphasics produced a significantly greater proportion of displacement errors than Broca's aphasics ($p < .02$).

The analysis of the distribution of all four types of errors within each group of subjects (Friedman test) allows us to say that Broca's aphasics produced a significantly smaller proportion of displacement errors than additions, omissions and substitutions ($p < .02$), whereas conduction aphasics did not show any statistically significant preferential tendency.

An examination of Kendall Tau finally showed that the distribution of the error types was not correlated in the two groups ($p = .167$).

2.2. Oral Reading.   No significant difference was found between Broca's and conduction aphasics on additions, displacements and substitutions (cf. Table 3.2b). However, a Mann-Whitney test yielded a significant difference between the two groups of subjects with respect to omissions, with Broca's aphasics producing proportionally many more errors of this type than conduction aphasics ($p < .02$).

TABLE 3.2a
Error Types, in Repetition,
in Broca's vs. Conduction Aphasics

	ADDITIONS *N = 364*		*OMISSIONS* *N = 552*		*DISPLACEMENTS* *N = 318*		*SUBSTITUTIONS* *N = 1,624*	
BROCA	159	16%	246	25%	26	3%	543	56%
N = 974	44%		45%		8%		33%	
CONDUCTION	205	11%	306	16%	292	15%	1,081	57%
N = 1,884	56%		55%		92%		67%	

TABLE 3.2b
Error Types, in Oral Reading,
in Broca's vs. Conduction Aphasics

	ADDITIONS N = 362		OMMISSIONS N = 313		DISPLACEMENTS N = 113		SUBSTITUTIONS N = 1,030	
BROCA	191	15%	269	22%	64	5%	724	58%
N = 1,248	53%		86%		57%		70%	
CONDUCTION	171	30%	44	8%	49	9%	306	54%
N = 570	47%		14%		43%		30%	

The analysis of the distribution of all four types of errors within each group of subjects (Friedman test) revealed that Broca's aphasics produced in proportion significantly fewer displacement errors than additions, omissions and substitutions ($p < .01$) than in repetition. Among conduction aphasics, on the other hand, additions and substitutions were significantly more frequent than omissions and displacements ($p < .01$), contrary to what had been observed in repetition.

As in repetition, Kendall Tau showed that distribution across "error types" was not correlated in the two groups of subjects ($p = .375$).

2.3. Repetition vs. Oral Reading. When comparing the distribution of error types in repetition and oral reading within each group of subjects, it appeared that the distribution was significantly correlated in both tasks in Broca's aphasics ($p < .05$, Kendall Tau) whereas it was not correlated in conduction aphasics ($p = .062$, Kendall Tau), a result which suggests the existence of more variability in the behavior of the conduction aphasics and of more stability in that of Broca's aphasics.

3. Number of Stimuli with (at least) One Error

As estimated on the basis of target items inducing at least one error, the average production of "distorted" stimuli did not appear to be significantly different in the two groups of subjects in repetition (cf. Table 3.3). This indicates that the fact that conduction aphasics generated many more errors than Broca's aphasics in this task (cf. table 1) cannot be accounted for in terms of an increase in the number of stimuli disturbed by the former group of subjects, but rather in terms of the presence of several errors within the context of the same "distorted" stimuli (see section 4).

TABLE 3.3
Percentages of Stimuli With At Least One Error

	REPETITION N = 300	ORAL READING N = 300
BROCA	49%	51.5%
CONDUCTION	39%	19%

As far as oral reading is concerned, though, there was a significant contrast between the two groups of subjects (p < .02, Mann-Whitney test), again emphasizing the fact that conduction aphasics were performing much better in that task than Broca's aphasics.

4. Number of Errors Within a Same Word

If we now consider the number of deviations generated by a patient in the production of a single target item, we come to the following conclusions:

4.1. Repetition. Intergroup comparisons show that Broca's aphasics produced significantly more frequently target items with only one deviation than conduction aphasics (p < .02, Mann–Whitney test), the latter tending to produce more frequently target items with more than two deviations than the former (unsignificant though) (cf. Table 3.4a).

With respect to an intragroup comparison, Broca's aphasics showed a significant tendency to produce proportionally more words with only one deviation than words with two deviations or more (p < .02, Freidman test). Conduction aphasics, on the contrary, did not show any preferential tendency.

TABLE 3.4a
Number of Errors Per Word in Repetition

	0 N = 1,423		1 N = 632		2 N = 314		> 2 N = 389	
BROCA	621	50%	392	32%	147	12%	81	6%
N = 1,241	44%		62%		47%		21%	
CONDUCTION	802	53%	240	16%	167	11%	308	20%
N = 1,517	56%		38%		53%		79%	

Kendall Tau finally showed that the distribution of erroneous words within the three above-mentioned categories (one deviation *vs.* two deviations *vs.* more than two deviations) was not similar in the two groups of subjects (*p* = .375).

4.2. Oral Reading. Broca's aphasics again produced significantly more frequently erroneous words with only one deviation than conduction aphasics (*p* < .02, Mann-Whitney test); no other significant difference was noted between the two groups of subjects (cf. Table 3.4b).

Broca's aphasics, as in repetition, produced significantly more erroneous words containing only one deviation than erroneous words containing two deviations or more (*p* < .04, Friedman test) but, this time, conduction aphasics behaved similarly (*p* < .04, Friedman test).

The latter observation was corroborated by Kendall Tau which indicated that the distribution of erroneous words within the three categories (1 vs. 2 vs. > 2 deviations) was similar in the two groups of subjects (*p* = 0.4). Now, whether such an apparent "quantitative" similarity reflects a "qualitative" pathogenetic similarity remains to be further assessed.

4.3. Repetition vs. Oral Reading. In both repetition and oral reading, Broca's aphasics showed significantly similar patterns of errors (*p* < .04, Kendall Tau). By contrast, no such similarity was observed between the two tasks among conduction aphasics, who produce more grossly off-target words in repetition than in oral reading (*p* = .375, Kendall Tau).

5. Monosyllabic vs. Polysyllabic Items

If we compare the number of deviations affecting monosyllabic items and polysyllabic items, we obtain the following results:

TABLE 3.4b
Number of Errors Per Word in Oral Reading

	0 N = 1,627		1 N = 539		2 N = 254		> 2 N = 197	
BROCA	601	46%	399	31%	170	13%	128	10%
N = 1,298	37%		74%		67%		65%	
CONDUCTION	1,026	78%	140	11%	84	6%	69	5%
N = 1,319	63%		26%		33%		35%	

TABLE 3.5a
Number of Errors on Monosyllabic vs. Polysyllabic Items in Repetition

	MONO N = 431		BI N = 259		TRI N = 309		TETRA N = 430	
BROCA	255	38%	112	17%	152	23%	155	23%
N = 674	59%		43%		49%		37%	
CONDUCTION	177	24%	147	18%	157	21%	272	37%
N = 753	41%		57%		51%		63%	

5.1. Repetition. Broca's aphasics produced in proportion significantly more deviations on monosyllabic items than conduction aphasics ($p < .04$, Mann–Whitney test) (cf. Table 3.5a). Conduction aphasics tended to produce proportionally more deviations on tetrasyllabic items but the tendency was not statistically significant.

Errors in relation to number of syllables present in the stimuli were found to be non-randomly distributed in Broca's aphasics ($p < .04$, Friedman test) as well as in conduction aphasics ($p < .04$, Friedman test).

An examination of Kendall's Tau nevertheless indicated that the distribution of our results within the four abovementioned categories (mono vs. bi vs. tri vs. tetra) was not the same for the two groups of subjects ($p = .167$). Broca's aphasics showed a greater proportion of errors on monosyllables whereas conduction aphasics showed a greater proportion of errors on tetrasyllables.

5.2. Oral Reading. Broca's aphasics (cf. Table 3.5b) produced significantly more frequently deviations on monosyllabic and bisyllabic items

TABLE 3.5b
Number of Errors on Monosyllabic
vs. Polysyllabic Items in Oral Reading

	MONO N = 347		BI N = 143		TRI N = 201		TETRA N = 252	
BROCA	282	44%	101	16%	126	19%	137	21%
N = 646	81%		71%		63%		54%	
CONDUCTION	65	22%	42	14%	75	25%	115	39%
N = 297	19%		29%		37%		46%	

than conduction aphasics (p < .02 in both cases, Mann–Whitney test). Conduction aphasics tended, as in repetition, to produce more deviations on tetrasyllabic items but such a tendency was not statistically significant.

The distribution of errors with regard to the number of syllables present in the stimuli was found to be "principled" in Broca's aphasics (p = .02, Friedman test) but not in conduction aphasics.

Again, as in repetition, the distribution of our results with respect to the four abovementioned categories was not similar over the two groups of subjects (p = .375, Kendall Tau).

5.3. Repetition vs. Oral Reading.   Once again, Broca's aphasics behaved similarly in both tasks, with a tendency to concentrate errors on monosyllables (p < .04, Kendall Tau). Conduction aphasics, on the contrary, did not show the same distribution of errors in the two tasks (p = .167, Kendall Tau): the distribution of errors within the four categories used for our analysis was less "principled" in oral reading (Friedman test unsignificant) than in repetition.

To summarize the results of the first five (general) analyses that we have just presented, it thus appears that:

1. Broca's aphasics' impairment affects repetition as well as oral reading.

2. The number and the nature of the errors generated by these subjects is similar for the two tasks.

3. The percentage of stimuli disturbed by Broca's and conduction aphasics is about the same, at least in repetition.

4. However, conduction aphasics produce more deviations on each of these "disturbed" stimuli, with two or more deviations being the rule. This leads these subjects to generate more grossly off-target words than Broca's aphasics.

5. In repetition still, conduction aphasics produce more displacement errors than Broca's aphasics and such errors, as could be expected, affect essentially the longest items.

6. Oral reading is less massively impaired than repetition among conduction aphasics, the nature of the errors being moreover partly different in both tasks, contrary to what is observed among Broca's aphasics who show a great coherence in their error patterns.

6. Error Patterns in Substitutions: Interphonemic Distance Analysis

An interphonemic distance (ID) analysis (Lecours & Lhermitte, 1969) corroborates the existence of different error patterns in the substitutions produced by the two groups of subjects.

TABLE 3.6a
Interphonemic Distance Analysis: Repetition

	$ID = 1$ $N = 862$		$ID = 2$ $N = 352$		$ID > 2$ $N = 410$	
BROCA	396	73%	101	19%	46	8%
$N = 543$	46%		29%		10%	
CONDUCTION	440	43%	261	23%	380	34%
$N = 1,081$	54%		71%		90%	

6.1. Repetition. Conduction aphasics (cf. Table 3.6a) generated a greater proportion of substitutions at $ID > 2$ (with more than two features differing between the two phonemes involved in such a type of error) than Broca's aphasics ($p \leqslant .02$, Mann–Whitney test), and thus produced, as already noted, more grossly off-target words.

Nevertheless, when comparing, for each group of subjects, the distribution of substitution errors within three arbitrarily defined categories ($ID = 1$ vs. $ID = 2$ vs. $ID > 2$), it remains that both Broca's aphasics and conduction aphasics tended to produce a greater proportion of substitutions at $ID = 1$ than substitutions at $ID = 2$ and $ID > 2$ ($p \leqslant .04$, Friedman test in both cases). However, since Friedman test is based on ranks rather than on raw data, some distributional differences (other than the value ranked first) together with raw quantitative differences (cf. Table 3.6a) tend to be neutralized. If Spitz L test (based on raw data and not on ranks) is applied to the data, the prevalence of substitutions at $ID = 1$ is clearly stronger among Broca's aphasics ($p \leqslant .001$) than among conduction aphasics ($p \leqslant .02$), the latter subjects producing 55% of substitutions at $ID = 2$ and $ID > 2$ (against 27% for Broca's aphasics).

TABLE 3.6b
Interphonemic Distance Analysis: Oral Reading

	$ID = 1$ $N = 603$		$ID = 2$ $N = 231$		$ID = > 2$ $N = 196$	
BROCA	468	65%	156	21%	100	14%
$N = 724$	78%		68%		51%	
CONDUCTION	135	44%	75	25%	96	31%
$N = 306$	22%		32%		49%	

6.2. Oral Reading. Broca's aphasics (cf. Table 3.6b) produced proportionally more substitutions at $ID = 1$ than conduction aphasics ($p \leqslant .02$, Mann-Whitney test); no other significant contrast was noted between the two groups of subjects, contrary to what was noted between the two groups of subjects, contrary to what was observed in repetition (cf. supra: $ID < 2$ in repetition).

As in repetition though, both Broca's and conduction aphasics tended to produce relatively more substitutions at $ID = 1$ than substitutions at $ID = 2$ and $ID > 2$; such a tendency was again stronger among Broca's aphasics ($p \leqslant .02$, Friedman test) than among conduction aphasics ($p \leqslant .04$).

6.3. Repetition vs. Oral Reading. Broca's aphasics showed exactly the same pattern of errors in both tasks ($p \leqslant .001$, Friedman test) with the following trend: $(ID = 1) > (ID = 2) > (ID > 2)$. Conduction aphasics also showed exactly the same pattern of errors in both tasks ($p \leqslant .001$, Friedman test) with the following trend (different from that of Broca's aphasics): $(ID = 1) > (ID > 2) > (ID = 2)$.

7. "Preferential" Consonantal Substitutions

The previous analysis revealed that, despite the existence of some differences between Broca's and conduction aphasics, both groups of subjects tended to produce relatively more substitutions between phonemes sharing all but one of their constituent features. However, such a partial similarity does not of course imply that the substitutions produced by the two groups of subjects be necessarily the same from a qualitative point of view, where target-phonemes are consistently and coherently replaced by the same erroneous segments. It is the aim of the present analysis to determine whether ID similarity correlates or not with stable phonemic substitutions.

7.1. Repetition. Kendall W test revealed that Broca's aphasics were coherent in their substitution patterns for 9 out of the 12 consonants presented in Figure 3.1[5]: *p, b, t, d, k, g, f, v,* and *s* (correlations with significance levels ranging from $p \leqslant .03$ to $p \leqslant .0001$) (cf. Fig. 3.1).

As presented in other publications by our group (Nespoulous et al., 1982, 1983a, 1984), two basic tendencies seem to characterize these subjects' errors:

1. voiced phonemes tend to be replaced by their unvoiced equivalents;
2. unvoiced phonemes, when involved in a substitution process, tend to be replaced by phonemes whose place of articulation is different.

---

[5] Although not shown on Figure 3.1, *E, l,* and *j* were also found to be coherently substituted.

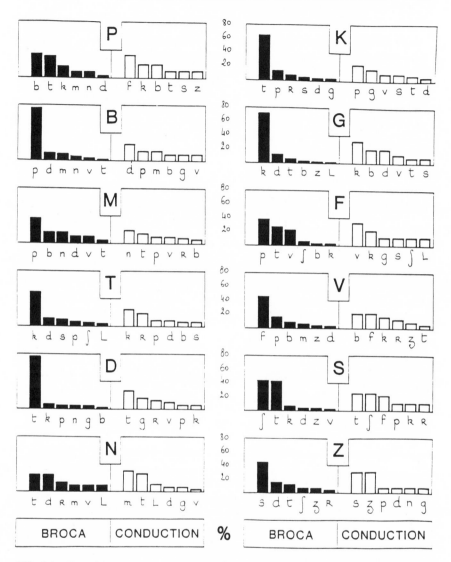

FIG. 3.1. Repetition.

The same statistical analysis revealed that, in conduction aphasics' substitution errors, only 3 consonants (out of 12) were coherently replaced by stable erroneous segments: *t, d,* and *m*[6] (Kendall *W* correlations with $p \leqslant$ 0.01, .04, .02, respectively).

---

[6] Again, although not shown in Figure 3.1, *R* was also found to be coherently substituted (*p* = .02).

It is thus reasonable to assume that there are indeed preferential tendencies in Broca's aphasics' substitution errors in repetition, whereas conduction aphasics' errors are definitely less homogeneous, despite the fact that many substitutions produced by the subjects involve an *ID* of 1 (see previous).

7.2. Oral Reading.   Kendall *W* test indicates that Broca's aphasics' substitutions are stable for all (12) consonants presented in Fig. 3.2[7] (correlations with significance levels from $p < .01$ to $p < .001$) (cf. Fig. 3.2).

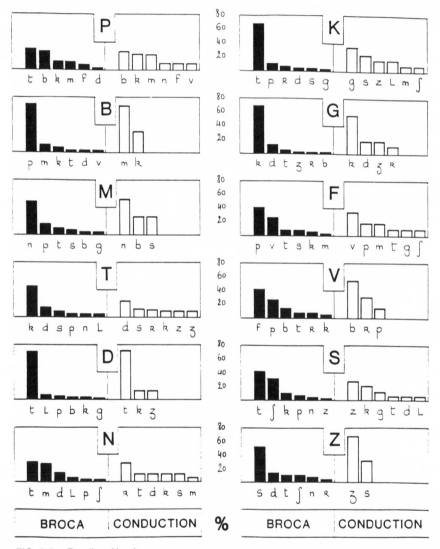

FIG. 3.2.   Reading Aloud.

----

[7] And on the consonants not shown here as well.

On the same statistical basis, conduction aphasics' substitution errors appear to be highly unsystematic, with no consonant regularly replaced by predictable erroneous segments.

Even more consistently than in repetition, Broca's aphasics' substitutions seem to be more highly constrained than those of conduction aphasics, which leads one to assume that there indeed exists an important difference in the basic underlying causality and determinism of errors generated by the two groups of subjects (see below).

8. Errors With vs. Without a Contextual Contamination Effect

A first analysis of context-sensitive errors concerned all deviant phenomena in which erroneous phonemes produced by the subjects were present elsewhere within the structure of the target words were numbered. Figure 3.3 presents the descriptive model that was used to analyze pre-positioning phonemic errors (the same applies of course to post-positioning phenomena).

8.1. Repetition. Even though both groups of subjects (cf. Table 3.7a) produced more errors without a contextual contamination effect, conduction aphasics generated significantly more "contextually-determined" errors than Broca's aphasics ($p < .02$, Mann–Whitney test).

8.2. Oral Reading. Even though, as in repetition, both groups of subjects produced proportionally more errors without a contextual contamination effect, conduction aphasics generated significantly fewer "non-contextually

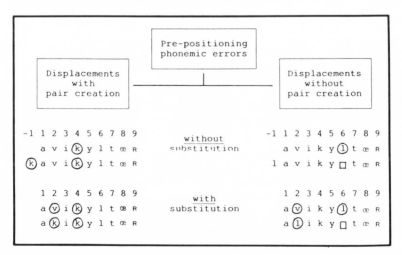

FIG. 3.3. Pre-positioning phonemic errors.
Target-word = "aviculteur", /avikyltoer/.

TABLE 3.7a
Errors With vs. Without A Contextual Contamination Effect: Repetition

	WITH CONTEXTUAL CONTAMINATION $N = 664$		WITHOUT CONTEXTUAL CONTAMINATION $N = 2,194$	
BROCA	138	14%	836	86%
$N = 974$		21%		38%
CONDUCTION	526	28%	1358	72%
$N = 1,884$		79%		62%

determined" errors than Broca's aphasics ($p < .02$ at Mann–Whitney test) (cf. Table 3.7b).

On the whole, it can thus be stated that, particularly in repetition, conduction aphasics tend to produce more "sequential errors" (Lecours & Lhermitte, 1969) than Broca's aphasics.

9. Anticipations vs. Perseverations

Corroborating our previous analysis, conduction aphasics (cf Table 3.8) were found to produce significantly more anticipations and perseverations than Broca's aphasics in repetition ($p < .02$, Mann-Whitney test) but not in oral reading.

TABLE 3.7b
Errors With vs. Without A Contextual
Contamination Effect: Oral Reading

	WITH CONTEXTUAL CONTAMINATION $N = 391$		WITHOUT CONTEXTUAL CONTAMINATION $N = 1,427$	
BROCA	195	16%	1053	84%
$N = 1,248$		50%		74%
CONDUCTION	196	34%	374	66%
$N = 570$		50%		26%

TABLE 3.8
Anticipations vs. Perseverations: Repetition

	ANTICIPATIONS N = 278		PERSEVERATIONS N = 386	
BROCA	60	43%	78	57%
N = 138	21%		20%	
CONDUCTION	218	41%	308	59%
N = 526	79%		80%	

A preferential tendency to anticipate or to perseverate was shown, though, neither between the two groups of subjects nor between the two tasks under study.

10. Errors With vs. Without Pair Creations

In this analysis (cf. table 3.9) two types of errors were distinguished: (a) "contextual errors" leading to pair creations (or assimilations, cf. Lecours & Lhermitte, 1969) and (b) "simple" displacements (cf. Figure 3.3).

Once again, conduction aphasics produced in proportion significantly more errors with and without pair creations than Broca's aphasics in repetition ($p < .02$, Mann-Whitney test) but not in oral reading.

Each Broca's aphasic tended to produce systematically more errors with than without pair creation in both repetition and oral reading although they generated relatively fewer errors of this type than conduction aphasics. In other words, while conduction aphasics generated both types of errors just

TABLE 3.9
Errors With vs. Without Pair Creations: Repetition

	WITH PAIR CREATIONS N = 354		WITHOUT PAIR CREATIONS N = 310	
BROCA	118	85%	20	15%
N = 138	33%		6%	
CONDUCTION	236	45%	290	55%
N = 526	67%		94%	

mentioned ((a) and (b)), Broca's aphasics showed a preferential tendency to produce bona fide consonantal assimilations.

The results of the analysis of the ten parameters presented above can be summarized as follows:

Broca's and conduction aphasics did not, in our corpus, show the same patterns of errors, particularly with respect to repetition.

Across-group comparisons revealed both quantitative and qualitative differences between the two groups of subjects:

1. Whereas no preferential error patterns were in evidence in phonemic substitutions produced by conduction aphasics, Broca's aphasics' error trends appeared to be very coherent, with a devoicing tendency being observed when target phonemes were voiced and a change of place of articulation when target phonemes were unvoiced.

2. Conduction aphasics produced significantly more "serial ordering" errors than Broca's aphasics.

Across-task comparisons, on the other hand, showed basically that while Broca's aphasics' errors were coherent and stable in both repetition and oral reading, conduction aphasics did not behave similarly in the two testing conditions. Particularly, percentages of "sequential errors", which differentiated clearly the two groups of subjects in repetition (conduction (15%) Broca's (3%)) were no longer quantitatively different in oral reading (conduction: 9% vs. Broca: 5%).

Even if our Interphonemic Distance analysis yielded significant differences between Broca's and conduction aphasics, it remains that the latter subjects produced more substitutions at $ID = 1$[8] than could be expected by chance. However, as stated above (cf. No. 7), even if such a tendency is likely to give important information about the underlying causality of the errors in both groups of subjects, it does not imply that such a determinism be the same in both cases. Indeed, when comparing "preferential substitution patterns" in our two groups of subjects (cf. No. 7), we are led to conclude that such a surface (quantitative) similarity is, in fact, misleading: Broca's aphasics' errors are highly systematic whereas no such coherence was observed among conduction aphasics' errors.

It is thus assumed that the pathogenesis of errors in Broca's and conduction aphasics is, at least partly, different in both groups of subjects, as intuitively felt by the pioneers of the French school of aphasiology (Alajouanine, Ombredane, & Durand, 1939).

---

[8] Although fewer than Broca's aphasics.

DISCUSSION

1. Pathogenesis of Errors in Broca's and Conduction Aphasia

Together with other results published by our group[9] and by such authors as Trost and Canter (1974), Burns and Canter (1977), Keller (1975, 1984), Martory and Messerli (1983), and MacNeilage (1982), the data presented here support the existence of different underlying determinisms at the origin of segmental errors observed amongst Broca's and conduction aphasics.

As far as Broca's aphasics are concerned, the presence of stable, coherent, preferential, (often) simplificatory errors might be appealing for whoever would like to advocate—like Sheila Blumstein (1973)—the existence of a markedness effect in these subjects' erroneous production. Such an interpretation would undoubtedly be most plausible if Broca's aphasics did not have massive arthric disorders, since one then could be led to consider that pathological phenomena find their origin in abstract, universal(?) properties of the phonological system. However, since most Broca's aphasics do have arthric impairments, it remains to be determined to what extent there might be a phonetic component in their speech errors.

Such an enterprise was carried out (among others) by MacNeilage (1982) in his attempt to account for devoicing errors found in Broca's aphasics (and not in conduction aphasics) in corpora borrowed from Johns and Darley (1970) and Trost and Canter (1974), corpora that yielded results very similar to the ones we have just presented. In his study, MacNeilage demonstrated (a) why voicing was physiologically more difficult to achieve during obstruents (fricatives and stop consonants) as compared with vowels and (b) how such a devoicing simplifying effect could be correlated with Broca's aphasics' slow rate of speech (Nespoulous et al., 1983a) and, maybe as well, with categorical perception artefacts from the transcribers. He was thus led to the conclusion that nonfluent aphasics "who are considered to have motor deficits . . . also show what he considers to be motor difficulties in their substitution error patterns" (MacNeilage, 1982), an interpretation which is similar to that of Alajouanine et al. (1939) and of Keller (1984), the latter showing "gesture simplification" to be evident in speech errors generated by Broca's (and not by conduction) aphasics.

MacNeilage's arguments, together with the results of the present study, make it reasonable to assume (a) that there is no abstract phonological

---

[9] See, in particular, our data on consonantal cluster production (Nespoulous et al., 1983b, 1983c, 1984): whereas Broca's aphasics tended to "destroy" clusters more often than to "create" new clusters, conduction aphasics did not show any preferential tendency; "cluster creations" were as frequent as "cluster destructions".

markedness effect in the speech errors of Broca's aphasics and (b) that there is instead a phonetic component in the pathogenesis of these subjects' errors. Now, whether such an interpretation enables us to account for *all* (simplificatory) errors observed in both consonantal segments (see above) and clusters (Nespoulous et al., 1984) generated by these subjects remains to be further assessed. Moreover, if, as it can be reasonably claimed, phonetic simplicity and complexity closely parallels abstract phonological simplicity and complexity, the task of distinguishing the respective role of both potential determinisms in Broca's aphasics' error production might very well turn out to be a bottomless chasm and, conceivably, an irrelevant venture. Both approaches—at least in the case of Broca's aphasics—seem therefore worthwhile for the time being.

As far as conduction aphasics are concerned, once a "phonetic" hypothesis[10] to account for the pathogenesis of their phonemic paraphasias is discarded, four observations have to be kept in mind when attempting to discover the more distal origin of their disturbances in a psycholinguistic model of speech production:

1. Conduction aphasics produce a high proportion of displacement errors, and such a type of errors clearly differentiated Broca's from conduction aphasics in repetition (see results, Sections 2 and 8);

2. Conduction aphasics—though less consistently than Broca's aphasics—produce phonemic substitutions at $ID = 1$ well above chance level (see Section 6); yet, such substitutions at $ID = 1$ do not show clear preferential patterns, contrary to what has been observed for Broca's aphasics[11];

3. Conduction aphasics tend to produce *more grossly off-target* words (see Section 4) and more *neologisms—which cannot be adequately analyzed in comparison to specific target words—(Nespoulous et al., 1983b and 1983c);*

4. Conduction aphasics' error patterns tend to be (at least partly) different when one compares repetition and oral reading (see results, Sections 2 and 8).

Thus, even if it clearly appears that the underlying determinism for the phonemic paraphasias of these subjects lies at a pre-motoric stage of psycholinguistic processing (MacNeilage, 1982; Nespoulous et al., 1984), the specific processes which happen to be disrupted in such patients constitute a matter largely open to discussion.

In former papers (Nespoulous et al., 1983b, 1983c, 1984), we have attempted to provide tentative explanations for (1) and (2) by resorting to

---

[10] Basically, such an hypothesis is discarded on account of (a) the fluency of these subjects' verbal output and (b) the absence of arthric disorders proper.

[11] In other words, no markedness effect whatsoever can be shown among conduction aphasics. Such an observation is consistent with the finding that consonantal substitutions in normals' speech errors—which, like the errors of fluent aphasics, are considered to be premotoric—do not show markedness effects (Shattuck-Hufnagel & Klatt, 1979).

Shattuck-Hufnagel's model (1979), and so has Buckingham in his most recent writings (1985). We thus hypothesized the disruption, in conduction aphasia, of the scan-copier mechanism postulated by Shattuck-Hufnagel to account for normal subjects' speech errors. If we assume that neologisms[12] are generated in a manner quite similar to phonemic paraphasias (Lecours, 1974), the disruption of this very same mechanism may be advocated as well for (3). Be that as it may, one is obviously in need of a specific and detailed psycholinguistic model of speech production to offer plausible explanations of all four abovementioned observations. Even if our attempt will sometimes restrict itself to laying out crucial questions that an "ideal" model should finally answer (and that we cannot fully answer right now), we will, in the next section of this chapter, confront our data and results with the leading existing psycholinguistic models of speech production in order to assess their adequacy to account for the erroneous phenomena generated by conduction aphasics.

2. Sublexical Processes Underlying Word and Sentence Production

The first question one would like to answer from the outset has to do with the nature of the lexical representation for open-class words as they are retrieved from the lexicon for sentence planning and production. We would submit that each individual lexical item comes out of the lexicon with its basic, canonical phonological properties: namely (a) its most abstract syllabic structure[13], which we would call its metrical geometry and (b) phonemic units (or segments) which are to be inserted into the different loci of such structural frames. For such a lexical item as "drapeau"—*dRapo* (= *"flag"*) we thus would have:

(a) *syllabic structure*

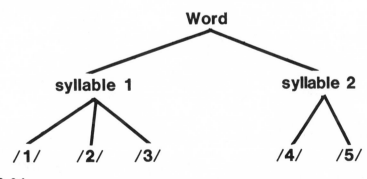

FIG. 3.4.

---

[12] Or, at least, some of them. See following for discussion.

[13] Independent of "later" resyllabifications.

in which the first syllable has a branching onset[14].

(b) *segments*

At this abstract level, the five segments to be retrieved from the subject's phonemic inventory would appear as feature matrices, each matrix leading to the "selection" of the specific phonemes required for a specific open class word.

In Garrett's model of sentence production (1975, 1976, 1980, 1981, 1982), such lexical items must then be inserted into the separately computed "phrasal geometry", thus building up the phonological representation of the sentence at the "positional level", a level of representation at which all linguistic units are linearly organized, as they will ultimately appear in the final utterance.

Processing disruptions generating such errors as the ones we have observed in our data (i.e., additions, omissions, substitutions and displacements) might logically occur at two distinct levels: (1) at the lexical level or (2) at the phrasal level. In the former case, one assumes that specific segments are mapped onto their syllabic loci before lexical insertion into the syntactic frames. In the latter case, one assumes that segment insertion into syllabic frames occur only at the "phrasal" level. The existence of across-word exchange errors[15] clearly indicates that the second hypothesis has to be retained, which does not imply that the first hypothesis has to be rejected (cf. intra word exchange errors). In other words, Shattuck-Hufnagel's scan-copier mechanism operates on several words, which are retrieved from the lexicon and are already abstractly assigned to phrasal "slots"[16]. Such a mechanism scans candidate segments from the whole set to be ordered and then copies these segments into their specific "slots" in the independently[17] computed syllabic matrices. Several monitors (a) prevent perseverative copying of given target segments by marking them as "used" after copying (cf. "check-off mechanism", Shattuck-Hufnagel, 1979) and (b) detect phonemic sequences that "might have arisen by error" ("error monitor", ibid.).

---

[14] Word stress would, of course, be specified at this level for languages (like English) in which stress assignment is phonologically and lexically relevant.

[15] Errors absent from our corpus for obvious reasons.

[16] As far as the "window" size upon which the scan-copier operates, see Blumstein (1978). In single word production, the window size is probably limited to the target lexical item—the phrasal level being absent from such a task—. It remains, though, to evaluate (a) to what extent, in repetition and oral reading of individual words, there would be partial "remanence" of the structural attributes of a preceding lexical item when the subject comes to encoding the following one and (b) to what extent aphasic may modify such a "window size" (= adaptive strategy) in order to better control their segmental production.

[17] See Shattuck-Hufnagel (1979).

Copying errors[18]—or erroneous segment assignment—can thus be viewed as:

1. the copying of one (or several), rightly selected segment(s) into inappropriate slots (exchange errors together with "contextually determined" additions and substitutions). In all these cases, it is of the highest interest to determine to what extent these "displacement errors" are constrained by structural properties of the abstract phonological representations extracted from the lexicon. Particularly, do the segments involved in the displacement process show metrical similarity (e.g. inter onset or inter coda exchange errors) or featural similarity (e.g. exchange errors involving two liquids)?

2. the copying of erroneous segments featurally similar to the target-segments but absent from the word (or rather from the "window") to be copied (contrary to (1)). In this second category of phonemic errors, one would find all $ID = 1$ phonemic substitutions (cf. results) together with non-contextually determined phonemic additions.

3. the consequence of the dysfunctioning of the "checkoff mechanism" and/or the "error monitor". Both monitors can, of course, be assumed to be at fault in most of the abovementioned types of phonemic paraphasias, otherwise the subject would obliterate such copying errors before "letting them out". But, there are two types of errors in which such a dysfunctioning seems to be particularly obvious: namely, additions and omissions. Indeed, in both cases, not only do we observe (as in substitutions and displacements) an erroneous assignment of phonemic segments but the syllabic structure of the whole string corresponding to a given "phrasal window" is altered, with plus or minus one phoneme; the "checkoff mechanism" having "lost" its count of the candidate-segments it has copied or is yet to copy[19]. It will be of particular interest in these latter cases to determine whether or not the subject violates the syllabic structural patterns characteristic of his mother tongue; most aphasiologists have so far considered that the answer should be negative (Lecours, 1974; Butterworth, 1979).

If what has just been proposed is correct to account for the pathogenesis of phonemic paraphasias (in which the underlying abstract phonological targets are both (a) recognizable (from surface production) by the observer and (b) probably accessible, in most cases, to subjects with conduction aphasia[20])

---

[18] Or, at least, some of them.

[19] How such an interpretation might correlate with a disturbance of verbal short-term memory remains to be investigated further (Caramazza et al., 1981; Saffran & Marin, 1975; Shallice & Warrington, 1970, 1974, 1977).

[20] See, as further evidence of this, the very many successive approximations produced by such subjects, thus indicating that the latter correctly realize the inadequacy of their verbal output as compared with the target (Joanette et al., 1980).

what is to be made of the underlying determinism of "neologisms" (Lecours, 1982a) produced by these subjects and by Wernicke's aphasics proper?

From the outset, it must be emphasized that it is far from obvious that all neologisms be pathogenetically alike, in individual subjects as well as across clinical groups of subjects (cf. conduction vs. Wernicke's aphasics in particular). Indeed, at least two possibilities are left open to account for the generation of such lexically unconventional items. It might very well be the case that both tentative explanations be adequate, but refer to *different types* of neologisms:

1. "Neologisms phonologically related to a target" (Butterworth, 1979), in which the subject is assumed to have retrieved from the lexicon either the correct item (or at least part of it) (as in phonemic paraphasias and perhaps formal verbal paraphasia) upon which inappropriate copying processes are subsequently applied[21]. In this first case, neologisms are believed to originate from the same disruption as phonemic paraphasias, the difference between the two phenomena being one of degree rather than of nature (Lecours, 1982a).

2. "Abstruse neologisms" (Lecours, 1982a), in which no target whatsoever is recognizable from the subject's verbal output and in which, if we adopt Butterworth's (1979) and Buckingham's (1985) opinion, the original pathological factor would be "anomia" (Buckingham & Kertesz, 1976; Kertesz & Benson, 1970; Kinsbourne & Warrington, 1963). Hence, we find a longer mean length of pauses before neologisms (indicating lexical search[22]), as opposed to shorter mean length of pauses (or to the absence of pausing) before phonemic paraphasias and verbal paraphasias, indicative of the absence of anomia (Butterworth, 1979). The production of abstruse neologisms would then be viewed as the outcome of the activation of a "generator" creating "quasi-randomly" phonotactically appropriate sequences of phonemes whenever lexical search reveals itself unfruitful after a delay of approximately 250 milliseconds (ibid). In such a case, it might be hypothesized that such "target-free" sequences would basically consist of unmarked, overproductive syllabic structures, as in most cases of non-aphasic glossolalia in which, as advocated here, there seems to be no underlying lexi-

---

[21] In some cases, though, it can be hypothesized that the item retrieved from the lexicon is itself wrong (as suggested by Lecours & Rouillon, 1976). In such cases, neologisms could be viewed as the outcome of erroneous phonemic copying applied on to an inappropriately selected lexical item.

[22] Alternative interpretations could, of course, be provided for such exaggerated pausing; such as (a) the impossibility, for the subject, to adequately inhibit wrongly selected lexical items (Rochford, 1974) or (b) the subject's "internal awareness" of the highly deviant nature of the "string" he has just abstractly encoded and that he is about to utter (Lecours, Travis, & Nespoulous, 1980).

cal target (Lecours, 1982b). This latter interpretation would also account for the frequent production in conduction and Wernicke's aphasia of neologisms "phonologically linked to other neologisms" (Butterworth, 1979), or even of "predilection neologisms" (Lecours & Vanier-Clement, 1976).

3. Repetition vs. Oral Reading

The stability (both quantitatively and qualitatively) of errors generated by Broca's aphasics makes it clear that these subjects' deficit is independent of the modality of input. As far as conduction aphasics are concerned, however, data interpretation appears, once again, more intricate. Quantitatively, these subjects clearly produced less errors in oral reading than in repetition (see results, Section 3.1.). Qualitatively, though, error trends tended to be most of the time the same in both tasks; the only clearcut discrepancy was that "preferential" error types were partly different in repetition and oral reading, and that additions were definitely more frequent than omissions in the latter task (as opposed to the former):

Repetition:	additions	<	displacements	<	omissions	<	substitutions
	(11%)		(15%)		(16%)		(57%)
Oral reading:	omissions	<	displacements	<	additions	<	substitutions
	(8%)		(9%)		(30%)		(54%)

Despite the slight qualitative difference, for which we have no definite interpretation to offer for the time being, it thus appears that the nature of the phonemic paraphasias observed in repetition and oral reading in conduction aphasia is basically the same while the number of errors produced in both tasks is substantially different. This twofold observation suggests (a) that the qualitative impairment responsible for phonemic paraphasias is the same in both tasks (and presumably in other tasks as well (spontaneous speech, naming)[23]; (b) that, as in Broca's aphasia, such an impairment is qualitatively independent from the modality of input, even though (c) oral reading, based on visual input, considerably reduces the number of errors generated by the subject.

On the latter issue, we will tentatively claim that, while the copying mechanisms are similarly impaired in repetition and oral reading, the permanence of the visual stimulus during oral production helps, to a certain extent, the subject's monitoring of the psycholinguistic processes whose aim is to build up the linear phonological representation (at Garrett's, 1982)

---

[23] Moreover, a complementary analysis of our data (in preparation) convinced that phonemic paraphasias produced in oral reading by conduction aphasics were by no means "visually induced" by the nature of the written stimuli. Indeed, very few errors (6% approximately) were of the following type: "drap" pronounced *drap* or "mord" pronounced *mord*.

"positional level" from the more abstract (and presumably nonlinear) lexico-phonological representation. The impairment of the "internal" checkoff mechanism and of the error monitor would thus be partly counterbalanced by "external" compensatory monitoring. If this statement is correct, then, not only would we have a tentative explanation for the production of fewer para-phasias in oral reading as opposed to repetition, but we might have as well a partial explanation for the decrease, in such a task, of such an error type as omission. In other words, the subject would be more accurate in its monitor-ing of which segments have to be copied or have already been copied for two complementary reasons: (a) the stimulus remains constant and (b) grapheme-phoneme correspondence, which is intact in our subjects, helps them to copy more efficiently the different segments required for the con-struction of linear phonological representations at the positional level. If this is so, we might predict that conduction aphasics who (contrary to ours) would only be briefly exposed to visual stimuli, would then make as many phonemic errors in oral reading as in repetition because "external" monitor-ing would then be impossible, the stimuli having lost in this case the per-manence they had in our testing procedure. Conversely, if such a prediction happened to be false, it would indicate that there are indeed important intrin-sic differences in (a) oral production from visual stimuli vs (b) oral produc-tion from auditory stimuli. Since the nature of phonemic errors produced was very similar in the two conditions in our data, we will, for the time being, stick to the above interpretation and claim that the impairment observed in conduction aphasia is unique, whatever the task proposed to the subject and whatever quantitative across-task discrepancies we may observe.

CONCLUSION

To conclude, we will summarize what appear to be the salient features of our study:

1. As claimed in former publications since the days of Alajouanine, there indeed exists a qualitative difference between segmental errors generated by Broca's aphasics and conduction aphasics;

2. Such a difference clearly indicates the existence of different pathogenetic causal factors in the two clinical groups of subjects under analysis:

- in Broca's aphasia, on one hand, the determining impairment has been interpreted as basically due to a relatively low-level "phonetic" deficit;
- in conduction aphasia, on the other hand, phonemic paraphasias have been presented as the outcome of the disruption of different mechanisms whose objective is to compute linear phonological representations (at

Garrett's positional level) from deeper, more abstract and probably non-linear lexico-phonological representations, retrieved from the lexicon (Caplan et al., in preparation);

3. Because of their overall insensitiveness to the modality of input (auditory vs. visual), the disturbances, in both groups of subjects, have been viewed as encoding deficits affecting psycholinguistic processes located at different levels in a model of word and sentence production, where the impairment of Broca's aphasics is more "peripheral" than that shown by conduction aphasics;

4. From a psycholinguistic point of view, our study, particularly that of conduction aphasia, finally tends to substantiate the adequacy (and proposes an interaction) of some leading present day models of word and sentence production devised to account for speech errors in normal speaking subjects for a better understanding of language disturbances in aphasia.

ACKNOWLEDGMENT

This work has been supported by Grant CRMC PG-28.

REFERENCES

Alajouanine, T. (1968). L'aphasie et le langage pathologique. Paris: Baillière.

Alajouanine, T., & Lhermitte, F. (1964). Essai d'introspection de l'aphasie: L'aphasie vue par les aphasiques. Revue Neurologique, 110, 609–621.

Alajouanine, T., Lhermitte, F., Ledoux, R., Renaud, D., & Vignolo, L. (1964). Les composantes phonémiques et sémantiques de la jargonaphasie. Revue Neurologique, 110, 5–20.

Alajouanine, T., Ombredane, A., & Durand, M. (1939). Le syndrome de désintégration phonétique dans l'aphasie. Paris: Masson.

Blumstein, S. (1973). A phonological investigation of aphasic speech. The Hague: Mouton.

Blumstein, S. (1978). Segment structure and the syllable in aphasia (pp. 113–154). In A. Bell & J. B. Hooper (Eds.), Syllables and segments (pp. 189–200). Amsterdam: North Holland.

Buckingham, H. W. (1985). Perseveration in aphasia. In S. Newman & R. Epstein (Eds.), Dysphasia (pp. 113–154). London: Churchill Livingstone.

Buckingham, H. W., & Kertesz, A. (1976). Neologistic jargon aphasia. Amsterdam: Swets & Zeitlinger.

Burns, M., & Canter, G. (1977). Phonemic behavior of aphasic patients with posterior cerebral lesions. Brain and Language, 4, 492–507.

Butterworth, B. (1979). Hesitation and the production of verbal paraphasias and neologisms in jargon aphasia. Brain and Language, 8, 133–161.

Caplan, D., Vanier, M., & Baker, C. (in preparation). Word production, verbal memory and sentence comprehension in a conduction aphasic.

Caramazza, A., Basili, A. G., Koller, J. J., & Berndt, R. S. (1981). An investigation of repetition and language processing in a case of conduction aphasia. Brain and Language, 14, 235–271.

80   NESPOULOUS, JOANETTE, SKA, CAPLAN, AND LECOURS

Delvaux, J. P. (1970). Calcul simplifié de la corrélation entre deux variables. *Revue de Psychologie et des Sciences de l'Education, 5,* 302-308.

Garrett, M. F. (1975). The analysis of sentence production. In B. Gordon (Ed.), *The psychology of learning and motivation: Advances in research and theory* (p. 133-177). New York: Academic Press.

Garrett, M. F. (1976). Syntactic processes in sentence production. In R. J. Wales & E. Walker (Eds.), *New approaches to language mechanisms* (pp. 231-256). Amsterdam: North Holland.

Garrett, M. F. (1980). Levels of processing in sentence production. In B. Butterworth (Ed.), *Sentence production* (pp. 177-220). London: Academic Press.

Garrett, M. F. (1981). *The organization of processing structure for language production: Applications to aphasic speech.* Paper presented at the Conference on Biological Perspectives on Language, Montreal.

Garrett, M. F. (1982). Production of speech: Observations from normal and pathological language use. In A. W. Ellis (Ed.), *Normality and pathology in cognitive functions* (pp. 19-77). London: Academic Press.

Joanette, Y., Keller, E., & Lecours, A. R. (1981). Sequences of phonemic approximations in aphasia. *Brain and Language, 11,* 30-44.

Johns, D., & Darley, F. (1970). Phonemic variability in apraxia of speech. *Journal of Speech and Hearing Research, 13,* 556-583.

Keller, E. (1975). *Vowel errors in aphasia.* Unpublished doctoral thesis, University of Toronto.

Keller, E. (1984). Simplification and gesture reduction in phonological disorders of apraxia and aphasia. In M. R. McNeil, J. C. Rosenbek, & A. E. Aronson (Eds.), *Apraxia of speech: Physiology, acoustics, linguistics, management* (pp. 221-256). San Diego: College-Hill Press.

Kertesz, A., & Benson, D. (1970). Neologistic jargon: A clinicopathological study. *Cortex, 6,* 362-396.

Kinsbourne, M., & Warrington, E. (1963). Jargon aphasia. *Neuropsychologia, 1,* 27-37.

Lecours, A. R. (1974). Linguistic analysis of paraphasias. *Neurosciences Research Program Bulletin, 12,* 555-569.

Lecours, A. R. (1982a). On neologisms. In J. Mehler, E. C. T. Walker, & M. F. Garrett (Eds.), *Perspectives on mental representation: Experimental and theoretical studies of cognitive processes and capacities* (pp. 217-248). Hillsdale, NJ: Lawrence Erlbaum Associates.

Lecours, A. R. (1982b). Simulation of speech production without a computer. In M. Arbib, J. Marshall, & D. Caplan (Eds.), *Neural models of language processes* (pp. 345-367). New York: Academic Press.

Lecours, A. R., & Lhermitte, F. (1969). Phonemic paraphasias: Linguistic structures and tentative hypotheses. *Cortex, 5,* 3, 193-228.

Lecours, A. R., & Lhermitte, F. (1979). *L'aphasie.* Paris: Flammarion.

Lecours, A. R., & Rouillon, F. (1976). Neurolinguistic analysis of jargonaphasia and jargonagraphia. In H. Whitaker & H. A. Whitaker (Eds.), *Studies in neurolinguistics* (Vol. 2, pp. 95-141). New York: Academic Press.

Lecours, A. R., Travis, L., & Nespoulous, J.-L. (1980). Néologismes et anosognosie. In *Etudes neurolinguistiques* (numero spécial de la revue Grammatica), Association des Publications de l'Université Toulouse-Le Mirail, 101-114.

Lecours, A. R., & Vanier-Clément, M. (1976). Schizophasia and jargonaphasia. A comparative description with comments on Chaika's and Fromkin's respective looks at schizophrenic language. *Brain and Language, 3,* 516-565.

MacNeilage, P. F. (1982). Speech production mechanisms in aphasia. In S. Grillner, B. Lindblom, J. Lubker, & A. Persson (Eds.), *Speech motor control* (pp. 43-60). New York: Pergamon Press.

Martory, M. D., & Messerli, P. (1983). Analyse phonologique comparée des troubles de l'expression orale. In P. Messerli, P. M. Lavorel, & J.-L. Nespoulous (Eds.), *Neuropsychologie de l'expression orale* (pp. 53–69). Paris: Editions du C.N.R.S.

Monoi, H., Fukusako, Y., Itoh, M., & S. Sasanuma, S. (1983). Speech sound errors in patients with conduction and Broca's aphasia. *Brain and Language, 20,* 175–194.

Nespoulous, J.-L., Joanette, Y., Beland, R., Caplan, D., & Lecours, A. R. (1984). Phonologic disturbances in aphasia: Is there a "markedness effect" in aphasic phonemic errors? In F. C. Rose (Ed.), *Advances in neurology, Vol. 42: Progress in aphasiology* (pp. 203–214). New York: Raven Press.

Nespoulous, J.-L., Lecours, A. R., & Joanette, Y. (1982). Stabilité et instabilité des déviations phonétiques et/ou phonémiques des aphasiques. *La Linguistique, 18,* 2, 85–97.

Nespoulous, J.-L., Lecours, A. R., & Joanette, Y. (1983a). La dichotomie phonétique/ phonémique a-t-elle une valeur nosologique? In P. Messerli, P. M. Lavorel, & J.-L. Nespoulous (Eds.), *Neuropsychologie de l'expression orale* (pp. 71–91). Paris: Editions du C.N.R.S.

Nespoulous, J.-L., Joanette, Y., Beland, R., Caplan, D., & Lecours, A. R. (1983b, June). *Is there a "markedness effect" in aphasic substitution errors?* Paper presented at the Sixth International Neuropsychological Society European Conference, Lisbon.

Nespoulous, J.-L., Joanette, Y., Beland, R., Caplan, D., Ska, B., & Lecours, A. R. (1983c). *Is there a markedness effect is aphasics' production of consonantal clusters?* Paper presented at the Academy of Aphasia Annual Meeting, Minneapolis.

Rochford, G. (1974). Are jargon disphasics disphasic? *British Journal of Disorders of Communication, 9,* 35–44.

Saffran, E. M., & Marin, O. S. (1975). Immediate memory for word lists and sentences in a patient with deficient auditory short-term memory. *Brain and Language, 5,* 420–433.

Shallice, T., & Warrington, E. K. (1970). Independent functioning of verbal memory stores: a neuropsychological study. *Quarterly Journal of Experimental Psychology, 22,* 261–273.

Shallice, T., & Warrington, E. K. (1974). Note. The dissociation between short-term retention of meaningful sounds and verbal material. *Neuropsychologia, 12,* 553–555.

Shallice, T., & Warrington, E. K. (1977). Auditory-verbal short-term memory impairment and conduction aphasia. *Brain and Language, 4,* 479–491.

Shattuck-Hufnagel, S. (1979). Speech errors as evidence for a serial-ordering mechanism in sentence production. In W. Cooper & E. C. T. Walker (Eds.), *Sentence processing: Psycholinguistic studies presented to Merrill Garrett* (pp. 295–342). Hillsdale, NJ: Lawrence Erlbaum Associates.

Shattuck-Hufnagel, S., & Klatt, D. H. (1979). The limited use of distinctive features and markedness in speech production: Evidence from speech error data. *Journal of Verbal Learning and Verbal Behavior, 18,* 41–55.

Siegel, S. (1956). *Nonparametric statistics for the behavioral sciences.* New York: McGraw Hill.

Trost, J. E., & Canter, G. (1974). Apraxia of speech in patients with Broca's aphasia: A study of phoneme production accuracy and error patterns. *Brain and Language, 1,* 63–80.

Damage to Input and Output Buffers—What's a Lexicality Effect Doing in a Place Like That?

4

Daniel Bub
Montreal Neurological Institute
Sandra Black
University of Toronto
Janice Howell
Andrew Kertesz
University of Western Ontario

ABSTRACT

The models of language most widely used to analyze functional damage are constructed in terms of discrete processing components that operate independently of each other. From this assumption, it follows that the stimulus dimensions affecting performance should point directly to the general location of the defective component within the language mechanism: Sensitivity to attributes involving only word-specific dimensions (e.g., the status of the target as a real word) would indicate the disturbance occurs after the level where the structural aspects of input and output codes are established. If variables related to structure (e.g., word length) do exert a major influence, the conclusion is that damage has taken place to encoding procedures which operate before the categorization of perceptual information as higher level units. We present evidence from three brain-damage patients that creates some difficulty for this general approach. Analysis of the cases suggests that relatively central components of the language mechanism are influencing ongoing events at more peripheral stages that compute a structural description. Such interactivity qualifies the notion of a completely transparent relationship between a disordered functional component and performance.

Information processing models are now widely used to analyse impairment caused by brain damage. Central to all these descriptions is the view of the language mechanism as a collection of discrete functional components that operate as independently of each other as possible. There is no inherent requirement for serially ordered processing, given this type of modular organization, but the simplest assumption (and the one most commonly entertained) is that information does proceed through the system in strict sequence. Each processing stage is completed before the next can begin, unconstrained by linguistic information specified at higher levels of representation in the system (see Marslen-Wilson, 1976; Tyler, 1982 for discussion of this approach).

Figure 4.1, adapted from several recent formulations (e.g., Morton & Patterson, 1980; Newcombe & Marshall, 1980), illustrates the functional pathways needed to carry out relatively simple language tasks such as repetition or reading of single words. The organization of the model respects the basic distinction between input/output mechanisms, which are concerned only with the physical description of a word (its constituent letters, phonemes, etc.) and more central levels of linguistic representation containing abstract knowledge about the word's orthographic, phonological, and semantic forms.

The assumption that the different components of the model function completely independently of each other allows us to determine whether a particular syndrome reflects damage to peripheral or central levels of processing in

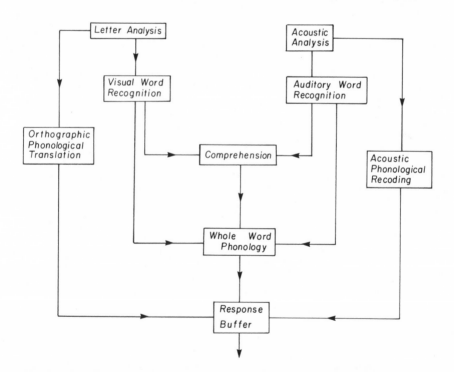

FIG. 4.1. Flow diagram of the language components mediating word recognition and pronunciation.

a reasonably straightforward manner, simply by noting which type of stimulus property (structural vs. linguistic) influences performance. As an example of this approach, consider the analysis of two very dissimilar acquired reading disorders, phonological dyslexia and letter-by-letter reading, which are quite clearly the result of impairment to separate, nonoverlapping components of the reading mechanism.

Phonological dyslexics show good to excellent recognition and pronunciation of individual words, but encounter extreme difficulty in retrieving the pronunciation of written nonsense words (Beauvois & Derouesné, 1979; Patterson, 1982). The variable of lexicality (i.e., wordness) is the only one that has been found to exert a clear cut effect on performance in this syndrome[1]: any letter array with a lexical representation is read aloud correctly, whereas unfamiliar but pronounceable strings cannot be accurately translated into sound.

Studies of letter-by-letter readers (Patterson & Kay, 1982; Warrington & Shallice, 1980) in contrast, have so far documented complete insensitivity to lexical status. This form of dyslexia is characterized by the inability to read without first laboriously spelling out (or in some cases, sounding out) each letter in succession. Words as well as nonsense words are decoded the same way, through sequential and explicit analysis of individual letters. Not surprisingly, the one variable found to exert massive effects on letter-by-letter reading is array length: the time taken for identification typically increases by 2 or 3 seconds for every additional letter making up a word.

The model outlined in Fig. 4.1 may be used to specify the approximate location of the functional disturbance for each dyslexic syndrome, if we have some idea which aspect of print is no longer reliably processed by the reading mechanism. Phonological dyslexics are only impaired when they are required to translate nonlexical spelling patterns into sound, so the damage must be confined to some part of the mechanism that derives orthographic units from print, assigns them a phonemic value and then blends the individual response elements into a single pronunciation. We can also argue that all the processes responsible for achieving lexical access remain intact, because phonological dyslexics have no trouble reading letter strings that form legitimate words.

This does not appear to be the case for the letter-by-letter reader; the fact that even very familiar words (e.g., *boy, tree, car*) are not identified directly (i.e., identified without painstaking attention to each letter) supports the conclusion that the functional disturbance has completely prevented normal access to the lexicon. The damage, on this interpretation, must be confined to

---

[1] Some phonological dyslexics are worse at reading individual function words and affixed words than other lexical items (e.g., the patient described by Patterson, 1982), but there are also cases that fail to show this pattern (Funnell, 1983).

the procedure achieving whole-word specification from letters: either the letter processing mechanism per se is no longer capable of dealing efficiently with multiple elements[2], or the transfer of graphemic code to the lexicon after letter encoding has been accomplished cannot encompass more than a single element at a time (Patterson & Kay, 1982). Alternatively, the disturbance may involve the actual description of whole-word orthographic forms (Warrington & Shallice, 1980). According to this argument, the letter-by-letter strategy occurs because information about word-specific orthography can still be retrieved from an intact spelling/writing mechanism, activated by a sequence of letter names or explicit letter identities.

A Fly In The Ointment

To establish the locus of impairment for the two syndromes, we applied the following axiom: A direct relationship exists between the particular level of the processing hierarchy that has been damaged and the pattern of variables affecting performance. In the most general terms, sensitivity to attributes involving only word-specific dimensions (e.g., lexical status) leads to the conclusion that the disturbance occurs beyond the level where the structural descriptions of input or output codes are established. When variables relating to structure (e.g., the number of letters in the word) do exert a major influence on the patient, we argue that the damage has occurred to encoding procedures which operate before the categorization of perceptual information as higher level units. Phonological dyslexia, therefore, must be the result of damage to a fairly "central" processing event, requiring orthographic and phonological knowledge. Letter-by-letter reading, however, is caused by a more peripheral disturbance that interferes with the activation of letter identities and/or their synthesis into lexical units.

The method of analysis just described is the one most commonly adopted in the attempt to uncover defective functional components underlying particular patterns of language breakdown. The validity of this approach to evaluating acquired language disorders rests entirely on the assumption of independence between the various processing modules of the system: information specified at one level of representation should not be used as feedback to determine analysis at another level.

To see why this constraint is so important, let us examine the possible consequence of damage to a processing system that operates with non-

---

[2] Warrington and Shallice (1980) argue that letter-by-letter reading cannot be due to defective encoding of multiple letter elements because their patients were generally capable of identifying a letter string presented for a relatively brief duration. It remains unclear, though, whether disturbed letter perception can be completely ruled out as a crucial aspect of the disorder; our own results suggest that perceptual synthesis, at least in some cases, is far from adequate (Bub, Black, Howell, & Kertesz, in preparation).

independent functional components. Strict independence could be violated, for example, if the outcome of one processing stage is checked against information specified at a higher level before the next stage begins. Alternatively, activation may spread passively back and forth through the system, so that analysis at lower levels is continuously influenced by knowledge at higher levels. Such a positive feedback mechanism is characteristic of the parallel network models recently developed to account for aspects of visual word recognition (McClelland & Rumelhart, 1981), skilled typing (Rumelhart & Norman, 1982) and speech production (Dell, 1985).

Suppose that an orthographic production system such as the one depicted in Fig. 4.2, operating with some interaction between components, sustains damage to a relatively peripheral stage of processing, say at the point where the letter codes mediating a written response are specified. Assume further that the major effect of the impairment is to weaken the durability of graphemic codes activated for production, so that letter-level information tends to decay abnormally quickly after formation in the output register (referred to in the figure as the letter output buffer).

What constraints are imposed by this type of functional disturbance on the writing mechanism? The stimulus dimensions affecting performance and the kinds of errors that occur must reflect the system's inability to always maintain letter descriptions long enough for correct output. We would certainly expect to find that structural properties of letter sequences are relevant, given the location of the impairment. For instance, we might anticipate more slips

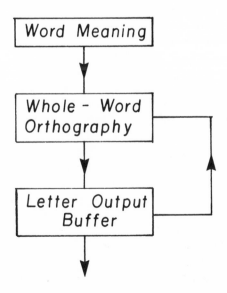

FIG. 4.2. Feedback between word- and letter-level components.

of the pen for longer words, which take more time to complete and therefore provide increased opportunity for information loss before letter codes can be converted to an overt response. Errors may also be more likely at terminal locations in the word, assuming that letters are retrieved serially and that trace decay occurs equally for each element over time. Finally, if the effects of information loss on retrieval are qualitatively similar to those observed in other short-term memory tasks (e.g., immediate memory for a sequence of digits), misspellings could include the omissions, additions, substitutions and inversions typical of serial list recall (Conrad, 1967; Ellis, 1980; Wickelgren, 1965).

The pattern of results we have described so far is consistent with the malfunctioning of a low level mechanism enlisted during the production of a written response. Our analysis, however, must still take into account the possible consequences of interactive feedback between this component of the writing mechanism and more central levels of representation.

Let us assume that letter codes generated for output can be referred directly back to whole word descriptions present in the orthographic lexicon. Such continuous access to information about the spelled form of words provides the basis for editing out potential mistakes prior to response production: as soon as an error develops, the pattern of activation at the letter level could be automatically adjusted to conform to the specification of the intended word. For example, the letters a-r-t might be selected as the target sequence at some point, but because of trace decay, the output codes may lack sufficient detail for the system to know whether a t or an f was specified as the final letter. The pattern a-r-f however, does not match any orthographic "logogen" (Morton, 1970) available to the writing mechanism, so the incorrect element (f) is quickly suppressed.

This type of monitoring device of course, will facilitate retrieval only when the target has lexical status—a nonsense word presented for a written response lacks the supporting influence of a permanent address in the orthographic lexicon and will not be correctly recovered once its structural description becomes ambiguous. In fact, the use of a word specific representation to facilitate performance could work against the successful production of a nonsense sequence because the system will tend to replace an unfamiliar pattern of activation with a pattern corresponding to a morpheme. Letters forming a nonsense word (e.g., *nop*) will often be altered to produce a word as the final outcome, which bears a close physical resemblance to the original (e.g., *mop*).

We can argue that impairment to a processing component dealing only with letter codes might well produce sensitivity to the effects of lexicality as well as structure, if information at relatively central levels of representation can be fed back to influence the activity of more peripheral input or output procedures.

Considerable evidence indicates that feedback of some kind does play a significant role in language performance. To take just a few examples: letters present in words are normally more resistant to the effects of central masking than randomly ordered letter strings (Reicher, 1969; Wheeler, 1970), a finding which points to greater recoverability of perceptual codes when access to a lexical framework is possible. Similar effects of whole word knowledge have been demonstrated on phonemic encoding; a dramatic instance of such feedback is revealed in the tendency to experience an utterance as intact (Warren, 1970), even though an extraneous sound has replaced some of the segments. The fact that restoration of missing phonemes occurs more strongly for words than nonsense words (Samuel, 1981) argues for a contextual effect on speech perception which is morpheme-specific in origin. Finally, there are results suggesting that the speech production mechanism also makes use of lexical feedback. Slips of the tongue involving exchanges or anticipations of initial consonants are much more likely if the outcome forms a pair of legitimate words (e.g., *queer old dean* for *dear old queen*) than a phonologically legal nonsense sequence (e.g., *heft lemisphere* for *left hemisphere*). This lexical bias effect, which has been observed in natural (Dell & Reich, 1980) as well as laboratory induced speech errors (Baars, Motley, & MacKay, 1975), provides support for the idea that phonemic output is monitored by word level components of the language system to check for possible planning errors. The editing mechanism will recognize and prevent slips that do not correspond to its morphemic inventory, but will fail to detect mistakes consisting of legitimate words.

Because lexical information can be brought to bear on lower level processors in the intact system, we must concede that feedback or monitoring may occur in the damaged system as well. This possibility complicates the attempt to analyse language breakdown in terms of impairment to discrete components of a processing model—we cannot always expect a transparent relationship between the location of a particular functional disturbance and the set of variables affecting performance.

To highlight the problem as it emerges in the interpretation of a processing disorder, we will describe three brain-damaged patients whose major difficulty is most reasonably attributed to the malfunctioning of a relatively peripheral processing stage, either at the level of encoding (*case 1*) or at the level of response production (*cases 2* and *3*). For each case we argue that the deficit must involve the failure to achieve a complete structural description of the input codes needed for perceptual synthesis or the output codes needed for accurately executing a response.

We have referred to these functional loci as input and output buffers in the title of this chapter, to reflect out conclusion that the breakdown is restricted to procedures with interface perceptual/motor systems with more central levels of representation. The term "buffer" is generally used to denote a processing device capable of maintaining information over a brief period. Although the results obtained from at least one of the patients do seem to implicate a disturbance caused by storage limitations, we do not claim that this explanation necessarily applies to all three cases. Our contention is only that the disorder must involve components of the language system establishing input/output codes, either because their representation is poorly specified at the outset or because traces deteriorate abnormally quickly once they have been established.

This type of impairment can produce a complex and potentially misleading pattern of experimental findings; performance is affected by those stimulus dimensions most typically associated with damage to a lower level process. But the lexical status of the material also has a major impact on the extent of the patients' disability. Nonsense words, encoded through the defective input or output channel, yield much less accurate responding than legitimate words, an outcome which at first glance could be interpreted as evidence for damage to a relatively central procedure taking place at a higher level than the computation of a structural description. The nature of the errors for nonsense words, however, along with other aspects of performance, weighs against two separate impairments; the lexicality effect in these patients appears directly linked to the buffer malfunction, which is diminished in severity if a lexical framework is available to support the activation of structural codes. The result suggest that whole word influences on components of perceptual analysis or response production can be a major feature of an acquired language disorder in certain instances. We discuss how this point qualifies the models currently used to analyse language breakdown after presenting a description of each of the three cases.

CASE #1 (M.M.): LETTER-BY-LETTER READING, WITH A DIFFERENCE

Letter-by-letter readers are only able to recognize words by laboriously spelling out each letter in succession. Thus, when faced with even a short, familiar word like *boy*, the patient will typically produce the response *b-o-y*, boy. Previous reports have emphasized the fact that this approach to recognition includes virtually every written word (and nonsense word); the letter-by-letter reader is almost never able to achieve a correct response unless each element is spelled, either aloud or subvocally. The present case, however, is unusual because reading does not invariably proceed letter-by-letter. M.M. is able to read some items without using a spelling strategy; we will see that the critical factor limiting performance appears to be whether a letter string can be unambiguously associated with a specific address in the orthographic input lexicon.

Description

M.M. is a 77-year-old, right-handed female who suffered a left subarachnoid hemorrhage in 1975. Severe vascular spasm resulted in a right homonymous hemianopia and global aphasia. A CT scan in 1978 revealed anterior and posterior left hemisphere infarcts involving the inferior frontal and precentral gyri, superior and middle temporal gyri and supramarginal and angular gyri. Currently her speech is fluent and well articulated, but she exhibits extreme word-finding difficulty. Her repetition is mildly impaired for single words and deteriorates for phrases. Comprehension is moderately affected. M.M. has good visual acuity, though her right field defect persists; no simultanagnosia was evident in her description of complex pictures.

Single Word Reading. M.M. reads slowly but accurately at the single word level. One hundred and sixty nouns, varying systematically in length (5, 6, 7, or 8 letters), in imageability and in spelling-sound regularity were presented to her for oral reading. She read 96% of these correctly; only five low frequency, low imagery nouns were spelled out prior to pronunciation.

Nonsense Word Reading. When asked to read pronounceable nonsense words, however, M.M. invariably names each letter before responding. She correctly read 34/38 nonwords consisting of 3-, 4- and 5-letter single syllable items in this way. Consistent with previous descriptions of letter-by-letter reading, her occasional errors were due to misidentification of individual letters; for example, shown the stimulus *lenk*, M.M. responded "*d-e-n-k, denk*".

Naming Latency. It is conceivable that the strikingly disparate approaches to reading words and pseudowords that M.M. reveals on the surface is more apparent than real. Perhaps she reads all items in a letter-by-letter fashion but adopts a more covert strategy (e.g., subvocal spelling) when words are encountered. We can easily check on this possibility, however, by examining the relative effects that stimulus length has on naming latency for words and pseudowords.

A characteristic of the letter-by-letter syndrome is that the time to read a word or pseudoword increases linearly with the length of the item, a result that confirms the fact that identification and pronunciation require sequential analysis of letters. To determine whether the difference observed between words and pseudowords in the present case reflects a genuine change in the way the two types of stimuli are processed, we assessed the influence of letter length on oral reading latency. If M.M. only uses a spelling strategy to pronounce written nonsense words, then we would expect that the effect of length will be very much greater for these items than for words.

Forty high and 40 low frequency nouns, comprising equal numbers of 3, 4, 5, and 6 letter stimuli were therefore presented individually to M.M. for oral reading. Naming latency correct to 1/100 second was obtained by means of a timer and voice activated relay. Word length and frequency were randomly varied over trials. Exposure duration was fixed at one second.

In addition, M.M. was asked to read aloud, as quickly and as accurately as possible, four lists of 15 pseudowords which were 4, 5, 6, or 7 letters in length respectively. The mean response latency per list was calculated from the overall times (determined by stopwatch) to read all 15 items. The effect of length on reading speech for words and nonsense words is shown in Table 4.1.

Performance for nonsense items is very much slower compared to words and reaction time increases linearly with length, but no such relationship between length and latency can be seen for words. Thus, although pronunciation of written nonwords is clearly based on a letter-by-letter spelling process, the evidence suggests that M.M. is still able to read words via a more direct procedure.

Recognition of Briefly Presented Words And Letters. Our impression on watching M.M.'s attempts to assemble a response for a written nonsense word was that her difficulty resulted from a perceptual rather than a linguistic impairment. There are several reasons for this assumption. First, we noted that when asked not to spell the pseudowords before reading them and to guess at their pronunciation, her errors often bore a strong visual resemblance to the target items (e.g., *pirt* read as *rirt, buke* as *burk, hain* as *hank, furg as thurch*). Second, if we allowed M.M. simply to copy a written nonsense word before requesting her to read it, she was immediately able to retrieve the correct pronunciation, a result which suggests that her limitation involves the identification of letters, rather than the conversion of graphemes into phonemes. Finally, limited exposure duration had a very deleterious effect on nonsense word reading, but a much less severe effect on words— M.M. was capable of correctly reading aloud 22/28 words (items were 4, 5,

TABLE 4.1
Naming Latency For Words And Pseudowords (Patient M.M.) As A Function Of Length (The number of errors is indicated in brackets)

	Length				
	3	*4*	*5*	*6*	*7*
High Frequency Words	1.89 sec (0)	1.90 sec (0)	2.04 sec (1)	1.63 sec (1)	—
Low Frequency Words	1.81 sec (0)	1.52 sec (0)	1.54 sec (2)	1.60 sec (1)	—
Nonsense Words	—	5.5 sec (3)	7.1 sec (2)	8.2 sec (2)	9.7 sec (4)

TABLE 4.2
Percent Correct Choice For Words And Random Strings (Patient M.M.) As A
Function Of Letter Position (Exposure duration was fixed at 80 msec)

	Letter Position				
	1	2	3	4	Mean % Correct
Words	100%	86%	93%	86%	91.0%
Random Strings	100%	73%	61%	65%	74.5%

6, or 7 letters in length and greater than 50 per million in frequency) when each was presented for 500 msec while only 4/20 written nonsense words could be correctly named at that exposure duration. Again, errors were visually similar to the actual stimuli; for example, *sog* was read as *sos*, *bap* as *bat*, *honse* as *horse*, *stroat* as *storth*.

In order to obtain further indication that letter encoding is impaired and to verify that processing of written words is less affected by the impairment, we tested M.M.'s recognition of briefly presented letters embedded either in a lexical framework or in a random array. Each trial consisted of a four letter stimulus which was exposed tachistoscopically in M.M.'s intact visual field; she was required immediately afterwards to distinguish between this and a foil that differed by only one letter from the actual target item. For example, if the stimulus was *wfrt*, M.M. might be shown the choices *wfrk* and *wfrt* and asked to indicate which of the two had been displayed. On word trials, a target like *cart* might be presented, say, followed by the choices *care* and *cart*. Foils were selected so that the letter identities in all four positions were tested equally often for both words and random strings. Target items were followed by a pattern mask[3] and exposure duration was adjusted during practice so that M.M. achieved an overall accuracy of 75% on random letter sequences. The experimental series comprised two blocks of 48 trials, with identification of letters in words tested first.

There are two aspects of the results (see Table 4.2) that are important. First, performance tends to become worse across letter target positions for random strings, suggesting that M.M. attempts to process items from left to right. Her comments during the experiment are consistent with this result; she remarked, "I can only get the first two letters and than I have to guess." This approach differs from the normal "ends-first" strategy, which typically produces a shallow bow-shaped function when recognition accuracy is plotted against serial position (Rumelhart & McClelland, 1982).

---

[3] The pattern mask in this type of experiment typically consists of a random display of letter segments flashed briefly after target offset to prevent further processing of the word or letter array.

A second point emerging from the data is that a lexical context can partially offset the loss of information at the letter level: M.M. is much better at identifying letters in words than random strings, across all four locations in the array. But the enhancing effect of lexical knowledge on M.M.'s ability to recover letter codes seems very fragile. Though she is able to read single words quite accurately, she finds reading text extremely arduous and produces numerous misidentifications when doing so. In addition, consider the outcome of reducing exposure duration on M.M.'s recognition of briefly presented words and letter sequences. Using the same forced choice paradigm as before but with target items presented for 40 msec instead of 80 msec, we now find that the word superiority effect obtained previously is considerably diminished (see Table 4.3), and the serial position effects characteristic of a left-to-right processing strategy can be seen for both words and random strings.

Synopsis

Results suggest that M.M.'s letter identification does not extend efficiently over multiple elements present in an array. Reading errors often involved confusion of form (e.g., *zeek* for *zeer*) or of letter position (e.g., *storth* for *stroat*) indicating that graphemic codes are only weakly activated with respect to their physical description and their correct location. Because the output of visual analysers for multiple letter codes is underspecified, M.M. relies on compensatory strategies to analyse the letters of an unfamiliar spelling pattern on a piecemeal basis. She therefore attempts to convert the visual array into a sequence of auditory letter identities when faced with a nonsense word, which she can then use to gain entry to other components of the reading mechanism. If asked to refrain from spelling out the letters to herself, we noticed on several occasions that she would trace them on the palm of her hand with her finger to generate kinesthetic feedback, instead of auditory cues, about their shape. Performance deteriorates markedly as soon as she cannot use these alternative methods of letter analyses: 12/15 single-syllable nonsense words were misread after M.M. was instructed to avoid oral spel-

TABLE 4.3
Percent Correct Choice For Words and Random Strings (Patient M.M.)
With Exposure Duration At 40 msec

	Letter Position				
	1	*2*	*3*	*4*	*Mean % Correct*
Words	100%	80%	70%	50%	75%
Random Strings	100%	70%	50%	50%	67.5%

ling and to place her hands with fingers outspread on the table. Consistent with our interpretation that her impaired reading stems from a perceptual deficit, the errors were all visually related to the target (e.g., *hair* for *haik*, *turk* for *furg*, *rirt* for *pirt*).

The processing disturbance that interferes so drastically with M.M.'s decoding of written nonsense words has a lesser impact on the reading of legitimate words. She does not have to rely on oral spelling to recognize a written morpheme (even a relatively low frequency one) and she can read the majority of words at an exposure duration that is brief enough to severely disrupt her identification of nonsense words.

The nature of this word superiority effect appears comparable to the effect observed in normal readers under perceptual conditions that reduce the quality of letter codes established at input (see Henderson, 1982, for a detailed review). Subjects are much better at reporting all the letters in words than nonsense words, if the stimuli are briefly presented before the onset of a central mask. Recognition errors are the same as M.M.'s; letters in nonsense words are confused during encoding with visually similar alternatives, and the outcome is often a real word which physically resembles the nonsense word target.

This experimental situation mimics, in our view, the kind of processing constraints M.M. faces even when allowed unrestricted viewing of the letter array. She is able to read words correctly because their letters make contact with an address in the orthographic lexicon, reinforcing the activation pattern which otherwise would be insufficient to provide an exact description of the target. For nonsense words, however, no single word specific representation can serve as a framework for perceptual synthesis, and consequently greater attention must be directed towards analysis at the letter-level. Because M.M.'s processing of letter strings is limited, the information extracted from a nonlexical spelling pattern will lack the specific detail needed for a correct response.

CASE #2 (M.V.): THE INS AND OUTS OF CONDUCTION APHASIA

The repetition difficulty characteristic of conduction aphasia quite often includes words as well as nonsense words, and in some cases can be equally severe for both types of stimuli (see for example Dubois, Hecaen, Angelergues, de Chatelier, & Marcie, 1964). It is unclear in these instances whether the syndrome involves a relatively peripheral phonemic sequencing disorder (Strub & Gardner, 1974), or whether more central components of language are implicated. If production of lexical items is inaccurate, the possibility exists that central levels of processing are compromised, since errors may reflect incorrectly specified output and knowledge sources incorporating the phonological forms of whole words. Indeed, consistent with the assumption that one source of paraphasic errors derives from a central impairment at the level of whole-word phonology, Allport (1984) has reported that patients with expressive lexical breakdown classified as conduction aphasics often failed to detect nonwords that were phonologically close approximations to real words in an auditory lexical decision task (also see Alajouanine & Lhermitte, 1964, for a very similar finding). This result suggests a very general inability to determine the phonology of lexical items with precision that affects recognition and speech output symmetrically.

We describe a conduction aphasic, however, whose repetition disorder cannot be due to a lexical disturbance, because words are reproduced with a high degree of accuracy, far higher than is usually seen in more typical instances of the syndrome. A large number of paraphasic errors occur, nonetheless, as soon as the patient is required to repeat meaningless phonemic sequences—these are often pronounced as words that sound similar to the target items (e.g. *lord* for *lird*). Evidence will be presented that rules out an explanation of the repetition disorder based on deficient perception or short-term storage; we argue instead that the processing limitation arises at a peripheral level of response production where articulatory information is maintained prior to a response.

DESCRIPTION

M.V. is a 66-year-old right-handed female who suffered a left hemisphere stroke in April, 1982. A CT scan showed an infarct mainly involving the inferior parietal region including the deep white matter. On initial language assessment with the Western Aphasia Battery, her object naming and repetition were impaired and she was classified as a conduction aphasic. On a recent follow up test, however, object naming and repetition scores have improved, so that she is now classified as an anomic aphasic. M.V.'s spontaneous speech is slow and somewhat hesitant and she displays word-finding difficulty and occasional paraphasic errors.

Word Repetition. One hundred and thirty monosyllabic words that sampled singleton consonants and consonant clusters in the initial and final positions, taken from Trost (1970), were administered to M.V. for repetition; performance was almost perfect (96% correct). A further list published by McCarthy and Warrington (1984), which systematically varied word frequency (A/AA or 40 per million) and syllable length (one, two, or three syllables) was also presented. Results show extremely good performance (see Table 4.4) for high frequency words and a somewhat lower level of accuracy for low frequency words. There are no consistent effects of syllable length, although repetition of low frequency, three syllable words was considerably worse than other items.

TABLE 4.4
Percent Correct Repetition For Words (Patient M.V) Varying In Syllable Length And Frequency (percentages were calculated from 30 trials per cell)

| | Number of Syllables | | | |
	1	2	3	Mean % Correct
High Frequency	96%	100%	96%	97.3%
Low Frequency	83%	83%	67%	78.0%

Nonsense Word Repetition. M.V.'s nonsense word repetition is extremely poor relative to her repetition of words; she correctly repeated only 8/12 single-syllable items and performance deteriorated markedly as syllable length increased (6/12 correct for bi-syllabic nonsense words and 2/12 for three syllable items). Number of syllables also exerted a pronounced effect when single consonant-vowel (CV) combinations were used as stimuli. Thus, M.V. could repeat 16/20 CV syllables (e.g., *bah*) but repeated only 8/20 when she was required to produce two such items (e.g., *bah ree*). Accuracy was also influenced by the delay between stimulus and response—M.V. repeated 12/20 monosyllabic nonwords on immediate retrieval but after a 5-second delay, accuracy dropped to 6/20. When subvocal rehearsal was prevented by asking her to count from 1 to 5 before responding, even fewer items (2/20) could be correctly reproduced.

Recognition of Phonemic Sequences. Recognition of nonwords was tested in order to determine whether encoding and/or retention difficulties contributed to M.V.'s defective pronunciation of nonsense sequences. A set of consonant-vowel stimuli (*pa, ba, ta, ca, da* and *ga*) were arranged in pairs to produce 20 trials. Half the pairs contained syllables that differed in place of articulation (e.g., *ba, ga*) or voicing (e.g., *ba, pa*), while on remaining trials, the members of each pair were phonologically identical. Trials were orally presented in random order, and pair members were separated by an interval of approximately one second. M.V.'s task was to decide if the two syllables comprising a trial were the same or different. Of 20 response, 19 were correct, indicating good phonemic discrimination.

We also assessed M.V.'s performance on a more difficult version of this task, which require some ability to maintain the phonological representation of the syllable for a brief interval. A 5-second delay was inserted between consonant-vowel pairs. In addition, we prevented M.V. from subvocally rehearsing during the interstimulus interval by asking her to begin counting softly after receiving the initial syllable until presented with the second one. Discrimination was not adversely affected by a delay introduced between the two syllables—M.V.'s same-different judgments were accurate on 19/20 trials.

When the number of comparison items per trial was doubled, M.V. continued to respond with a high level of accuracy. Twenty trials were administered consisting of a pair of syllables (e.g., *poo, ba*), followed by two additional CV items that were exactly the same or differed by one consonant from the original pair. The four CV stimuli were pseudo-randomly presented so that a syllable did not always stay in the same relative position between pairs. In judging whether the test items were the same or different, M.V. obtained a score of 17/20 correct.

Finally, we asked M.V. to compare two nonsense words with a more complex phonological structure. Pairs were either one, two, or three syllables in length and the discrepant phonemes occurred equally often at initial, medial, or final positions within the nonsense string. The items comprising a pair were separated by a delay of 5 seconds and during this interval, M.V. either remained silent or counted aloud. She was able to perform correctly on 16/18 trials with an unfilled delay between pair members. When the delay was accompanied by articulatory suppression, 21/24 responses were correct.

Reading Versus Repetition.   It seems quite unlikely that M.V.'s difficulty stems from an impairment to processes establishing or maintaining the internal representation of a dictated nonsense word. She is capable of adequate phonemic discrimination, and retains phonological information long enough (i.e., for at least 5 seconds) to rule out the possibility that poor auditory short-term memory is the basis for her flawed repetition.

A second aspect of performance also weighs against an explanation based on misperception or forgetting of speech input. M.V. encounters similar difficulty in producing nonsense words when they are presented as written targets; by contrast, her ability to read legitimate words aloud is virtually intact. She correctly pronounced 149/160 (88%) written nouns varying in imageability, frequency and spelling-sound regularity. No effects of imageability or regularity were found but high frequency items were read somewhat better than low frequency items (92% correct vs. 80% correct). She could read only 42% of 266 monosyllabic nonwords, however. Mispronunciations were quite often real words that closely approximated the written target (e.g., *monk* for *munt*); these lexicalizations accounted for 62% of her errors. We administered a further set of 240 nonwords (also monosyllables) for repetition, to compare performance in the two modalities. M.V. accurately repeated 53% and lexicalized on 49% of her incorrect responses.

A more detailed analysis of all her mispronunciations shows a definite correspondence between the error patterns obtained for reading and repetition. We classified mistakes as consonant or vowel substitutions, omissions, additions, or transpositions. Roughly two-thirds of her mispronunciations involved only one error type (reading, 71%; repetition, 69%) and in one-third there were two deviations from the target (reading, 29%; repetition,

31%). As can be seen in Table 4.5, substitutions predominated, constituting 80% of her reading errors and 62% of her repetition errors. Single phoneme omissions, the next most common type of error, occurred primarily for non-words with consonant clusters (reading 23%; repetition 12%). Phoneme additions comprised approximately 10% of errors and were mostly obtained for lexicalizations. Transpositions were very uncommon.

These results point to a combined impairment of nonlexical reading and repetition—the damaged procedure must therefore be a component of print-to-sound as well as acoustic-phonological translations. We can specify the locus of the breakdown within the language system more precisely by taking the following considerations into account:

TABLE 4.5
Comparison Of Error Types (Patient M.V.) In Nonsense
Word Reading And Repetition

1. READING	LIST A	LIST B NO CLUSTERS	LIST C CLUSTERS	TOTAL
No. Administered	108	57	101	266
No. Correct	48 (44%)	28 (49%)	35 (35%)	111 (42%)
Error Type (%):				
Substitutions (Cons.)	37	59	38	41
Substitutions (Vowel)	24	28	16	21
Total Substitutions	61	83	54	62
Omissions	15	5	39	23
Additions	18	12	7	12
Transpositions	6	0	0	3

2. REPETITION	LIST I	LIST II NO CLUSTERS	LIST III CLUSTERS	TOTAL
No. Administered	40	88	112	240
No. Correct	20 (50%)	53 (60%)	54 (48%)	127 (53%)
Error Type (%):				
Substitutions (Cons.)	50	49	49	49
Substitutions (Vowel)	35	36	26	31
Total Substitutions	85	85	75	80
Omissions	9	2	19	12
Additions	6	13	6	8
Transpositions	0	0	0	0

1. First, M.V.'s adequate retrieval of whole-word pronunciation clearly indicates that the deficit arises subsequent to the activation of lexical phonology;

2. The phonological process common to the transcoding of both written and orally presented nonsense words occurs at the level of speech *production* (see Figure 4.1), where phonemes are activated and assembled for overt articulation;

3. The difficulty must in fact originate before the actual programming of output in articulatory form because the articulatory mechanism per se appears to be intact. There is no reason to assume, moreover, that an articulatory disturbance alone could interfere more with the production of nonsense words than real words.

Our assumption, given these comments, is that M.V.'s disability reflects a phonemic planning impairment; she fails to read or repeat a nonsense word because the response buffer, which activates and maintains pre-articulatory code (cf. Morton, 1970), can no longer organize the exact description of an unfamiliar speech sequence. Additional evidence reveals that the processing disturbance still allows M.V. to approximate the pronunciation of a nonsense word, but not capture it fully. Recall that her most common error type is the substitution of one phoneme in the nonword stimulus with another phoneme (see Table 4.5). This kind of error is also frequently made by aphasics with impaired speech production at the whole-word level. Subphonemic analyses of these paraphasic responses have shown that they are by no means randomly determined—in general, consonant substitutions differ from the target by one (or at most two) distinctive features (Blumstein, 1973; Burns & Canter, 1977; Monoi, Fukusako, Itoh, & Sasanuma, 1983).

The same method of analysis was applied to M.V.'s nonsense word errors: we employed a four-feature scheme of place, manner, nasality and voicing, similar to that used by Trost and Canter (1974) for determining the distinctive feature distance between substituted and target consonants. The large majority of substitutions made by M.V. were one feature away from the nonword target for reading (74% of 66 errors) as well as repetition (88% of 56 errors). A distance of two features was found for only 20% of her reading errors[4] and 10% of her repetition errors (see Fig. 4.3). Interestingly, this pattern of results occurred for lexicalizations as well as for nonlexical responses: most of the substitutions differed from the target consonant by one distinctive feature alone, including the errors that change nonmorphemic targets into legitimate words.

---

[4] A more fine-grained, four-feature analysis was also carried out to further subdivide place and manner. Place was categorized as bilabial, labiodental, interdental, alveolar, palatal, velar and glottal; manner was subdivided into stops fricatives, affricates, liquids, glides and vowels. A slightly different pattern of results was obtained, with the majority of errors divided equally

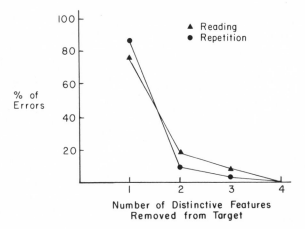

FIG. 4.3. Percentage of errors involving one, two, three, and four distinctive features from the target.

Synopsis

The nature of M.V.'s incorrect attempts at pronouncing words reveals that the elements organized for a response are underspecified. This does not arise because of a problem in phonological synthesis at the perceptual level; her poor repetition of nonsense words, as we have noted, is not linked to a corresponding deficit in identifying the description of the target segments. Furthermore, M.V. is obviously well aware of her failure to retrieve the exact pronunciation of a nonword, both in reading and in repetition, since she frequently comments on her own errors (e.g. *wabe* (written presentation)—"*wade,* but that isn't quite right"; *snark* (auditory presentation)—"*snort,* no that ain't it, I can't say it".

The functional impairment seems to be one of actually programming phonemic output codes within the response buffer; a simple and direct interpretation is that the buffer has become susceptible to an abnormal degree of noise or interference, so that it cannot always deliver the exact form of an

---

between responses that varied from the target either by one or two features. The strong correspondence between M.V.'s reading and repetition still occurred, however.

We also checked whether M.V.'s reading substitution errors may have been phonemically close to the nonsense words simply because of a fortuitous correlation between visual and acoustic similarity for letters. Thus, the letters N and M, for example, are close phonemically, but they also happen to look similar as well. If M.V's mispronunciations of nonsense words were actually visual errors, the effect of phonemic distance would be spurious. To take this possibility into account, we re-analyzed the data after excluding all substitutions for letters that were physically close. The overall pattern remained unaltered even when we discounted mistakes that could have been visual in origin.

unfamiliar speech sequence. We note, however, that M.V.'s deficit has left her with considerable ability to retrieve the pronunciation of items when they are represented as legitimate words. Our contention is that this relative sparing of word-specific output provides another instance of lexical constraints on more peripheral language procedures, in this case on processes assembling pre-articulatory information for speech production.

Activated speech segments for words deteriorate within the response buffer, just as do segments for nonsense words. M.V. has sufficient higher-level information about the target word, however, to offset the loss of trace quality at the phonemic level. Presumably, the compensatory information includes both lexical and semantic descriptions of the word, as lexical feedback alone would probably be insufficient to always successfully disambiguate the contents of the buffer. The speech output codes for a word like *card,* for example, could not be easily recovered once confusion begins about their exact specification, because the lexical entries *cord, guard, cart,* etc. are so close phonologically that they would often substitute for the intended target. If semantic criteria are also applied to the phonemic sequence (cf. Motley, 1980), only one morpheme will qualify as the most reasonable candidate for output. M.V.'s tendency to pronounce nonsense words as similar-sounding words can be seen as a further outcome of lexical feedback. Noise or distortion in the output traces for a meaningless sequence would also trigger the feedback mechanism. The system can only operate by activating a whole-word address that matches, as closely as possible, the information in the phonemic buffer. We should expect many of M.V.'s responses, then, to be words that approximate the phonology of the nonsense targets.

CASE #3 (C.H.): PHONOLOGICAL AGRAPHIA, BUT NOT REALLY

A few cases of agraphia have been described in the literature that are clearly the result of a very peripheral disturbance to the writing system, so peripheral that specification of the graphemic code is intact and impairment is almost entirely restricted to later stages of processing concerned with realizing the spelling information as a sequence of letters on the page. The distinguishing feature in all these reports, which confirms the fact that graphemic representation is preserved, is that oral spelling is relatively accurate, whereas written responding produces numerous errors. The nature of the errors varies with the type of impairment to lower level output mechanisms—the patient described by Margolin and Binder (1984) for example, has a deficit which apparently affected the retrieval and execution of motor patterns, since writing consisted of grossly distorted letters that were almost totally illegible. Rosati and de Bastiani (1979), however, reported a case of agraphia with relatively good letter formation and numerous omissions, substitutions and repetitions that occurred when words were written. According to the model developed by Ellis (1982), the impairment must have arisen between the graphemic output buffer and the processing of graphic motor patterns, at the stage responsible for selecting and maintaining the appropriate letter forms in spatial code (allographs).

The writing disorder of the patient we describe in this section also originates at the level of allographic processing, because (a) oral spelling is much better than writing and (b) errors involve the retrieval of letter sequences as words rather than the actual production of the letters themselves. Although the impairment must be entirely peripheral in this case of pure agraphia, however, there are aspects of performance which are strikingly reminiscent of the central disturbance seen in phonological agraphia— CH's writing is considerably more accurate when high frequency words are presented for dictation than low frequency words and correct transcription of dictated nonsense words is extremely impaired. The effect of lexical status is not seen for oral spelling in contrast, which as indicated, is far superior to written performance.

Case Description

A 64-year-old woman with a past history of lung cancer experienced sudden onset of aphasic symptoms associated with a left-sided headache. On admission, she had minimal right face and arm weakness and word-finding difficulty in spontaneous speech. Confrontation naming, repetition, and comprehension were all good. She made a few errors on reading aloud and comprehended written material well. Her most notable impairment was in writing, where spelling errors abounded. At 2 weeks her symptoms had virtually resolved except for persisting dysgraphia, and she scored in the mild anomic range (AQ 94.6) on the Western Aphasia Battery. CT scan on day one was normal and angiography revealed no significant lesions. Nuclear magnetic resonance (NMR) scanning 4 days later in the transverse plane showed a small lesion deep to the central sulcus involving the white matter of the pre- and post-central gyrus. On coronal views the lesion was superior and medial to the insula and involved the superior longitudinal (arcuate) fasciculus. A follow-up CT and further NMR scanning at two months confirmed this localization. The patient died from complications of her lung cancer shortly thereafter and the lesion looked macroscopically to be an infarct at autopsy.

Writing.   Forty-eight words varying from four to seven letters in length were presented to C.H. for both oral writing and spelling on separate occasions. Half the words were high frequency items (greater than 50 per million) while half were low frequency (less than 10 per million). In addition a separate list of pseudowords (lengths of three, four, five, or six letters) were administered for writing and spelling. Results are shown in Table 4.6.

Numerous errors occurred in C.H.'s written responses, principally due to letter omissions (e.g., *bar* for *bear*), substitutions (*caoton* for *cotton*), transposition (*fligth* for *flight*), insertions (*parriot* for *parrot*) and perseverations (*hammmock* for *hammock*). A pronounced effect of lexical status can be seen—62.5% of high frequency words are correctly written, but only 29% of low frequency words, and nonsense words yield an even lower level of accuracy (17% correct). While a clear effect of frequency and wordness emerges for writing, oral spelling is relatively preserved and does not vary with stimulus type.

The Nature of Allographic Impairment.   What aspect of allographic processing has been impaired to produce this pattern of results? One possibility is that errors occur because a word registered in the allographic buffer decays too rapidly for C.H. to correctly retrieve all the letters as motor output. Support for this conclusion could be obtained by examining the effect of serial position on writing errors—we would expect paragraphias to occur more frequently at the ends of words if loss of information from a short term allographic store is responsible for mistakes, as letters in terminal locations would have been maintained for a longer period (and would therefore be subject to greater decay) in the output buffer than initial letters.

To explore the relationship between letter position and error rate, we presented C.H. with a series of 4, 5, and 6 letter words for dictation. Frequency was balanced across groups and items were administered in random order. The percentage of correct responses in each location for the different word lengths is displayed in Fig. 4.4.

The evidence supports the conclusion that one source of C.H.'s writing difficulty is the pronounced temporal decay of memory traces from a short-term output buffer; her ability to correctly retrieve a letter deteriorates significantly across letter positions.

TABLE 4.6
Percentage Correct For Writing And Spelling (Patient C.H.) Of High
Frequency, Low Frequency and Nonsense Words

| | *Stimulus* | | | |
	HF Words	*LF Words*	*Nonsense Words*	*Mean % Correct*
Writing	62.5%	29%	17%	36%
Oral Spelling	83.0%	79%	90%	84%

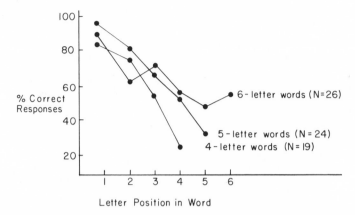

FIG. 4.4. Percentage of correct letter responses as a function of position in the word. Numbers in brackets indicate sample size for each word length.

Synopsis

There is good reason to assume that the writing mechanism includes a component for temporarily storing the actual letter sequences making up a word (Ellis, 1982; Wing & Baddeley, 1980). The production of a handwritten response takes place quite slowly, and the system must have some way of maintaining output codes until their corresponding motor programs are retrieved and executed.

Recently, Nolan and Caramazza (1983) have utilized the concept of a written output buffer in their analysis of an agraphic patient (V.S.) whose writing disturbance, they argue, occurred because the buffer's capacity had become impaired. They base their conclusion primarily on the fact that V.S. could recognize and correct many of her own spelling errors when they were later presented to her. According to the authors, the patient retained a knowledge of whole word orthography but was unable to successfully retrieve the information for output.

It is not possible to reach any definite conclusion about the nature of the agraphia in this particular instance, however. The major difficulty for interpretation is that V.S. did *not* demonstrate better oral spelling than written spelling, so we lack convincing evidence that she could generate the spelled form of the target for writing. Her agraphia may well have been due to a retrieval difficulty, but this could involve defective access to the lexicon itself rather than poor retention of abstract letter codes.

C.H.'s preserved word spelling clearly indicates that she does retrieve the graphemic description of a word or nonsense word. Her agraphia must occur because of damage to processes organizing the letter codes for a written response. She had no trouble capturing the form of individual letters, so the problem was not one of locating their spatial or allographic representation. The fact that writing errors occurred more often towards the end of a word leads us to argue that C.H. cannot retain a sequence of allographs long enough to process them as motor output. The effect of the storage impairment is significantly greater for unfamiliar words and nonsense words—the presence of lexical information, more readily available for high frequency words, acts on the contents of the allographic buffer and allows successful completion of the response.

DISCUSSION

All three of the patients described show effects of structural variables on performance: M.M.'s naming latency for written nonsense words strongly depends on their length; M.V. is much less accurate in repeating a three-syllable nonsense word than a monosyllabic one, and C.H.'s writing errors are more numerous at the terminal locations in the words. These results are consistent with damage to relatively peripheral input or output devices establishing the codes for lexical access or response production.

The impairment caused by the functional damage was found to be much more severe when the patients attempted to process unfamiliar words or nonsense words. There must be some means, then, by which lexical knowledge can partially offset the malfunction at the peripheral level. What assumptions are needed for a model of the language mechanism to account for these results?

We might try to retain the view that processing components operate sequentially and without interaction, by arguing that the procedures that accomplish a structural description for a familiar word are not necessarily the same as those needed for a nonsense word. Seymour and MacGregor (1984), for example, suggest that two lexical reading routes exist: one system, the "logographic" route, discriminates among familiar words on the basis of visual features, but does not rely on individual graphemes. The other route, which is alphabetic, uses letter identities to accomplish word recognition and to assemble the pronunciation of written nonsense words.

Seymour and MacGregor have applied this model to analysing developmental reading disorders; they consider that certain cases of "visual-analytic" dyslexia are the result of a defective alphabetic encoding process, so that reading is more dependent on the logographic route. This dyslexia has the following characteristics:

1. A letter-by-letter approach is used to process nonsense words. The authors interpretation is that nonsense words require more detailed segmental

analysis of individual graphemes (Seymour & May, 1981) than words. The alphabetic route cannot perform this operation efficiently and letters are processed slowly and in sequence.

2. When words are spatially distorted (e.g., written vertically) they are also decoded through prolonged sequential analysis of individual letters.

Seymour and MacGregor propose that distortion interferes with the logographic processor, forcing the visual-analytic dyslexic to use the deficient alphabetic route.

There appears to be an obvious parallel between this syndrome and our description of M.M.—she reads words wholistically but relies on a letter-by-letter procedure to read nonsense words. Could her dyslexia be explained in terms of a distinction between separate logographic and alphabetic processing components?

We can check on this possibility by looking at M.M.'s reading performance under spatial distortion. Naming latency for 3-, 4-, 5-, and 6-letter words was measured for both horizontal and vertical presentation formats. There were no effects of length on reaction time in either condition. We can reject the hypothesis, then, that M.M.'s reading is logographic.

If the effect of lexicality cannot be easily attributed to a distinct type of encoding device for morphemes, perhaps we may still be able to keep matters simple in accounting for our results by focussing on the input/output buffers themselves as a source of knowledge about the statistical relationship between word segments. Letters or phonemes that are repeatedly associated may establish representational units that facilitate the processing of elements with a history of frequent co-occurrence. It may be the case that nonsense words were more difficult for our patients because we happened to generate stimuli with low-probability constituents.

While there is good reason to believe that the associative strength between segmental units does have an influence on word recognition (see Henderson, 1982 for details) and even production (Motley & Baars, 1975), this cannot be the primary reason for the patients' greater difficulty with nonsense words. We assessed the effect of bigram frequency (Mayzner & Tresselt, 1965) on M.M.'s ability to read words. Neither speed nor accuracy were influenced by this variable. C.H.'s poor writing of nonsense words could also not have been due to their lower bigram frequency; many of these items had a transitional probability which equalled that of the high frequency words used as stimuli. Her writing was still much worse for these nonsense words than the familiar words. We also examined whether M.M. was less capable of repeating nonsense words with infrequent constituent phonemes. Monosyllabic nonsense words (CVC patterns) were presented with terminal segments found in very few words (less than five) or in a large number of words (greater than 50). We found no relationship between a segment's frequency of occurrence and M.V.'s repetition accuracy.

Our conclusion then, is that the lexicality effect we have documented comes from the status of the targets as whole words. The patients could read, write, or repeat true words better than nonsense words because the processing of structure is determined not just by analysis of lower-level codes but also by higher-level information about their probable lexical representation. We should point out that this type of interaction does not necessarily imply that all functional components of the language system communicate unrestrictedly. The present results indicate only that whole-word knowledge can facilitate the activity of processors that operate at the interface between input or output devices and the lexicon. The implications for understanding language disorders are important, however. The results obtained from certain patients may mimic those indicative of central disturbances, but instead reflect the influence of lexical feedback on lower level components.

ACKNOWLEDGMENTS

This chapter was written while the first author held a Postdoctoral Fellowship from the Medical Research Council of Canada.

REFERENCES

Alajouanine, T., & Lhermitte, F. (1964). Les composantes phonémiques et sémantiques du langage jargonaphasique. *International Journal of Neurology, 4,* 277–286.

Allport, D. A. (1984). Auditory-verbal short-term memory and conduction aphasia. In H. Bouma & D. G. Bouwhuis (Eds.), *Attention and Performance X,* (pp. 313–326). Hillsdale, NJ: Lawrence Erlbaum Associates.

Baars, B. J., Motley, M. T., & MacKay, D. G. (1975). Output editing for lexical status from artificially elicited slips of the tongue. *Journal of Verbal Learning and Verbal Behavior, 14,* 382–391.

Beauvois, M. F., & Derouesné, J. (1979). Phonological alexia: Three dissociations. *Journal of Neurology, Neurosurgery and Psychiatry, 42,* 1115–1124.

Blumstein, S. (1973). *A phonological investigation of aphasic speech.* Mouton: Paris.

Bub, D., Black, S., Howell, J., & Kertesz, A. (1984). *Letter-by-letter reading: A re-analysis. Niagara Falls: Babble.*

Burns, M. S., & Canter, G. J. (1977). Phonemic behavior of aphasic patients with posterior cerebral lesions. *Brain and Language, 4,* 492–507.

Conrad, R. (1967). Interference or decay over short retention intervals? *Journal of Verbal Learning and Verbal Behavior, 6,* 49–54.

Dell, G. S. (1985). Positive feedback in hierarchical connectionist models: Applications to language production. *Cognitive Science, 9,* 75–112.

Dell, G. S., & Reich, P. A. (1980). Toward a unified theory of slips of the tongue. In V. A. Fromkin (Ed.), *Errors in linguistic performance: Slips of the tongue, ear, pen and hand* (pp. 273–286). New York: Academic Press.

Dubois, J., Hecaen, H., Angelergues, R., de Chatelier, A. M., & Marcie, P. (1964). Etude neurolinguistique de l'aphasie de conduction. *Neuropsychologia, 2,* 9–44.

Ellis, A. W. (1980). Errors in speech and short-term memory: The effects of phonemic similarity and syllable position. *Journal of Verbal Learning and Verbal Behavior, 19,* 624–634.

Ellis, A. W. (1982). Spelling and writing (and reading and speaking). An A. W. Ellis (Ed.), *Normality and pathology in cognitive functions* (pp. 113–146). London: Academic Press.

Funnell, E. (1983). Phonological processes in reading: New evidence from acquired dyslexia. *British Journal of Psychology, 74,* 159–180.

Henderson, L. (1982). *Orthography and word-recognition in reading.* London: Academic Press.

Margolin, D. I., & Binder, L. (1984). Multiple component agraphia in a patient with atypical cerebral dominance: An error analysis. *Brain and Language, 22,* 26–41.

Marslen-Wilson, W. D. (1976). Linguistic descriptions and psychological assumptions in the study of sentence perception. In R. J. Wales & E. Walker (Eds.), *New approaches to language mechanisms* (pp. 203–229). Amsterdam: North-Holland.

Mayzner, M. S., & Tresselt, M. E. (1965). Tables of single-letter and digram frequency counts for various word-length and letter-position combinations. *Psychonomic Monograph Supplements, 1,* 13–32.

McCarthy, R., & Warrington, E. K. (1984). A two-route model of speech production: Evidence from aphasia. *Brain, 107,* 463–485.

McClelland, J. L., & Rumelhart, D. E. (1981). An interactive activation model of context effects in letter perception: Part 1. An account of basic findings. *Psychological Review, 88,* 375–407.

Monoi, H., Fukusako, Y., Itoh, M., & Sasanuma, S. (1983). Speech sound errors in patients with conduction and Broca's aphasia. *Brain and Language, 20,* 175–194.

Morton, J. (1970). A functional model for memory. In D. A. Norman (Ed.), *Models of human memory* (pp. 203–260). New York: Academic Press.

Morton, J., & Patterson, K. E. (1980). A new attempt at an interpretation, or, an attempt at a new interpretation. In M. Coltheart, K. E. Patterson, & J. C. Marshall (Eds.). *Deep dyslexia* (pp. 91–118). London: Routledge and Kegan Paul.

Motley, M. T. (1980). Verification of "Freudian Slips" and semantic pre-articulatory editing via laboratory-induced spoonerisms. In V. A. Fromkin (Ed.), *Errors in linguistic performance* (pp. 133–148). New York: Academic Press.

Motley, M. T., & Baars, B. J. (1975). Encoding sensitivity to phonological markedness and transitional probability: Evidence from spoonerisms. *Human Communication Research, 2,* 351–361.

Newcombe, F., & Marshall, J. C. (1980). Transcoding and lexical stabilization in deep dyslexia. In M. Coltheart, K. E. Patterson, & J. C. Marshall (Eds.), *Deep dyslexia* (pp. 176–188). London: Routledge and Kegan Paul.

Nolan, K. A., & Caramazza, A. (1983). An analysis of writing in a case deep dyslexia. *Brain and Language, 20,* 305–328.

Patterson, K. E. (1982). The relation between reading and phonological coding: Further neuropsychological observations. In A. W. Ellis (Ed.), *Normality and pathology in cognitive functioning* (pp. 77–111). London: Academic Press.

Patterson, K. E., & Kay, J. (1982). Letter-by-letter reading: Psychological descriptions of a neurological syndrome. *Quarterly Journal of Experimental Psychology, 34A,* 411–441.

Reicher, G. M. (1969). Perceptual recognition as a function of meaningfulness of stimulus material. *Journal of Experimental Psychology, 81,* 274–280.

Rosati, G., & de Bastiani, P. (1979). Pure agraphia: A discrete form of aphasia. *Journal of Neurology, Neurosurgery and Psychiatry, 42,* 266–269.

Rumelhart, D. E., & McClelland, J. L. (1982). An interactive activation model of context effects in letter perception: Part 2. The contextual enhancement effect and some tests and extensions of the model. *Psychological Review, 89,* 60–94.

Rumelhart, D. E., & Norman, D. A. (1982). Simulating a skilled typist: A study of skilled cognitive-motor performance. *Cognitive Science, 6,* 1–36.

Samuel, A. G. (1981). Phonemic restoration: Insights from a new methodology. *Journal of Experimental Psychology: General, 110,* 474–494.

Seymour, P. H. K., & MacGregor, C. J. (1984). Developmental dyslexia: A cognitive experimental analysis of phonological morphemic and visual impairments. *Cognitive Neuropsychology, 1,* 43–82.

Seymour, P. H. K., & May, G. P. (1981). *Locus of format effects in word recognition.* Paper presented at the meeting of the Experimental Psychology Society, Oxford.

Strub, R. L., & Gardner, H. (1974). The repetition defect in conduction aphasia: Mnestic or linguistic? *Brain and Language, 1,* 241–255.

Trost, J. E. (1970). *A descriptive study of verbal apraxia in patients with Broca's aphasia.* Unpublished doctoral dissertation, Northwestern University.

Trost, J. E., & Canter, G. (1974). Apraxia of speech in patients with Broca's aphasia: A study of phonemes, production accuracy and error patterns. *Brain and Language, 1,* 63–80.

Tyler, L. K. (1982). Serial and interactive theories of sentence processing. *Theoretical Linguistics, 8,* 29–65.

Warren, R. M. (1970). Perceptual restoration of missing speech sounds. *Science, 167,* 392–392.

Warrington, E. K., & Shallice, T. (1980). Word-form dyslexia. *Brain, 103,* 99–112.

Wheeler, D. D. (1970). Processes in word recognition. *Cognitive Psychology, 1,* 59–85.

Wickelgren, W. A. (1965). Similarity and intrusion in short-term memory for consonant-vowel digrams. *Quarterly Journal of Experimental Psychology, 17,* 241–246.

Wing, A. M., & Baddeley, A. D. (1980). Spelling errors in handwriting: A corpus and distributional analysis. In U. Frith (Ed.), *Cognitive processes in spelling* (pp. 252–273). New York: Academic Press.

5 Phonological Representations in Word Production

David Caplan
Montreal Neurological Institute
and
Laboratoire Théophile-Alajouanine

ABSTRACT

The case of a reproduction conduction aphasic patient, R.L., is presented. R.L. produces phonemic paraphasias in single word repetition, reading aloud, and picture naming, which are qualitatively similar inasmuch as they are strongly influenced by the number of syllables in the word to be produced. R.L. makes similar errors in repeating nonwords, but his performance is more impaired than with words. This pattern is discussed in relationship to several theories of the abnormalities in single word production leading to phonemic paraphasias. The results are inconsistent with many models, and suggest that there is a common stage of abstract phonological representations that is accessed in repetition, reading, and naming. It is hypothesized that this abstract representation is an underlying phonological representation.

In this chapter I make a suggestion about the structure of the word production system on the basis of several observations of word production in a conduction aphasic. I argue that the data suggest the existence of a level of underlying phonological representations in word production. The nature of my argument is indirect: I consider a variety of analyses and argue that all are inadequate to account for the patient's performance, leaving the model I suggest as the only remaining account of word production that will accommodate this patient's errors. I also argue that this account is consistent with current linguistic theory.

111

My suggestions are restricted to preliminary hypotheses about the nature of the representations involved in word production and the sequence whereby they are activated. I have no data which bear on the question of the mechanisms that activate these representations, such as serial search (Forster, 1976); activation to threshold of the resting activity level of a representation (McClelland & Rumelhart, 1981; Morton, 1970; Morton & Patterson, 1981); or more complex interactional mechanisms (Gordon, 1983). Investigation of these different mechanisms requires observations which have not been made in this patient.

METHOD

The patient studied is R.L., a 55-year-old right-handed male carpenter with an eighth grade education who had a stroke involving the temporal parietal area of the left hemisphere in March of 1983. He was studied on two separate occasions, in April and May of 1983, and in December, 1983. R.L.'s native language is French. He was also fluent in English prior to his stroke. He was tested entirely in French. On a French translation of the Boston Diagnostic Aphasic Examination (Goodglass & Kaplan, 1972), he showed fluent speech, with pauses before content words and phonemic paraphasias in the production of content words. He had perfect comprehension of single spoken words, but showed some difficulties in the comprehension of "complex ideational material." Repetition showed a considerable number of phonemic paraphasias at both the single word and sentence level. Phonemic paraphasias were also noted in reading aloud. Comprehension of single written words was excellent. initially R.L. showed a dysgraphia consisting of both slow and inaccurate letter formation and errors in the choice of individual letters. R.L. falls into the category of "conduction aphasia" on the basis of these performances.

R.L.'s word production was studied in three situations: word repetition, reading, and picture naming. Repetition of nonwords was also studied. The word list used for repetition and reading is the one constructed by Lecours (see also Nespoulous, Joanette, Ska, Caplan, & Lecours, this volume). It consists of 300 French words, 150 of which are mono-syllabic, 50 bi-syllabic, and 100 tri- and quadri-syllabic. Half the tri- and quadri-syllabic words contained consonant clusters and half did not. The words in this list are not controlled for frequency, major lexical category (function word vs. context word), concreteness, imagibility, or morphological complexity. In general, the tri- and quadri-syllabic words are less frequent and more abstract, and they are the only words which have derivational morphological features. Despite these limitations, I believe R.L.'s pattern of results on this list can be adequately interpreted for my purposes. The stimuli for naming consisted of 60 pictures of common concrete objects. Twenty pictures were designated by words of one syllable, 20 by words of two syllables and 20 by three syllable words. Words were matched for frequency. The list of non-words was constructed from the original list of 300 French words by substituting and permuting consonants and syllables, and therefore maintains the number of syllables of the original word. Obviously problems of concreteness, imagibility, frequency, and morphological complexity do not arise in non-word lists. The degree of similarity of non-words to existing words was not controlled.

RESULTS

Results are presented in Tables 5.1 through 5.4.

TABLE 5.1
Word Repetition

Number of Syllables:	1	2	3
Correct	148/150	38/50	65/100
Phonemic Paraphasias	2/150	12/50	35/100

TABLE 5.2
Naming

Number of Syllables	1	2	3
Correct	20/20	17/20	6/20
Phonemic Paraphasias	0	3/20	9/20
Omission (No Response)	0	0	5/20

TABLE 5.3
Word Reading

Number of Syllables	1	2	3
Correct:	30/30	28/30	19/30
Phonemic Paraphasias	0	2/30	10/30
Omission (No Response)	0	0	1/30

TABLE 5.4
Nonword Repetition

Number of Syllables	1	2	3
Correct:	50/50	39/50	15/50
Phonemic Paraphasias:	0	11/50	35/50

Tables 5.1, 5.2, and 5.3 indicate a strong syllable effect in word production. In repetition and reading, the number of phonemic paraphasias strikingly increases as syllable length increases from 1 to 3. In naming, in addition to the increase in the number of phonemic paraphasias, there are also a large number of omissions which are entirely found in three syllable words. Performance in reading is slightly better than in repetition (see also Nespoulous et al., this volume). Table 5.4 shows the same syllable effect in repetition of non-words as seen in word production in Tables 5.1, 5.2, and 5.3. In addition to showing the syllable effect, nonword repetition is more prone to the production of phonemic paraphasias than is word repetition, especially for words of three and more syllables.

The presence of a syllable effect in repetition of nonwords and in naming, where the various factors confounded with syllable length in the word repetition and reading tasks are either absent or controlled, is evidence that the syllable effect in word repetition and reading exists independently of any other factor. Similarly, the existence of a slight but definite increase in the number of phonemic paraphasias in words of two syllables compared to one syllable in repetition and reading cannot be due to factors of abstractness or derivational morphology, and indicates that the syllable effect is truly present in the determination of phonemic paraphasias.

A more detailed description of R.L.'s abnormalities in word production has been undertaken by R. Beland (personal communication, 1984), in connection with her doctoral dissertation. Beland has constructed lists of words containing four phonemes which vary from 1 to 3 syllables. Twelve different consonantal and vocalic patterns are present in this list, ranging from words of the form CCVC (*crêpe*-one syllable) to VVCV (*ahuri*-3 syllables). Beland's data confirm the effect of syllable length. Beland has also undertaken a close phonetic transcription of her entire corpus. This transcription indicates that R.L. is capable of subtle aspects of phonetic detail in the realization of both consonants and vowels. For instance, vowels are appropriately lengthened before voiced consonants in R.L.'s production. R.L. also consistently produced the phonetic features particular to the accent found in his socioeconomic class and age group. There are no features of his speech that could be considered dysarthric, once these accent-specific features are taken into account. Beland's corpus also confirms the presence of a significant number of phonemic paraphasias, in repetition and reading aloud.

DISCUSSION

The remainder of this chapter deals with the implications of these data for models of the word production process. As is usual in studies of aphasics, I shall approach this question by considering where errors such as these could occur in the process of word production. I shall pursue this analysis by considering four different accounts of the errors in conduction aphasia that have been found in the recent literature. These accounts are the "decoding" theory (Strub & Gardner, 1974); the "disconnection" theory (Kinsbourne, 1972); the short term memory theory (Shallice & Warrington, 1970, 1977; Warrington & Shallice, 1969); and the "production" theory (Dubois et al., 1964; Lecours & Lhermitte, 1969, and others).

The "decoding" theory of conduction aphasia maintains that some aspect of "input side" processing of words is defective in the syndrome and is responsible for the problems in overt production of sounds. Strub and Gardner (1974) have made a number of suggestions along these lines, such as that the simultaneous maintenance of the semantic representation of a word and the transfer of the auditory representation of a word to the motor apparatus are impossible for this type of patient. There is good evidence that R.L.'s problem is not of this sort, and does not arise on the input side. His BDAE results show that word-picture matching was excellent and the results in Table 5.2 and 5.3 indicate that naming and reading are affected in the same way as repetition. This rules out a disturbance of auditory input side processing as the sole locus of R.L.'s disturbance.

The "disconnection" model, originally proposed by Wernicke (1874), and Lichtheim (1885), which has been implicit in much of the clinical literature (see Geschwind, 1965; Morton, 1984, for discussion), has been recently readvocated by Kinsbourne (1972). Kinsbourne argues that his patients showed a disturbance of the connection between auditory-verbal representations and motor speech output. This analysis cannot apply to R.L., whose problems also occur in reading and naming. One way to adapt the disconnection analysis so that it can apply to R.L. would be to maintain that in both reading and naming "auditory-verbal representations" are accessed prior to the engagement of the motor speech apparatus. This sort of analysis is found in Wernicke's and Lichtheim's original models but not in the more recent version proposed by Kinsbourne. We shall return to this possibility.

The third theory of conduction aphasia is the "short-term memory" deficit analysis suggested by Shallice and Warrington (1977); Saffran and Marin (1975); Caramazza et al. (1981), and others. This analysis accounts for the repetition disturbance in this syndrome by relating it to a demonstrated failure of STM. R.L. does not fall into this subtype of Conduction Aphasia on several grounds. He shows significant disturbances in the production of single words, which is not characteristic of the (relatively) pure cases of this subgroup. Furthermore, though his recall is limited by his production of phonemic paraphasias and omissions, his recognition memory is excellent for lists of words and non-words and for recognition of serial order of words and non-words in lists, up to lists of six items (Caplan et al., 1986). STM failure will not account for R.L.'s disturbance in single word production.

The fourth set of possibilities regarding the locus of disturbance in conduction aphasia is that the problem occurs during the process of production. The essential claim of the authors who advocate this analysis is that the processes of word recognition, lexical access from nonverbal stimuli such as pictures or objects, the recognition of the phonological characteristics of nonwords, and the maintenance of these lexical and nonlexical representations in very short term memory (at least when dealing with individual stimuli) is not the source of the phonemic paraphasias seen in single word production in Conduction Aphasia. Some investigators who advocate the "production" model of the deficit would allow that these "input side" processes may not be entirely normal, but the production theory denies that input side processing is sufficiently disturbed to account for the extent and nature of the errors found in these patients. The "production" theory has several advocates whose models differ slightly from each other.

The first production model is that of Dubois et al. (1964). Dubois et al. claim that the disturbance in conduction aphasia lies in the process of constructing the level of representation termed the "first articulation", which is the level of linguistic representation corresponding to phrases and sentences. This formulation is inadequate to account for R.L.'s problems because, although R.L. does have a problem in sentence repetition and in sentence production, he also has a problem in single word production. (The case reported in Dubois et al.'s (1964) paper also had a problem at the single word level and it is hard to see why the authors conclude that the problem in conduction aphasia lies only at the level of the first articulation.)

The second version of the production theory has been developed by Garrett (1984). His suggestion is that conduction aphasia have a problem in the process of accessing lexical phonology from lexical semantics. In his terminology, this would be a problem in a "linking address" from lexical semantics to lexical phonology. Garrett supports this analysis by pointing to the fact that conduction aphasics recall first syllable of words that they cannot produce more frequently than anomics do (data reported in Goodglass et al., 1976) and that conduction aphasics show a phenomenon of successive approximations to the target, which clearly indicates that a good deal of word form is retained despite the patient's inability to produce it (the "conduite d'approches" phenomenon is analysed in Joanette et al., 1980). The problem with this analysis in R.L.'s case is that repetition and reading are also affected, and there is no reason to believe that R.L. necessarily uses a semantic route in these tasks. Thus, a failure to link lexical semantics and lexical phonology would not account for R.L.'s disturbances in these tasks. Moreover, R.L. has a qualitatively similar and quantitatively worse disturbance in the repetition of nonwords, where the linking address analysis cannot apply. If we maintain a single source for the disturbances shown by R.L., we cannot accept this version of the production theory.

A third version has been proposed by Buckingham (1982), who has suggested that phonemic paraphasias arise because of a failure of the "scan copying mechanism" that Shattuck-Hufnagel (Shattuck-Hufnagel, 1979) has postulated. Shattuck-Hufnagel has suggested that it is reasonable to postulate a mechanism which scans lexical segmental phonology and inserts it into phrase makers and that errors in such a mechanism could account for the occurrence of phonological slips of the tongue in normals (see Shattuck-Hufnagel, this volume). As with Dubois et al.'s suggestion (1964), the problem with this suggestion in R.L.'s case is that R.L.'s problems arise at the single world level.

The plausibility of the scan copier mechanism as a component of a normal speech production requires that two levels of phonemic representation be identified, one to be scanned, and the other to receive the copy. In Shattuck-Hufnagel's theory, the first of these levels is associated with lexical structure and the second with phrasal and sentence structure. In normals, sound-based errors in sentence production show great influence from surrounding words, and can reasonably be thought to arise as part of the process of inserting lexical phonology into sentence and phrasal contexts. However, in the case of single word production, the second of these two levels of representation is not obviously present. In the case of naming, as well as single word repetition and reading aloud, if the process of lexical access results in a phonological representation, there is no need to copy this phonological representation into a phrase marker. Thus, postulating a disturbance in the scan copier mechanism, as is done by Buckingham, cannot account for the occurrence of phonemic paraphasias at the single word level.

The last version of the production model is that of Lecours (Lecours & Lhermitte, 1969). Lecours' model claims that a substitution-concantenation operation occurs over segmental phonological representations in words. This substitution-concatenation operation is an error-generating mechanism, and Lecours has argued that it is constrained by a similarity and distance metric defined over at least the consonants of the target word. The reservation that has been expressed about this model is similar to the one just formulated regarding Buckingham's proposal: there is no obvious process in normal word production at which such substitution-concatenation function could apply. It is, of course, possible that such an error-generating function arises *de novo* in conduction aphasia as a result of brain injury (Caplan, 1981). If so, errors of this sort in conduction aphasia would not be relevent to models of normal word production.

It thus appears that none of the four variants of the "production" model are able to account for the type of error found in R.L.'s naming, repetition and reading of single words, and repetition of nonwords. We are thus left with a contradiction. We have eliminated the "input side" disturbances and "short-term memory" disturbances as the source of R.L.'s phonemic paraphasias, but we cannot accommodate his phonemic paraphasias to any of the "output side" models presented in the literature. The solution I propose is a modification of the production model on the basis of R.L.'s performance.

What is needed to account for R.L.'s production disturbances is a model which has two features. The first is that there be a stage of phoneme-to-phoneme mapping in the production of single words. This stage must not be one at which phonemes are mapped on to phonetic details in word production, because this is an operation that R.L. accomplishes well. Furthermore, the second level of phoneme representation cannot be necessarily linked to lexical insertion into phrases and sentences, because R.L.'s problem arises at the level of single word production. Rather, this second level of the phoneme-to-phoneme mapping must be part of the production process for the tasks of naming, reading, and repetition of isolated words.

The second requirement of the model is that the stage of phoneme-to-phoneme mapping has to be one which is more easily traversed by an existing word than by a nonword, because R.L. is better at the repetition of words than nonwords. This requirement rules out a whole class of models of word production that have the basic architecture of the Logogen model (Morton, 1969, 1970; Morton & Patterson, 1981). The Logogen model and all models that have their architecture of stages do provide the opportunity for phoneme-to-phoneme mappings at the single word level and for non-words, but because of the sequences of stages specified in these models, words should always be more subject to an error process affecting these mappings than non-words. As the reverse is the case in R.L., and many cases of conduction aphasia (see Bub, this volume, for similar concerns), models with this architecture cannot provide an account of the errors found in R.L. and similar cases.

A model of word production that has these two properties is inspired by linguistic theory (see Shattuck-Hufnagel, this volume, for similar reliance upon linguistic theory in the development of a production model). All modern versions of phonology postulate both underlying and superficial phonological representations. The superficial phonological representations are not simply phonetic. The two levels of representation differ with respect to such features as vowel quality, diphthongization, certain aspects of the realization of consonantal quality, the presence of stress in languages where stress is predictable (with attendant changes in vowel quality), vowel harmony, and other phonological features. Underlying representations are either not specified for certain of these features or have phonological specifications that are changed by rules of word level phonology to yield superficial phonological representations. Phonetic details, such as lengthening of vowels before voiced consonants, deaspiration of unvoiced stops that follow initial spirants, or occur at the ends of words, etc., occur after superficial phonological representations are specified. This division of phonological representations into underlying and superficial phonological levels antedates work within the framework of generative phonology, but it is clearly evident in the earliest works in generative phonology such as Chomsky and Halle (1968), and has been continued through more recent approaches, such as metrical phonology (Liberman & Prince, 1977) and autosegmental phonology (Goldsmith, 1976).

Given that lexical phonology involves both an underlying and a superficial phonological level, it is now possible to accommodate the errors seen in R.L. to a model of word production which includes both these levels. The errors seen in R.L. at the single word level would, on this view, arise in the process of achieving a superficial phonological representation from an underlying phonological representation.

On this model, the underlying phonological representation can be seen as the permanent lexical representation of a word, from which superficial phonological representations are produced during the process of word production. By the same token, the underlying phonological representations, being permanent lexical representations directly linked to semantic and syntactic features of a word (as in Chomsky, 1965, 1981; Chomsky & Halle, 1968), have been suggested to be the targets of perceptual processes involved in recognition of lexical items. This has been proposed for reading (Chomsky & Halle, 1968; Henderson, 1982), and it seems reasonable to extend the proposal to auditory word recognition as well. The underlying phonological representation would be a natural target for perceptual processes, since its immediate link to semantics and syntax makes it the phonological representation most useful in achieving access to those lexical features—syntax and semantics—that are relevent to understanding a word and its contribution to sentential semantics.

This model is presented in Fig. 5.1 in which abstract letter identities superficial phonology and lexical semantics are all necessarily linked to underlying lexical phonology. In this model, errors such as those seen in single word production in R.L. can all be accounted for by an error generating process located between underlying phonological representations and surface phonological representations. Whether the error generating process in R.L. is a pathologically induced exaggeration of the process that makes for occasional phonological errors in single word production in normals, or is some new process related to brain injury, and whether its operations are exactly those postulated by Lecours or are constrained by the kinds of factors specified by Shattuck-Hufnagel, remain to be determined.

The greater difficulty in repetition of nonwords than words can be accounted for on this model by observing that the attempt to find an underlying representation for a nonword involves processes which are different from such an attempt in the case of an existing word. This process can be more difficult for nonwords than for words. Words have permanent underlying representations in the lexicon, whereas nonwords do not. On the proposed

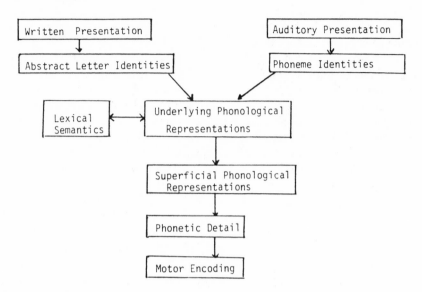

FIG. 5.1. A Simplified Model of Stages in Word Recognition and Production.

model, all stimuli recognized as linguistic are subject to a process that attempts to compute an underlying phonological representation. In the case of words that exist in the language of an individual, this process must involve a matching operation whereby the underlying phonology computed from the presented word is matched against the underlying phonology in the permanent mental lexicon. In the case of a nonword, there is no confirmatory match of this sort. On the one hand, the existence of this confirmation may make further processing of the computed underlying phonology simpler, and, on the other hand, processing of underlying phonological representation subsequent to this confirmatory matching process can take place on the actual lexical representation, rather than the computed underlying phonological representation, only in the case of words. For both reasons, processing of existing lexical underlying phonological representations may be easier than processing of computed underlying phonological representations for nonwords.

I conclude with a brief discussion of several implications of this model. First, this model bears a resemblance to the earliest psycholinguistic processing models proposed on the basis of aphasic data, such as that of Wernicke (1874) and Lichtheim (1885). This model is reproduced in Fig. 5.2. These authors postulated the existence of a "storehouse for auditory patterns of words", which was necessarily evoked during the process of repetition, oral reading, and naming. Similar models have been proposed consistently in the neurolinguistic literature to the present (Caramazza et al., 1981). The question of the nature of "auditory verbal representation" (Caramazza et al., 1981) or "the storehouse for the auditory form of words" has never been

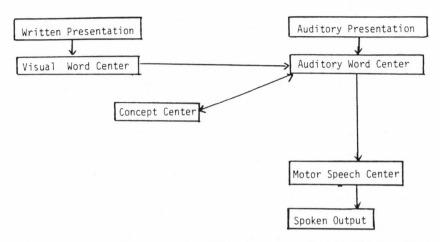

FIG. 5.2. Wernicke's and Lichtheim's Model of Stages in Word Production. The "Concept Center", "Visual Word Center", and "Auditory Word Center" correspond roughly to "Lexical Semantics", "Abstract Letter Identities", and "Phoneme Identities" in Fig. 5.1. The model developed in the text argues that word recognition and production converge on a more abstract level of phonological representation than suggested by this model.

clarified. On the present model, this structural level can be considered to be the level of underlying phonological representations of words. However, the representations that I am postulating are quite different from those implicit in the models of Wernicke, Lichtheim, Caramazza et al., and others. As far as I can tell, these theorists have in mind a relatively superficial level of phonological representation, one which can be considered to be "auditory" in some sense. Possibly these authors have in mind a representational system which incorporates some actual auditory or acoustic information, though it is unclear what such information might be or what role such information might play in the processes of reading and naming. At the least, these authors seem to have in mind a fully specified (hence superficial) phonological representation. In contrast, the model I propose postulates that a very abstract level of representation, distantly related to the physical properties of sound and closely linked to semantic and syntactic features of words, is the representational level universally computed in the process of word recognition and word production.

Second, a model of this sort has implications for analysis of several normal and pathological processes. In particular, it has implications for theories of dyslexia. For instance, the model I have proposed does not allow for a direct route from abstract letter identities to superficial phonology. The standard view of grapheme/phoneme correspondence rules is thus cast into doubt, if GPCs are thought to convert graphemes into surface phonemes. Grapheme/phoneme correspondence rules must convert Abstract Letter Identities to underlying phonological representations on this model. Surface dyslexia might be due to a particular form of disturbance in the conversion of Abstract Letter Identities to underlying phonological representations. In many cases, this would be indistinguishable from the present analysis, but some patterns of reading impairment might distinguish these two models. One such case is that of Schnitzer (1972), in which approximately 50% of the dyslexic errors could be most parsimoniously accounted for by postulating disturbances in underlying phonological representations which then led to complex abnormalities in the sound pattern of individual words. This disturbance can be easily accounted for on the present model by postulating that the patient could not achieve normal underlying phonological representations from abstract letter identities. The case is more complex, because Kehoe and Whitaker (1973) have reported that errors occurred almost exclusively in reading words with Latinate derivational morphology and not in equally long words of Anglo-Saxon or American-Indian origin or nonwords with Latinate derivational endings. These additional features cannot be accounted for by a model as simple as that presented in this paper, and suggest that what I have called "underlying phonological representations" must be further divided along a variety of linguistic lines, perhaps following theories of lexical morphology and phonology currently under development (Kiparsky, 1982).

In summary, I have presented a model of the word production process that incorporates a level of underlying phonological reproductions as a necessary part of word production. This model allows for the location of the disturbance in the patient I have presented within the normal process of word production. The model has implications for theories of dyslexia, normal reading, and normal recognition of auditorily presenting words and then processing of nonwords. Perhaps the most important feature of this model is that it incorporates a level of linguistic representation into the processes of word recognition in production, justified on structural grounds, that has occasionally been postulated to play a role in psycholinguistic processing models. I have deliberately restricted my presentation of this model to its essential features, and considerable elaboration of the notion of an underlying phonological representation is possible. The further development of models of planning of word phonology on the basis of data from aphasia incorporating a larger number of structural levels discovered in linguistics, will depend on more detailed observations and analyses of the deficits in phonological processing in aphasic patients.

REFERENCES

Buckingham, H. W. (1982). Perseveration in aphasia. In S. Newman & R. Epstein, (Eds.), *Dysphasia*. Churchill Livingston, London.

Caplan, D. (1981). On the cerebral localization of linguistic functions. *Brain and Language, 14,* 120–137.

Caplan, D., Vanier, M., & Baker, C. (1986). A case study of reproduction conduction aphasia: I. Word production. *Cognitive Neuropsychology, 3,* 99–128.

Caramazza, A., Basili, A. G., Koller, J. J., & Berndt, R. S. (1981). An investigation of repetition and language processing in a case of conduction aphasia. *Brain and Language, 14,* 235–271.

Chomsky, N. (1965). *Aspects of the theory of syntax.* Cambridge, MA: MIT Press.

Chomsky, N. (1981). *Lectures on government and binding.* Dordrecht: Foris.

Chomsky, N., & Halle, M. (1968). *The sound pattern of English.* New York: Harper & Row.

Dubois, J., Hecaen, H., Angelergues, R., Maufras du Chatelier, A., & Marcie, P. (1964). Étude neurolinguistiques de l'aphasie de conduction. *Neuropsychologia, 2,* 9–44.

Forster, K. I. (1976). Accessing the mental lexicon. In E. C. T. Walker & R. J. Wales (Eds.), *New approaches to language mechanisms.* Amsterdam: North-Holland.

Garrett, M. F. (1984). The organization of processing structure for language production: Applications to aphasic speech. In D. Caplan, A. R. Lecours, & A. Smith (Eds.), *Biological perspectives on language.* Cambridge, MA: MIT Press.

Geschwind, N. (1965). Disconnection syndromes in animal and man. *Brain, 88,* 237–294.

Goldsmith, J. A. (1976). *Autosegmental phonology.* Bloomington, IN: Indiana University of Linguistics Club, Bloomington, Indiana.

Goodglass, H., & Kaplan, E. (1972). *The assessment of aphasia and related disorders.* Philadelphia: Lea & Febiger.

Goodglass, H., Kaplan, E., Weintraub, S., & Ackerman, N. (1976). The "tip of the tongue" phenomenon in aphasia. *Cortex, 12,* 145–153.

Gordon, B. (1983). Lexical access and lexical decision: Mechanisms of frequency sensitivity. *Journal of Verbal Learning and Verbal behaviour, 22,* 24–44.

Henderson, L. (1982). *Orthography and word recognition in reading.* London: Academic Press.

Joanette, Y., Keller, E., & Lecours, A. R. (1980). Sequences of phonemic approximations in aphasia. *Brain and Language, 11,* 30–44.

Kehoe, W. J., & Whitaker, H. A. (1973). Lexical structure disruption in aphasic: A case study. In H. Goodglass & F. Blumstein (Eds.), *Psycholinguistics and aphasia.* Baltimore: John Hopkins University Press.

Kinsbourne, M. (1972). Behavioural analysis of the repetition deficit in conduction aphasia. *Neurology, 22,* 1126–1132.

Kiparsky, P. (1982). From cyclical phenology to cyclical morphology. In H. van der Hulst & V. Smith (Eds.), *The structure of phonological representations.* Foris, Dordrecht.

Lecours, A. R., & Lhermitte, F. (1969). Phonemic paraphasias: Linguistic structures and tentative hypotheses. *Cortex, 5,* 193–225.

Liberman, M., & Prince, A. (1977). On stress and linguistic rhythm. *Linguistic Inquiry, 8,* 249–336.

Lichtheim, L. (1885). On aphasia. *Brain, 7,* 433–488.

McClelland, J. L., & Rumelhart, D. E. (1981). An interactive activation model of context effects in letter perception. Part I: An account of basic findings. *Psychological Review, 88,* 375–407.

Morton, J. (1969). The interaction of information in word recognition. *Psychological Review, 76,* 165–178.

Morton, J. (1970). A functional model for memory. In D. A. Norman (Ed.), *Models for human memory.* New York: Academic Press.

Morton, J. (1984). Brain based on non-brain based models of language. In D. Caplan, A. R. Lecours, & A. Smith (Eds.), *Biological perspectives on language.* Cambridge, MA: MIT Press.

Morton, J., & Patterson, K. (1981). An attempt at a new explanation, or a new attempt at an explanation. In. M. Coltheart, J. C. Marshall, & K. Patterson (Eds.), *Deep dyslexia.* London: Routledge.

Saffran, E. M., & Marin, O. S. M. (1975). Immediate memory for word list sentences in a patient with deficient auditory short-term memory. *Brain and Language, 2*, 420-433.

Schnitzer, M. L. (1972). *Generative phenology evidence from aphasia. University Park, PA: The Pennsylvania State University Studies 34, Pennsylvania State University.*

Shallice, T., & Warrington, E. K. (1970). Independent functioning of the verbal memory stores: A neuropsychological study. *Quarterly Journal of Experimental Psychology, 22*, 261-273.

Shallice, T., & Warrington, E. K. (1977). Auditory verbal short-term memory impairment and conduction aphasia. *Brain and Language, 4*, 479-491.

Shattuck-Hufnagel, S. (1979). Speech errors as evidence for a serial order mechanism in sentence production. In W. Cooper & E. C. T. Walker (Eds.), *Sentence processing: Psycholinguistic studies presented to Merrill Garrett,* (pp. 295-342). Hillsdale, NJ: Lawrence Erlbaum Associates.

Strub, R. L., & Gardner, H. (1974). The repetition defect in conduction aphasia: Mnestic or Linguistic? *Brain and Language, 1*, 241-255.

Warrington, E. K., & Shallice, T. (1969). The selective impairment of auditory verbal short-term memory. *Brain, 92*, 885-896.

Wernicke, C. (1874). *Der Aphasische Symptomen complex.* Breslau: Taschen.

6 The Cortical Representation of Motor Processes of Speech

Eric Keller
Université du Québec à Montréal
and
Centre de recherche
Centre Hospitalier Côte-des-Neiges

ABSTRACT

This chapter proposes, first, a synthesis of the contemporary premises of speech motor control, and second, an analysis of the neurological disturbances of this function. It is proposed that during language acquisition, the motor system stores contractile and temporal relations that define the articulatory actions of speech. These relations are thought to be the basis of local synergies between muscle groups in various portions of the vocal tract (mediated by the primary motor cortex), and of global synergies that coordinate the actions of the entire vocal tract (mediated by the secondary motor cortex). In the post-acquisitional phase, these synergies are thought to constitute some of the basic building blocks of the articulatory utterance chain.

The relational aspect of these synergies suggests a number of verifiable hypotheses for neurological impairments of language. For instance, it predicts that certain neurological lesions may disrupt the relational aspect of the programming of articulatory events; as a result, speech would become dysfluent and dyscoordinated. These predictions are supported by research on Broca's aphasia, which is characterized by excessive dysfluency and by disruptions of interarticulatory coordination. Further, the hypothesized differentiation of local and global synergies predicts known differences between certain types of aphasia and dysarthria. Specifically, the global phonemic disturbances of conduction aphasia are found to contrast with the typically more local phonetic disturbances of spastic dysarthria.

Throughout the history of psycholinguistics, the study of neurological disorders of adult speech has held out the promise of contributing to the understanding of the relationship between linguistic performance and the neural structures mediating this performance. However, a number of factors have retarded progress in establishing direct relationships between language performance and its neurophysiological substrate. Chief among these are the great variation between apparent localization of functions in various speakers, the difficulty of inferring normal speech function from disordered function, the impossibility of conducting crucial neurophysiological experiments with human subjects, and a long history of terminological confusions.

To remedy these problems, arguments have been made for abandoning the localizationist frame of reference as primary conceptual map in favor of a psycholinguistic process frame of reference. This is because all speakers of a given language must engage in fairly similar performance processes, such as discourse structuring, lexical selection, syntactic and morphological structuring, phonological and articulatory phonetic processing. For speakers of a given language, one may assume similar interrelations between processing events, despite differences in the number of available lexical or syntactic elements. Within this framework, neurogenic language production disorders are seen as selective impairments of one or several psycholinguistic processes, regardless of site and size of the underlying lesion. This approach, which ensures greater comparability of disorders from one patient to another, facilitates the construction of measuring instruments for aphasia and dysarthria, and shows promise of reducing terminological confusions.

Despite its usefulness, this approach does not replace or abviate research on the relationship between language and its physiological substrate. Indeed, there are circumstances and research purposes where it is promising to link functional hypotheses to pertinent neuroanatomical and neurophysiological information. This is the case with motor processes of speech, where subject-to-subject variation in localization of language production processes appears to decrease with proximity to the final output. Further, the neurophysiology underlying motor control is better understood than that which mediates cognitive systems, and can thus provide some indications of how speech motor control might be organized. Finally, there is a growing body of research that ties observations on neurogenic speech disturbances to neurophysiological principles of motor control.

Thus two distinct theoretical approaches to neurogenic language impairments have emerged, on one hand, computationally oriented hypotheses arising from formal linguistics, cognitive psychology, or artificial intelligence; and on the other, neurophysiologically oriented hypotheses originating in articulatory phonetics, physiological psychology, and neurophysiology. The research purposes served by these two approaches are fundamentally different. The purpose of computationally oriented hypotheses is to state formally and explicitly how linguistic units interact in speech production without reference to neurophysiological events. Neurophysiologically oriented hypotheses, by contrast, state general principles of operation and explain a number of observations by means of a single, coherent set of assumptions. They attempt to show the general form of the interaction of linguistic units, as much as possible with reference to it neurophysiological matrix. Although of no immediate interest to formal linguistics, computational cognitive psychology, or artificial intelligence, such hypotheses are indispensable for orienting future physiologically oriented research on speech motor control in neurophysiology, physiological psychology and articulatory phonetics, as well as to the clinical understanding of neurogenic speech disturbances.

This chapter is an attempt to formulate a neurophysiologically oriented hypothesis. It proposes that one of the fundamental cortical functions in speech motor control is to learn to execute articulatory movements by abstracting and storing relations (or "synergies") between commands for individual articulatory muscle groups[1]. It further argues that toward the end of the speech motor acquisition period, the major function of the cortex in speech motor control shifts to the selection of such synergies, and to their adjustment to environmental conditions. This view is contrary to that of some other authors (e.g., Abbs & Cole, 1982), who maintain that, rather than producing speech segments from a large number of stored movement patterns, movement patterns are generated afresh each time they are required[2].

In the first part of this chapter contemporary functional and neurophysiological perspectives of speech motor control are synthesized. In the second part, the hypothesis is outlined, and some predictions for neurogenic speech disorders are examined. Most of the findings and principles leading up to the hypothesis are well established, although they are presented here in the condensed form of a personal synthesis of the field. The hypothesis itself is more explicit and in some respects more comprehensive than previous, similar accounts (Abbs & Cole, 1982; Keller, 1984; Kelso & Tuller, 1981), and the examination of its predictions for neurogenic disorders is original[3]. To render this contribution accessible to as wide and diverse an audience as possible, little specialized knowledge concerning motor control, neurophysiol-

---

[1] In this chapter, the term *muscle command* refers to an internally regulated neurological impulse train, related to and preceding a peripheral contraction in a coherent muscle group. It is assumed that such a command represents the coordinated output of a large number of motoric neuronal cells.

[2] In all fairness to authors such as Abbs and MacNeilage who have in the past defended the "generating afresh" hypothesis, they have generally done so with a fair bit of caution. Far less careful of this issue have been a number of authors in the clinical domain (cited by Goehl & Kaufman, 1984); assuming not only fresh generation but also total dependence on feedback for each articulation, these authors appear to have uniformly (and erroneously) predicted severe deterioration of speech production subsequent to impairments of a feedback channel, as through adventitious deafness.

[3] This chapter incorporates and clarifies concepts previously sketched out in Keller (1975, 1978, 1979, 1984).

ogy, and neurogenic language disorders has been assumed, and the use of technical terms has been restricted to a minimum.

A. BASIC ASSUMPTIONS I: THE FUNCTIONAL ORGANIZATION OF SPEECH

1. The Variable of Time, The Planning/motor Processes Distinction and the Automaticity of Motor Actions

All consideration of language performance is ultimately tied to the parameter of time. Production processes do not only occur in "real time," but they are constrained and shaped by time limits—limits that are partly due to social and communicative needs and conventions, and are partly the result of physical inertial and oscillatory aspects of articulatory movements.

As an example of a socially imposed time limit, asking a question usually sets up a time constraint for the answer; if the answer is not produced within that time, it may be ignored or discounted. As an example of an inertial and oscillatory time constraint, one may think of the articulatory rhythm imposed by the weight and the contractile characteristics of the speech musculature on a continuous, rapid (diadochokinetic) repetition of "dadada . . ." (see also Kelso & Tuller, this volume). Due to such constraints, audible spontaneous speech is typically (a) restricted to certain time slots and (b) produced at a fairly rapid and rhythmic rate.

In order to be able to produce such well-paced utterances, speakers plan out portions of their utterances beforehand. Evidence for this is that the search for a difficult-to-remember word may take more time than is indicated by its prompt appearance in the appropriate spot in the utterance; in fact, normal anticipation errors such as ". . . *T*anadian from *T*oronto . . ." (Fromkin, 1973) indicate that planning events may precede execution events by a considerable margin, and may thus involve processes that are functionally separate from execution processes. In this view, planning and motor processes in continuous discourse operate concurrently (in parallel), while operating on linguistic information sequentially.

This by now well-established psycholinguistic notion (e.g., Foss & Hakes, 1978; Keller, 1979; MacKay, 1970) corresponds to our introspective awareness, and accounts satisfactorily for a number of normal speech phenomena (e.g., anticipatory speech errors, hesitations). In the present context, the notion of differential time constraint further permits us to delimit speech motor processes from speech planning processes by the criterion of automaticity. Due to the rigid time constraints imposed on motor processes by the processing mechanics, motor processes must deal primarily with highly repetitive, not-too-varied and predictable relationships which can be automatized through learning. Examples are: processes for translating the chain into executable and coordinated articulatory movements, for adjusting the output to actual speaking conditions, and for muscular execution. These processes involve fewer and more frequent elements than do planning processes, and can thus be highly automatized.

By contrast, the planning stage appears to involve above all those processes that cannot easily be automatized, because they involve the manipulation of unpredictable or infrequent processing variables. Decisions for the implementation of various aspects of the speaker's discourse, the selection of lexical items, and many syntactic and morphological decisions are complex and involve a great variety of infrequent elements that are not easily automatized.

It merits pointing out that the present distinction between planning and motor processes is not synonymous with the difference between supraphonological and phonological levels, characteristic of most linguistic descriptions. Phonological anticipation errors indicate that planning must be concerned with phonological information, whereas motor processing can be shown to be concerned with selected morphological events.

For example, evidence from spontaneous speech errors indicates that the morphophonological choice between the indefinite articles "a" and "an", preceding words beginning with consonants and vowels, is usually made during motor processing (see Fromkin, 1973, pp. 229 & 259). If it can be assumed from the model of the anticipatory errors that most speech errors occur at the interface between planning and motor processes, an adjustment in the "a/an" choice subsequent to the speech error implies that the "a/an" choice is a motoric process. Fromkin's data show, for example, that "an ice cream cone" became "a kice ream cone," and "a history of an ideology" became "an istory of a hideology." In those cases, the spontaneous speech errors apparently created inputs to the motor processes to which the *a/an* selection process adapted instantaneously, evidently during the process of motoric outputting.

Similarly, by the automaticity criterion, the selection of the most common closed-class (function) words could be performed during motor processing, whereas the selection of most open class (lexemic) words could be performed during planning. This is because the selection of closed class words is highly predictable and makes use of frequently used manipulanda, while the selection of open class (lexical) words involves a large inventory of words of generally lesser frequency of occurrence. Consequently, the selection of closed-class words can be more easily automatized than the selection of open class items, and can be integrated more readily into time-critical speech production processes.

The overall speech production framework to emerge from these considerations is somewhat different from traditional conceptions of speech production. Early linguistic models were constructed around the separability of semantic, morpho-syntactic and phonological levels, yet all but ignored time constraints and related concepts of processing complexity and automaticity. Within an online processing model, considerations of time constraints became primordial, since the possibilities of buffering information decrease with proximity to final output. The more peripheral motoric processes are thus seen to be more time-critical than the more central cognitive processes. As a consequence, the demarcations between semantic, morpho-syntactic and phonological types of processing become obscured, and the distinctions between more or less predictable (and thus more or less automatizable) processes of any type become more pronounced.

Although the notions of time constraints and automaticity have not yet been extensively investigated, there are some indications that this conceptualization makes the right predictions for both normal and neurogenically impaired speech. In normal speech, for instance, the degree of vowel reduction appears to be determined in part by the degree of automaticity of the syllable in question; unstressed syllables are shorter in duration and involve lesser articulatory movements than stressed syllables (Delattre, 1969; Ostry, Keller, & Parush, 1983). The vowels of unstressed syllables are thus said to be "reduced" in comparison to those of stressed syllables. But similar reductions in syllable duration and articulatory gestures have also been observed for closed-class words, as compared to their open-class homonyms. In pilot data from our laboratory, the French closed-class items "la" [la] (the) and "vers" [vɛR] (toward) have been found to be produced in a shorter time than their homonymous lexemes "las" [la] (weary) and "vers" [vɛr] *"worm"* in the sentence *"le vers las rampe vers la cabane"* *(the weary worm crawls toward the hut"* *("vers": paired t* = 5.8, *p* < .025, one-tailed, *n* = 5; "las/la": paired *t* = 3.2, *p* < .05, one-tailed, *n* = 4).

Predictions for neurogenically impaired speech are similarly encouraging. If closed-class items can indeed be inserted into the speech chain during the motor processing stage, it would follow that lesions affecting motoric output processing should in some proportion of cases also affect closed-class processing, while leaving essentially intact open-class processing. Syndromically, this prediction corresponds to clinical experience: although only a subset of patients with motoric types of aphasia show agrammatism (i.e., impairments in the processing of predictable, easily automatized closed-class items), those that do show agrammatism without fail also experience motoric speech impairments. Further, the recent documentation of two aphasic patients who showed agrammatism without comprehension deficit of closed-class items (Miceli, Mazzucchi, Menn, & Goodglass, 1983; Nespoulous & Dordain, 1985), further supports the notion that this type of disorder may take its origin in motoric processing.

We conclude from these arguments that motor processes are differentiated from cognitive processes primarily by their responsiveness to time constraints, and are by implication limited to automatizeable processes operating on predictable and high frequency items.

2. Perceptual Goals

Traditionally, the motor processes of speech have been seen as performing a simple translation between a planned utterance and its muscular and acoustic equivalent. Partly because of our robotic preconceptions, this has seemed to be nothing more than a mechanical task, consisting of "looking up" and executing typical motor equivalents or stereotyped muscle actions in response to given demands.

However, the research of the last 15 years on articulatory motion in speech (the so-called "kinematics of speech") has shown that the likely course of events is quite different. Most importantly, it has been found that a given perceptual goal can be achieved by different muscle actions, depending on momentary and local requirements. As far back as 1955, Stevens and House calculated formant frequencies for a vocal tract simulation and showed that a given vowel does not require a unique vocal tract configuration (Fig. 6.1). They found that a vowel formant pattern typical of a given phoneme could be obtained with a whole range of vocal tract configurations by manipulating the degree of mouth opening, the radius of minimal constriction, and the distance between the glottis and the point of maximal linguo-palatal constriction ("point of constriction").

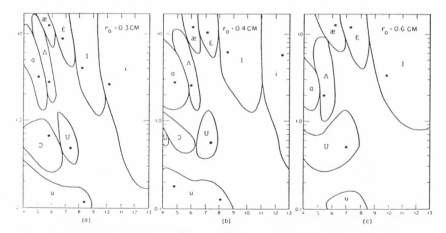

FIG. 6.1. Different configurations of the vocal tract capable of producing the complex acoustic waveforms of certain English vowels (Stevens & House, 1955). These results derived from calculations for a simulated vocal tract, indicate that the full set of English vowels can be produced by various combinations of maximal intra-oral constriction (panels a to c), the distance between the larynx and the point of maximal contribution (x axis) and the degree of mouth opening (y axis). (From Stevens & House, 1955.)

Subsequently, observational and experimental data gave further credence to the notion that two tokens of the same perceived acoustic category can be produced with widely differing gestures. A number of authors demonstrated covariance between two participating articulatory structures, such as when the lips show a small movement in performing an oral closure at times when the lower jaw performs a large movement, and a large movement when the lips show a small movement (Hughes & Abbs, 1976; cited in Abbs, 1982). Also, it was found with various articulatory gestures that the placing of an unexpected interference on an articulator produces short-latency compensatory movements in an unaffected coarticulator. In an experiment that has become a classic in this domain, Folkins and Abbs (1975, 1976) put an unexpected load on the jaw during the jaw closure for p in [hæpæp] and observed compensatory behavior in the two lips, implemented so rapidly that there was a satisfactory oral closure despite the arrested jaw movement (Fig. 6.2). Oral closures resulting in the same perceived phoneme were always performed in these experiments, no matter whether they involved varied movements of the lips, or compensation by one structure for another.

This suggests that the ultimate criterion (the "goal") of articulatory performance is not articulatory, but perceptual. Under this hypothesis, a typical speaker would consider his motor performance to be satisfactory as long as his output conforms largely to the perceptual categories he has internalized for the given language. His ultimate criterion would be perceptual, even though his internal and automatic self-correction processes may depend upon criteria that integrate auditory with correlated proprioceptive information. At

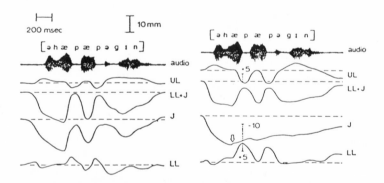

FIG. 6.2. Compensatory lip movements with perturbation of the jaw trajectory during the articulation of the stimulus phrase "Say a [hæpæp] again." On the left panel, the upper lip (UL) descended during the transition from [hæ] to [p], while the jaw (J) and the lower lip (LL) rose. On the right panel, the jaw action was impeded at the moment indicated by the arrow. The two lips compensated this perturbation by performing relatively greater movements (additional displacement for each lip: 5 mm). The audio trace indicates that despite this maneuver, the lip occlusion was sufficient to block all speech sounds. (Folkins & Abbs, 1975.)

the segmental level, the perceptual category boundaries presumably correspond to phonemic category boundaries, whereas at supersegmental levels, they may correspond to category boundaries established according to the particularities of the language in question (viz., syllabic structure, stress, and/or intonational contour patterns). We thus expect a speaker to correct himself primarily when the perceptual category boundaries are violated and only rarely when they are not. Although systematic examinations remain to be performed, this prediction receives some support from the predominance of phonemic over sub-phonemic exchange errors in normal speech (Shattuck-Hufnagel, 1983).

The perceptual goal thus occupies a key position in the present theoretical framework. At the same time, acoustic or perceptual category boundaries should not be considered to be inviolable; some speakers of English can be observed to habitually neutralize even stressed vowels, while others systematically transgress phoneme boundaries due to an articulatory handicap. I have observed a patient with congenital cerebral palsy who lacked facial nerve (cranial nerve VII) muscle control but who had intact glossopharyngeal (c.n. IX) and hypoglossal nerve (c.n. XII) control. He was incapable of controlling his lips, but could produce effective alveolar and oral stops and nasals. While speaking, he regularly substituted alveolar for labial consonants. Although his speech was clearly affected by these phonemic substitutions, it was surprisingly understandable, especially after some auditory training. Evidently, listeners will tend to auditorily compensate the breach of perceptual categories as long as the redundancy in the message permits. Yet it remains that generally, speakers will tend to respect such perceptual boundaries, particularly when it is important that they be well understood.

3. The Notion Of Motor Equivalence

These observations on speech motor control can be summarized by the concept of motor equivalence (Hebb, 1949). In its original formulation, motor equivalence captured the principle underlying the finding that rats, trained to run a certain maze, will subsequently show superior performance in swimming a similarly laid-out water maze. More recently, the term has been applied to motor function in the sense that a given motor objective can be implemented by a number of different muscle contractions, or different muscle groups, on condition that contractions combine to achieve a given goal.

In this view, the motor system does not mechanically translate a conceptual goal into a set of muscular contractions. Rather, its responsibilities is to learn command structures defining combinations of muscular contraction which can implement a perceptual goal, to select structures appropriate to the present circumstances from the family of structures that have previously been successful, and to adjust or bias, the selected commands in terms of the prevailing circumstances. The crucial concept inherent in this formulation is that there are whole families of commands to be learned, selected, and adjusted, whereby each family is united by a single goal. Motor equivalence is a general principle of motor action, and can be documented for actions as divergent as speaking, playing golf, or shooting rifles, each being characterized by achievement goals that are remote from the anatomical structure involved in its implementation.

The motor system thus has no direct link with the achievement goal. Because the system can only control muscle contractions, its task is to learn—perhaps through perceptually guided, successive approximations—the combinations of contractions which can achieve the given perceptual goal. Under these circumstances, the nervous system will discover a set of systematic relations between commands to various muscle groups, and between the muscle commands and the achievement of the remote goal. In doing so, the system learns to set its contractions of muscle groups in such a way that the combined effect falls within the boundaries set for the achievement of the goal; in the process, the system abstracts relations, or "synergies", between the various "successful" muscle contractions, and by implication, between the commands that implemented them.

The central concept is that movement commands are fundamentally defined as learned relations between specifications for the contraction of individual muscles. Informally, this knowledge can be envisaged to be relationships of the type "if degree of contraction in muscle group A is relatively small, then there must be a greater degree of contraction in muscle group B, in order to implement the goal correctly and with maximal efficiency," or "contraction in muscle group A must be initiated when contraction in muscle group B has attained degree x." These relations are seen as hierarchically organized, whereby the two levels of greatest importance to speech motor control are that of the movement aggregate, associated with the motor programming stage and responsible for an entire speech gesture, and that of the grouping of individual muscle commands for a given speech tract valve, characteristic of the execution stage and responsible for aspects of the speech gesture, such as nasality, voicing or labial closure.

4. The Reduction Of The Degrees Of Freedom

In order to implement the multitude of relations between muscle commands in a real-time speech event, the system must set the degree of muscle contraction for each muscle group, taking into account the named local and general conditions. Since there are around 60 identifiable muscle groups in the human vocal tract, each capable of a range of contractions, and cooperating to produce around 10 to 15 phonemes a second, the system encounters considerable computational complexity. This problem is known as the "degree of freedom" problem.

To briefly summarize arguments presented in great detail by Kelso and colleagues (e.g., Kelso & Tuller, 1981; Kelso et al., 1983), physiological systems faced with this problem will attempt to reduce computational complexity by establishing "coordinate structures", which are links, or predictable relations, between the freely varying variables. This is comparable to a "program" for movement synergies, phrased in terms of sequential, overlapping and parallel relationships between muscle commands. These programs permit the system to simplify its task by letting learned links between muscle commands take care of predictable relations for a given condition.

Two important consequences of reducing the system's degrees of freedom are first, that movements become more stereotyped (through the loss of degrees of freedom of movement), and second, that the gain in simplicity translates into greater speed of operation (unless the system is specifically "set" for slowness). We may speculate that the speed obtained by applying this type of knowledge results from eliminating repeated complex calculations of sequential organization and degree of muscle contractions.

5. Are Movement Parameters Produced From Storage Or Calculated Anew In Speech Production?

The present proposal emphasizes that movement information is learned, which in turn implies that normal, skilled articulation involves selecting aggregates of muscle commands from a store of commands, rather than generating afresh all the movement information each time a speech articulation is to be produced[4]. This position is somewhat controversial. Some authors would maintain that the number of movement aggregates to be stored is necessarily excessive, because there are several hundreds of thousands of possible phoneme-to-phoneme movement transitions to be stored away, just counting possible CVC combinations. In their view, this is an unlikely and inefficient account of normal speech production.

However, this argument loses some of its punch if one takes into account the unequal distribution of phoneme transitions in the language. Roberts' (1965) frequency tables for phoneme-to-phoneme transitional frequencies indicate, for instance, that out of 512 possible phoneme-to-phoneme transitions involving at least one vowel, just 37 transitions (or 7%) capture 51.4% of all transitional events. Other types of transitions are similarly unequally distributed. It therefore does not seem impossible for a neurological system to learn of the order of several hundred or several thousand of the most fre-

---

[4] In line with theories that view memory storage as occuring in close conjunction with neuron pools involved in a given process, the store for articulatory movement aggregates is assumed to be a facilitation process for previously used neuron interactions. "Selection from store" can thus be understood as "the activation of those neuron interactions that have been potentiated through previous use".

quent phoneme sequences, leaving the least frequent transitions to be calculated as the need arises.

The second argument brought against the "learning and storing" view of muscle commands is the demonstrated presence of fast compensations to unexpected perturbations in the vocal tract (see section on Perceptual Goals). It is argued that this is evidence that the system calculates movements in an ongoing fashion, taking into account all current, past and future conditions in the vocal tract, including unexpected perturbations.

However, it can be argued that the presence of compensations does not negate the learning and storing away of articulatory movement information. It is equally possible that generally, the system produces skilled speech from storage, but retains the option to bias it just before outputting, in order to compensate potential perturbations and to learn new movement patterns as the need arises. This view is concordant with relatively recent views on feedback in speech and with some pertinent findings on neurogenic disorders (see below). It also has the non-negligible advantage of embracing the concept of motor learning inherent to all language learning, be it the learning of a specific language, or learning to compensate for a regular encumbrance in the speech tract.

6. The Variability Of Feedback

Feedback processes assume the responsibility of informing the system about preceding local conditions in the vocal tract, and of initiating corrective action if necessary. Their organization is still in some dispute, because there is seemingly contradictory evidence on the importance of feedback information to the motor processes of speech. On the one hand, the efficient, short-latency compensations to perturbations obtained by Abbs and his coworkers indicate that in the normal speaker, the system has continuous and rapid access to sensory feedback on conditions in the vocal tract.

On the other hand, experimental or pathological interference with various types of feedback from the vocal tract has relatively little effect on the quality of speech, even when auditory and proprioceptive channels are impaired simultaneously. Borden (1979), for instance, reviews experiments in which auditory, tactile and proprioceptive feedback was distorted or interrupted by a variety of means, such as providing delayed auditory feedback, testing with noise conditions, or blocking sensory feedback through nerve anesthesia. The overwhelming impression conveyed by these experiments is that spontaneous speech in normal adults under predictable conditions does not crucially depend on feedback, despite some loss of precision when feedback is impaired (Gracco & Abbs, this volume). Convergent results derive from studies of the adventitiously deaf; adults who undergo sudden loss of hearing do not lose their ability to speak. Other than minor difficulties with fricatives and with judging voice amplitude, such persons show essentially intact speech; in blind listening conditions, their speech cannot be reliably distinguished from normal speech (Goehl & Kaufman, 1984).

Borden resolves this paradox by postulating that interference with feedback has only minor effects when speech is produced in predictable conditions (i.e., head upright and vocal tract unimpeded in an experienced speaker), but seriously hampers the compensation of unpredictable conditions and the calculation of less habitual movements (i.e., the presence of unpredictable vocal tract conditions in an experienced speaker, or a speaker inexperienced with a given language or set of vocal tract conditions). In this view, feedback recedes for the most part to a surveillance position in the motorically proficient adult, while it contributes directly to the calculation of articulatory movements during a motor learning phase, be it in childhood or in adult life. In support of this position, Borden summarizes studies showing that young children learning their first language and adults learning a second language are more severely affected by disruptions of auditory feedback than are adults speaking their native language (see MacNeilage, Rootes, & Chase, 1967). This notion is also supported by Oller and MacNeilage's (1983) reports that children are less capable than adults at compensating the presence of bite blocks between their teeth.

We note that this hypothesis does not address the question of feedback in the traditional either–or terms of "closed loop" or "open loop" operation (operating with or without feedback control), but it suggests that the exact degree of involvement of feedback information depends on the present state of the speaker's motor competence. In addition to being compatible with the notion that skilled movements in predictable conditions are produced from storage, this flexible view of feedback incorporates the speed advantage of movements selected from storage with reduced calculation load. At the same time, it accounts for results obtained with the perturbation paradigm by permitting a selected movement to be biased to compensate for unexpected perturbations and inhabitual steady-state conditions in the speech tract.

B. BASIC ASSUMPTIONS II: THE PHYSIOLOGICAL ORGANIZATION OF SPEECH

1. The Relation Between Limb And Speech Motor Control

Because much previous work in motor neurophysiology has concentrated on limb control, it is important to open this section by discussing the appropriateness of using neurophysiological findings on limb control in an exploration of speech motor control.

In terms of anatomy and neurophysiology, there are important differences between limb and speech articulations. The limb control system is fundamentally concerned with relatively gross bone movement, whereas the speech control system involves principally fine movement of muscular tissue; further, limb movement typically involves rotation around a pivot, accomplished by a group of lateralized muscles operating in a dominant agonist/ antagonist muscle mode, whereas speech articulation involves a large number of bilaterally attached minor muscle groups serving to shape several muscular masses (e.g., tongue, lips, velum) by means of complex agonist/antagonist formations. These differences bear on the lateral versus bilateral nature of final cortical motor control, and they may be expected to have consequences upon the degree of complexity in coordination, accomplished by the respective neurological control structures.

Another difference concerns the locus of control for the two systems. At least with respect to subhuman hind limb control, contemporary thinking distributes the main loci of control between the cortex and the spinal cord. Because decerebrate cats (spinal cord sectioned off from the brain) can be induced to walk on a treadmill while they are unable to walk on their own, it is argued that the so-called "spinal mechanism" of neural control must contain most of the "program" for the walking sequence (Carew, 1981), while the higher brain centers coordinate reflex activity with voluntary motor action and mediate spinal cord mechanisms by switching back and forth between different phases of the walking program (between the "swing phase", when the foot is off the ground and the "stance" phase, when the foot touches ground.

By contrast, there is little evidence for homologues to spinal mechanisms in speech motor control. For one thing, brainstem-based reflexes bear no obvious functional similarity to articulatory movement, since they have primarily vegetative and protective functions (e.g., to keep the teeth from biting the tongue or to keep water out of the lungs) (Abbs & Cole, 1982). Secondly, relatively short delay times (15 to 20 ms) are possible between the cortex and the articulatory musculature, enabling the cortex to adjust the articulatory program to perturbations within the constrained time frames of speech execution (Abbs & Cole, 1982; Cole & Abbs, 1983).

In view of such evidence, and taking into account the probable difference in evolutionary origins for limb and speech motor control, we assume that (a) the final output control over speech articulators tends toward bilaterality, although it is probably more unilateral in the case of the limbs, (b) the cortical component of neural control is more important for speech than it is for hind limb motor control, and (c) feedback for speech motor control is mediated primarily by the cortex, whereas it is handled more extensively at the spinal level in the case of certain forms of limb control. Evidence from neurophysiological experiments on limb control must therefore be interpreted with care and cannot automatically be presumed to be a standard model for speech control.

These differences in motor control design are not taken to be at odds with the similarities between limb and speech articulator movement that have been documented for aspects of displacement and velocity in speech and limb movement (Ostry & Cooke, this volume; Ostry, Keller, & Parush, 1983). If the two types of movements show kinematic similarities at the same time that neurophysiological evidence indicates differences at the level of the control structures, we must assume that the measured kinematic parameters do not address differences in locus or nature of the control structure, but that they are indicative of another level of motor functioning, or the effect of physical laws or physiological regularities governing any movement mediated by muscular tissue.

2. Somatotopic Organization, Direct Neural Innervation, And The Fractionation Of Movement

It is well known that the neural tissue making up the cortex is somatotopically organized. In the case of the motor system, this generally means that the surface stimulation of adjacent neural cells in certain areas of the cortex tends to produce simple, observable motor responses in closely situated muscular groups. With respect to sensory processing, this means, in the case of experiments with humans, that the stimulation of closely situated portions of certain areas of the cortex gives rise to perceived sensations in adjacent parts of the body; in the case of experiments with animals, however, it means that tactile stimulation of adjacent parts of the body tends to produce increased neural responses in neighboring parts of the cortex. The immediate motor and sensory responsibilities can be mapped out on the cortical area in question, or can be summarized by homunculi drawn on the cortical surface, with body parts proportional to the area of associated motor or sensory cortex.

The somatotopic organization of the human cortex differs from that of other mammals in ways that may bear on speech motor processing and its disturbances. First, there is much greater separation between motor and sensory representations in the human cortex than in that of other mammals. Ghez (1981) reports that there is complete overlap of motor and sensory representations in the hedgehog, a mammal whose anatomy seems to have remained unchanged for millions of years. With phylogenetic development, separate areas emerge in which either motor or sensory functions are dominant; in the cortex of higher primates including man, the frontal lobe is the site of primarily motoric functions, while the parietal and superior temporal lobes are dominant for sensory functions.

Parallel to the appearance of dominant (but not exclusive) areas for motor and sensory functions in the cortex, there is a development of increased direct cortical innervation of the peripheral musculature, with an associated increase of fine motor control over separate body parts (Ghez, 1981). This development is known as the "fractionation of movement." Lower mammals, including cats, present corticospinal motor innervations that terminate exclusively in the dorsal portions of the spinal cord where they do not make any direct connection with the motoneurons originating in the spinal cord. Progressively, as one examines prosimians, monkeys, apes and humans, there appear corticospinal tracts making monosynaptic contact with motoneurons of the distal limb musculature, and later, of the proximal musculature.

Similarly, there is indirect evidence to suggest that vocal tract control is more elaborate in humans than in lower mammals; the portion of motor cortex devoted to the vocal tract is found to be proportionally greater in humans than in apes, with about 30% of the human primary motor cortex devoted to direct innervation of the vocal tract, while the comparable figure for the simian primary motor cortex is about 18% (calculation based on homunculi shown in illustrations in Eyzaguirre & Fidone, 1975).

These indicators further support the notion that the human motor cortex is particularly well equipped to serve the speech functions described above. The frontal lobe has undergone the greatest phylogenetic development in man, it is motorically dominant and suited to fine motor control, and it is the site of a disproportionally large area concerned with vocal tract control. This area thus appears to be specialized for the mediation of fine motor control in the vocal tract, available above all for speech motor processing.

3. Primary And Secondary Motor Cortex

Another well established concept of importance to speech disorders is the difference between primary and secondary motor cortex. The primary motor cortex (Brodmann area 4) is situated bilaterally, immediately anterior to the central sulcus (Rolandic fissure). Electrical surface stimulation of this type of cortex elicits controlateral, discrete movements in a freely suspended anesthetized animal (Thompson, 1967). The secondary motor cortex is less clearly circumscribed. In animals, stimulation of parietal lobe areas dominant for sensory function will also tend to evoke muscle contractions, even when cortico-cortical connections to the primary motor cortex are ablated. However, contractions are evoked only at stimulation levels much superior to those used in the primary motor cortex (Thompson, 1967). Lesion studies in a variety of animals further suggest more complex motor programming by anterior frontal lobe cortex than is performed by the primary motor cortex (Denny-Brown, 1951), and more recent single-cell experiments have identified neuronal units in the parietal cortex related to specific classes of movements (Stein, 1978).

Penfield and Roberts' (1959) reports on the effects of stimulation of the exposed human brain during open-brain surgery indicate that with respect to speech as well, the primary and the secondary motor cortex may fulfill largely different functions. They report that stimulation of the primary motor cortex on either hemisphere resulted in uncontrollable vocalization and slurring of speech (although the right-hemisphere data are less convincing than those of the left hemisphere; see also Bhatnagar and Andy, 1983). By contrast, stimulation of the nonprimary speech areas, exclusively on the language-dominant hemisphere (perisylvian precentral, parietal, and temporal cortex), produced hesitations and perseverations on naming. Further stimulation effects dominantly but not exclusively related to the secondary motor cortex, were the repetition of syllables and serious distortions of speech (plus interference with a number of speech planning processes).

Although Penfield and Roberts used fairly powerful levels of stimulation by modern standards, an inspection of their figures indicates that these effects are fairly exclusive to either the primary or the secondary motor cortex. Further, this type of data is complementary with anatomical evidence concerning the origin of the cortico-bulbar pathway fibres, as well as with more recent localization indicators of ongoing brain activity (e.g., magnetography, see Beatty, Richer and Barth, in press; or blood flow studies, see various articles in vol. 9, no. 1 of *Brain and Language,* 1980).

These differences between stimulation effects in the primary and secondary cortex are quite revealing if interpreted in terms of relations between muscle commands during speech processing (cf. Fig. 6.1). Both vocalization and slurring, occurring with primary motor cortex stimulation, can be interpreted to involve primarily muscle commands affecting a single speech valve (speech valves are functionally-defined synergistic muscular units, such as those controlling the laryngeal, velo-pharyngeal, linguo-palatal and labial ports). In vocalization, articulators assume a relatively fixed position for the period of stimulation, devoid of the dynamic characteristics of normal speech motor action, while the laryngeal valve alone is active (in conjunction with the thoracic musculature, of course). Similarly, at least one manner of provoking slurring is to pose a steady impediment to the air stream by means of the linguo-palatal valve, possibly through a relaxation of the valve's entire musculature.

By contrast, perseverations and repetitions, provoked by secondary motor cortex stimulation, must involve entire movement aggregates (producing phonemes or syllables). This means that stimulation in the secondary motor cortex can mobilize motor units regulating the entire speech musculature. Penfield and Roberts' results may thus be interpreted to say that the primary cortex appears to be more directly concerned with synergistic contractions of functionally related muscular structures (valves), giving rise to friction, nasality, vocalization, etc., whereas the remaining perisylvian speech motor areas, particularly in the frontal lobe, are more directly concerned with the organization of larger aggregates of movements involving the whole speech musculature, that is, units at the phonemic and higher levels of phonological organization. These data are thus in support of the distinction between programming and execution stages in motor processing, introduced previously (section 6.A1).

The present interpretation of the responsibilities of the primary and secondary motor areas is also supported by more recent open brain stimulation experiments conducted by Ojemann and colleagues (e.g., Ojemann, 1980; Ojemann & Mateer, 1979). The stimulation of motor cortex in both hemispheres led to speech arrest and to impairments in mimicking single as well as multiple orofacial movements. In the dominant hemisphere, global mimicking impairments extended to the immediate premotor cortex. However, stimulation outside of this region in a wider area of peri-Sylvian cortex in the dominant hemisphere affected only the mimicking of sequences of orofacial movements, and left intact the mimicking of single movements. Areas where stimulation led to speech arrest and to impairment of all mimicking thus correspond to primary motor areas, whereas areas where only sequential mimicking was impaired correspond to secondary motor areas. Finally, results reported by Ojemann (1980) indicate that the extent of the primary motor cortex shows less inter-subject variation that of the secondary motor cortex.

4. Movement Versus Muscle Control: Intracortical Stimulation Experiments In Monkeys

The hypothesized concept of speech valve control in the primary motor cortex is also supported by neurophysiological investigations on cortically induced wrist movements in the monkey. Such movements are under direct cortical fine motor control and are thus probably more comparable to articulatory movements than motions partly mediated by spinal mechanisms (such as walking movements in the cat).

Meticulous studies by such researchers as Asanuma and Evarts (e.g., Asanuma, 1973; Evarts, 1974) have shown that certain neurons of the primary motor cortex relate directly to specific muscle groups at the periphery. By means of microelectrode investigations applying minimal stimulation currents inside the top four millimeters of cortical tissue, these authors were able to stimulate muscles groups independently of other groups to perform movements like thumb flexion, extension, adduction, and abduction (Asanuma, 1973). Such neurons are arranged in columnar arrays, called *cortical efferent zones,* which contain thousands of neurons and typically project to separate muscles around a single joint (Henneman, 1974).

Efferent zones with excitatory muscular effect are often situated close to zones with inhibitory effect on antagonist muscles, but neuron pairs with reciprocal excitatory and inhibitory effect are seldom situated within the same efferent zone. Each of these zones also receives proprioceptive and tactile sensory information from a large number of adjoining muscular areas, situated again primarily around a specific joint. Results obtained from the motor cortex of cats and monkeys were similar, except that monkeys showed a greater incidence of overlap between efferent zones for antagonist muscles, a finding probably related to their ability to fix a joint by simultaneously contracting antagonist muscles, such as when holding an object (Asanuma, 1973).

The primary motor cortex concerned with limb movement therefore appears to be "hard-wired" for producing individual muscle contractions, and it seems to be "programmable" for movements; further, the primary motor cortex appears to be anatomically "predisposed" for programming musculature involved in synergistic action around a given joint. The somatotopic organization of efferent zones insures that movements can be easily programmed by intra- and inter-columnar communications, if necessary with reference to sensory information arriving from the periphery. If this structural arrangement generalizes to vocal tract control in humans, it would appear that the architecture of the primary motor cortex favors, or at least does not impede, the hypothesized learning of relations governing synergistic contractions within specific speech tract valves.

In this sense we may have an answer to a question debated by neurophysiologists for close to a century, i.e., whether the cortex is organized so as to control individual muscle contractions, or whether it is organized in terms of controlling whole movements or even aggregates of movements. In retrospect, it appears that this was an unfortunate manner of posing the question. Since the cortex evidently controls both individual contractions and whole movements, it now turns out to be more profitable to specify to which degree, and in which parts of the brain, the system is "hard-wired", "programmed", or "predisposed toward spontaneous development of programs" to handle muscle contractions, movements or aggregates of movements.

As applied to speech production, the question is whether and to which degree there is predisposition for the development of articulatory programs. As we saw, evidence extrapolated from simian finger movement appears to favor a "predisposition" conception for the development of valve-related synergistic programs at the primary motor cortex level, and a "programming" conception for the higher-level organization of speech motor movement at the secondary motor cortex level.

C. THE HYPOTHESIS

At this point, the various strands of argumentation may be coalesced into an hypothesis on the cortical functions in the motor processing of speech.

First, we retain from the neurophysiological considerations that the cortex is the kingpin of the neurophysiological system subserving speech motor control. There is an absence of evidence for a speech homologue to the spinal mechanisms found for walking in subhuman animals, and the advanced level of the fractionation of vocal tract movement in humans indicates that the cortex is well-equipped to learn motor control over complex articulatory movements. Probably available to this learning process are neuronal structures permitting direct interactions between motor and sensory types of information; also, feedback delays between the periphery and the cortex are sufficiently short, so as to permit control over ongoing articulatory movement within the cortex.

Second, we retain from the functional considerations that the motor processing system: (a) uses and abstracts relations, or links, between the actions of different muscle groups, in line with given perceptual goals, and (b) takes into account preceding, ongoing and anticipated vocal tract conditions, as well as predominating local and external conditions. Both the need to reduce the system's degrees of freedom of operation and the multiple interplays between articulators impose the development of a network of predictable relations between muscle commands. As a result, speech motor action is mediated by families of linked commands, united by common perceptual goals and by similar articulatory movement characteristics. Three central aspects of speech motor control are therefore learning which, how, and under what circumstances muscle commands are grouped, selecting appropriate muscle command groups in skilled speech, and adjusting them to environmental conditions to the degree that they diverge from commands used in predictable speech articulations.

Third, we postulate that the bilateral primary motor cortices are concerned with more elementary aspects of speech motor control than is the unilateral secondary motor cortex in the language-dominant hemisphere. It would seem that the primary motor cortices are predisposed to develop linkages between muscle groups within individual speech tract valves (the labial, linguo-palatal, velo-pharyngeal, and laryngeal ports), whereas the secondary cortex is concerned with relations within organized movement aggregates involving the entire speech musculature. We retain that the anatomical extent of the primary and secondary cortices was functionally defined in this paper, and that these areas may show considerable subject-to-subject variation, particularly in the case of areas serving secondary motor function.

Finally, we postulate that in skilled speech production, and under predictable circumstances, the cortex selects commands for the most part without having to calculate muscle contraction settings on the basis of feedback information; however, in the initial stages of speech motor control, movement information is calculated on the basis of ongoing feedback about local and general environmental conditions. We also postulate that at the skilled stage, feedback continues to be used for calculating compensation biases for unexpected perturbations, for infrequent phoneme-to-phoneme transitions, and for inhabitual steady-state conditions in the vocal tract.

D. AN EXAMINATION OF PREDICTIONS FOR CORTICAL NEUROGENIC DISORDERS

1. Definitions

For the purposes of this section, it is important to define a few terms. Descriptively speaking, neurogenic disorders of speech motor processes tend to cause two rather different, but not mutually exclusive, impairments. On the one hand, a patient may produce distorted speech, whereby the entire speech chain is affected in the same manner, and where deviations from the norm for the most part fall within categorical (phonemic) bounds set by the perceptual goal. In their pure form, such phonetic disorders are seen in patients affected by various types of dysarthria.

On the other hand, a patient may produce phonologically disordered speech; that is, speech characterized among other things by a variety of errors affecting individual phonemes or groups of phonemes. These errors transgress the categorical bounds of the perceptual goal to form phoneme substitutions ("literal paraphasias"); further, there are repetitions, additions, and omissions of phonemes or groups of phonemes. In their pure form, such phonemic disorders are seen in patients affected by various types of aphasia.

Syndromically, phonetic disorders are typically seen in patients showing lesions of subcortical structures (extrapyramidal system, cerebellum, brain stem, and lower motor neurons). One type of dysarthria (pseudobulbar palsy) is caused by a lesion of the cortico-bulbar pathways (upper motor neurons) (Darley, Aronson, & Brown, 1975). Because these pathways originate largely in the bilateral primary motor cortex, it is also common to observe certain cortically-lesioned patients showing similar phonetic disorders, (i.e., continuous distortion of the speech chain) in addition to other language impairments, such as phoneme substitutions. In its pure form, this type of cortical dysarthric difficulty is described as "anarthrie pure" in the French literature, a term which will be used here in its English translation of "pure anarthria" (désintégration phonétique" in Alajouanine, Ombredane, & Durand, 1939). In its less pure forms, it is known as "trouble arthrique" or "arthric difficulty".

Syndromes characterized by phonemic disorders are seen in a variety of patients, showing various cortical or, more rarely, subcortical lesions, particularly in association with two major syndromes: (a) a syndrome characterized by slowness of speech and arthric difficulty, sometimes by agrammatism (the underuse of function or "closed-class" words), and by relatively intact comprehension (a syndrome known as "Broca's aphasia"), and (b) a syndrome whose main characteristic is a phonemic disorder associated with a severe repetition deficit, but devoid of arthric difficulty ("conduction aphasia"). A third common syndrome is characterized by a lack of arthric difficulty, by comprehension deficits, by word finding difficulties, and by paragrammatic speech (short stretches of grammatically correct speech within a deficient overall grammatical and discourse structure) ("Wernicke's aphasia"). Patients of this type show fewer phonemic difficulties than do those marked by other syndromes.

Although statistical differences have been demonstrated for these different types of neurogenically disordered speech (Keller, 1984; Nespoulous, Joanette, Ska, Caplan, & Lecours, this volume; Nespoulous, Lecours, & Joanette, 1983), no overall hypothesis has been advanced which successfully predicts the observed differential phenomena. The present neurofunctional hypothesis predicts many of the hitherto unexplained differences between syndromes as a consequence of impairments of the speech production processes defined here and of their underlying relational structure.

2. Difficulties Of Relating Neurogenic Language Disorders To Speech Production Processes

Despite this optimistic outlook, the major aphasic and dysarthric syndromes are not easily related to the speech production processes which have above been distinguished on functional, anatomical and experimental grounds. The major problem is that syndrome-process relationships are, for the most part, not one-to-one; some syndromes appear to affect several processes at a time, while others seem to interfere with processes affecting the transfer of information from one process to the next, and thus appear to argue in favor of processes not previously differentiated.

Patients with Broca's aphasia, for instance, show evidence of impairments at both the motor programming and the motor execution levels. Their frequent phonemic substitutions, their occasional productions of nonnative sounds, and their propensity towards consonant cluster simplification (Keller, 1984) indicate severe deficits at the motor programming level; at the same time, the continuous phonetic distortions (slurring, nasality, breathiness, etc), which typically affect their entire speech chain, are indicative of problems at the command execution level.

Conduction aphasia, on the other hand, appears to affect primarily the interface between planning and motor processes. One of the most characteristic impairments of these patients is that they often execute erroneous phonemes or syllables, but attempt to correct them immediately. Both correct and erroneous phonemes and syllables tend to be motorically intact (at least to the transcriber's ear), and their frequent, immediate attempts at correction indicate that their awareness of the intended utterance must be reasonably good (see also Joanette, Keller, & Lecours, 1980, for further evidence of intactness of planned phonemic targets). Analyzed in terms of the speech processes proposed above, it must be assumed that with respect to phonemic substitutions, their essential problem is neither at the planning or at the motor programming level; rather, it may very well occur at the point where the planned utterance is mapped, or "scan-copied", into the motor processes, in other words, at the interface between the two types of processes.

Essentially two analytical procedures are available to the theoretician faced with this problem. Either, processes are postulated directly on the basis of neurologically impaired language (an approach exemplified by Marshall and by Paradis in the present volume), or the attempt is made to relate externally motivated processes to the speech disorders of these patients (the approach chosen here). Both approaches have their advantages and their drawbacks. The advantage of the first approach is that all impairments and their derivative postulated processes are guaranteed to have "neurofunctional reality" in at least one patient. On the other hand, this approach can lead to an enormous proliferation of processes, with the attendant possibility that significant similarities between processes be obscured. Further, this approach may lead to the postulation of nongeneralizable processes, since there is no guarantee that all patients use exactly the same mental processes in those cases where alternative psycholinguistic strategies are possible.

The alternative approach chosen here may not be able to relate processes to disorders quite as directly, but its inherent lack of expliciteness is compensated by the pertinence assured by the multiple motivations for fewer, but better known processes (such as planning, motor programming and motor execution). This approach also appears preferable in view of a further difficulty in interpreting neurogenically impaired speech, which arises from the fact that this type of speech is not only characterized by the impairments themselves, but also by adjustments to the disorder, such as actions taken to overcome, compensate or circumvent a difficulty occasioned by the pathology. Observed pathological behaviors are often indeterminate as to whether they take their origin in the lesion itself, or in the adjustment to the lesion; an approach devoid of external motivation may thus run the risk of interpreting adjustment behaviors as lesion-impaired behaviors.

To illustrate, the fact that French and English Broca's aphasics tend to simplify their consonant clusters (Keller, 1984) was cited above in support of the notion that Broca's aphasics suffer from problems in motor programming. In this interpretation (which I believe to be correct), such patients have a lesion-induced difficulty in programming the complex and time-critical transitions between two or three consonants of a consonant cluster. Yet the same phenomenon could also be interpreted as a compensatory strategy. Since much of English and French phonological structure is characterized by the CV alternation pattern, it can be hypothesized that patients who are habitually faced with motoric difficulty, would tend to preferentially select those articulatory sequences which are in conformity with the CV alternation pattern, and thus to favor single consonants over consonant clusters. Uncertainty with respect to these alternatives is reduced if interpretation proceeds from independently-motivated speech production processes to impaired speech.

In the following sections, the adequacy of predictions from the present hypothesis will be examined with respect to (a) some typical major lesion effects, (b) effects on speech rate, and (c) effects on inter-articulatory organization (cf. Fig. 6.1). Also, we examine some of the predictions concerning the difference between primary and secondary motor cortex and concerning feedback from the vocal tract.

3. Predictions Concerning Typical Major Lesion Effects On Planning And Motor Processes In Speech

The Difference Between Planning and Motor Processes.   The distinction between motor and planning processes has been attributed to two criteria, precedence and automaticity.   Precedence is the notion that planning processes must feed into motor processes, while automaticity captures the idea that motor processes involve time-critical operations, while the planning stage groups those that are less time-critical.   Planning processes can thus deal with non-repetitive, less-automatized operations on open-ended classes of linguistic units, while motor processes were seen to be constrained to repetitive and automatized operations on relatively small classes of linguistic units.

It can be seen that automaticity can account for the difference between anomia and agrammatism. Anomia (word-finding difficulty) is an impairment in the selection and/or representation of open-class or lexical words, and is particularly frequent in Wernicke's aphasia, while agrammatism is an impairment in the selection and/or representation of closed-class or function words and is most often found in Broca's aphasia.

This analysis is thus supportive of the traditional syndrome distinctions which characterized Wernicke's aphasia as a pre-motor impairment, and Broca's aphasia as a motor deficit. However in contrast to previous accounts associating agrammatism with a motor deficit (e.g., Goodglass, Fodor, & Schulhoff, 1967, who suggested that agrammatism was an inhibition due to motoric difficulty), the present analysis provides an explicit, time-based rationale for viewing agrammatism as one aspect of faulty motor processing, and for associating this disorder with one and not the other of the two aphasic syndromes in question. In further support of the motoric quality of agrammatism is the fact that agrammatism can be found to affect exclusively the productive modality (Miceli et al., 1983; Nespoulous & Dordain, 1985).

The criterion of precedence can account for a number of further differences between the two syndromes, particularly those relating to phonological impairments. Because planning is thought to be concerned with the preparation of the phonological representation of certain utterance segments, a disruption of these processes should in Wernicke's aphasia lead to impaired phonological representations in the planned utterance segments. This in turn should be reflected in an impaired self correcting ability, and in a distinctive pattern of phonological substitution or omission errors. By contrast, Broca's aphasics should show relatively intact self correcting ability, and a pattern of phonological disorders indicative of motor processing impairment.

These predictions appear to be supported. The results on successive approximations to a target (e.g., "*A moh-, ma-m, mail, mail box*") indicate that among Wernicke's, conduction and Broca's aphasics, Wernicke's aphasics were least able to correct their phoneme substitutions (Joanette et al., 1980). Also, these patients had particular difficulties articulating phonemes when two succeeding target words contained several similar phonemes (e.g., *caramel* and *camera*) (Guyard, Sabouraud, & Gagnepain, 1981). This suggests that because of an insufficient internal representation, Wernicke's aphasics have been difficulty in selecting the right phoneme at the appropriate moment. Further, the phonological errors of Wernicke's aphasics are suggestive of open-class word selection difficulties (a planning problem), as their phonologically grossly abnormal (i.e., jargonaphasic) utterance tend to occur when they look for appropriate words (Buckingham & Kertesz, 1974).

By contrast, the phonological problems of Broca's aphasics show evidence of motor impairment, such as exceptional difficulties in phoneme-to-phoneme transitions and in the selection and articulation of infrequent phonemes. As already indicated, the simplification tendencies found with Broca's, and not with Wernicke's aphasics, are probably related to their phoneme-to-phoneme transition difficulties. Further, Guyard et al. (1981) found that Broca's aphasics had a greater error susceptibility than Wernicke's aphasics for pairs of articulatorily difficult stimuli (e.g., for French "pull" [sweater], "poule" [hen], or for "truite" [trout]—"huitre" [oyster]). However unlike Wernicke's aphasics, they had relatively few problems with selecting phonemes from competing phonemes in the planned utterance segments (i.e., few difficulties with syntagmatically difficult stimuli like "couturière" or "institutrice"). Finally, the phoneme substitutions of Broca's aphasics show less evidence of contextual contamination than do those of Wernicke's aphasics (Blumstein, 1973), indicating again that these patients are impaired in the processing of the ongoing articulatory string, rather than in the selection of phonemes from the internal representation of the planned utterance segments.

Again, these characterizations are by and large in accord with previous accounts (e.g., Guyard et al., 1981, Joanette et al., 1980; Keller, 1979; 1984; Nespoulous et al., 1983; etc); however, in contradistinction to those analyses, the present account does not seek to explain processing phenomena on the basis of neurogenic data, but proceeds from a hypothesis built on normal speech behaviors and neurophysiological data to a verification of its predictions for neurogenically impaired speech. This externally motivated hypothesis, specific as to the relational nature of motor output operations, promises not only greater robustness for the proposed theoretical constructs, but also a better understanding of the causes and effects of neurogenic speech impairments.

The Difference Between Motor Programming and Motor Execution. Within motor processing, the hypothesis predicts differences in the impairments of motor programming and motor execution. However, in view of the lack of one-to-one relationships between syndromes and proposed processes, direct empirical tests of this difference are difficult to obtain. Accordingly, we must report to more indirect analyses.

The neurogenic speech disorder most clearly associated with a disorder of motor execution is spastic dysarthria (found in pseudobulbar palsy) (Darley et al., 1969, 1975). This type of dysarthria is due to a lesion in the upper motor neurons, which have their origin in the primary motor cortex. Through retrograde degeneration, an entire upper motor neuron disintegrates, if it is lesioned anywhere along its pathway from the primary motor cortex to brain stem synapses with the given lower motor neuron; spastic dysarthria is therefore a cortical as well as a subcortical disorder.

In accordance with the neurophysiologically based hypothesis for primary motor cortex function, an upper motor neuron lesion should thus cause disorders in the synergistic commands to functional groupings of speech musculature, such as those controlling respiration, laryngeal activity, lingual and labial activity. In terms of our hypothesis, this impairment occurs because of a loss or impairment of learned links between muscle commands. Clinical reports are in support of these notions. Darley et al. (1975) report on a number of studies indicating respiratory insufficiency in patients of this type, due to "too-rapid breathing, difficulty in taking a deep inhalation, difficulty in controlling a prolonged exhalatory movement, antagonistic diaphragmatic-abdominal and thoracic movements, and involuntary movements in the respiratory musculature" (p. 137), all disorders that can be interpreted in terms of an impairment of muscular synergies of local groups to muscle tissue. Further, the laryngeal muscles appear to be subjected to hyptertonus, a sign that can be interpreted as abnormal co-contraction of musculature that normally functions antagonistically. This state manifests itself perceptually in a number of prominent signs, such a harsh voice, low pitch, and a strained and strangled voice (p. 142).

With respect to differences between the programming and the execution stage of motor processing, it is probably best to examine observed differences between Broca's and conduction aphasia. It will be recalled that both types of aphasics show phonemic errors, but only Broca's aphasics show phonetic impairments extending over the entire speech chain (arthric effects). Accordingly, Broca's aphasics can be expected to show disorders in both programming and execution, while conduction aphasics can be expected to show primarily programming disorders and impairments related to the copying of information from planning to motor processes (see section D.2.).

The study in this volume by Nespoulous, Joanette, Ska, Caplan, and Lecours presents a number of findings that appear to support the present hypothesis (none seem to contradict it). Let us recall that at the interface between planning and motor processings, we assume a "scan-copying" process (impaired by conduction aphasia), and at the motor processing level, a sequential organization of the speech chain in terms of movement commands, and their interpretation in terms of synergistic aphasia). Because scan-copying is essentially a process of activating selective phonemes among others (see e.g., Guyard et al., 1981; Lecours & Lhermitte, 1969), while motor processing is by and large sequential, we would expect that scan-copying errors produce phoneme substitutions which take their origin in the surrounding phonemes ("syntagmatic" or "displacement" errors), while motor processing errors should be less seriously affected by syntagmatic influences. Indeed, Nespoulous et al. (this volume) showed conduction aphasics to have more displacement errors than Broca's aphasics.

Also, the phonemic errors of Broca's aphasics showed a devoicing tendency, and a change of place of articulation when target phonemes were unvoiced, while the errors of conduction aphasics did not show such a tendency. This is in accord with the loss of synergistic muscle control over specific valves postulated for impairments of motor execution processes: in this view, a largyngeal hypertonus tends to prevent voicing, and synergistic aberrations give rise to changes in place of articulation. Conduction aphasics, who are not assumed to show any major motor execution problems, lack such selective impairment.

In summary, the major lesion effects examined here appear to be in excellent accord with predictions derived from the hypothesis. Wernicke's aphasia appears to be an impairment at the level of the planning processes, conduction aphasia seems to interfere primarily with the scan-copying process between planning and motor processes, Broca's aphasia interferes most clearly with a variety of motor programming and motor execution processes, and spastic dysarthria impairs the synergistic aspect of commands to functional groupings of articulatory musculature.

4. Predictions Concerning Lesion Effects On Speech Rate

Because it has been hypothesized that learned relations defining movement and muscle commands are stored in the motor cortex areas, a further prediction of the hypothesis is that lesions of these areas would impair the use of relations between muscle commands, in proportion to the tissue lost. The system would thus be forced to calculate movements anew by means of the remaining brain tissue.

The effect on movement is predictable from the degrees of freedom hypothesis (section A.4.). Because such a lesion would to some degree undo the effects of learning, one would expect an increase in the number of degrees of freedom, which would be reflected in a loss of speed of integrated movements and in a reduction of stereotyping of movements. In terms of articulatory movement, one would expect a slow speech rate and dyscoordinated movements in the articulators. A reduction in speech rate is particularly likely, because recalculations might have to be performed by neural tissue that previously was not involved in the calculation of articulatory events.

This prediction is well supported. Excessive slowness of speech articulation is one of the most reliable and most distinctive signs associated with impairments of the motoric aspect of speech. Goodglass and Kaplan (1972), for example, use nonfluency as one of the defining characteristics of Broca's aphasia. Also, as would be expected from the discussion in the previous section, slow speech rate is a serious impairment in the spastic type of dysarthria (upper motor neuron disorder). Darley et al., (1969, 1975), for instance, ranked spastic dysarthria (pseudobulbar palsy) as more severely affected by slowness than flaccid dysarthria (bulbar palsy, lower motor neuron disorder), hypokinetic dysarthria (parkinsonism) or ataxic dysarthria (cerebellar disorder). By contrast, cortically-lesioned patients with a minimum of impairments of processes associated with the motor phase of speech, such as Wernicke's aphasics, do not show any slowness of speech (Goodglass & Kaplan, 1972).

Moreover, it is illustrative to compare Broca's aphasia with conduction aphasia. The speech of Broca's aphasics is often described as continuously labored, in other words, the slowness affects the entire speech chain, and may be accentuated at transitions between phonemes or syllables (Luria, 1962/1966). By contrast, the slowness of conduction aphasics typically results from difficulties in chaining short utterance segments, and not in executing individual phonemes. Goodglass and Kaplan (1972) say that "the fluency may be restricted to brief bursts of speech" (p. 68). Analyzed in terms of the processes proposed above, conduction aphasics seem to run into difficulties at the point where they chain phonemes, syllables or even longer segments into a continuous speech output (interface between planning and motor processes), and Broca's aphasics suffer from an impairment of the learned characteristics of articulatory motor commands (motor programming and motor execution processes).

5. Predictions Concerning Lesion Effects On Inter-articulatory Organization And Synergistic Muscle Action

Another predicted effect of a motor aphasia is a breakdown in sequential relations within organized command aggregates. As a result, one would expect impairments in the (a) coordination of the action of various speech tract valves and (b) synergistic action of the musculature of such valves. As an example of an interarticulatory coordination problem, one would expect disorders in voice onset time (VOT, coordination of the linguo-palatal and the laryngeal valves), and as an example of a breakdown in muscle synergy, one would expect co-contractions of normally antagonistic musculature.

To the degree that this prediction has been investigated, it is well supported. Recently, two research teams have examined the VOT performance of patients with and without motoric impairment. Blumstein and her colleagues (Blumstein, Cooper, Goodglass, Statlender, & Gottlieb, 1980) report that a sample of American Broca's aphasics failed to clearly differentiate VOTs for voiced and unvoiced stops, which indicates that the sequential relations between the linguopalatal articulatory valve and the laryngeal valve were impaired. By contrast, Wernicke's patients did differentiate VOTs in the voiced and the unvoiced condition, although it must be noted that in comparison to normal subjects, their differentiations were exaggerated. Itoh and his colleagues (Itoh, Sasanuma, Tatsumi, Murakami, Fukusako, & Suzuki, 1982) (Fig. 6.3) document similar results for comparable groups of Japanese patients.

Itoh, Sasanuma, Hirose, Yoshioka, & Ushijima (1980) also present X-ray microbeam measurements for velum and tongue dorsum action in a patient with a motoric impairment. For the sound n in [$d\mathcal{E}$:n$\mathcal{E}$:], a normal person lowers the velum at the same time as he raises the tongue tip towards the hard palate and depresses the tongue dorsum (top panel of Fig. 6.3). However, the patient with motor impairment does not show this relationship. Unfortunately, no data on the tongue tip is available. Yet with respect to the relationship between the velum and the tongue dorsum, the patient is seen to raise his tongue dorsum, instead of lowering it, at the time that the velum is lowered (bottom panel of Fig. 6.3).

With respect to a breakdown of muscular synergy, Fromm, Abbs, McNeil, and Rosenbek (1982; Fig. 6.4) present direct EMG evidence from a comparable patient showing pathological co-contraction in muscles which in normals function antagonistically (orbicularis oris inferior and depressor labii inferior in bilabial closure). These data illustrate very powerfully the neurophysiological calculation errors which are at the basis of the articulatory errors of these patients.

6. Predictions Concerning Processing In The Primary And Secondary Motor Cortex

The differences between phonetic disorders found in patients showing arthric effects, and phonemic disorders found in aphasia patients without anarthria probably relate to the difference between primary and secondary motor cortex impairment. In view of the direct control over individual muscle groups

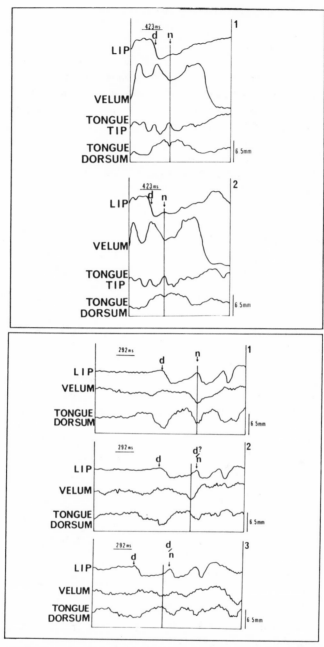

FIG. 6.3. Displacements of several articulators for the Japanese stimulus [dɛ:nɛ:] (top panel: a normal subject; bottom panel, a patient with Broca's aphasia ["apraxia of speech"]). The vertical lines indicate the moment of maximal velar lowering for the nasal consonant [n]. The time scale for the top panel is different from that for the bottom panel. It can be seen that the patient raised his tongue dorsum, instead of lowering it, at the time that the velum was lowered. (Itoh, Sasanuma, Hirose, Yoshioka, & Ushijima, 1980.)

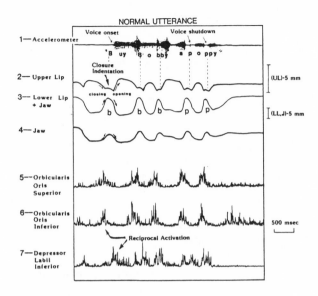

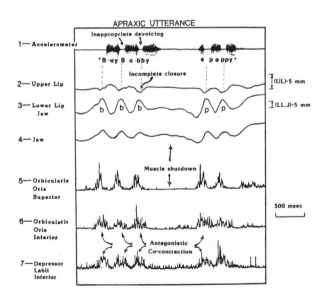

FIG. 6.4. Muscle activity and labial-mandibular movement signals obtained from a normal subject (top panel) and a patient with Broca's aphasia ("apraxia of speech") (bottom panel). The bottom three traces of each panel show the integrated EMG. The patient showed co-contraction in muscles which in the normal subject functioned antagonistically. (Fromm, Abbs, McNeil, & Rosenbek, 1982)

reported for primary efferent zones in higher mammals, the function of the primary motor cortex was seen to be concerned with synergistic relations between commands for individual muscle contractions, whereas the secondary cortex was seen to be concerned with the sequential organization of larger aggregates of movements.

In speech, a disorder of synergy due to primary cortex lesion should result in a continuous impairment of muscular execution in specific speech valves; this would correspond to the phonetic impairments in dysarthria and in the arthric effects found in Broca's aphasia. By contrast, a lesion of the secondary motor cortex should impair sequential relations between command aggregates for the entire speech musculature, to produce substitutions, omissions, additions and repetitions of phonemes, syllables or larger utterance stretches. We recall that these are the signs of phonemic motor disturbances in aphasia (see also Johns & Darley, 1970).

In further support of the difference between impairments of the primary and the secondary motor cortex, we would predict a predominance of phonetic over phonemic impairments with lesions of the non-dominant hemisphere. This prediction receives some support from a study of 42 patients with cortical lesions in the right, non-dominant hemisphere; 7 of the patients were affected by marked arthric effects, while none showed frequently recurring phonemic disturbances (Joanette, Lecours, Lepage, & Lamoureux, 1983; Joanette, personal communication, 1985).

7. Predictions Concerning The Impairment Of Feedback-based Speech Motor Processing

The fourth aspect of the hypothesis concerned the flexible status of feedback in motor learning and processing. One of the few examples in the literature of the impairment of speech motor learning or processing due to a lesion of feedback pathways, is found in Linke (1976). He describes a relatively clear case which illustrates the crucial role feedback plays in compensating perturbations, at the same time as it demonstrates the non-use of feedback under predictable circumstances.

A patient with bilateral operative lesion of the trigeminal nerve (cranial nerve V), which provides primarily sensory input from the face, was found to be incapable of lip control for eating, for holding a cigarette, or for liprounding on command; at the same time, there was no demonstrable impairment for normal speech, even when speaking in a white noise condition. The movements involved in eating, holding a cigarette, and liprounding on command probably involve calculations for muscle contractions based on momentary circumstances in the vocal tract, fed back to the central nervous system via the sensory input; speech in predictable circumstances probably involves the use of learned relations defining articulatory movement, relatively independent of sensory input.

As expected, this patient experienced difficulties when speaking in inhabitual conditions; indeed, he was found to have excessive difficulties when speaking with a pencil in his mouth, a condition which normal speakers can easily compensate. Further, when a non-painful electrical stimulation was applied to the lips, normal subjects were able to compensate the perturbation easily, while this patient reacted with a complete breakdown of speech for the ensuing 300 to 500 ms.

Although these results provide good support for the present hypothesis, more extensive studies on the use and importance of feedback in speech motor processing are clearly called for.

E. CONCLUSION

In this chapter, a synthesis of findings derived from the functional and neurophysiological studies of speech motor control, and tested with respect to findings on neurogenic impairment of speech, has led to an hypothesis of cortical functioning with respect to normal and neurogenically impaired speech.

It was proposed that the acquisition of speech motor control involves the abstracting of relations between those commands for muscle contractions that have been previously successful in implementing perceptually circumscribed speech targets. Skilled speech, by contrast, was seen as involving the retrieval of stored relations, and the calculation of additional movement biases in order to compensate for unpredictable and infrequent conditions in the vocal tract. The difference between the acquisitional and the skilled stage of speech production necessitated a flexible view of the contribution of the feedback mechanism. Finally, it was proposed that these functions were mediated primarily by the cortex; the secondary motor cortex in the speech-dominant hemisphere was seen to be concerned primarily with the sequential organization of command aggregates involving the entire speech musculature, while the bilateral primary motor cortices were seen to be concerned principally with synergistic relations between constituents of functionally related muscular structures (speech tract valves).

Predictions arising from this proposal with respect to patients with neurological cortical damage were shown to be supported by available data. It was seen that classical expressive symptoms of various groups of aphasic patients were well predicted by the theoretical framework elaborated from non-aphasic evidence. Further, some specific predictions relating to speech rate and interarticulatory organization were seen to be borne out. Since the hypothesis suggests that relations between muscle commands are learned in order to obtain a speed advantage associated with a reduction of the system's degrees of freedom, it can be expected that the impairment of such relations through cortical damage leads to a slowing of the speech rate; indeed, slowness of speech is one of the most reliable symptoms of the motor control disorder found in Broca's aphasia and in spastic dysarthria.

Also, available direct indications on the breakdown of the sequential organization and synergistic contraction patterns in neurogenic speech disorders show the hypothesis to be supported. Recent VOT and cinefluorographic experiments show that patients with Broca's aphasia suffer more directly from errors in the sequential coordination of different speech articulators than other types of aphasics. The predicted breakdown of synergistic relations between muscle commands were also briefly documented.

The difference between primary and secondary motor cortex responsibilities, derived from animal studies and from electrical stimulation of the exposed cortex, are supported by the difference between phonemic and phonetic types of articulatory breakdown, associated respectively with impairments of sequential organization of speech tract motor commands, and synergistic commands to speech tract valves.

Finally, the proposed flexible view of feedback was shown to be further supported by a rather unusual and illustrative case of bilateral (sensory) trigeminal nerve ablation who showed intact speech in predictable speech conditions, but in contrast to normal subjects, was unable to deal with inhabitual vocal tract conditions or unexpected perturbations.

Despite its comprehensiveness, it is evident that the present account leaves many unanswered questions. It may be useful to list just a few:

1. The central hypothesis, that the acquisition of speech motor control is fundamentally the learning of relational information, should be examined systematically, preferably by means of EMG and kinematic records in children, adults and adults with various types of neurological lesion.

The present hypothesis predicts that disorders based on a breakdown of relational muscle command specifications would be seen primarily with disorders of the primary and secondary motor cortices; what are the VOT characteristics of various types of subcortically-impaired dysarthric patients? Of patients with lesions in non-speech areas? Do they back up the present theoretical notions?

2. What are the theoretical implications of viewing agrammatism as a motor disorder due to a breakdown in learned automaticity? Is it possible to apply the relational paradim elaborated here for the muscular command structure, to the context of grammatical relations?

3. At present, the empirical basis for verifying the predicted lack of stereotypy of articulatory movement is relatively weak. Recently-developed, improved recording techniques for articulatory movement (e.g., X-ray microbeam, ultrasound, magnetic tracking, etc.) may be successfully applied to this question.

4. The exact extent of a "functional grouping of speech musculature," here globally characterized as a "speech tract valve," should be explored for

each group. Can cases be found in which the abnormality affects just one speech tract valve? If so, what is the anatomical extent of affected musculature?

5. Unaffected portions of the speech production system probably adjust their operations to the effects of a disorder "further up" or "down" in the system. What is the nature of this adjustment?

6. How does the present account articulate with other models of speech production, such as those derived from normal speech errors in spontaneous speech?

7. What are the speech motor functions of various subcortical brain structures, such as the extrapyramidal loop involving the basal ganglia and the thalamus, the cerebellum and the brain stem nuclei? How do they integrate with the processes proposed here?

Despite the many unanswered questions and the (fully avowed) great uncertainties about what has been proposed here, it would seem that the present account makes an attempt to present an integrated view which coherently explains findings from a large number of experiments, from observations on normal and neurogenically impaired speech, and from the neurophysiology of motor control in general. It provides logical and responsible links between a variety of related scientific domains, and furnishes a global conceptual framework for normal, acquisitional and disordered processes in speech motor control.

The major challenges awaiting these hypothesis are, first of all, intensive direct testing of its specific predictions by means of experiments on the learning and the utilization of motor control in normal and impaired speech condition; and secondly, the theoretical integration of these findings into a larger model of speech production.

ACKNOWLEDGMENTS

Portions of this chapter have been substantially modified as a result of fruitful discussions with Jean-Luc Nespoulous, Yves Joanette, André Roch Lecours, Sylviane Valdois, Marie-Joséphe Tainturier, Frédérique Gardye, David Caplan, and Marie Vanier, and on the basis of the insightful suggestions offered by Betty Tuller, Vince Gracco, Myrna Gopnik, and Jack Ryalls. Some of these researchers may not share certain opinions expressed here. Further direct discussions with the author about this chapter are invited. This work has been completed while the author was on sabbatical leave from the Université du Québec à Montréal. It was supported by funding from the Fonds FCAC (équipes) of the Government of Quebec and by the intramural funding organization of the Université du Québec à Montréal (Programme d'aide financière aux chercheurs et aux créateurs).

REFERENCES

Abbs, J. H. (1982). A speech motor system perspective on nervous system control variables. *Speech Motor Control Laboratories Preprints, Fall-Winter* (University of Wisconsin, Madison), 91–93.

Abbs, J. H., & Cole, K. J. (1982). Consideration of bulbar and suprabulbar afferent influence upon speech motor coordination. In S. Grillner, B. Lindblom, J. Lubker, & A. Persson (Eds.), *Speech motor control* (pp. 159–186). New York: Pergamon Press.

Alajouanine, T., Ombredane, A., & Durand, M. (1939). *Le syndrome de désintégration phonétique dans l'aphasie.* Paris: Masson.

Asanuma, H. (1973). Cerebral cortical control of movement. *The Physiologist, 16,* 143–166.

Beatty, J., Richer, F., & Barth, D. A. (in press). Magnetoencephalography. In M. G. H. Coales, S. W. Porges, & E. Donchin (Eds.), *Psychophysiology: Systems, processes and applications. Vol. 1: Systems:* New York: Guilford Press.

Bhatnagar, S., & Andy, O. J. (1983). Language in the nondominant right hemisphere. *Archives of Neurology, 40,* 728–731.

Blumstein, S. (1973). *A phonological investigation of aphasic speech. The Hague: Mouton.*

Blumstein, S. E., Cooper, W. E., Goodglass, H., Statlender, S., & Gottlieb, J. (1980). Production deficits in aphasia: A voice-onset time analysis. *Brain and language, 9,* 153–170.

Borden, G. J. (1979). An interpretation of research on feedback interruption in speech. *Brain and Language, 7,* 307–319.

Buckingham, H. W., Jr., & Kertesz, A. (1974). A linguistic analysis of fluent aphasia. *Brain and Language, 1,* 43–62.

Carew, T. J. (1981). Descending control of spinal circuits. In E. R. Kandel & J. H. Schwartz (Eds.), *Principles of neural science* (pp. 312–322). New York: Elsevier/North-Holland.

Cole, K. J., & Abbs, J. H. (1983). Intentional responses to kinesthetic stimuli in orofacial muscles: Implications for the coordination of speech movements. *Speech Motor Control Laboratories Preprints, Spring-Summer,* (University of Wisconsin, Madison), 1–22.

Darley, F. L., Aronson, A. E., & Brown, J. R. (1969). Differential diagnostic patterns of dysarthria. *Journal of Speech and Hearing Research, 12,* 246–269.

Darley, F. L., Aronson, A. E., & Brown, J. R. (1975). *Motor speech disorders.* Philadelphia: W. B. Saunders.

Delattre, P. (1969). An acoustic and articulatory study of vowel reduction in four languages. *IRAL, 7,* 295–325.

Denny-Brown, D. (1951). The frontal lobes and their functions. In A. Feiling (Ed.), *Modern trends in neurology,* (pp. 13–89). London: Butterworth.

Evarts, E. V. (1974). Sensorimotor cortex activity associated with movements triggered by visual as compared to somesthetic inputs. In F. O. Schmitt & F. G. Worden (Eds.), *The neurosciences,* (Vol. 3, pp. 327–337). Cambridge, MA: MIT press.

Eyzaguirre, C., & Fidone, S. J. (1975). *Physiology of the nervous system: An introductory text.* Chicago: Year Book Medical Publishers.

Folkins, J. W., & Abbs, J. H. (1975). Lip and jaw motor control during speech: Responses to resistive loading of the jaw. *Journal of Speech and Hearing Research, 18,* 207–220.

Folkins, J. W., & Abbs, J. H. (1976). Additional observations on responses to resistive loading of the jaw. *Journal of Speech and Hearing Research, 19,* 820–821.

Foss, D. J., & Hakes, D. T. (1978). *Psycholingusitics: An introduction to the psychology of language.* Englewood Cliffs, NJ: Prentice-Hall.

Fromkin, V. A. (1973). The non-anomalous nature of anomalous utterances. In V. A. Fromkin (Ed.), *Speech errors as linguistic evidence* (pp. 215–242). The Hague: Mouton.

Fromm, D., Abbs, J. H., McNeil, M. R., & Rosenbek, J. C. (1982). Simultaneous perceptual-physiological method for studying apraxia of speech. *Speech Motor Control Laboratories Preprints, Fall-Winter,* (University of Wisconsin, Madison), 155–171.

Ghez, C. (1981). Introduction to the motor systems. In E. R. Kandel & J. H. Schwartz (Eds.), *Principles of neural science* (pp. 271–283). New York: Elsevier/North-Holland.

Goehl, H., & Kaufman, D. K. (1984). Do the effects of adventitious deafness include disordered speech? *Journal of Speech and Hearing Disorders, 49*, 58–64.

Goodglass, H., Fodor, I. G., & Schulhoff, C. (1967). Prosodic factors in grammar—evidence from aphasia. *Journal of Speech and Hearing Research, 10*, 5–20.

Goodglass, H., & Kaplan, E. (1972). *The assessment of aphasia and related disorders.* Philadelphia: Lea & Febiger.

Guyard, H., Sabouraud, O., & Gagnepain, J. (1981). A procedure to differentiate phonological disturbances in Broca's aphasia and Wernicke's aphasia. *Brain and Language, 13*, 19–30.

Hebb, D. O. (1949). *The organization of behavior.* New York: Wiley.

Henneman, E. (1974). Motor functions of the cerebral cortex. In V. B. Mountcastle (Ed.), *Medical physiology* (Vol. 1, pp. 747–782). St. Louis, MO: The C.V. Mosby.

Hughes, O., & Abbs, J. H. (1976). Labial-mandibular coordination in the production of speech: Implications for the operation of motor equivalence. *Phonetica, 44*, 199–221.

Itoh, M., Sasanuma, S., Hirose, H., Yoshioka, H., & Ushijima, T. (1980). Abnormal articulatory dynamics in a patient with apraxia of speech: X-ray microbeam observation. *Brain and Language, 11*, 66–75.

Itoh, M., Sasanuma, S., Tatsumi, I. F., Murakami, S., Fukusako, Y., & Suzuki, T. (1982). Voice onset time characteristics in apraxia of speech. *Brain and Language, 17*, 193–210.

Joanette, Y., Keller, E., & Lecours, A. R. (1980). Successive approximations in aphasia. *Brain and Language, 11*, 30–44.

Joanette, Y., Lecours, A. R., Lepage, Y., & Lamoureux, M. (1983). Language in right-handers with right-hemisphere lesions: A preliminary study including anatomical, genetic, and social factors. *Brain and Language, 20*, 217–249.

Johns, D. F., & Darley, F. L. (1970). Phonemic variability in apraxia of speech. *Journal of Speech and Hearing Research, 13*, 556–583.

Keller, E. (1975). *Vowel errors in aphasia.* Unpublished doctoral thesis, University of Toronto.

Keller, E. (1978). Parameters for vowel substitutions in Broca's aphasia. *Brain and Language, 5*, 265–285.

Keller, E. (1979). Planning and execution in speech production. *Recherches Linguistiques à Montréal, 13*, 34–51.

Keller, E. (1984). Simplification and gesture reduction in phonological disorders of apraxia and aphasia. In J. C. Rosenbek, M. R. McNeil, A. E. Aronson (Eds.), *Apraxia of speech: Physiology, acoustics, linguistics, management* (pp. 221–256). San Diego: College-Hill Press.

Kelso, J. A., & Tuller, B. (1981). Toward a theory of apractic syndromes. *Brain and Language, 12*, 224–245.

Kelso, J. A., Tuller, B., & Harris, K. (1983). A "dynamic pattern" perspective on the control and coordination of movement. In P. F. MacNeilage (Ed.), *The production of speech* (pp. 137–173). New York: Springer-Verlag.

Lecours, A. R., & Lhermitte, F. (1969). Phonemic paraphasias: Linguistic structures and tentative hypothesis. *Cortex, 5*, 193–228.

Linke, D. (1976). Ein Störtest zur Differentialdiagnose motorischer Aphasien. In G. Peuser (Ed.), *Interdisziplinäre Aspekte der Aphasieforschung.* (pp. 91–102). Cologne, FRG: Rheinland-Verlag, GMBH.

Luria, A. R. (1966). *Higher cortical function in man* (B. Haigh, Trans.). New York: Basic Books. (Original work published in 1962)

MacKay, D. G. (1970). Spoonerisms: The structure of errors in the serial order of speech. *Neuropsychologia, 8*, 323–350.

MacNeilage, P. F., Rootes, T. P., & Chase, R. A. (1967). Speech production and perception in a patient with severe impairment of somesthetic perception and motor control. *Journal of Speech and Hearing Research, 10*, 449–467.

Miceli, G., Mazzucchi, A., Menn, L., & Goodglass, H. (1983). Contrasting cases of Italian agrammatic aphasia without comprehension disorders. *Brain and Language, 19*, 65–97.

Nespoulous, J.-L., Lecours, A. R., & Joanette, Y. (1983). La dichotomie phonétique/ phonémique a-t-elle une valeur nosologique? In P. Messerli, P. M. Lavorel, & J.-L. Nespoulous (Eds.), *Neuropsychologie de l'expression orale* (pp. 71–91). Paris: Editions du C.N.R.S.

Nespoulous, J.-L., & Dordain, M. (1985). L'agrammatisme: Trouble syntaxique et/ou déficit morphématique? Une étude de cas. *Rééducation Orthophonique, 23*, 163–175.

Ojemann, G. A. (1980). Brain mechanisms for language: Observations during neurosurgery. In J. S. Lockard & A. A. Ward, Jr. (Eds.), *Epilepsy: A window to brain mechanisms* (pp. 243–260). New York: Raven Press.

Ojemann, G., & Mateer, C. (1979). Human language cortex: Localization of memory, syntax, and sequential motor-phoneme identification systems. *Science, 205*, 1401–1403.

Oller, D. K., & MacNeilage, P. F. (1983). Development of speech production: Perspectives from natural and perturbed speech. In P. F. MacNeilage (Ed.), *The production of speech* (pp. 91–108). New York: Springer-Verlag.

Ostry, D. J., Keller, E., & Parush, A. (1983). Similarities in the control of the speech articulators and the limbs: kinematics of tongue dorsum movement in speech. *Journal of Experimental Psychology: Human Perception and Performance, 9*, 622–636.

Penfield, W., & Roberts, L. (1959). *Speech and brain-mechanisms.* New York: Atheneum.

Roberts, A. H. (1965). *A statistical linguistic analysis of American English.* The Hague: Mouton.

Shattuck-Hufnagel, S. (1983). Sublexical units and suprasegmental structure in speech production planning. In P. F. MacNeilage (Ed.), *The production of speech* (pp. 109–136). New York: Springer-Verlag.

Stein, P. S. G. (1978). Motor systems, with specific reference to the control of locomotion. In W. M. Cowan, Z. W. Hall, & E. R. Kandel (Eds.), *Annual review of neuroscience, 1* (pp. 61–82). Palo Alto, CA: Annual Reviews.

Stevens, K. N., & House, A. S. (1955). Development of a quantitative description of vowel articulation. *Journal of the Acoustical Society of America, 27*, 484–493.

Thompson, R. F. (1967). *Foundations of physiological psychology.* New York: Harper & Row.

7 Programming and Execution Processes of Speech Movement Control: Potential Neural Correlates

Vincent L. Gracco
James H. Abbs
Speech Motor Control Laboratories
University of Wisconsin-Madison

ABSTRACT

Explicit consideration of nervous system anatomy and physiology underlying speech and language is critical to provide a more concrete basis for linguistic and behavioral theories of communication. The purpose of the present paper is to provide a data-based neuroanatomical model for the nervous system actions associated with the motor programming and execution of speech movements. Recent studies indicate that speech motor control requires the integration of multiple sensory signals with internally specified, general motor goals. Results from these recent investigations of speech sensorimotor control and considerations of neuroanatomical and neurophysiological findings from nonhuman primates offer some specific hypotheses regarding underlying nervous system operations. In particular, it is possible to evaluate the speech motor programming and execution contributions of the premotor, primary motor, and supplementary motor cortical areas, and the inputs to these important cortical sites from the cerebellum, basal ganglia, and other cortical regions. Although this model is based on data obtained primarily from the perioral region and its CNS representations, the hypotheses provided are sufficiently basic to reflect general operations of the nervous system in this critically human function.

INTRODUCTION

Scientists investigating the processes underlying human speech and language behavior face a difficult problem. The superficial manifestations of oral communication can be observed rather directly. However, the underlying neural processes, seemingly critical to optimal understanding, are almost wholly opaque. Although it is possible to draw certain inferences concerning these neural processes from speech and language deficits associated with focal brain damage, these inferences are limited inherently by the rapid and substantial reorganizational processes that occur with loss of nervous system tissue (cf. Asanuma & Arissian, 1984; Glassman, 1978; Laurence & Stein, 1978). To overcome these difficulties, multiple and often complementary approaches have evolved. Commonly, these approaches include:

1. Identification of various hypothetical constructs or abstractions from linguistic or information processing models,
2. Classification of oral communication patterns in relation to those constructs, and
3. Interpretation of those patterns (or deficits thereof) to hypothesized subcomponents of the unobservable processes.

The constructs or abstractions commonly employed include planning, programming, serial and parallel processing, parsing, syntax, phonology, modularity, etc. Implicit in the use of such hypothetical constructs or abstractions is the assumption that they reflect essential aspects of underlying nervous system organization and function. Indeed, one major difference among the various theoretical and methodological approaches to understanding speech and language behavior appears to be the degree to which hypotheses and dependent measures explicitly reflect extant knowledge of the nervous system. From our perspective, explicit consideration of nervous system anatomy and physiology is critical if we are to make long-term progress in this area. Without this constraint, it is all too easy to conjure up a large number of equally plausible, abstract hypotheses to explain a given set of communication behaviors or deficits thereof. Despite the intellectual exercise that is provided by such effects, one must recognize that little may be gained in understanding the critical nervous system functions for speech and language.

In the study of speech motor control and nervous system control of movement in general, some hypothetical constructs also guide the ongoing research. However, the primary goal is focused more explicitly on determining functional brain behavior relations. For example, most investigators recognize that the overall motor control process includes several stages or levels. These stages commonly are identified as planning, programming, and execution involving what are thought to be distinct operations occurring prior to or during generation of a motor output. While definitions of these constructs often are operationalized and the terms are not always used uniformly, there is basic agreement regarding their importance and their general sequence within the motor act. Moreover, active research is under way in many laboratories to determine the neurophysiological correlates of these processes. Planning, for example, is considered an early process preceding programming, primarily involving processes that include general identification of motor goals (Paillard, 1983). By contrast, the programming process appears to include the selection and adjustment of the nervous system circuits required to achieve the precise muscular, kinematic, and temporal requirements for the intended motor act (Paillard, 1983; Schmidt, 1982). Finally, the execution process is thought to involve the actual generation of the final descending neural signals, including their moment-to-moment shaping by continuous afferent input.

In this context, one purpose of the present paper is to review some recent physiological data from speech motor control which appear to reflect two of these hypothesized processes; motor programming and execution. As suggested by the present authors (cf. Abbs, 1986; Abbs, Gracco, & Cole, 1984) in speech motor control, these two processes would seem to lie immediately downstream from linguistic planning stages and hence reflect the implementation of phonological goals. In contrast to much of the work on neural mechanisms underlying the upstream language processes, these data on speech motor programming and execution were obtained in normal subjects, utilizing techniques adapted from studies of limb motor control in waking animals and man. Moreover, based upon these experimental data and previous neuroanatomic and neurophysiologic studies in nonhuman primates, it is possible to consider the neural structures that might underlie the processes of speech motor programming and execution. As such, a second purpose of this paper is to refine the neuroanatomical and neurophysiological foundation for further investigations of speech motor control, speech neuropathologies, and voluntary motor behavior in general. In consideration of these neuroanatomical and neurophysiological data, we feel that the advantages of incorporating extant biological data into models of speech and language processes will be apparent.

FUNCTIONAL SENSORIMOTOR PROCESSES IN SPEECH MOVEMENT CONTROL

A fundamental premise of the present paper is that the generation of movements for speech involves the continuous utilization of sensory information from the muscle receptors and cutaneous mechanoreceptors that are distributed throughout the respiratory, laryngeal, and orofacial systems. The suggestion that sensory information is continuously utilized does not imply that this is the sole means by which speech movements are generated. Rather, recent data indicate that the rich supply of orofacial, respiratory, and laryngeal afferents continually interact with central operations (e.g., programs) to yield the speech movement patterns associated with oral communication. In the discussion immediately following, we will review briefly the various data that address this pivotal point and illustrate how it is possible to document the critical operation of sensorimotor control processes by selectively perturbing speech movements and observing the muscle and movement "corrections" that occur in response to those induced errors.

The control of multiarticulate movements such as speech demands the temporal spatial interaction of multiple structures. As such, controlling the movements of speech is not a unidimensional process, but must also include the coordination among multiple structures necessary for this skilled motor behavior. Recent results have implicated the contribution of afferent-dependent mechanisms in both the control of individual speech movements and in the coordination among them (Abbs & Gracco, 1984; Folkins & Abbs, 1975, 1976; Gracco & Abbs, 1985; Kelso, Tuller, Bateson, & Fowler, 1984). These studies have demonstrated the presence of task-dependent, functionally organized, short latency compensatory responses to unanticipated mechanical perturbations applied prior to or during a speech movement. Comparable sensorimotor actions have been demonstrated for other complex motor behaviors; e.g., rapid postural adjustments (Marsden, Merton, & Morton, 1981; Nashner & Cordo, 1981; Nashner, Woollacott, & Tuma, 1979), compensatory eye-head interactions (Bizzi, Kalil, & Tagliasco, 1971; Morasso, Bizzi, & Dichgans, 1973), wrist-thumb actions (Traub, Rothwell, & Marsden, 1980), and thumb-finger coordination (Cole, Gracco, & Abbs, 1984).

These recent results are in contrast to earlier investigations of sensory contributions to speech motor control that primarily involved experimental interference with various afferent inputs. For example, following anesthetic reduction in oral sensation, global measures indicate that overall speech production capability is disrupted only in subtle ways (Gammon, Smith, Daniloff, & Kim, 1971; Ringel & Steer, 1963; Scott & Ringel, 1971). Additionally, reduced or distorted auditory information results in only mildly distorted speech motor output (Kelso & Tuller, 1983; Lane & Tranel, 1971). Estimates of afferent-to-efferent neural transport delays via analyses of reaction times, coupled with the apparent ballistic nature and short duration of many speech movements, have also led some to the position that speech movements are primarily preprogrammed; i.e., sensory information is used only in long-term adaptation or speech skill acquisition (cf. Borden, 1979; Keller, this volume; Kent & Moll, 1975; see, however, Cole & Abbs, 1983). From this alternate perspective, speech movements would be generated from preset motor patterns or programs and executed independently of any afferent information. Similar theoretical positions have been postulated from limb studies demonstrating that functionally deafferented animals (Fentress, 1973; Polit & Bizzi, 1979; Taub & Berman, 1968) and man (Rothwell, Traub, Day, Obeso, Thomas, & Marsden, 1982) are capable of executing certain learned motor tasks (cf. Marsden, Rothwell, & Day, 1984 for review). One must be cautious in the interpretation of motor performance observed under conditions of sensory deficit. Such observations are not interpretable in relation to what the removed portion of the nervous system does, but rather what the rest of the nervous system does without the part in question (cf. Asanuma &

Arissian, 1984; Berenberg, 1984; Dostrovsky, Millar, & Wall, 1976; Glass-man, 1978). Furthermore, recent studies have shown that movements exe-cuted in the absence of afferent information often are only grossly normal, essentially lacking their normal precision (Sanes & Evarts, 1983). Finally, more natural, multijoint behaviors appear more disrupted by reduced afferent input than stereotypic behaviors or movements around a single joint (Bos-som, 1974; Polit & Bizzi, 1979; Rothwell et al., 1982). Although it is apparent that the observations in sensory deficit studies cannot be interpreted easily, the results do indicate that certain motor tasks can be carried out, in a somewhat crude manner, despite reduced or absent afferent input. Hence, these data suggest that the nervous system is capable of prespecifying some muscle contraction and movement parameters (i.e., as in a "generalized motor program," cf. Schmidt, 1982), albeit in a somewhat imprecise form.

Integrating these latter findings into a theory of speech motor coordination and control thus requires the inclusion of an interactive process between ascending afferent signals and a generalized motor program. As suggested by Abbs et al. (1984), afferent information may be used to refine certain parameters of an abstract motor program in relation to the varying state of the periphery, yielding a more specific and detailed set of motor commands for actual motor execution (also cf. Abbs, 1979; MacNeilage, 1980). Support for this position has come from recent studies in which distinctly different compensatory response patterns are observed at different times prior to and during the motor execution of a speech movement gesture (Gracco & Abbs, 1982a, 1982b, 1985), seemingly reflecting the differential contribution of afferent mechanisms in the programming and execution of speech move-ments.

Prior to considering these most recent data, it is helpful to review the most salient findings of previous studies specifying the basic sensorimotor processes of speech. Our major approach to this problem has involved the adaptation and refinement of what has been shown to be a powerful tech-nique available for investigation of sensorimotor mechanisms in human subjects—the unanticipated perturbation paradigm. Small, precisely con-trolled errors are introduced during the movement for a particular voluntary gesture, and the resulting muscle activity and movement changes are analyzed to determine the nature of the underlying sensorimotor actions. If applied carefully, this approach is not susceptible to confounding problems of adaptation and compensation associated with many other paradigms for evaluating sensory contributions; e.g., local anesthesia, masking of auditory feedback, fixing the jaw, etc. Additionally, unanticipated perturbation in con-junction with single neural unit recording has been used extensively in awake animals to determine the nervous system pathways and processes accompany-ing sensorimotor control in nonhuman primates (Conrad, 1978; DeLong, Alexander, Georgopoulos, Crutcher, Mitchell, & Richardson, 1984; Evarts &

Fromm, 1978; Evarts & Tanji, 1976; Georgopoulos, Kalaska, Caminiti, & Massey, 1983; Tatton & Bawa, 1979; Thach, 1978). These latter data support the contribution of ascending afferent signals to the motor control functions of the primary motor cortex, the somatic sensory cortex, the basal ganglia, the cerebellum, and as such permit more meaningful interpretation from parallel studies in man.

Application of the unanticipated perturbation technique in the investigation of speech motor control processes has revealed that when a small mechanical perturbation is applied to one speech structure, compensatory adjustments are observed in both the perturbed structure as well as the coactive unperturbed structures (Folkins & Abbs, 1975, 1976; Folkins & Zimmermann, 1982; Gracco & Abbs, 1985; Kelso et al., 1984). For example, if a perturbation is introduced to the lower lip during the elevation for a bilabial stop, compensatory adjustments are observed in both the upper lip and jaw. These data imply that sensory information is used not only to correct errors in individual movements, but also to make adjustments among the multiple movements involved in a given speech motor gesture; the latter observation thus suggests that sensorimotor actions contribute also to the coordination of speech movements. Compensatory adjustments in perturbed and unperturbed coactive structures are illustrated in Fig. 7.1; perturbation applied to the lower lip results in lower lip as well as upper lip adjustments. These upper and lower lip adjustments to lower lip perturbation have been defined previously as reflecting afferent-dependent open loop and closed loop control processes, respectively (Abbs & Gracco, 1984) or more recently as nonautogenic and autogenic sensorimotor actions (Abbs et al., 1984). That is, adjustments observed in the perturbed structure are designated as autogenic, while compensatory adjustments in a coactive but unperturbed structure are designated as nonautogenic. The terms autogenic and nonautogenic adjustments may be preferred because they do not limit the conceptualization of the underlying neural processes to extant engineering control schemes.

The responses presented in Fig. 7.1 and to be discussed subsequently were obtained during rapid lip closure for the production of a bilabial speech sound. Subjects were not aware of the purpose of the experiments and showed these compensations the first time they experienced a perturbation. The subjects' task consisted of sustaining the vowel *ae* and, upon hearing a tone, to close their lips as rapidly as possible and generate a *b*. Once the bilabial stop was produced, subjects resumed producing the vowel, and responded again when the tone was heard. Effectively, subjects were producing rapid lip closure from a static posture. Unanticipated perturbations were delivered to the lower lip on approximately 15% of the trials within a restricted time interval, as shown in Fig. 7.2; this 100 ms target interval was chosen for introduction of the perturbations to minimize contamination of natural control processes by voluntary adjustment.

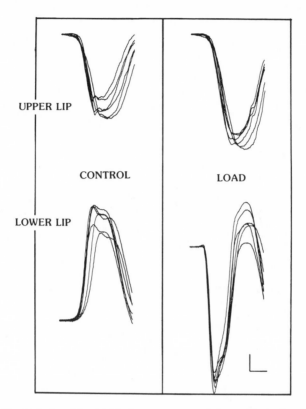

FIG. 7.1   Six control and load trials from a representative subject. Loads were intro-duced approximately 20ms before OOI onset. Load magnitude is 45gms. Calibration bars represent 1mm (vertical) and 50ms (horizontal).

Utilizing this paradigm, we have conducted a series of related studies involving the introduction of small unanticipated loads (10-40 grams) to the upper and lower lips prior to or during bilabial or labial-dental speech ges-tures. Load-induced movement changes (displacement, velocity, duration) and EMG changes (magnitude, latency) have been quantified to discern the operation of sensorimotor actions in the control of these speech gestures and their response characteristics. In the refinement of this paradigm, a number of issues have been explored formally and informally to determine its viabil-ity in revealing "normal" sensorimotor processes of speech movement con-trol. The key observations, obtained from over 40 naive subjects, include:

1. *All subjects* compensated for unanticipated loads the first time they were introduced,

2. There were no trials for which speech was disturbed in any perceptible manner,

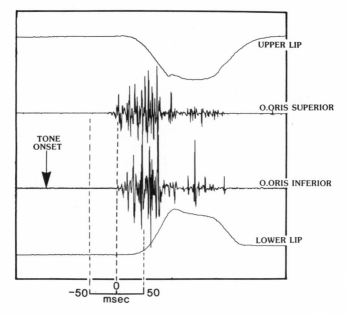

INTERVAL FOR LOADS RE: O.ORIS ONSET

FIG. 7.2   Target interval for the placement of lower lip perturbations.

3. Subjects were *unable* to suppress a compensatory response if given instructions to "not respond" to the loads, indicating the ingrained nature of the underlying sensorimotor processes,

4. Compensatory patterns to perturbations introduced early in an experimental session did not differ, qualitatively or quantitatively, from those introduced near the end of a session,

5. Consistent and statistically significant changes in EMG and movement were observed *in all subjects studied,* even for loads as small as 10 gms (yielding perturbation displacements of 1.0 to 2.5 mm),

6. Magnitudes of compensatory displacement changes in the upper and lower lips were significantly and positively correlated to the magnitudes of the perturbation displacement,

7. *Inter*subject variability was remarkably small when factors such as range of normal lip movement, load magnitude and load onset time were normalized.

The aforementioned observations collectively support the power of this technique in revealing sensorimotor mechanisms involved in goal-directed speech motor actions. Additionally, parallel observations indicate that these sensorimotor actions vary functionally with different speech tasks. For example, if lower lip perturbations are introduced during a labial dental articulation for [f], upper lip responses (as shown in Figure 7.1) are absent (Abbs et al., 1984). Similarly, when jaw loads are introduced for [b] and [z] articulations, compensatory responses were task-specific, i.e., confined to the muscles and movements of the lips and tongue, respectively (Kelso et al., 1984). These latter data suggest that these patterns of sensorimotor action are a component of the phonetic intention or motor program of the speaker (cf. Abbs, 1986). Given these results, we felt justified to utilize this paradigm to address the hypothesis that sensory information is used differently in the motor programming for speech movements, as contrasted to its moment-to-moment utilization during movement execution (cf. Abbs et al., 1984; Gracco, 1984).

TEMPORAL VARIATIONS IN SENSORIMOTOR ACTIONS FOR SPEECH MOVEMENT CONTROL

In order to distinguish sensory contributions during the different stages of motor "preparation," motor programming and motor execution, unanticipated perturbations were introduced at different times prior to and during the initiation of a multimovement speech gesture. Perturbations introduced "early" (i.e., well before agonist EMG onset) presumably would yield compensations indicative of a pre-execution or programming process, while later perturbations would tap the stage of motor execution. In comparing the system responses under these two conditions, clear and consistent time-dependent variations in the form and loci of the compensatory responses were observed. Comparisons of nonautogenic (e.g., upper lip responses to a lower lip load) and autogenic (lower lip responses to a lower lip load) compensation revealed consistent differences in kinematic adjustments and latencies that varied with the time the load was introduced re: the onset of agonistic muscle EMG. An example of the kinematic changes accompanying load onset timing differences is presented in Fig. 7.3. These two single load/control comparisons reflect upper and lower lip movement changes to an early (38 ms prior to voluntary EMG onset) and a late (8 ms prior to voluntary EMG onset) lower lip perturbation. As can be seen, the autogenic lower lip response predominates for the early load, while the nonautogenic upper lip response predominates for the later occurring perturbation. Figure 7.4 shows the separate upper and lower lip perturbation adjustments (expressed as a ratio of perturbation displacement to compensatory change in displacement) for a group of five subjects. As shown, the lower lip provides greater relative compensation for loads introduced prior to muscle activation (10-55 ms pre-EMG onset) than the upper lip. These data also indicate that for early loads compensatory adjustments yield proportional and relatively consistent increases in both upper and lower lip displacements.

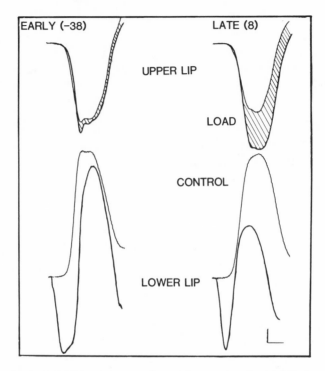

FIG. 7.3   A single load/control comparison demonstrating the load timing changes in the compensatory response. As can be seen, early occurring loads (before OOI onset) result in a larger increase in the lower lip response. Conversely, later occurring loads (after OOI onset) result in a larger increase in the upper lip response. Calibrations are the same as in Fig. 7.1.

An important aspect of the compensatory responses that occurred prior to muscle activation was their lack of time-locked response. That is, early loads do not result in fixed latency responses in the upper and lower lip muscles. Rather, the muscle changes are apparently incorporated into the previously programmed voluntary response at a wide range of latencies. Further, for these early loads, introduced 40 or 50 ms prior to EMG onset, compensatory responses from the upper and lower lips are adjusted as a unit apparently reflecting an overall modification of the parameters of a·previously programmed voluntary action (Abbs et al., 1984; Gracco, 1984; Gracco & Abbs, 1985). Later occurring perturbations (after OOI onset) result in a lower lip response that is markedly reduced; by contrast, the upper lip contributes disproportionally as the load is introduced after muscle activation. As such, it appears that for perturbations introduced after motor execution has been initiated, the upper and lower lip contributions to the compensatory response reflect a different form of multimovement coupling than was

GAIN

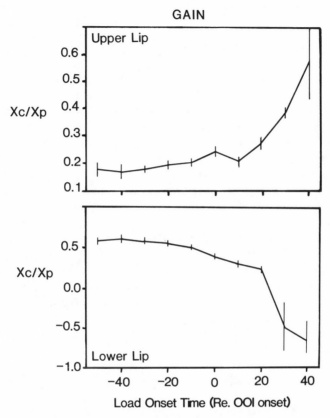

FIG. 7.4 Ratio of compensation displacement (Xc) to perturbation displacement (Xp) as a function of lower lip onset re: o. oris inferior onset. Motor task was /aba/. Compensation displacement (Xc) is the difference between the peak displacement of the upper or lower lip for the perturbed trial re: the preceding control trial. Data represent 509 trials from 5 subjects. Upper and lower lip gains were significantly different ($p < .01$) except at load onset time 20 ms post-OOI onset.

apparent for the early occurring perturbations. Instead of a proportional rescaling of both the upper and lower lip, it appears that responses to perturbations introduced immediately prior to or after the onset of muscle contraction actually reflect a functional decoupling of the two movements involved in this gesture.

SPEECH MOTOR PROGRAMMING AND EXECUTION

Given the above data, it might be hypothesized that perturbations introduced in the early phase of the motor act, seemingly prior to the activation of pyramidal neurons for initiation of the movement, reflect the operation of a nervous system process characterized as "parameter estimation" (cf. Arbib, 1981); i.e., setting up the motor "program" to best fit the peripheral conditions. In contrast, compensatory responses to later loads (following muscle activation) reflect a predominantly predictive control mode characterized by nonautogenic adjustments. This later interval, presumably after the motor cortex has initiated its action, represents the time during which the motor task is being executed. A number of considerations, such as a high correlation between perturbation displacement and compensation displacement in the early interval and a reduction of that correlation in the later interval, reflect differences between these two processes.

These recent findings also augment the distinction we made in previous studies between autogenic (or corrective) and nonautogenic (or predictive) sensorimotor actions; these two processes appear to reflect two different nervous system control operations. In a more theoretical and evolutionary vein, a similar position has been recently offered by Goldberg (in press). Goldberg hypothesized that the nervous system is organized according to projectional (or predictive) and responsive (or corrective) control modes, representing extremes or poles of action. Based on our results of compensatory variations to lip perturbation, it appears that the compensatory responses to early loads (prior to muscle activation) reflect a predominant corrective (responsive) control mode characterized primarily by autogenic adjustments. In relation to the classical distinctions between corrective and predictive control processes (Houk & Rymer, 1981; Miles & Evarts, 1979; Rack, 1981), the predictive (projectional) actions have been suggested to be more robust under greater time constraints, as one might anticipate. Subsequently once motor action is initiated, the autogenic corrective actions, perhaps subject to the inherent instability of closed-loop delays, appear to be reduced in gain; their contribution is significantly less in the later interval. Consequently, the predominant control mode during execution appears to involve predictive nonautogenic adjustments. These observations suggest that the production of voluntary speech movements involves different sensorimotor actions during programming and execution. That is, for complex voluntary behaviors such as speech, the control mode or mode of action appears to involve both corrective and predictive sensorimotor actions (cf. Abbs & Gracco, 1984; Abbs et al., 1984, Gracco & Abbs, 1985).

The relative contribution of one control mode over the other is most probably dependent on several factors. For example, the task or context may influence the relative predominance of one control mode over the other. A task requiring precise manipulation with no speed or time requirement may rely exclusively on corrective or autogenic adjustments. Conversely, a time-critical task, such as speech production, may rely more heavily on the use of predictive adjustments. Secondly, these two opposite but overlapping control modes further delineate the basic motor programming and execution stages in speech motor control. That is, the programming of an action appears to involve reactive or corrective actions utilizing afferent-dependent refinement of a generalized motor program (cf. Abbs et al., 1984; Schmidt, 1982). The actual execution of the program involves predictive actions utilizing afferent information to shape or fine-tune the previously programmed response through preset transfer functions included as part of the program. In this respect, we do not view the motor program as a detailed specification of the motor "commands" for a particular pattern of muscle contractions and movements. Rather, in our view, the motor program is an algorithm which sets up the system for a process whereby on-line sensory input and general motor command prespecifications are "mixed" dynamically to yield appropriate intended goals (cf. Abbs et al., 1984 for a more detailed discussion of this important point). Finally, the ability to modify speech movements throughout the motor act indicates that movement control is a real-time continuous process and is sensitive to inputs during both pre-execution and movement times (cf. Georgopoulos, Kalaska, & Massey, 1981).

NEUROANATOMICAL CORRELATES

From the previous discussion, it appears that there are multiple sensorimotor actions underlying the generation of movements for speech production. In this section, drawing from research in both human and nonhuman primates, we will consider some of the potential neuroanatomic structures or pathways that might underlie these multiple sensorimotor processes. Due to the extent of this literature, the limited scope of this chapter, and the extensive interconnection among nervous system components, we will only consider pathways that appear to be most directly involved in speech motor control. As such, this analysis must be considered a simplification primarily intended to illustrate that (a) sensory input is utilized in multiple ways in motor control, and (b) certain sensorimotor pathways appear to be preferentially involved in motor programming while others appear to be involved preferentially in motor execution. It needs to be emphasized at this juncture that a strict division between motor execution and motor programming is not realistic nor ultimately productive, hence the use of the qualifying term, preferential. In addition, we will focus upon these pathways and their functions in a unidirectional manner, from sensory input to motor output. As such, the reciprocal nature of most CNS interconnections will be ignored.

SENSORIMOTOR CONTROL OF SPEECH MOVEMENT EXECUTION

In considering the sensorimotor mechanisms of speech motor execution, one is motivated to examine those pathways whereby sensory input gains most direct (and short latency) access to motor neurons. Such direct access is important, for as noted in the observations reviewed above, motor execution is a time-critical process and perturbations introduced just prior to or after the onset of muscle contraction yield shorter latency responses than those introduced earlier.

Brainstem Pathways

For the lips, the shortest and most direct route by which afferents affect motor output is through the trigeminal afferent-to-facial MN connections in the lower brainstem, i.e., the perioral reflex pathway. As reflected in our previous analyses (Abbs & Gracco, 1984; Gracco & Abbs, 1982b), it appears that this seemingly most direct route (via brainstem connections) is not operative during orofacial speech motor behaviors. That is, using stimuli which are within the range of lip movement kinematics for speech (i.e., velocity, acceleration), there is a notable absence of short latency perioral reflex responses (Abbs & Gracco, 1984; Gracco & Abbs, 1982b). Lower lip perturbations occurring prior to agonist muscle onset (OOI) do not result in a reflex response at brainstem-mediated perioral reflex latencies (12-18 ms). Rather, it appears that the EMG changes in response to the perturbation occur over a wide range of latencies (22-85 ms). These latency values and the lack of perioral reflex contributions to these compensatory responses support a previous suggestion by Abbs and Cole (1982) that perioral system control for speech relies more heavily on supranuclear sensorimotor pathways. The reduction in the magnitude of lower lip EMG and movement responses for loads after the onset of OOI EMG is also notable (cf. Fig. 7.4), particularly since this variation is the opposite of what one might predict if the afferent influences were acting directly on the facial motor neurons. That is, if these responses were mediated via direct afferent input at the brainstem level, one would predict that the magnitude of the response would be proportional to the excitability of the motoneuron pool (cf. Houk, 1978). The observed reduction in response magnitude at a time when the motoneuron pool is most excited (immediately prior to and following EMG onset) is apparently due to influences that are out of phase with MN pool excitability, i.e., supranuclear centers. Given the acknowledged importance of multiple supranuclear sites in speech motor control, this is not surprising.

Cortical Sensorimotor Pathways

Recent neuroanatomical findings suggest several alternative supranuclear routes over which perioral afferents might influence coordination and control of speech movements during motor execution. These various pathways, discussed below, are illustrated schematically in Fig. 7.5. Our approach here is to begin at the orofacial motoneurons and proceed upstream to the sensory inputs.

For almost all voluntary movement, the major motor outputs of the central nervous system are directed through the primary motor cortex, MI. As reflected in Fig. 7.5, for orofacial cortical regions, the pyramidal cells of layers V and VI of the primary motor cortex make monosynaptic connections to cranial motor nuclei (lips, tongue and jaw) (Kuypers, 1958). Estimates of the minimal latencies of these descending pathways from the motor cortex to orofacial motoneurons have been obtained from observations with intracortical microstimulation (ICMS) in nonhuman primates. Using ICMS, Sirisko, Lucier, Wiesendanger, and Sessle (1980) reported EMG activation of facial muscles with latencies ranging from 7-22 ms. Similarly, Hoffman and Luschei (1980) reported response latencies of 6.5 to 7.0 ms in jaw muscles with intracortical microstimulation of a primary motor cortex jaw area. These direct connections suggest that the motor cortex output directly underlies execution of speech movements; i.e., the motor cortex is the final stage of

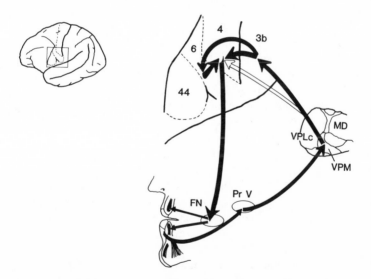

FIG. 7.5 Highly simplified orofacial "transcortical" pathways underlying the execution of speech movements. Abbreviations used include: PrV—Principal sensory nucleus of the trigeminal; Thalamic nuclei—VPM—ventral posteromedial VPLc—ventral posterolateral, caudal part; MD—dorsomedial; Cortical areas—3b—Somatic sensory, 6—lateral premotor, 4—precentral motor. FN—facial nucleus. The undarkened arrow reflects a possible direct thalamocortical pathway based on data reported by Asanuma et al., 1979 (see text).

supranuclear control.[1] In this context, determining the supranuclear structures contributing to the sensorimotor processes of speech execution involves examining those sensory pathways that have the most direct influence on the pyramidal cells.

As illustrated in Fig. 7.5, there is a direct route from sensory receptors located in the periphery (cf. Evarts, 1981; Wiesendanger, 1978) to the primary motor cortex pyramidal cells (i.e., the so-called transcortical pathway). This input to motor cortex from muscle afferent and cutaneous stimuli is very powerful and appears largely to be somatotopically organized. For example, primary motor cortex pyramidal cells projecting to a given peripheral region (e.g., the index finger) preferentially receive sensory input from the muscles and skin associated with movement of that region (Asanuma & Rosen, 1972; Rosen & Asanuma, 1972). This pathway, originally suggested by Hammond (1956, 1960) from observations in human subjects, and more recently by Phillips (1969), may traverse two different routes, as shown in Fig. 7.6 (cf. Asanuma & Arissian, 1984; Evarts, 1981 for discussion). That is, the transcortical pathway is considered to involve sensory input directed to the motor cortex pyramidal cells both via SI and directly, the latter through either the nucleus ventralis posterolateralis pars oralis (VPLo) subdivision of the thalamus (Asanuma & Arissian, 1984; Asanuma, Larsen, & Yumiya, 1979; Lemon & van der Burg, 1979; Rosen & Asanuma, 1972) or the nucleus ventralis posterolateralis caudalis (VPLc) (Asanuma, Thach, & Jones, 1983).

Sensory impulses originating from the perioral region also project to numerous thalamic and hence cortical sites. Perhaps the most secure and rapid transmission of sensory input from orofacial sites is via the trigeminothalamic projections, originating from the main sensory nucleus and subnucleus oralis of the trigeminal complex. Based on the types of trigeminothalamic synaptic junctions and terminal distribution of corticobulbar fibers, the main sensory nucleus represents the bulbar homologue of the dorsal horn (Kuypers, 1981). That is, similar to the dorsal column system, the trigeminothalamic system transmits information regarding touch and kinesthesia and this ascending information can be modulated through descending corticobulbar influences. In most species, including monkey and man, trigeminothalamic projections terminate in the ventral posteriomedial (VPM) nucleus of the thalamus (Smith, 1975). These large-diameter crossed and uncrossed projections are somatotopically organized (Kaas et al., 1984) and have been shown to reflect peripheral stimuli with a high degree of

---

[1] Although not dealt with specifically in this view, it is known that there are projections from the orofacial regions of MI and premotor cortex to the parvocellularis portion of the red nucleus, which in turn appears to project to the ipsilateral inferior olive (Humphrey, Gold, & Reed, 1984; Kuypers & Lawrence, 1967). The magnocellular division of the red nucleus also receives MI input (Humphrey et al., 1984; Kennedy, Gibson, & Houk, 1984; Kuypers & Lawrence, 1967) primarily from the leg and arm areas, and has been shown to project to the facial nucleus (Miller & Strominger, 1973) and to the interpositus nucleus of the cerebellum.

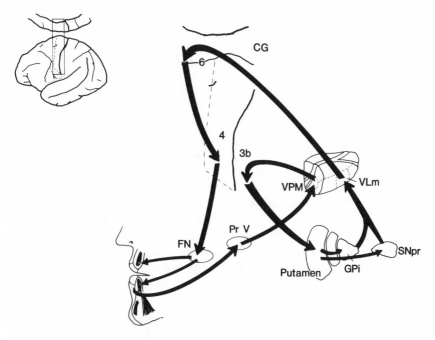

FIG. 7.6 Proposed pathway for speech motor programming incorporating the known basal ganglia—supplementary motor area (SMA) relations. Abbreviations used include: PrV—Principal sensory nucleus of the trigeminal; VPM—Ventral posteromedial nucleus of the thalamus, VLm—Ventral lateral nucleus, medial part; GPi—globus pallidus, inner segment, SNpr—substantia nigra pars reticulata; Cortical areas—3b—somatic sensory, 6—mesial premotor (SMA), 4—precentral motor; FN—facial nucleus; CG—cingulate gyrus.

reproductibility (Darian-Smith, 1966), indicating limited preprocessing and minimal convergence. Information transmitted through the trigeminal system via this pathway is in turn relayed to cortical somatic sensory areas 3b and 1 (Felleman, Nelson, Sur, & Kaas, 1983; Kaas, Nelson, Sur, Dykes, & Merzenich, 1984; Merzenich, Kaas, Sur, & Lin, 1978).[2]

The sensory projections from the perioral region to the somatic sensory cortex have been examined primarily by recording evoked potentials on the exposed cortex (Dreyer, Loe, Metz, & Whitsel, 1975); unfortunately, the latencies of these pathways have often not been reported. In one study (O'Brien, Pimpaneau, & Albe-Fessard, 1971), evoked potentials in the somatic sensory cortex of chloralose anesthetized monkeys to labial electrical stimulation were observed at latencies ranging from 5-12 ms. These authors

---

[2] It should be mentioned that Asanuma et al. (1979) reported the presence of a few facial VPM thalamic neurons activated antidromically from the motor cortex, suggesting the presence of a direct trigeminothalamic projection to MI independent of SI.

also reported responses in the face area of the motor cortex at slightly longer latencies (7-14 ms). Similarly, Hoffman and Luschei (1980) were able to activate motor cortex pyramidal cells by stretching the jaw closing muscles; the sinusoidal stretch used by these investigators yielded responses that were sensitive to the dynamic phases of the mechanical perturbation and were presumably of short latency. Given these data, it appears that direct ascending and descending pathways via the cortex are available with minimal loop times of as short as 14-20 ms (e.g., sensory ascending latencies of 7-10 ms and descending motor latencies of approximately this same minimum value). It should be noted that this sensorimotor pathway for the orofacial system is not well-elucidated; only a single study has reported both corticopetal and corticofugal responses in the same experiment and that experiment focused on the masticatory system (Hoffman & Luschei, 1980). Moreover, modern neuroanatomical techniques (e.g., axoplasmic tracing) have not focused specifically on supranuclear representations of orofacial mechanisms. However, the available data suggest that there are orofacial analogs to the so-called transcortical pathways which would involve minimal latencies and minimal processing; these pathways would be ideal for control during the time-critical processes of motor execution. In that respect, it would appear reasonable to suggest that the orofacial sensory projections to motor cortex (i.e., a transcortical pathway) are a major candidate for the autogenic sensorimotor adjustments observed in response to the later loads observed in our previous experiments. While the sensory pathways to primary motor cortex pyramidal cells are the most direct, there are sensory projections to other areas of the cortex that also may underlie the moment-to-moment adjustments necessary for motor execution. In this vein, the classical transcortical pathway traditionally has been considered to underlie autogenic or corrective adjustments; as such, other pathways may be involved in the prominent nonautogenic adjustments (i.e., upper lip responses to lower lip perturbations) just described.

One possible pathway for the nonautogenic adjustments is via sensory inputs to the cortical cytoarchitectonic area 6 (premotor cortex) in lateral regions of the precentral cortex (Fig. 7.7). This lateral premotor area has been shown to receive somatic sensory input from the orofacial region and in turn projects to the primary motor cortex. Neuroanatomically, the route for this sensory input to the lateral premotor cortex is ambiguous. However, electrophysiological data are quite compelling. For example, O'Brien et al. (1971) and Rizzolatti, Scandolara, Gentilucci, and Camarda (1981a) demonstrated that:

1. Lateral premotor responses to peripheral orofacial stimulation are almost as short in latency as those to the primary motor cortex (10-12 ms), and

2. This region of cortex is particularly sensitive to more complex, multimovement goal oriented stimuli (as contrasted to the primary motor cortex).

That is, this region of cortex appears to receive the kind of converging orofacial somatic sensory projections necessary for adjustments in the upper lip to lower lip perturbations or adjustments in the lips or tongue to perturbations applied to the jaw. Muakkassa and Strick (1979) and others have shown also that the face region of this premotor area has direct projections to primary motor cortex. As such, it might be suggested that one pathway underlying nonautogenic (intermovement) adjustments during the execution phases of the speech motor act is via orofacial somatic sensory projections to premotor cortex and, in turn, to the primary motor regions. Interestingly, select lesions of the orofacial premotor regions in monkeys result in dramatic deficits in the coordination of the lips, jaw, and tongue (cf. Larson, Byrd, Garthwaite, & Luschei, 1980; Luschei & Goodwin, 1975; Watson, 1975).

These considerations suggest that the nonautogenic sensorimotor compensations described previously in this paper may be mediated via a second cortical-cortical pathway, i.e., via the premotor cortical region. In this context, it is especially intriguing to consider how such adjustments are organized and reorganized with variations in phonetic goals (e.g., *p* vs. *f*) on a moment-to-moment basis. Seemingly, such variations would involve the processes referred to earlier as motor programming. In this case, the instructions for task-dependent sensorimotor actions (cf. Abbs et al., 1984; Kelso et al., 1984) would be "down-loaded" from other CNS structures for implementation in primary and nonprimary motor cortical regions. Responses to perturbations introduced well in advance of muscle activation would appear to reflect operations associated with these down-loaded processes. This consideration, of course, leads to the second central motor process of interest in the present paper, speech motor programming.

SENSORIMOTOR PROCESSES IN SPEECH MOTOR PROGRAMMING

There are several alternate and more indirect routes over which sensory input gains access to the primary motor cortex, possibly involving sensory processing and integration for purposes other than moment-to-moment adjustments of motor execution. Several of these indirect pathways involve brain sites thought to be important for motor control in a more executive capacity. Consideration of these pathways thus offers some preliminary hypotheses on some of the supranuclear structures potentially involved in speech motor programming. The two subcortical structures most often implicated in movement programming are the basal ganglia and the cerebellum (Allen &

Tsukahara, 1974; Brooks, 1979; Brooks & Thach, 1981; DeLong & Georgopoulos, 1981; Kemp & Powell, 1971; Paillard, 1983). Further, Schell and Strick (1984), based on their own neuroanatomic findings and reinterpretation of earlier data, suggest that the orofacial representations of the basal ganglia and cerebellum project in a topographic and segregated fashion to two different nonprimary motor cortical regions; the supplementary motor and premotor areas, respectively. Inasmuch as the primary motor cortex receives strong somatotopically segregated projections from premotor and supplementary motor cortices (Matelli, Camarda, Glickstein, & Rizzolatti, 1984; Muakkassa & Strick, 1979), these latter data suggest that afferents from the basal ganglia and the cerebellum influence the primary motor cortex via these nonprimary motor areas. Collectively, these data thus provide a basis for considering how orofacial sensory input might influence the process of speech motor programming. In the discussion that follows, we review these more recent neuroanatomical and neurophysiological findings which suggest that these subcortical and nonprimary motor areas comprise two major motor systems over which afferent input from the orofacial region gains access to motor output.

Basal Ganglia/Supplementary Motor Contributions

As noted, one sensorimotor pathway potentially underlying speech motor programming involves the basal ganglia. From this perspective, the basal ganglia are viewed as being upstream from the motor cortex and involved in task specifications that occur prior to a completed movement. Damage to the basal ganglia is known to result in numerous muscle tone and movement problems (cf. DeLong & Georgopoulos, 1981; Marsden, 1982). Although there has been controversy regarding a motor versus cognitive role of the basal ganglia, it now seems clear that the basal ganglia are composed of two functional subsystems; i.e., the caudate and putamen, serving "complex" and motor functions, respectively (cf. DeLong & Georgopoulos, 1981; DeLong et al., 1984). As illustrated in Fig. 7.6, the following discussion focuses primarily on the sensory input, orofacial representation, and motor output of the putamen in relation to its potential influences on motor cortex output. It should be noted that although many investigators view the basal ganglia as having a programming function, their potential role in moment-to-moment adjustments for motor execution is an issue of continuing interest (cf. Iansek & Porter, 1980; Liles, 1983).

The putamen receives sensory information from three major sources: (a) the substantia nigra pars compacta (SNpc), (b) the intralaminar nuclei of the thalamus, and (c) multiple cortical sites including the somatosensory, motor, and premotor areas (Dray, 1980; Jones, Coulter, Burton, & Porter, 1977; Künzle, 1975, 1976, 1977). Shown in Fig. 7.6 is only one of many possible projections to the basal ganglia. Neurons in the putamen have been shown to respond to both passive and active limb movements at latencies between 25 and 50 ms (Crutcher & DeLong, 1984a, 1984b; DeLong & Georgopoulos, 1979). Similarly, studies of somatosensory input to the basal ganglia have shown that putamen neurons also respond to natural orofacial stimuli (DeLong & Georgopoulos, 1979). In the cat, Schneider, Morse, and Lidsky (1982) found that 42% of the units responsive to orofacial stimulation had a mean latency of 18 ms. The latency of basal ganglia responses to somatosensory stimuli, as compared to somatic sensory and motor cortex responses (cf. Evarts, 1973 [monkey]; Landgren & Olsson, 1980 [cat]), suggests an indirect, multisynaptic input pathway.

The major output from the putamen is directed through the inner segment of the globus pallidus and the pars reticulata portion of the substantia nigra (SNpr) (Nauta & Mehler, 1966). As reflected in Fig. 7.6, neurons related to orofacial movements have been found in the lateral portion of the SNpr and the ventrocaudal segment of the GPi (DeLong, Crutcher, & Georgopoulos, 1981; DeLong & Georgopoulos, 1979); cells in SNpr have been observed to discharge in relation to natural orofacial movements (DeLong et al., 1984; Mora, Mogenson, & Rolls, 1977). Further, it has been shown that portions of the basal ganglia associated with orofacial movements (SNpr) have a major efferent projection to a subdivision of the centrolateral thalamus, ventrolateralis medialis (VLm) (Carpenter & McMasters, 1964; Carpenter, Nakano, & Kim, 1976; Carpenter & Peter, 1972). As noted, recent work by Schell and Strick (1984) partially completes this picture demonstrating segregated inputs from VLm to the face area of the supplementary motor area (SMA) (cf. Fig. 7.6). The final set of data to this point are those of Muakkassa and Strick (1979) that demonstrate reciprocal connections between the face subregion of SMA and primary motor cortex. Inasmuch as anatomic and electrophysiologic studies have indicated an absence of direct projections from the SMA to facial, motor trigeminal or hypoglossal nuclei (Künzle, 1978; Macpherson, Marangoz, Miles, & Wiesendanger, 1982; Penfield & Welch, 1951), SMA influences on orofacial actions presumably are exerted via primary motor cortex. Hence, it appears that face area projections from the basal ganglia exert their motor control influence on MI via the SMA. As such, one way somatic sensory inputs to the basal ganglia can influence the control of orofacial movements for speech is via ascending projections to SMA, and, in turn, to primary motor cortex.[3]

---

[3] It should be noted that corticofugal projections via SNpr also are directed onto numerous brainstem sites including the superior colliculus, and reticular formation sites with the midbrain pons and medulla (Kuypers, 1981). Based on recent evidence from our laboratory (Gracco & Abbs, 1984) indicating the abnormal presence of perioral reflex responses to lower lip perturbation in Parkinson patients, it might be suggested that the inhibitory function often associated with the basal ganglia (cf. DeLong & Georgopoulos, 1981) may be mediated by these descending influences. The dysfunction of such hypothesized inhibitory influences is consistent with Parkinson patients' inability to suppress the mid-latency response to muscle stretch (Mortimer & Webster, 1979; Tatton & Lee, 1975).

Based on these data and consideration of the anatomical connections of the SMA with primary motor cortex, the suggestion that SMA is involved in executive level function relative to the primary motor cortex (Brinkman & Porter, 1979; Jürgens, 1984; Roland, Larsen, Lassen, & Skinhøj, 1980; Tanji, 1984) appears warranted. In addition to the basal ganglia inputs, the SMA also receives projections from numerous cortical sites including premotor, primary motor, somatic sensory, and parietal cortices (areas 1, 2, and 5) (Jones & Powell, 1970; Jürgens, 1984; Pandya & Vignolo, 1971). As with basal ganglia responses to peripheral stimuli, SMA latencies have been shown to be longer (greater than 20 ms from arm area; Brinkman & Porter, 1979) than for MI (7–15 ms from the fingers; Lemon, 1981). Additionally, SMA is less responsive to peripheral stimuli than MI (Brinkman & Porter, 1979; Lemon & Porter, 1976; Wise & Tanji, 1981), and apparently more selective. Tanji and Kurata (1982) reported SMA neurons to be selectively active dependent on the modality of the stimulus; i.e., visual, auditory, or somatosensory. This observation is in contrast to MI for which no such modality specificity has been reported. Timing of SMA activity has been shown to be related to movement with neurons responding both before and after the onset of muscular activity (Brinkman & Porter, 1979; Smith, 1979). The onset of neuronal activity in response to visual or auditory cues to move are earlier than those of precentral neurons, suggesting that SMA is involved in the earlier stages of premovement sensorimotor processing. Additionally, SMA has been shown to be involved primarily in movement sequences or complex movements; its apparent unresponsiveness to passive peripheral stimuli may merely reflect the multisynaptic and task-specific nature of the SMA contribution. Finally, as shown by Tanji and colleagues (Tanji & Kurata, 1982; Tanji, Taniguchi, & Saga, 1980), SMA activity is related to the actual motor preparation and not to the stimulus used to signal the initiation of a motor act.

Based upon observations in normal and impaired humans, the basal ganglia SMA pathway obviously is important for speech motor control and motor control in general. For example, it has been shown that basal ganglia dysfunction leads to speech and limb movement aberrations (Darley, Aronson, & Brown, 1975; Evarts, Teräväinen, & Calne, 1981; Flowers, 1976; Hunker, Abbs, & Barlow, 1982; Marsden, 1982; Wilson, 1925). These data, obtained exclusively in individuals with Parkinson's disease, range from perceptually observed deficits (e.g., imprecise consonants, monopitch, and monoloudness, cf. Darley et al., 1975) to reductions in amplitude and velocity of movements (Evarts et al., 1981; Hunker et al., 1982; Hunker & Abbs, 1984), elongated movement times (Evarts et al., 1981), and an apparent inability to utilize sensory information normally in scaling movement amplitude and force (Gracco & Abbs, 1984; Tatton, Eastman, Bedingham, Verrier, & Bruce, 1984). These observations are consistent with the suggestion that the basal ganglia ultimately influence the scaling of EMG and subsequent kinematic parameters (DeLong et al., 1984; Horak & Anderson, 1984a, 1984b).

Interestingly, as noted previously, several investigators have suggested a similar executive function for the motor portions of the basal ganglia (cf. DeLong & Georgopoulos, 1981; Marsden, 1982). Moreover, there are similarities in the motor deficiencies of individuals with Parkinson's disease and SMA damage. Those basal ganglia-SMA dysfunction similarities include speech motor aberrations, ranging from speech arrest to imprecise articulation (Arseni & Botez, 1961; Caplan & Zervas, 1978; Damasio & Van Hoesen, 1980; Darley, Aronson, & Brown, 1975; Masdeu, Schoene, & Funkenstein, 1978).

In contrast to observable motor deficits resulting from basal ganglia dysfunction, the motor contributions of the SMA are less clearly documented. Changes in cerebral blood flow (CBF) have been used to identify cortical areas active during certain complex motor gestures including speech (Larsen, Skinhøj, & Lassen, 1978; Orgogozo & Larsen, 1979; Roland, Larsen, Lassen, & Skinhøj, 1980). Subjects instructed to count or recite the days of the week displayed increased blood flow in the primary motor and supplemental motor cortex of both cerebral hemispheres. Blood flow changes were noted in SMA, basal ganglia (putamen and globus pallidus), and motor cortex during execution of independent finger movements, but not during simpler motor tasks such as repetitive flexion of a single finger or during sustained isometric contractions (Orgogozo & Larsen, 1979; Roland et al., 1980; Roland, Meyer, Shibasaki, Yamamoto, & Thompson, 1982). Similarly, electrical stimulation of the SMA in man produces a transient inability to speak (Penfield & Roberts, 1959). Damage to the anterior cerebral artery primarily results in volitional speech disturbances often described as a motor or transcortical aphasia (Gelmers, 1983; Rubens, 1975). In a summary of 12 patients with well-defined tumors involving the SMA, Arseni and Botez (1961) report two categories of speech disturbances; one affecting the functioning of the motor mechanism of speech and the other a more "dysphasic disorder." Similar observations had been made earlier by Critchley (1930); Chusid, de Gutiérrez-Mahoney, & Margules-Lavergne (1954); and Laplane, Talairach, Meininger, Bancaud, & Orgogozo (1977). Although the studies reporting speech symptoms associated with SMA damage are not as numerous or, more importantly, as detailed, it appears that the motor aberrations in these patients may be similar to aberrations associated with basal ganglia damage.

Cerebellar/Premotor/Contributions

The second potential pathway by which sensory input may influence motor programming is via the cerebellum, a structure classically considered to be involved in coordination of complex movements (cf. Holmes, 1922). Because of the parallel sensory projections to the cerebellum and somatic sensory cortex, one is led to believe that the former inputs are involved in functions other than moment-to-moment control of motor execution. Indeed a number of investigators have shown that cerebellar output via the dentate nucleus reflects more complex motor functions such as "motor set" (Hore & Vilis, 1984; Strick, 1978, 1983). Until very recently, however, the exact projections from the orofacial portions of the cerebellum to the motor cortex were ambiguous; earlier studies primarily utilized degenerative or destructive neuroanatomical techniques. Recent neuroanatomical and physiological observations, as summarized later, offer a more coherent picture of these projections.

As illustrated schematically in Fig. 7.7, the cerebellum receives orofacial sensory information from the periphery via direct trigeminal routes as well as more indirect cortical projections (Allen, Gilbert, & Yin, 1978; Allen & Tsukahara, 1974). Afferent input to the cerebellum terminates on the cerebellar cortex (Cody & Richardson, 1978; Miles & Wiesendanger, 1975; Snider & Stowell, 1944) and on the deep cerebellar nuclei (Chan-Palay, 1977; Eller & Chan-Palay, 1979). In the forelimb, somatic sensory stimuli have been

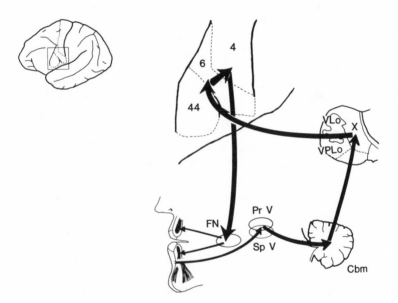

FIG. 7.7 Proposed pathway for speech motor programming incorporating the known cerebellar—premotor area (PMA) relations. Abbreviations used include: PrV—principal sensory nucleus of the trigeminal, spV—spinal portion of the trigeminal (interpolaris subdivision); Cbm—cerebellum (lateral dentate nucleus—although not indicated in the figure, the trigeminal projections terminate on the cerebellar cortical surface as well as directly to the deep nuclei; see text for detail); X—thalamic nucleus X, VPLo—ventral posterolateral nucleus, oral part, VLo—ventral lateral nucleus, oral part; Cortical areas—same as previous figures; FN—facial nucleus.

recorded in dentate and interpositus nuclei with latencies of 30-50 ms and 20-40 ms, respectively (Harvey, Porter, & Rawson, 1979; Strick, 1978). Cutaneous facial stimulation results in short latency input to Crus I and II and the paramedian lobule of the cerebellar cortex (Huerta, Frankfurter, & Harting, 1983), which contains the most expansive facial map (Shambes, Gibson, & Welker, 1978). In addition, retrograde HRP labelling in the monkey has shown direct and bilateral monosynaptic connections from the main sensory and spinal nucleus of V to cerebellar dentate nucleus (Chan-Palay, 1977). Similar HRP injections into the interpositus nucleus resulted in retrograde labelling in the mesencephalic nucleus, containing jaw muscle spindles, but not in the main sensory or spinal nucleus of V (Chan-Palay, 1977). However, facial representations in the interposed nuclei are reported by Thach, Perry, and Schieber (1982) in the monkey and Richardson, Cody, Paul, and Thomas (1978) in the cat. Thach et al. (1982) reported neurons in the posterior portion of dentate and interpositus that discharged in relation to facial movements. Recordings in the cat cerebellum have demonstrated projections onto interpositus nuclei from supraorbital, infraorbital, mental, and masseteric nerve branches (Richardson et al., 1978). These data indicate that orofacial afferents project directly to the dentate nucleus as well as indirectly to dentate and interpositus via the cerebellar cortex.

While precise somatotopy has not been described for the hemispheres of the cerebellar cortex, the lateral nuclei are known to contain a facial representation primarily located in caudal and posterior regions (Stanton, 1980; Thach et al., 1982).[4] As reflected in Fig. 7.7, the caudal portion of the dentate nucleus, which includes this facial representation, projects primarily to the ventrolateral thalamus area (Asanuma et al., 1983; Stanton, 1980) with a noticeable lack of cerebellar terminations in VLm (Schell & Strick, 1984) which receives basal ganglia projections as noted above. These thalamic projections from the caudal dentate are coextensive and overlap with corticothalamic projections from the face areas of the primary and nonprimary motor cortices (Kievit & Kuypers, 1977; Kuypers & Lawrence, 1967). Based on their retrograde HRP tracing study and considering the physiological studies of Sasaki et al. (1976, 1979), Schell and Strick (1984) indicate that the caudal dentate nuclei (the orofacial representation) project to the premotor cortex via thalamic area X. Thus, it appears that the caudal dentate does not project directly to motor cortex, but rather to the premotor area (cf. Fig. 7.7). Moreover, as noted previously, Muakkassa and Strick (1979) demonstrated direct inputs from the face area of premotor cortex to MI. As such, sensory inputs to the cerebellum appear to influence motor cortex output to orofacial motoneurons indirectly via the premotor cortex.

---

[4] Both interpositus and dentate nuclei project to thalamus; however, we will focus on the dentate projections as the literature suggests that dentate is more involved in motor programming (Allen & Tsukahara, 1974; Brooks & Thach, 1981; Thach, 1978).

Analyses of cerebellar outputs, as reflected in activity of the deep nuclei, reflect the executive role of this structure. Dentate activity appears to be governed by the "willed" action of the animal and related to the intended movement, seemingly independent of activity at the motor cortex or the lower motor neuron pool. More specifically, Thach (1978) demonstrated dentate activity which was correlated with position of the limb and the direction of the intended next movement. In contrast, interpositus activity was best related to the pattern of muscular activity of the limb, the reflexive behavior of neurons in motor cortex or in muscles when a stimulus (perturbation) is delivered (Thach, 1978). Strick (1978, 1983) has reported data on single unit recordings in dentate nucleus during several contrastive motor tasks, and suggested that this output of the cerebellum was involved preferentially in "motor set". In particular, it was demonstrated that single neural units in dentate did not vary directly with a sensory stimulus (as apparently do cortical cells), but rather responded to predetermined combinations of the intended movement and sensory stimuli. Similarly, Hore and Vilis (1984) eliminated components of EMG responses attributed to set by cooling the dentate nucleus. These latter data suggest that lateral cerebellar nuclear output to the motor cortex is not related to the particular parameters of movement (as would be predicted if this structure were involved in motor execution), but to the conditions under which a given movement was generated. Finally, prior to a voluntary movement, cells within the dentate have been shown to discharge earlier than cells within the motor cortex (Thach, 1975), and cooling of the dentate delayed both onset of voluntary movement as well as movement-related activity in motor cortex (Meyer-Lohmann, Hore, & Brooks, 1977). These data augment the suggestion that cerebellar output, as manifested in dentate, is upstream from and precedes activity in motor cortex. Further, data such as these strongly implicate the lateral cerebellar nuclei in the programming of voluntary movements.

The role of the cerebellum as a brain center underlying coordination of movement and the effects of premotor cortical lesions lend credence to the concept that the cerebellum and the orofacial region of premotor cortex work in conjunction, perhaps in a serial fashion. The influence of this cerebellar-premotor pathway in orofacial control and speech is apparent from several sets of data. For example, damage to the cerebellum results in an ataxic dysarthria (Darley et al., 1975; Kent & Netsell, 1975; Kent, Netsell, & Abbs, 1979; Lechtenberg & Gilman, 1978) seemingly characterized by a breakdown in normal speech movement generation. Further, speech aberrations following frontal lobe damage suggest that the premotor area is also involved in the control of orofacial movements (cf. Fromm, Abbs, McNeil, & Rosenbek, 1982; Itoh, Sasanuma, Hirose, Yoshioka, & Ushijima, 1980; Schiff, Alexander, Naeser, & Galaburda, 1983; Tonkonogy & Goodglass, 1981). As noted by Mohr (1976):

a 'restricted' lesion to these areas (lateral premotor) leads one to view their function as mediating a more traditionally postulated role as a premotor association cortex region concerned with acquired skilled oral, pharyngeal, and respiratory movements, involving speaking as well as other behaviors but not essentially language or graphic behavior, per se. (p. 22)

Similarly, single neural unit and behavioral studies in nonhuman primates have shown the premotor area to be involved in the guidance of movements based on sensory signals (Godschalk, Lemon, Nijs, & Kuypers, 1981; Halsband & Passingham, 1982; Rizzolatti, Scandolara, Matelli, & Gentilucci, 1981b). Similar to cerebellar studies, the premotor cortex has been shown to reflect activity associated with motor set or programming (cf. Weinrich & Wise, 1982; Weinrich, Wise, & Mauritz, 1984). Parallel to the earlier suggestion that the basal ganglia-SMA damage may produce some comparable speech movement aberrations, it also has been suggested that cerebellar and premotor cortical damage may yield similar speech movement aberrations (cf. Kent & Rosenbek, 1982 for discussion based on acoustical analyses). The movement discoordination noted by Fromm et al. (1982) in a study of apraxia of speech and the dysprosodic similarities between ataxic dysarthrics and apraxic patients described by Kent and Rosenbek (1982) appear to support such a suggestion. Based on the behavioral data presented here and the parallel neuroanatomical considerations, it appears that the cerebellar-premotor system occupies an executive position relative to the primary motor cortex and may perform overlapping or related functions in the programming of speech. Obviously, however, more detailed investigations are needed.

SYNTHESIS AND IMPLICATIONS

As discussed previously and summarized in Fig. 7.8, there is substantial neuroanatomical and functional evidence for the operation of multiple somatic sensory contributions to the processes of speech motor control. These multiple sensory influences upon orofacial motor output dramatically highlight suggestions over the last 10 years by many neuroscientists that our current challenge is no longer to determine whether sensory input is utilized in control of motor output, but rather to determine the exact nature of this important contribution (cf. Abbs & Cole, 1982; Evarts, 1982; Grillner, 1975). In that spirit, the present paper provides an initial neuroanatomical and neurophysiological framework within which to consider the differential contribution of sensory inputs to the operations of motor programming and motor execution. However, these two processes in turn each appear to be served by more than one set of pathways. For motor execution, there may be as

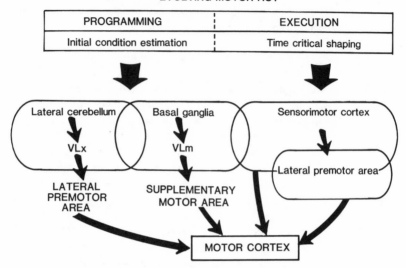

FIG. 7.8 Schematic summary illustrating the hypothesized multiple sensorimotor processes and neuroanatomical substrate involved in the programming and execution of speech.

many as three major sensorimotor pathways involved, including inputs to motor cortical pyramidal cells (the "upper motor neuron pool") via the somatic sensory cortex, the premotor cortex, and directly via the thalamus. All of these pathways appear to have the requisite short latencies and input/output characteristics to contribute to the time-critical adjustments for motor execution.

In parallel, it appears that while both the cerebellum and basal ganglia also receive sensory input, these centers, in conjunction with the nonprimary motor areas, may participate in more executive functions related to the programming of movement. Extrapolating from available data in the limbs, it appears that the cerebellum may be involved in establishing the necessary temporal-spatial relationship among the speech articulators (Soechting, Ranish, Palminteri, & Terzuolo, 1976) (i.e., the scaling of the upper lip, lower lip, and jaw for bilabial production) as well as initiating the timing between agonist and antagonist muscles (Brooks, Kozlovskaya, Atkin, Horvath & Uno, 1973; Meyer-Lohmann et al., 1977; Soechting et al., 1976; Trouche & Beaubaton, 1980). Several recent papers have provided very specific data to this point; e.g., the cerebellum appears to control the spatial gain between the head and eye movements in the vestibular-ocular reflex as an off-line controller (cf. Lisberger, 1984). On the other hand, the basal ganglia sensorimotor pathway may influence the generated movement by scaling the EMG activity in the agonist and antagonist muscles (Horak & Anderson, 1984a, 1984b) to yield movements of appropriate magnitude and velocity.

The integration of sensory input with the motor programs via the basal ganglia and cerebellum may correspond, neuroanatomically, to the parameter estimation process suggested by Arbib (1981) (cf. Abbs et al., 1984). Interestingly, both of these subcortical systems influence the motor system via nonprimary motor areas that in turn impinge on the primary motor cortex. In this context, it needs to be reemphasized that, in our particular view, a motor program is not a representation of detailed movements and specific muscle contractions. Rather, we consider a motor program more as an "implementation algorithm" for carrying out motor execution, including appropriate modulation and gating of sensorimotor pathways. One could argue that these algorithms, including appropriate gating for on-line sensorimotor adjustments during motor execution, are down-loaded to the premotor and supplementary motor cortex and are ultimately manifest only indirectly in the observable motor output. These nonprimary motor areas have long been considered to have significant roles in motor control, particularly in the preliminary programming of complex movements.

Together, these results and discussion point to a dynamic hierarchical model of speech motor control utilizing distributed motor control processes and interacting neural subsystems. This hierarchical organization, as depicted graphically in Fig. 7.8, is dynamic from the standpoint that once the goal has been established, the locus of system control is time-dependent. Specifically, it is suggested that the cerebellar-premotor system is involved early in the programming process with little influence once execution has been initiated. In contrast, the basal ganglia-SMA system is predominantly involved late in the programming process and its influence appears to span both programming and execution. The remaining hypothesized pathways are preferentially involved in the execution of the motor program providing on-line sensorimotor adjustments. This flexible hierarchical organization allows for the operation of multiple, parallel subtask actions, each down-loaded and implemented via actions in the nonprimary and primary motor cortices. Together these distributed sensorimotor systems appear to interact dynamically to produce the coordinated movements of human speech.

ACKNOWLEDGMENTS

The authors express their gratitude to Eric Keller for his comments on an earlier version of this manuscript. Gratitude also is expressed to our bioengineer Richard Konopacki for his technical assistance.

This work was supported by National Institute of Neurological and Communicative Disorders and Stroke Grants NS20668, NS13274 and National Institute of Child Health and Human Development Grant HD-3352.

REFERENCES

Abbs, J. H. (1979). Speech motor equivalence: A need for a multilevel control model. *Proceedings 9th International Congress of Phonetics, Vol. II.* Copenhagen, 318–324.

Abbs, J. H. (1986). Invariance and variability in speech production: A distinction between linguistic intent and its neuromotor implementation. In J. Perkell & D. Klatt (Eds.), *Invariance and variability of speech processes* (pp. 202–218). Hillsdale, NJ: Lawrence Earlbaum Associates.

Abbs, J., & Cole, K. (1982). Consideration of bulbar and suprabulbar afferent influences upon speech motor coordination and programming. In S. Grillner, B. Lindblom, J. Lubker, & A. Persson (Eds.), *Speech motor control* (pp. 159–186). New York: Pergamon Press.

Abbs, J. H., & Gracco, V. L. (1984). Control of complex motor gestures: Orofacial muscle responses to load perturbations of the lip during speech. *Journal of Neurophysiology, 52*(4), 705–723.

Abbs, J. H., Gracco, V. L., & Cole, K. C. (1984). Control of multimovement coordination: Sensorimotor mechanism in speech motor programming. *Journal of Motor Behavior, 16*(2), 195–232.

Allen, G. I., Gilbert, P. F. C., & Yin, T. C. T. (1978). Convergence of cerebral inputs onto dentate neurons in monkey. *Experimental Brain Research, 32,* 151–170.

Allen, G. I., & Tsukahara, N. (1974). Cerebrocerebellar communication systems. *Physiological Reviews, 54*(4), 957–1005.

Arbib, M. A. (1981). Perceptual structures and distributed motor control. In J. M. Brookhart & V. B. Mountcastle (Eds.), *Handbook of physiology: Sec. 1. The nervous system: Vol. 2. Motor control, Part 2* (pp. 1449–1480). Bethesda, MD: American Physiological Society.

Arseni, C., & Botez, M. I. (1961). Speech disturbances caused by tumors of the supplementary motor area. *Acta Psychiatrica Neurologica Scandinavica, 36,* 279–298.

Asanuma, H., & Arissian, K. (1984). Experiments of functional role of peripheral input to motor cortex during voluntary movements in the monkey. *Journal of Neurophysiology, 52*(2), 212–227.

Asanuma, H., & Rosen, I. (1972). Topographical organization of cortical efferent zones projecting to distal forelimb muscles in the monkey. *Experimental Brain Research, 14,* 243–256.

Asanuma, H., Larsen, K., & Yumiya, H. (1979). Direct sensory pathways to motor cortex in the monkey: A basis of critical reflexes. In H. Asanuma & V. J. Wilson (Eds.), *Integration in the nervous system* (pp. 223–237). Tokyo: Igaku Shoin.

Asanuma, C., Thach, W. T., & Jones, E. G. (1983). Distribution of cerebellar terminations and their relations to other afferent terminations in the ventral lateral thalamic region of the monkey. *Brain Research Reviews, 5,* 237–265.

Berenberg, R. A. (1984). Recovery from partial deafferentation increases 2-deoxyglucose uptake in distant spinal segments. *Experimental Neurology, 84,* 627–642.

Bizzi, E., Kalil, R., & Tagliasco, V. (1971). Eye-head coordination in monkeys: Evidence for centrally patterned organization. *Science, 173,* 452–454.

Borden, G. J. (1979). An interpretation of research on feedback interruption in speech. *Brain and Language, 7,* 307–319.

Bossom, J. (1974). Movement without proprioception. *Brain Research, 71,* 285–296.

Brinkman, C., & Porter, R. (1979). Supplementary motor area in the monkey: Activity of neurons during performance of a learned motor task. *Journal of Neurophysiology, 42*(3), 681–709.

Brooks, V. B. (1979). Motor program revisited. In R. E. Talbott & D. R. Humphrey (Eds.), *Posture and movement: Perspectives for integrating sensory and motor research on the mammalian nervous system* (pp. 13–49). New York: Raven Press.

Brooks, V. B., Kozlovskaya, I. B., Atkin, A., Horvath, F. E., & Uno, M. (1973). Effects of cooling dentate nucleus on tracking-task performance in monkeys. *Journal of Neurophysiology, 36*, 974–995.

Brooks, V. B., & Thach, W. T. (1981). Cerebellar control of posture and movement. In J. M. Brookhart & V. B. Mountcastle (Eds.), *Handbook of physiology: Sec. 1. The nervous system: Vol. 2. Motor control, Part 2* (pp. 877–946). Bethesda, MD: American Physiological Society.

Caplan, L. R., & Zervas, N. T. (1978). Speech arrest in a dextral with a right mesial frontal astrocytoma. *Archives of Neurology, 35*, 252–253.

Carpenter, M. B., & McMasters, R. E. (1964). Lesions of the substantia nigra in the rhesus monkey. Efferent fiber degeneration and behavioral observations. *American Journal of Anatomy, 114*, 293–320.

Carpenter, M. B., Nakano, K., & Kim, R. (1976). Nigrothalamic projections in the monkey demonstrated by autoradiographic techniques. *Journal of Comparative Neurology, 165*, 401–416.

Carpenter, M. B., & Peter, P. (1972). Nigrostriatal and nigrothalamic fibers in the rhesus monkey. *Journal of Comparative Neurology, 144*, 94–166.

Chan-Palay, V. (1977). *Cerebellar dentate nucleus: Organization, cytology and transmitters.* New York: Springer-Verlag.

Chusid, J. G., de Gutiérrez-Mahoney, C. G., & Margules-Lavergne, M. P. (1954). Speech disturbances in association with parasagittal frontal lesions. *Journal of Neurosurgery, 11*, 193–204.

Cody, F. W. J., & Richardson, H. C. (1978). Mossy and climbing fibre projections of trigeminal inputs to the cerebellar cortex in the cat. *Brain Research, 153*, 351–356.

Cole, K. J., & Abbs, J. H. (1983). Intentional responses to kinesthetic stimuli in orofacial muscles: Implications for the coordination of speech movements. *Journal of Neuroscience, 3*(12), 2660–2669.

Cole, K. J., Gracco, V. L., & Abbs, J. H. (1984). Autogenic and nonautogenic sensorimotor actions in the control of multiarticulate hand movements. *Experimental Brain Research, 56*, 582–585.

Conrad, B. (1978). The motor cortex as a primary device for fast adjustments of programmed motor patterns to afferent signals. In J. E. Desmedt (Ed.), *Cerebral motor control in man: Long loop mechanisms, Vol. 4, Progress in Clinical Neurophysiology* (pp. 123–140). Basel: Karger.

Critchley, M. (1930). The anterior cerebral artery, and its syndromes. *Brain, 53*, 120–165.

Crutcher, M. D., & DeLong, M. R. (1984a). Single cell studies of the primate putamen. II. Functional organization. *Experimental Brain Research, 53*, 233–243.

Crutcher, M. D., & DeLong, M. R. (1984b). Single cell studies of the primate putamen. II. Relations to direction of movement and pattern of muscular activity. *Experimental Brain Research, 53*, 244–258.

Damasio, A. R., & Van Hoesen, G. W. (1980). Structure and function of the supplementary motor area. *Neurology, 30*, 359.

Darian-Smith, I. (1966). Neural mechanisms of face sensation. *International Review of Neurobiology, 9*, 301–395.

Darley, F. L., Aronson, A. E., & Brown, J. R. (1975). *Motor speech disorders.* Philadelphia, PA: Saunders.

DeLong, M. R., Alexander, G. E., Georgopoulos, A. P., Crutcher, M. D., Mitchell, S. J., & Richardson, R. T. (1984). Role of basal ganglia in limb movements. *Human Neurobiology, 2,* 235-244.

DeLong, M. R., Crutcher, M. D., & Georgopoulos, A. P. (1981). Relations between movement and single cell discharge in the substantia nigra of the behaving monkey. *Journal of Neuroscience, 3*(8), 1599-1606.

DeLong, M. R., & Georgopoulos, A. P. (1979). Motor function of the basal ganglia as revealed by studies of single cell activity in the behaving primate. *Advances in Neurology, 24,* 131-140.

DeLong, M. R., & Georgopoulos, A. P. (1981). Motor functions of the basal ganglia. In J. M. Brookhart & V. B. Mountcastle (Eds.), *Handbook of physiology: Sect. 1. The nervous system: Vol. 2. Motor control, Part 2* (1017-1062). Bethesda, MD: American Physiological Society.

Dostrovsky, J. O., Millar, J., & Wall, P. D. (1976). The immediate shift of afferent drive of dorsal column nucleus and spinal cord. *Experimental Neurology, 52,* 480-495.

Dray, A. (1980). The physiology and pharmacology of mammalian basal ganglia. *Progress in Neurobiology, 14,* 221-335.

Dreyer, D. A., Loe, P. R., Metz, C. B., & Whitsel, B. L. (1975). Representation of head and face in postcentral gyrus of the macaque. *Journal of Neurophysiology, 38,* 714-733.

Eller, T., & Chan-Palay, V. (1979). Afferents to the cerebellar lateral nucleus: Evidence from retrograde transport of horseradish peroxidase after pressure injections through micropipettes. *Journal of Comparative Neurology, 166,* 285-302.

Evarts, E. V. (1973). Motor cortex reflexes associated with learned movement. *Science, 179,* 501-503.

Evarts, E. V. (1981). Role of motor cortex in voluntary movements in primates. In V. B. Brooks (Ed.), *Handbook of physiology, Section 1. Vol. II: Motor control, Part 2* (pp. 1083-1120). Bethesda, MD: American Physiological Society.

Evarts, E. V. (1982). Analogies between central motor programs for speech and limb movements. In S. Grillner, B. Lindblom, J. Lubker, & A. Persson, *Speech motor control* (pp. 19-41). Oxford: Pergamon Press.

Evarts, E. V., & Fromm, C. (1978). The pyramidal tract neuron as summing point in a closed-loop system in the monkey. In J. E. Desmedt (Ed.), *Cerebral motor control in man: Long-loop mechanisms, Vol. 4, Progress in Clinical Neurophysiology* (pp. 56-69). Basel: Karger.

Evarts, E. V., & Tanji, J. (1976). Reflex and intended responses in motor cortex pyramidal tract neurons of monkey. *Journal of Neurophysiology, 39,* 1069-1080.

Evarts, E. V., Teräväinen, H., & Calne, D. B. (1981). Reaction time in Parkinson's disease. *Brain, 104,* 167-186.

Felleman, D. J., Nelson, R. J., Sur, M., & Kaas, J. H. (1983). Representations of the body surface in areas 3b and 1 of postcentral parietal cortex of cebus monkeys. *Brain Research, 268,* 15-26.

Fentress, J. C. (1973). Development of grooming in mice with amputated forelimbs. *Science, 179,* 704-705.

Flowers, K. A. (1976). Visual 'closed-loop' and 'open-loop' characteristics of voluntary movement in patients with parkinsonism and intention tremor. *Brain, 99,* 269-310.

Folkins, J., & Abbs, J. (1975). Lip and jaw motor control during speech: Responses to resistive loading of the jaw. *Journal of Speech and Hearing Research, 18,* 207-220.

Folkins, J., & Abbs, J. (1976). Additional observations on responses to resistive loading of the jaw. *Journal of Speech and Hearing Research, 19,* 820-821.

Folkins, J., & Zimmermann, G. (1982). Lip and jaw interaction during speech: Responses to perturbation of lower-lip movement prior to bilabial closure. *Journal of the Acoustical Society of America, 71,* 1225-1233.

Fromm, D., Abbs, J. H., McNeil, M., & Rosenbek, J. C. (1982). Simultaneous perceptual-physiological method for studying apraxia of speech. In R. Brookshire (Ed.), *Proceedings of the Annual Clinical Aphasiology Conference* (pp. 155–171). Minneapolis, MN: BRK Publishers.

Gammon, S. A., Smith, P. J., Daniloff, R. G., & Kim, C. W. (1971). Articulation and stress/juncture production under oral anesthetization and masking. *Journal of Speech and Hearing Research, 14,* 271–282.

Gelmers, H. J. (1983). Non-paralytic motor disturbances and speech disorders: The role of the supplementary motor area. *Journal of Neurology, Neurosurgery, and Psychiatry, 46,* 1052–1054.

Georgopoulos, A. P., Kalaska, J. F., Caminiti, R., & Massey, J. T. (1983). Interruption of motor cortical discharge subserving aimed arm movements. *Experimental Brain Research, 49,* 327–340.

Georgopoulos, A. P., Kalaska, J. F., & Massey, J. T. (1981). Spatial trajectories and reaction times of aimed movements: Effects of practice, uncertainty, and change in target location. *Journal of Neurophysiology, 46,* 725–743.

Glassman, R. B. (1978). The logic of the lesion experiment and its role in the neural sciences. In S. Finger (Ed.), *Recovery from brain damage: Research and theory* (pp. 3–31). New York: Plenum.

Godschalk, M., Lemon, R. N., Nijs, H. G. T., & Kuypers, H. G. J. M. (1981). Behavior of neurons in monkey peri-arcuate and precentral cortex before and during visually guided arm and hand movements. *Experimental Brain Research, 44,* 113–116.

Goldberg, G. (in press). Response and projection: A reinterpretation of the premotor concept. In E. A. Roy (Ed.), *Advances in psychology: Apraxia of neuropsychology and related disorders.* Amsterdam: Elsevier North-Holland, Inc.

Gracco, V. (1984). *Time varying sensorimotor processes of the perioral system during speech.* Unpublished doctoral dissertation, University of Wisconsin-Madison.

Gracco, V., & Abbs, J. (1982a). Compensatory response capabilities of the labial system in relation to variation in the onset of unanticipated loads. *Journal of the Acoustical Society for America, 71,* S34.

Gracco, V., & Abbs, J. (1982b). Temporal response characteristics of the perioral system to load perturbations. *Society for Neuroscience Abstracts, 8,* 282.

Gracco, V., & Abbs, J. (1984). Sensorimotor dysfunction in Parkinson's disease: Observations from a multiarticulate speech task. *Society for Neuroscience Abstracts, 10,* 906.

Gracco, V., & Abbs, J. (1985). Dynamic control of the perioral system during speech: Kinematic analyses of autogenic and nonautogenic sensorimotor processes. *Journal of Neurophysiology, 54,* 418–432.

Grillner, S. (1975). Locomotion in vertebrates—central mechanisms and reflex interaction. *Physiological Reviews, 55,* 247–304.

Halsband, U., & Passingham, R. (1982). The role of premotor and parietal cortex in the direction of action. *Brain Research, 240,* 368–372.

Hammond, P. M. (1956). The influence of prior instruction to the subject on an apparently involuntary neuromuscular response. *Journal of Physiology, 132,* 17–18.

Hammond, P. M. (1960). An experimental study of servo action in human muscular control. In *Proceedings of III International Conference on Medical Electronics* (pp. 190–199). London: Institute of Electrical Engineers.

Harvey, R. J., Porter, R., & Rawson, J. A. (1979). Discharges of intracerebellar nuclear cells in monkeys. *Journal of Physiology, 297,* 559–580.

Hoffman, D. S., & Luschei, E. S. (1980). Responses of monkey precentral cortical cells during a controlled jaw bite task. *Journal of Neurophysiology, 44,* 333–348.

Holmes, G. (1922). Clinical symptoms of cerebellar disease and their interpretation. The Croonian lectures I. *Lancet, 1,* 1177–1182.

Horak, F. B., & Anderson, M. E. (1984a). Influence of globus pallidus on arm movements in monkeys. I. Effects of kainic acid-induced lesions. *Journal of Neurophysiology, 52*(2), 290–304.

Horak, F. B., & Anderson, M. E. (1984b). Influence of globus pallidus on arm movements in monkeys. II. Effects of stimulation. *Journal of Neurophysiology, 52*(2), 305–322.

Hore, J., & Vilis, T. (1984). Loss of set in muscle responses to limb perturbations during cerebellar dysfunction. *Journal of Neurophysiology, 51*(6), 1137–1148.

Houk, J. C. (1978). Participation of reflex mechanisms and reaction-time processes in the compensatory adjustments to mechanical disturbances. In J. E. Desmedt (Ed.), *Cerebral motor control in man: Long-loop mechanisms, Vol. 4, Progress in clinical neurophysiology* (pp. 193–215). Basel: Karger.

Houk, J., & Rymer, W. (1981). Neural control of muscle length and tension. In J. M. Brookhart & V. B. Mountcastle (Eds.), *Handbook of physiology: Sec. 1. The nervous system: Vol. 2. Motor control, Part 1* (pp. 257–323). Bethesda, MD: American Physiological Society.

Huerta, M. F., Frankfurter, A., & Harting, J. K. (1983). Studies of the principal sensory and spinal trigeminal nuclei of the rat: Projections to the superior colliculus, inferior olive, and cerebellum. *Journal of Comparative Neurology, 220,* 147–167.

Humphrey, D. R., Gold, R., & Reed, D. J. (1984). Sizes, laminar and topographic origins of cortical projections to the major divisions of the red nucleus in the monkey. *Journal of Comparative Neurology, 225,* 75–94.

Hunker, C. J., & Abbs, J. H. (1984). Physiological analyses of parkinsonian tremors in the orofacial system. In M. R. McNeil, J. C. Rosenbek, & A. Aronson (Eds.), *The dysarthrias: Physiology-acoustics-perception-management.* San Diego, CA: College-Hill Press.

Hunker, C. J., Abbs, J. H., & Barlow, S. M. (1982). The relationship between parkinsonian rigidity and hypokinesia in the orofacial system: A quantitative analysis. *Neurology, 32,* 755–761.

Iansek, R., & Porter, R. (1980). The monkey globus pallidus: Neuronal discharge properties in relation to movement. *Journal of Physiology, 301,* 439–455.

Itoh, M., Sasanuma, S., Hirose, H., Yoshioka, H., & Ushijima, T. (1980). Abnormal articulatory dynamics in a patient with apraxia of speech: X-ray microbeam observation. *Brain and Language, 11,* 66–75.

Jones, E. G., Coulter, J. D., Burton, H., & Porter, R. (1977). Cells of origin and terminal distribution of corticostriatal fibers arising in the sensory-motor cortex of monkeys. *Journal of Comparative Neurology, 173,* 53–80.

Jones, E. G., & Powell, T. P. S. (1970). An anatomical study of converging sensory pathways within the cerebral cortex of the monkey. *Brain, 93,* 793–820.

Jürgens, U. (1984). The efferent and afferent connections of the supplementary motor area. *Brain Research, 300,* 63–81.

Kaas, J. H., Nelson, R. J., Sur, M., Dykes, R. W., & Merzenich, M. M. (1984). The somatotopic organization of the ventroposterior thalamus of the squirrel monkey, saimiri sciureus. *Journal of Comparative Neurology, 226,* 111–140.

Kelso, J. A. S., & Tuller, B. (1983). "Compensatory articulation" under conditions of reduced afferent information: A dynamic formulation. *Journal of Speech and Hearing Research, 26,* 217–224.

Kelso, J. A. S., Tuller, B., Bateson, E. V. & Fowler, C. A. (1984). Functionally specific articulatory cooperation following jaw perturbations during speech: Evidence for coordinative structures. *Journal of Experimental Psychology: Human Perception and Performance, 10,* 812–832.

Kemp, J. M., & Powell, T. P. S. (1971). The connections of the striatum and globus pallidus: Synthesis and speculation. *Philosophical Transactions of the Royal Society of London, Series, B, 262,* 441–457.

Kennedy, P. R., Gibson, A. R., & Houk, J. C. (1984). Contrast between the 2 major divisions and 3 cell types of monkey red nucleus. *Society for Neuroscience Abstracts, 10,* 537.

Kent, R., & Netsell, R. (1975). A case study of an ataxic dysarthric: Cineradiographic and spectrographic observations. *Journal of Speech and Hearing Disorders, 40*(1), 115–133.

Kent, R. D., & Moll, K. L. (1975). Articulatory timing in selected consonant sequences. *Brain and Language, 2,* 310–323.

Kent, R. D., Netsell, R., & Abbs, J. H. (1979). Acoustic characteristics of dysarthria associated with cerebellar disease. *Journal of Speech and Hearing Research, 22,* 627–648.

Kent, R. D., & Rosenbek, J. C. (1982). Prosodic disturbance and neurologic lesion. *Brain and Language, 15,* 259–291.

Kievit, J., & Kuypers, H. G. J. M. (1977). Organization of the thalamocortical connections to the frontal lobe in the rhesus monkey. *Experimental Brain Research, 29,* 299–322.

Künzle, H. (1975). Bilateral projections from precentral motor cortex to the putamen and other parts of the basal ganglia. An autoradiographic study in macaca fascicularis. *Brain Research, 88,* 195–209.

Künzle, H. (1976). Thalamic projections from the precentral motor cortex in macaca fascicularis. *Brain Research, 105,* 253–267.

Künzle, H. (1977). Projections from the primary somatosensory cortex to basal ganglia and thalamus in the monkey. *Experimental Brain Research, 30,* 481–492.

Künzle, H. (1978). An autoradiographic analysis of the efferent connections from premotor and adjacent prefrontal regions (Areas 6 and 9) in macaca fascicularis. *Brain Behavior and Evolution, 15,* 185–234.

Kuypers, H. G. J. M. (1958). Corticobulbar connections to the pons and lower brainstem in man: An anatomical study. *Brain, 81,* 364–388.

Kuypers, H. G. J. M. (1981). Anatomy of the descending pathways. In J. M. Brookhart & V. B. Mountcastle (Eds.), *Handbook of physiology: Sec. 1. The nervous system: Vol. 2. Motor Control, Part 2* (pp. 597–666). Bethesda, MD: American Physiology Society.

Kuypers, H. G. J. M., & Lawrence, D. G. (1967). Cortical projections to the red nucleus and the brainstem in the rhesus monkey. *Brain Research, 4, 151–188.*

Landgren, S., & Olsson, K. A. (1980). Low threshold afferent projections from the oral cavity and the face to the cerebral cortex of the cat. *Experimental Brain Research, 39,* 133–147.

Lane, H. L., & Tranel, B. (1971). The Lombard sign and the role of hearing in speech. *Journal of Speech and Hearing Research, 14,* 677–709.

Laplane, D., Talairach, J., Meininger, V., Bancaud, J., & Orgogozo, J. M. (1977). Clinical consequences of corticectomies involving the supplementary motor area in man. *Journal of the Neurological Sciences, 34,* 301–314.

Larsen, B., Skinhøj, E., & Lassen, N. (1978). Variations in regional cortical blood flow in the right and left hemispheres during automatic speech. *Brain, 101,* 193–209.

Larson, C. R., Byrd, K. E., Garthwaite, C. R., & Luschei, E. S. (1980). Alterations in the pattern of mastication after ablations of the lateral precentral cortex in rhesus macaques. *Experimental Neurology, 70,* 638–651.

Laurence, S., & Stein, D. G. (1978). Recovery after brain damage and the concept of localization of function. In S. Finger (Ed.), *Recovery from brain damage. Research and theory* (pp. 369–407). New York: Plenum.

Lechtenberg, R., & Gilman, S. (1978). Speech disorders in cerebellar disease. *Annals of Neurology, 3,* 285–290.

Lemon, R. N. (1981). Functional properties of monkey motor cortex neurones receiving afferent input from the hand and fingers. *Journal of Physiology, 311,* 497–519.

Lemon, R. N., & Porter, R. (1976). Afferent input to movement-related precentral neurones in conscious monkeys. *Proceedings of the Royal Society of London* (Series B), *194*, 313–339.

Lemon, R. N., & van der Burg, J. (1979). Short-latency peripheral inputs to thalamic neurones projecting to the motor cortex in the monkey. *Experimental Brain Research, 36,* 445–462.

Liles, S. L. (1983). Activity of neurons in the putamen associated with wrist movements in the monkey. *Brain Research, 263,* 156–161.

Lisberger, S. G. (1984). The latency of pathways containing the site of motor learning in the monkey vestibulo-ocular reflex. *Science, 225,* 74–76.

Luschei, E. S., & Goodwin, G. M. (1975). Role of monkey precentral cortex in control of voluntary jaw movements. *Journal of Neurophysiology, 38,* 146–157.

MacNeilage, P. F. (1980). Distinctive properties of speech motor control. In G. E. Stelmach & J. Requin (Eds.), *Tutorials in motor behavior* (pp. 607–627). Amsterdam: North Holland.

Macpherson, J. M., Marangoz, C., Miles, T. S., & Wiesendanger, M. (1982). Microstimulation of the supplementary motor area (SMA) in the awake monkey. *Experimental Brain Research, 45,* 410–416.

Marsden, C. D. (1982). The mysterious motor function of the basal ganglia: The Robert Wartenberg lecture. *Neurology, 32*(5), 514–539.

Marsden, C. D., Merton, P. A., & Morton, H. B. (1981). Human postural responses. *Brain, 104,* 513–534.

Marsden, C. D., Rothwell, J. C., & Day, B. L. (1984). The use of pheripheral feedback in the control of movement. *Trends in NeuroSciences,* 253–257.

Masdeu, J. C., Schoene, W. C., & Funkenstein, H. (1978). Aphasia following infarction of the left supplementary motor area: A clinicopathologic study. *Neurology, 28,* 1220–1223.

Matelli, M., Camarda, R., Glickstein, M., & Rizzolatti, G. (1985). Interconnections within the postarcuate cortex (area 6) of the macaque monkey. *Brain Research, 310,* 388–392.

Merzenich, M. M., Kaas, J. H., Sur, M., & Lin, C. S. (1978). Double representation of the body surface within cytoarchitectonic areas 3b and 1 in "SI" in the owl monkeys (Aotus trivirgatus). *Journal of Comparative Neurology, 181,* 41–74.

Meyer-Lohmann, J., Hore, J., & Brooks, V. B. (1977). Cerebellar participation in generation of prompt arm movements. *Journal of Neurophysiology, 40,* 1038–1050.

Miles, F. S., & Evarts, E. V. (1979). Concepts of motor organization. *Annual Review of Psychology, 30,* 327–362.

Miles, T. S., & Wiesendanger, M. (1975). Climbing fibre inputs to cerebellar Purkinje cells from trigeminal cutaneous afferents and the S1 face area of the cerebral cortex in the cat. *Journal of Physiology, 245,* 425–445.

Miller, R. A., & Strominger, N. L. (1973). Efferent connections of the red nucleus in the brainstem and spinal cord of the rhesus monkey. *Journal of Comparative Neurology, 152,* 327–346.

Mohr, J. P. (1976). Broca's area and Broca's aphasia. In H. Whitaker & H. Whitaker (Eds.), *Studies in neurolinguistics, Vol. 1* (pp. 201–236). New York: Academic Press.

Mora, F., Mogenson, G. J., & Rolls, E. T. (1977). Activity of neurons in the region of the substantia nigra during feeding in the monkey. *Brain Research, 133,* 267–276.

Morasso, P., Bizzi, E., & Dichgans, J. (1973). Adjustments of saccade characteristics during head movements. *Experimental Brain Research, 16,* 492–500.

Mortimer, J. A., & Webster, D. D. (1979). Evidence for a quantitative association between EMG stretch responses and parkinsonian rigidity. *Brain Research, 162,* 169–173.

Muakkassa, K. F., & Strick, P. L. (1979). Frontal lobe inputs to primate motor cortex: Evidence for four somatotopically organized 'premotor' areas. *Brain Research, 177,* 176–182.

Nashner, L. M., & Cordo, P. J. (1981). Automatic postural responses. *Experimental Brain Research, 43,* 395–405.

Nashner, L. M., Woollacott, M., & Tuma, G. (1979). Organization of rapid responses to postural and locomotor-like perturbation of standing man. *Experimental Brain Research,, 36,* 463–476.

Nauta, W. J. H., & Mehler, W. R. (1966). Projections of the lentiform nucleus in the monkey. *Brain Research, 1,* 3-42.

O'Brien, J. H., Pimpaneau, A., & Albe-Fessard, D. (1971). Evoked cortical responses to vagal, laryngeal and facial afferents in monkeys under chloralose anaesthesia. *Electroencephalography and Clinical Neurophysiology, 31,* 7-20.

Orgogozo, J. M., & Larsen, B. (1979). Activation of the supplementary motor area during voluntary movement in man suggests it works as a supramotor area. *Science, 206,* 847-850.

Paillard, J. (1983). Introductory lecture: The functional labelling of neural codes. In J. Massion, J. Paillard, W. Schultz, & M. Wiesendanger (Eds.), *Neural coding of motor performance* (pp. 1-19). Berlin Heidelberg: Springer-Verlag.

Pandya, D. N., & Vignolo, L. A. (1971). Intra- and interhemispheric projections of the precentral, premotor and arcuate areas in the rhesus monkey. *Brain Research,, 26,* 217-233.

Penfield, W., & Roberts, L. (1959). *Speech and brain mechanisms.* Princeton, NJ: Princeton University Press.

Penfield, W., & Welch, K. (1951). The supplementary motor area of the cerebral cortex. A clinical and experimental study. *Archives of Neurology and Psychiatry, 66,* 289-317.

Phillips, C. G. (1969). The Ferrier lecture, 1968. Motor apparatus of the baboon's hand. *Proceedings of the Royal Society [Biology], 173,* 141-174.

Polit, A., & Bizzi, E. (1979). Characteristics of motor programs underlying arm movements in monkeys. *Journal of Neurophysiology, 42,* 183-194.

Rack, P. M. (1981). Limitations of somatosensory feedback in control of posture and movement. In V. B. Brooks (Ed.), *Handbook of physiology, Section 1, Vol. II: Motor control, Part 1* (pp. 119-256). Bethesda, MD: American Physiological Society.

Richardson, H. C., Cody, F. W. J., Paul, V. E., & Thomas, A. G. (1978). Convergence of trigeminal and limb inputs onto cerebellar interpositus nuclear neurones in the cat. *Brain Research, 156,* 355-359.

Ringel, R., & Steer, M. (1963). Some effects of tactile and auditory alterations on speech output. *Journal of Speech and Hearing Research, 6,* 369-378.

Rizzolatti, G., Scandolara, C., Gentilucci, M., & Camarda, R. (1981a). Response properties and behavioral modulation of 'mouth' neurons of the postarcuate cortex (area 6) in macaque monkeys. *Brain Research, 255,* 421-424.

Rizzolatti, G., Scandolara, C., Matelli, M., & Gentilucci, M. (1981b). Afferent properties of periarcuate neurons in macaque monkeys. I. Somatosensory responses. *Behavioral Brain Research, 2,* 125-146.

Roland, P. E., Larsen, B., Lassen, N. A., & Skinhøj, E. (1980). Supplementary motor area and other cortical areas in organization of voluntary movements in man. *Journal of Neurophysiology, 43,* 118-136.

Roland, P. E., Meyer, E., Shibasaki, T., Yamamoto, Y. L., & Thompson, C. J. (1982). Regional cerebral blood flow changes in cortex and basal ganglia during voluntary movements in normal human volunteers. *Journal of Neurophysiology, 48*(2), 467-480.

Rosen, I., & Asanuma, H. (1972). Peripheral afferent inputs to the forelimb area of the monkey motor cortex: Input-output relations. *Experimental Brain Research, 14,* 257-273.

Rothwell, J., Traub, M., Day, B., Obeso, J., Thomas, P., & Marsden, C. (1982). Manual motor performance in a deafferented man. *Brain, 105,* 515-542.

Rubens, A. B. (1975). Aphasia with infarction in the territory of the anterior cerebral artery. *Cortex, 11,* 239-250.

Sanes, J., & Evarts, E. V. (1983). Regulatory role of proprioceptive input in motor control of phasic or maintained voluntary contractions in man. In J. Desmedt (Ed.), *Motor control mechanisms in health and disease* (pp. 47-59). New York: Raven Press.

Sasaki, K., Jinnai, K., Gemba, H., Hashimoto, S., & Mizuno, N. (1979). Projection of the cerebellar dentate nucleus onto the frontal association cortex in monkeys. *Experimental Brain Research, 37,* 193-198.

Sasaki, K., Kawaguchi, S., Oka, H., Sakai, M., & Mizuno, N. (1976). Electrophysiological studies on the cerebellocerebral projections in monkeys. *Experimental Brain Research,, 24,* 495–507.

Schell, G. R., & Strick, P. L. (1984). The origin of thalamic inputs to the arcuate premotor and supplementary motor areas. *Journal of Neuroscience, 4*(2), 539–560.

Schiff, H. B., Alexander, M. P., Naeser, M. A., & Galaburda, A. M. (1983). Aphemia: Clinical-anatomic correlations. *Archives of Neurology, 40,* 720–727.

Schmidt, R. A. (1982). *Motor control and learning.* Champaign, IL: Human Kinetics Publishers.

Schneider, J. S., Morse, J. R., & Lidsky, T. I. (1982). Somatosensory properties of globus pallidus neurons in awake cats. *Experimental Brain Research, 46,* 311–314.

Scott, C. M., & Ringel, R. L. (1971). Articulation without oral sensory control. *Journal of Speech and Hearing Research, 14,* 804–818.

Shambes, M., Gibson, M., & Welker, W. (1978). Fractured somatotopy in granule cell tactile areas of rat cerebellar hemispheres revealed by micromapping. *Brain, Behavior and Evolution, 15,* 94–140.

Sirisko, M., Lucier, G., Wiesendanger, M., & Sessle, B. (1980). Multiple representation of face, jaw, and tongue movements in macaca fascicularis as revealed by cortical microstimulation. *Neuroscience Abstracts, 6,* 342–424.

Smith, A. M. (1979). The activity of supplementary motor area neurons during a maintained precision grip. *Brain Research, 172,* 315–327.

Smith, R. L. (1975). Axonal projections and connections of the principal sensory trigeminal nucleus in the monkey. *Journal of Comparative Neurology, 163,* 347–376.

Snider, R. S., & Stowell, A. (1944). Receiving areas of the tactile, auditory, and visual systems in the cerebellum. *Journal of Neurophysiology, 7,* 331–357.

Soechting, J. F., Ranish, N. A., Palminteri, R., & Terzuolo, C. A. (1976). Changes in a motor pattern following cerebellar and olivary lesions in the squirrel monkey. *Brain Research, 105,* 21–44.

Stanton, G. B. (1980). Topographical organization of ascending cerebellar projections from the dentate and interposed nuclei in macaca mulatta: An anterograde degeneration study. *Journal of Comparative Neurology, 190,* 699–731.

Strick, P. L. (1978). Cerebellar involvement in "volitional" muscle responses to load changes. In J. Desmedt (Ed.), *Cerebral motor control in man: Long-loop mechanisms, Vol. 4. Progress in clinical neurophysiology* (pp. 85–93). Basel: Karger.

Strick, P. L. (1983). The influence of motor preparation on the response of cerebellar neurons to limb displacements. *Journal of Neuroscience, 3*(10), 2007–2020.

Tanji, J. (1984). The neuronal activity in the supplementary motor area of primates. *Neurochemistry, 42,* 71–79.

Tanji, J., & Kurata, K. (1982). Comparison of movement-related activity in two cortical motor areas of primates. *Journal of Neurophysiology, 48*(3), 633–653.

Tanji, J., Taniguchi, K., & Saga, T. (1980). Supplementary motor area: Neuronal response to motor instructions. *Journal of Neurophysiology, 43*(1), 60–68.

Tatton, W. G., & Bawa, P. (1979). Input-output properties of motor unit responses in muscles stretched by imposed displacements of the monkey wrist. *Experimental Brain Research, 37,* 439–457.

Tatton, W. G., Eastman, M. J., Bedingham, W., Verrier, M. C., & Bruce, I. C. (1984). Defective utilization of sensory input as the basis for bradykinesia, rigidity and decreased movement repertoire in parkinson's disease: A hypothesis. *Canadian Journal of Neurological Sciences, 11,* 136–143.

Tatton, W. G., & Lee, R. G. (1975). Evidence for abnormal long-loop reflexes in rigid parkinsonian patients. *Brain Research, 100,* 671–676.

Taub, E., & Berman, A. J. (1968). Movement and learning in the absence of sensory feedback. In S. J. Freedman (Ed.), *The neurophysiology of spatially oriented behavior.* Homewood, IL: Dorsey.

Thach, W. T. (1975). Timing of activity in cerebellar dentate nucleus and cerebral motor cortex during prompt volitional movement. *Brain Research, 88,* 233–241.

Thach, W. T. (1978). Correlation of neural discharge with pattern and force of muscular activity, joint position, and direction of intended next movement in motor cortex and cerebellum. *Journal of Neurophysiology, 41*(3), 654–676.

Thach, W. T., Perry, J. G., & Schieber, M. H. (1982). Cerebellar output: Body maps and muscle spindles. *Experimental Brain Research, Suppl. 6,* 440–453.

Tonkonogy, J., & Goodglass, H. (1981). Language function, foot of the third frontal gyrus, and rolandic operculum. *Archives of Neurology, 38,* 486–490.

Traub, M. M., Rothwell, J. C., & Marsden, C. D. (1980). A grab reflex in the human hand. *Brain, 103,* 869–884.

Trouche, E., & Beaubaton, D. (1980). Initiation of a goal-directed movement in the monkey. Role of the cerebellar dentate nucleus. *Experimental Brain Research, 40,* 311–322.

Watson, C. (1975). *The role of precentral gyrus in the control of facial movement in Macaca mulatta.* Unpublished doctoral dissertation, University of Chicago.

Weinrich, M., & Wise, S. P. (1982). The premotor cortex of the monkey. *Journal of Neuroscience, 2*(9), 1329–1345.

Weinrich, M., Wise, S. P., & Mauritz, K.-H. (1984). A neurophysiological study of the premotor cortex in the rhesus monkey. *Brain, 107,* 385–414.

Wiesendanger, M. (1978). Comments on the problem of transcortical reflexes. *Journal of Physiology, Paris, 74,* 325–330.

Wilson, S. A. K. (1925). Disorders of motility and muscle tone, with special reference to the striatum. *Lancet, 2,* 1–53, 169, 215, 268.

Wise, S. P., & Tanji, J. (1981). Supplementary and precentral motor cortex: Contrast in responsiveness to peripheral input in the hindlimb area of the unanesthetized monkey. *Journal of Comparative Neurology, 195,* 433–451.

Intrinsic Time in Speech Production: Theory, Methodology, and Preliminary Observations

8

J. A. S. Kelso
Betty Tuller
Florida Atlantic University and
Haskins Laboratories

ABSTRACT

A continuing challenge to our understanding of speech production and perception is the fact that utterances with markedly different acoustic, kinematic, and electromyographic characteristics can nevertheless be perceived as the "same" word. In this chapter, we first discuss the importance of examining articulation relative to an intrinsic, activity-defined metric, and show how such an analysis of intervocalic consonant timing across different speaking rates and stress patterns significantly reduces both interspeaker and intraspeaker variability. Next, we explore whether the observed relative temporal stability can be achieved without reference to an extrinsic clocking device, but rather in terms of the dynamic topology of the system's behavior. To this end, using a phase plane description of articulatory motion, we show how the temporal analysis originally offered can be redescribed in terms of critical position-velocity states (or, in polar coordinates, phase angles) for interarticulator cooperation. Such coordination, we propose, can be captured in terms of events that are intrinsic to the system's dynamics, not in terms of conventional durational metrics.

1.0 INTRODUCTION

One primary focus of speech production research has been to understand how the many articulatory degrees of freedom are temporally organized. In traditional (and many current) theories, the problem is "explained" by invoking the notion of a program, a representation of the behavior coded in some mental or neural device that exists before the behavior is realized in the real world (see Kelso, 1981; Kelso, Tuller, & Harris, 1983; Kugler, Kelso, & Turvey, 1980, for criticisms). The function of the temporal program is to instruct the articulators when to become active and for how long. For example, in the early, influential theories proposed by Kozhevnikov and Chistovich (1966) and Lindblom (1963), execution of discrete linguistic units was thought to be triggered by an independent "rhythm generator" or "timing program," which timed the units with respect to one another. More recently, so-called central pattern generators have been thought to be the neural embodiment of timing programs.

This class of theory can be termed indicational (cf. Reed, 1981); that is, the role of the plan is to indicate, instruct, or command the articulators how and when they should be active. The emphasis of indicational theories is placed firmly on the symbolic mode of description with little or no attention paid to the detailed dynamical processes that the symbol mode is said to indicate or direct. To use a favorite example (cf. Pattee, 1977), a stop sign indicates to a driver that the car should be stopped, but provides no detailed information about how to stop the car; i.e., how, where, and by how much to decelerate, apply the brakes, etc. Thus, the symbolic or indicational mode greatly underdetermines the information actually required to perform an activity. In the case of speech, indicational theories pay no regard to the dynamical behavior of the articulatory system; i.e., the ordered motions of the articulators in space and time. The timing program or rhythm generator concept emphasizes the symbolic, indicational mode and provides no account of how the multiple degrees of freedom of the articulatory system are actually coordinated in the course of an activity.

Indicational theories (which are pervasive in biology and psychology) not only ignore, in large part, dynamical processes, but also lack a rationale for how it is and by what means one particular symbol string is created rather than another (cf. Kugler, Kelso, & Turvey, 1980, 1982; Turvey & Kugler, 1984). In speech research, different variants of an indicational theory include features, segments, or syllables as candidates for units of articulation. What is missing, then, is an account of the symbolic mode that is not arbitrary with respect to the dynamics that it instructs. The origins of the symbolic mode must, it seems, be lawfully derived from dynamics.[1]

The foregoing arguments serve to focus attention on dynamics as a source of understanding natural activities, such as speaking, whose spatiotemporal

---

[1] We see efforts to explore the origins of language in terms of more fundamental processes, such as particular perception-production mappings, as entirely consistent with this view (e.g., Lindblom, 1983a, in press; Lindblom, MacNeilage, & Studdert-Kennedy, 1983).

organization is the main concern of this paper. Dynamics, by definition, means simply motion and change in space/time. Maxwell (1877/1952) described dynamics as the "simplest and most abstract description of the motion of a system." Thus, and this is important, there is no logical reason why dynamics, although rate-dependent, cannot be conceived of as abstract. One reason why dynamics has been undervalued is that it has been interpreted as local and concrete (purely biomechanics?) rather than global and abstract. Yet recent developments in the field of dynamical systems indicate otherwise: Systems possessing huge numbers of dimensions can be abstractly characterized in a low-dimensional space (cf. Abraham & Shaw, 1982; Haken, 1983). Moreover, it is certainly possible, in principle, to characterize the global behavior of a dynamical system using symbolic representations (e.g., Crutchfield & Packard's, 1983, "symbolic dynamics"). Here again, however, the question of the non-arbitrary or privileged coupling between a symbolic representation of the dynamics and the dynamics itself remains.

In this chapter, we try to accomplish three goals, all of which relate to a dynamic perspective on speech production with particular emphasis on its temporal aspects (see also Kelso & Tuller, 1984a, 1984b). First, we review some of our recent research, which reveals that the relative timing among articulatory events is a significant index of the stable performance of the speech motor system across suprasegmental changes in stress and speaking rate. This ubiquity of relative timing, not only in speech production but other activities as well, raises a number of issues about the role of time in biological systems (e.g., conventional questions about how the system meters and monitors time, how duration is controlled, etc.). The whole question of time has been a subject of fascination since the dawn of modern thought. Aristotle is said to have associated time with motion, yet also advocated "a soul which counts" (cf. Prigogine, 1984). In the second main part of the chapter, we argue that the soul that counts (today's temporal program?) can be usefully replaced by a view of time that is intrinsic to a sequence of events, and whose units are defined entirely in terms of the state variables of the system.

Fowler (1977; see also Fowler, Rubin, Remez, & Turvey, 1980) has proposed an intrinsic timing account of speech production that, though appealing, has lacked an empirical methodology for its detailed evaluation. In the third part of the paper, we ground the notion of intrinsic time empirically by recasting our relative timing data into a phase plane description of articulator trajectories, in which time itself does not appear explicitly. In our final remarks we address the advantages—both theoretical and experimental—of this methodology in which intrinsic time is revealed by the geometry of the system's dynamical behavior. This dynamical perspective stresses different observables and motivates a simpler and more elegant account of relative timing in speech production.

2.0 RELATIVE TIMING OF ARTICULATORY GESTURES

Our basic intuition is that it is probably incorrect to assume, as conventional accounts do, that speech timing is based on standard temporal units, such as milliseconds. This intuition is strengthened by well known facts: namely, that the absolute duration of individual electromyographic, kinematic, and acoustic speech events can change dramatically as a function of speaking rate, syllable stress, and phonetic context, among other things, yet the perceptual identity of constituents is preserved (e.g., Fry, 1955, 1958; Lehiste, 1970; Lindblom, 1963). This suggests that time might usefully be measured in relative, rather than absolute, temporal units that are, in a sense, "normalized" to the activity being performed.

The notion that the relative timing of articulatory events provides a more appropriate metric than their absolute durations is mirrored by the importance of relative acoustic durations for perception of speech. For example, the duration of the interval between release of supraglottal occlusion and the onset of glottal pulsing, the so-called voice onset time, is a strong cue to the voicing category of a stop consonant (Lisker & Abramson, 1964). However, perception of the voicing category does not switch when some absolute interval duration of voice onset time is reached. Rather, the category boundary is perceived relative to the overall speech rate (Summerfield, 1975; see also Port, 1979). Similarly, the duration of formant transitions is a strong distinguishing cue between perception of /b/ and /w/ in word initial position (Liberman, Delattre, Gerstman, & Cooper, 1956). But again, the absolute duration of these transitions is less important than the transition duration relative to syllable duration, interpreted as speech rate (Miller & Liberman, 1979).

Other evidence that time is relative in motor control comes from analyses of nonspeech activities in which the timing of individual events appears to be constrained relative to a longer, activity-defined period. This relative temporal stability of muscle activities, or kinematic events, is apparent over scalar changes in rate or force of production that often result in large variations in absolute duration. Although early demonstrations of relative temporal stability were provided from activities that are qualitatively repetitive and potentially pre-wired (e.g., locomotion, respiration, and mastication; see Grillner, 1977, for review), more recent work has revealed that less repetitive activities show the same organizational features (e.g., two-handed movements, typing, handwriting, postural control, and speech-manual coordination; Hollerbach, 1981; Kelso, Southard, & Goodman, 1979a, 1979b; Kelso, Tuller, & Harris, 1983; Lestienne, 1979; Nashner, 1977; Schmidt, 1982; Shapiro, Zernicke, Gregor, & Diestel, 1981; Viviani & Terzuolo, 1980).

In recent papers, we have presented data suggesting that the production of speech can be described by a similar style of organization (Harris, Tuller, &

Kelso, 1986; Tuller & Kelso, 1984; Tuller, Kelso, & Harris, 1982, 1983). This demonstration should be of some interest to neuroscience and neuropathology, because it supports the idea that a single set of organizational principles may underlie very different motor skills, including one as highly symbolic as human speech (e.g., see contributions by Grillner, Evarts, and Granit in Grillner, Lindblom, Lubker, & Persson, 1982; Ostry & Cooke, this volume; Ostry, Keller, & Parush, 1983). The data are also interesting, we believe, because they highlight the importance of a commensurate vocabulary for the symbolic description of an activity, and the activity itself, and offer an activity-sensitive metric for measuring timing in speech production.

In our work on speech production, we varied two suprasegmental aspects of speech that are believed to be particularly important—syllable stress and speaking rate—in an effort to discover underlying articulatory invariance across speech segments. We approached this problem by examining kinematic and acoustic recordings of speakers' productions of two-syllable nonsense utterances embedded in the carrier phrase "It's a _____ again." The utterances under discussion here were /ba#Cab/, and /bæ#Cab/, where the medial C was from the set /b, p, w/. Half of the tokens were produced with primary stress placed on the first syllable and half were produced with primary stress on the second syllable. Twelve repetitions of each utterance were produced at each of the two stress patterns and at two self-selected speaking rates, conversational and somewhat faster.

Kinematics of articulatory movements were monitored in the up-down direction using an optical tracking system that followed the movement of lightweight, infrared, light-emitting diodes (LEDs) attached to the subject's lips, jaw, and nose. In order to minimize head movements during the experiment, output of the LED on the nose was displayed on an oscilloscope placed directly in front of the subject, who was told to keep the display on the zero line. The movement records were recorded on multichannel FM tape for later computer analysis. For each token, displacement maxima and minima (corrected for head movements) and the times at which they occur, were obtained individually for the jaw, the upper lip, and the lower lip.

The spatiotemporal coordination among articulator events was analyzed to determine whether stable relative timing of kinematic events is characteristic of speech. This analysis requires demarcation of some period of articulatory activity and the latency of an articulatory event within the defined period. Although we examined relative timing of nine different articulatory events, linguistic evidence suggests that temporal stability among phonetic segments will be defined relative to the period between successive vowels. For example, when short silent intervals are inserted into a sentence, listeners notice the insertions only when they disrupt the relative timing of the stressed vowels (Huggins, 1972). Here we discuss only the timing of consonant production relative to the interval between flanking vowels, by far the most stable of our measures. Over linguistic variations, in this case stress and rate, these intervals change in their absolute durations. The question is whether they change in a systematically related manner.

Figure 8.1, taken from Tuller and Kelso (1984), shows one subject's data for production of the utterances /babab/, /bapab/, and /bawab/. The data were similar for all four subjects. The x-axis represents the interval (in ms) from the onset of jaw lowering for the first vowel to the onset of jaw lowering for the second vowel. The y-axis is the interval from the onset of jaw lowering for the first vowel to the onset of upper lip lowering for the medial labial consonant. In this figure, the jaw component has been subtracted from the lower lip movement. Each point on the graph is one token of an utterance type. A Pearson product-moment correlation was calculated for each distribution. The high correlations obtained (.97, .97, and .89) signify that the relative timing of these articulatory events was maintained over the large variation apparent in their absolute durations. For utterances with / æ / as the first vowel, we find the same results as for the utterances displayed in Fig. 8.1; the temporal changes are highly correlated ($r = .90$, .89, and .84, for medial consonants b, p, and w, respectively).

Although Fig. 8.1 illustrates the data from only a single subject, the three other subjects showed essentially the same pattern. Values obtained for the other subjects by correlating the period between the onsets of successive vowel articulation ranged from .84 to .97 whether the onset of consonant articulation was defined by the raising gesture of the lower lip or by the lowering gesture of the upper lip. In all cases, the calculated correlation was significantly higher ($ps < .05$) than what would be expected solely on the basis of changes in vowel duration or part-whole correlations (cf. Barry, 1983; Munhall, 1985; Tuller & Kelso, 1984; Tuller, Kelso, & Harris, 1983). Note, however, that the relationship is not ratiomorphic—lip latency varies systematically with jaw cycle deviation, plus some intercept value that changes with speaker and phonetic context. This basic description has recently been replicated and extended to tongue gestures produced by English speakers (Harris et al., 1986; Munhall, 1985), and lip and jaw gestures produced by speakers of French and Swedish (Gentil, Harris, Horiguchi, & Honda, 1984; Lubker, 1983; see also Linville, 1982). Let us underscore again that this strong relationship holds even though other aspects of the movements, such as their displacement, velocity, and absolute duration, change substantially. For example (in agreement with the acoustic/phonetic literature), the production of destressed syllables shows smaller displacement, lower velocity, and shorter duration movements than the same phonetic segment spoken with primary stress (e.g., Harris, 1971, 1978; Kent & Netsell, 1971; Lindblom, 1963; MacNeilage, Hanson, & Krones, 1970; Mermelstein, 1973; Stone, 1981; Sussman & MacNeilage, 1978; Tuller, Harris, & Kelso, 1982).

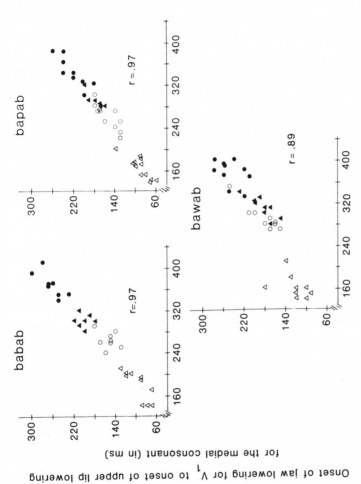

FIG. 8.1. Timing of upper lip lowering for medial consonant articulation as a function of the vowel-to-vowel period for one subject's productions of the indicated utterances. Each point represents a single token of the utterance. (•) primary stress on the first syllable, spoken at a conversational rate; (○) primary stress on the second syllable, spoken at a conversational rate; (△) primary stress on the first syllable, spoken at a faster rate; (▲) primary stress on the second syllable, spoken at a faster rate (from Tuller & Kelso, 1984).

209

These relative timing results indicate, we believe, a functional constraint on movement—a coordinative structure (cf. Easton, 1972; Fowler, 1977; Kelso et al., 1979a, 1979b; Turvey, 1977) or unit of action (cf. Ghiselin, 1981)—in which a system possessing a large number of potential degrees of freedom is compressed into one that requires few control decisions (Bernstein, 1967). During a movement, the timing of individual elements is constrained within a particular relationship. Flexibility can then be attained by adjusting control parameters over the total unit.

3.0   INTRINSIC VERSUS CONVENTIONAL METRICS FOR THE ANALYSIS OF TIMING

The ubiquity of stable relative timing in so many different types of activities, including speech production, raises a number of fundamental questions about the underlying basis of timing regularity in biological systems. For example, is the duration of each articulatory movement controlled directly via an extrinsically-imposed timing program, or is the duration of an articulator's movement a consequence of some other parameter, as yet unspecified? If not controlled by an extrinsic clock, what is the informational basis for the observed temporal stability? How, in a complex system of articulators, does a given articulator "know" when it should be activated in relation to other active articulators? With respect to our relative timing data, for example, what information is needed for the upper lip (a remote, non-mechanically linked articulator) to move in appropriate temporal relation to the jaw? Although an intrinsic timing theory of speech production has been proposed (Fowler, 1980), a generalized methodology for evaluating "intrinsic time" has yet to be offered. Before proposing such a methodology and applying it to experimental data, let us first clarify the basic notion of intrinsic time (cf. Richardson & Rosen, 1979).

Although it is convenient to measure time intervals between events as durations, this is purely a convention, because, it can be argued and shown, time itself has no unique dimension. A few examples will clarify what we mean. Consider a primitive clock, such as a candle. Time in this case corresponds to a change in a spatial variable, namely, the length of the candle that is burned. The units of time intrinsic to this particular dynamical system are inches. Similarly, in a water clock, the unit of time corresponds to number of drops. We see very quickly from these simple but intuitive examples that time itself is not, strictly speaking, a fundamental observable; rather, it is intrinsically determined by the particular system involved. Thus, paraphrasing Richardson and Rosen (1979), time is demarcated by defining some state variable appearing in the events; it is intrinsic to that sequence, that is, to a dynamical process, and takes its units from the system's state variables. This kind of intrinsic time is quite different from conventional time, which is imposed on a system regardless of its particular dynamics. Conventional or mechanical time (measured in seconds, hours, etc.) plays a role when it is necessary to determine the relationship between the intrinsic times of two devices whose dynamic parameters are very different. In such cases, a standard is introduced. For example, 1/86,400 of the earth's rotation is, by convention, called a second. Again, according to convention, all harmonic oscillators are calibrated in terms of seconds, not in terms of an event that is intrinsic to all harmonic oscillators, namely, the cycle.

We want to stress that calibration and convention, though important, are not the central issues of concern here. Our aim, rather, is to define an intrinsic metric in terms of the dynamical behavior of a biological system, in this case that of speech production. The examples of the candle and the clock indicate how a given system can generate its own intrinsic time entirely according to its constitutive parameters. We recently came across similar sentiments expressed in a rather different context, namely irreversible thermodynamics and nonequilibrium physics. There, Prigogine (1984) uses the concept of internal time. In Prigogine's words, "to grasp the intuitive meaning of internal time, think about a drop of ink in a glass of water. The *form* the drop takes gives us an idea of the interval of time that has elapsed." (p. 6; italics added). And later: "The internal time T is quite different from the usual mechanical time, since it depends on the global topology of the system" (p. 7). The drop of ink, the candle, and the water clock do not possess any knowledge of their own dynamics, nor do these systems contain an explicit representation of time. Time evolves from the "playing out" of the dynamics, but there is no programming, time control, or time representation anywhere (see also Kelso & Holt, 1980; Kelso, Tuller, & Harris, 1986; Kelso, V.-Bateson, Saltzman, & Kay, 1985). These terms are simply not descriptions appropriate to the concept of intrinsic time.

4.0 GROUNDING INTRINSIC TIME IN THE GEOMETRY OF THE SPEECH SYSTEM'S DYNAMICS

Let us now follow through with the claim that the notion of intrinsic time is open to measurement and evaluation. This requires that we characterize articulator motion in terms of certain state variables (see Section 3.0). To do this, we introduce a phase portrait methodology developed originally by Poincaré and Liapounov for many-body problems in dynamics, and employed by us and others for analyses of movements (e.g., Kelso et al., 1985). The phase portrait captures the forms of motion (a purely geometric/kinematic description) produced by an underlying dynamic organization (cf. Abraham & Shaw, 1982). But first let us consider the standard representation of our speech timing data (see Section 2.0).

Consider the simple case we have described in which the latency (in ms) of onset of lower lip motion for a medial consonant is measured relative to the interval (in ms) between onsets of jaw motion for flanking vowels. As we have shown, the two events are highly correlated across rate and stress in different speakers. Although this strictly temporal description has been useful, it does not necessarily imply that the speech motor control system is keeping track of the duration of articulator motions. In contrast, preliminary work suggests that the data can be understood without recourse to an extrinsic timer or timing metric (more extensive analyses are currently underway). Here we describe in general terms how, using a phase portrait description of articulator trajectories on the phase plane, a very different view of articulator "timing" emerges (see also Kelso et al., 1986).

The phase plane is the space of all possible states of the system, in the plane whose axes are the articulator's position (x) and its velocity ($\dot{x}$). The position and velocity values act as coordinates of a point on the articulator in two dimensional space. As time varies, the point P ($x,\dot{x}$) describing the motion of the articulator moves along a certain path on the phase plane.

Figure 8.2 illustrates the mapping from time domain to phase plane trajectories. Hypothetical jaw and upper lip trajectories (position as a function of time) are shown for an unstressed /bab/ (Fig. 8.2a, left) and a stressed /bab/ (Fig. 8.2b, left). On the right are shown the corresponding phase plane trajectories. In this figure and those following we have reversed the typical orientation of the phase plane so that position is shown on the vertical axis and velocity on the horizontal axis. Thus, downward movements of the jaw are displayed as downward movements of the phase path. The vertical crosshair indicates zero velocity and the horizontal crosshair indicates zero position (midway between minimum and maximum displacement). As the jaw moves from its highest to its lowest point (from A to C in Fig. 8.2), velocity increases (negatively) to a local maximum (B) then decreases to zero when the jaw changes direction of movement (C). Similarly, as the jaw is raised from the low vowel /a/ into the following consonant constriction, velocity peaks approximately midway through the gesture (D) then returns to zero (A).

Note that time, although implicit and usually recoverable from the phase plane description, does not appear explicitly. For different initial conditions (such as starting position or the level of articulator stiffness) there will be different corresponding paths, and the totality of all possible trajectories constitutes the full phase portrait of the system's dynamic behavior. It is useful to transform the Cartesian $x,\dot{x}$ coordinates into equivalent polar coordinates, namely, a phase angle, $\phi = \tan^{-1}[\dot{x}/x]$, and a radial amplitude, $R = [x^2 + \dot{x}^2]^{1/2}$. These polar coordinates are indicated on the phase planes shown in Fig. 8.2. The phase angle will be a key concept in our re-analysis of interarticulator timing because it signifies position on a cycle of states (cf. Abraham & Shaw, 1982; Garfinkel, 1983).

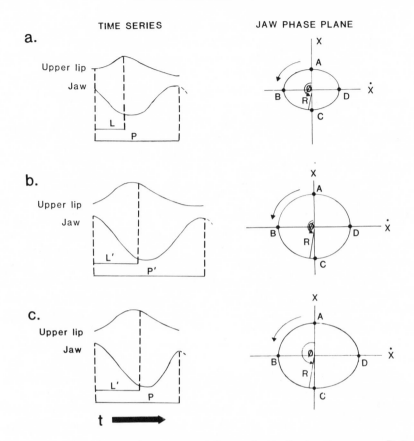

FIG. 8.2. Left: Time series representations of idealized utterances. Right: Corresponding jaw motions, characterized as a simple mass spring and displayed on the 'functional' phase plane (i.e., position on the vertical axis and velocity on the horizontal axis). Parts a, b, and c, represent three tokens with vowel-to-vowel periods (P and P′) and consonant latencies (L and L′) that are not linearly related. Phase position of upper lip movement onset relative to the jaw cycle is indicated (see text).

The phase plane trajectory preserves some important differences between stressed and unstressed syllables. For example, maximum lowering of the jaw for the stressed vowel is greater than lowering for the unstressed vowel and maximum articulator velocity differs noticeable between these two orbits (e.g., Kelso et al., 1985; MacNeilage et al., 1970; Stone, 1981; Tuller, Harris, & Kelso, 1982). In contrast, the different durations taken to traverse the orbit as a function of stress are not represented in this description. To reiterate, a crucial point about this description is that duration does not appear explicitly. Jaw cycles of different durations are still characterized as a single orbit on the plane, i.e., they are topologically the same.

Now we can rephrase the question of how the lip "knows" when to begin its movement for the medial consonant by asking where on the cycle of jaw phase angles the lip motion for medial consonant production begins. One possibility is that lip motion begins at the same phase angle of the jaw across different jaw motion orbits (i.e., across rate and stress). This outcome is not necessarily entailed, or predicted by, the relative timing results. For example, Fig. 8.2a through 8.2c shows three utterances whose vowel-to-vowel periods and consonant latencies do not change in a linearly related fashion. Nevertheless, the phase angle at which upper lip motion begins relative to the cycle of jaw states is identical in the three cases. Thus, the information for "timing" of a remote articulator (e.g., the upper lip) may not be time itself, nor absolute position of another articulator (e.g., the jaw), but rather a relationship defined over the position-velocity state (or, in polar coordinates, the phase angle) of the other articulator. Although this conceptualization is intriguing, we want to re-emphasize that it constitutes an alternative description of the relative timing data set. For example, Fig. 8.3 illustrates the converse of Fig. 8.2, namely, that two (hypothetical) utterances with identical vowel-to-vowel periods (P) and consonant latencies (L) can nonetheless show very different phase positions for upper lip movement onset. To be specific, the phase angle analysis incorporates the full trajectory of motion; the relative timing analysis is independent of trajectory once movement has begun and is based only on the onsets and offsets of events.

We also want to emphasize that the jaw motion need not be perfectly sinusoidal in order to apply a phase angle analysis. In fact, the motions actually observed are usually not sinusoidal; position at zero velocity is affected by the stress and rate characteristics of the surrounding vowels (see Fig. 8.2 and 8.4). For this reason, each jaw cycle is normalized by determining the minimum and maximum jaw positions for the consonant-vowel gesture. The midpoint between them is used as the best approximation of the equilibrium or zero position for that syllable. Similarly, jaw velocity (from zero to peak lowering velocity) is normalized for each cycle.

Figure 8.4 shows jaw motion on the phase plane for the first syllable of /'ba#bab/ (top) and /ba#'bab/ (bottom) produced at a fast rate. Each token shown is the first instance produced of the utterance type. On the left is the entire jaw cycle for each stress pattern; on the right, the jaw cycle is reproduced only until the point of onset of upper lip movement downward for production of the medial bilabial consonant, as measured from the first deviation from zero velocity. The calculated phase position at which upper lip motion begins is indicated for each token. Notice that the jaw displacement and velocity are both greater for the stressed than the unstressed syllable. Nevertheless, upper lip motion begins at essentially the same phase angle for both tokens. If upper lip motion began at a phase angle of 180°, it would be synchronous with the jaw "turnaround" point.

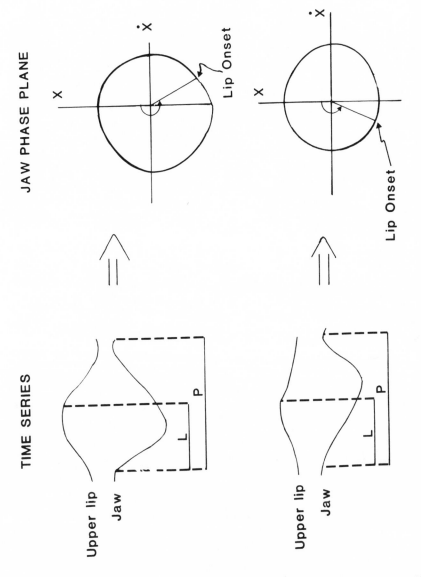

FIG. 8.3. Two hypothetical utterances having identical vowel-to-vowel periods (P) and consonant (upper lip) latencies (L) but different phase angles of upper lip onset (see caption Fig. 8.2).

215

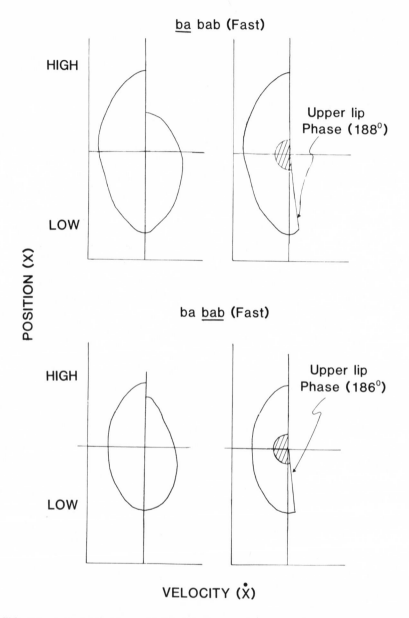

FIG. 8.4. Left: Jaw cycle on the phase plane for the first token produced of stressed /bab/ (top) and unstressed /bab/ (bottom), spoken at a fast rate. Right: Jaw cycle until the onset of upper lip lowering for the second /b/.

Figure 8.5 shows the mean data and the standard error of the mean from the same speaker whose relative timing data were shown in Fig. 8.1. The phase angle subtended, in degrees, is shown on the y-axis; stress-rate condition on the x-axis. A 2 × 2 ANOVA for each utterance type showed no significant main effects or interactions on the phase angle of upper lip onset

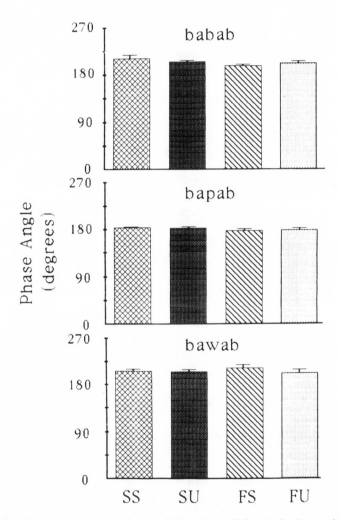

FIG. 8.5. Mean phase angles of upper lip lowering relative to the jaw cycle for one subject's productions of /ba#bab/. Standard error of the mean is also shown. SS: slow, first syllable stressed; SU: slow, first syllable unstressed; FS: fast, first syllable stressed; FU: fast, first syllable unstressed.

for medial consonant production. For /babab/ Fs $(1,27)$ = 2.50, 0.03, and 1.85; for /bapab/ Fs $(1,30)$ - 2.39, 0.01, and 0.10; for /bawab/, Fs $(1,29)$ = 0.06, 1.16, and 0.61. F-ratios are for rate, stress, and their interaction respectively, $ps > .5$[2].

There are at least two empirical advantages of this result over our relative timing description. First, in the relative timing analysis, the overall correlations across rate and stress conditions are very high, but the within-condition slopes tend to vary somewhat. In the phase analysis, on the other hand, the mean phase angle is the same across conditions. Second, remember that the relative timing scenario was described by two parameters, a slope and an intercept. The phase description requires only a single parameter. Thus, if nothing else, the phase description is to be preferred on grounds of parsimony.

The phase conceptualization also has a number of theoretical advantages over our original relative timing analysis. First, once articulatory motions are represented geometrically on the phase plane, duration is normalized across speaker, stress, speaking rate, etc. Strictly speaking, the system's topology is unaffected by durational changes. For example, the "down-up" cycle of the phase plane description is independent of the duration required for the gesture. This potentially provides a grounding for so-called intrinsic timing theories of speech production (e.g., Fowler, 1980; Fowler et al., 1980). Second, neither absolute nor relative durations have to be extrinsically monitored or controlled in this formulation. There is no need to posit any kind of time-keeping mechanism or time controller. As an aside, it has never been clear how the speech system could keep track of time, at least peripherally, because there is no known afferent basis (such as time receptors) for time-keeping in the articulatory structures themselves (Kelso, 1978). On the other hand, an informational basis (e.g., in position and velocity sensitivities of muscle spindle and joint structures) is a physiological given in the phase angle characterization. It might well be the case that certain critical phase angles provide information for coordination between articulators (beyond those considered here) and/or vocal tract configurations, just as phase angles of the leg joints provide coupling information for locomotory coordination (Shik & Orlovskii, 1965). Thus, the temporal orchestration of articulatory events in the speech motor system unfolds as a consequence of its dynamic parameters. By extension, it seems unlikely that the symbol structure for speech production includes a specification of durational rules defined in conventional mechanical time. As in a candle and a watch, time is not a possessed, programmed, or represented property of the speech production system.

---

[2] Subsequent analyses showed identical results for three additional speakers. These data are reported in detail in Kelso, Saltzman, and Tuller (in press).

ACKNOWLEDGMENTS

The research referred to here was supported by National Institutes of Neurological Communicative Diseases and Strokes Grants NS-17778 and RR-05396 to Cornell University Medical College, NS-13617 to Haskins Laboratories, and by a grant from the Ariel and Benjamin Lowin Medical Research Foundation, directed through the Stuttering Center, Department of Neurology, Baylor College of Medicine. The first author was also supported by U. S. Office of Naval Research Contract No. N0014-83-K-00. Elliot Saltzman gave us extremely helpful comments on this paper, for which we are grateful.

REFERENCES

Abraham, R. H., & Shaw, C. D. (1982). *Dynamics—The geometry of behavior.* Santa Cruz, CA: Aerial Press.

Barry, W. J. (1983). Some problems of interarticulator phasing as an index of temporal regularity in speech. *Journal of Experimental Psychology: Human Perception and Performance, 9,* 826–828.

Bernstein, N. A. (1967). *The coordination and regulation of movements.* London: Pergamon Press.

Crutchfield, J. P., & Packard, N. H. (1983). Symbolic dynamics of noisy chaos. *Physica, 7D,* 201–223.

Easton, T. A. (1972). On the normal use of reflexes. *American Scientist, 60,* 591–599.

Fowler, C. (1977). *Timing control in speech production.* Bloomington, IN: Indiana University Linguistics Club.

Fowler, C. A. (1980). Coarticulation and theories of extrinsic timing control. *Journal of Phonetics, 8,* 113–133.

Fowler, C. A., Rubin, P., Remez, R. E., & Turvey, M. T. (1980). Implications for speech production of a general theory of action. In B. Butterworth (Ed.), *Language production* (pp. 373–420). New York: Academic Press.

Fry, D. B. (1955). Duration and intensity as physical correlates of linguistic stress. *Journal of the Acoustical Society for America, 27,* 765–768.

Fry, D. B. (1958). Experiments in the perception of stress. *Language and Speech, 1,* 126–152.

Garfinkel, A. (1983). A mathematics for physiology. *American Journal of Physiology: Regulatory, Integrative, and Comparative, 14,* R455–R466.

Gentil, M., Harris, K. S., Horiguchi, S., & Honda, K. (1984). Temporal organization of muscle activity in simple disyllables. *Journal of the Acoustical Society of America, 75,* S23. (Abstract)

Ghiselin, M. T. (1981). Categories, life, and thinking. *The Behavioral and Brain Sciences, 4,* 269–313.

Grillner, S. (1977). On the neural control of movement—A comparison of different basic rhythmic behaviors. In G. S. Stent (Ed.), *Function and formation of neural systems* (pp. 197–224). (Life Sciences Research Reports, Vol. 6). Berlin: Dahlem.

Grillner, S., Lindblom, B., Lubker, J., & Persson, A. (Eds.). (1982). *Speech motor control.* Oxford: Pergamon Press.

Haken, H. (1983). *Synergetics.* Heidelberg: Springer-Verlag.

Harris, K. S. (1971). Vowel stress and articulatory reorganization. *Haskins Laboratories Status Report on Speech Research, SR-28,* 167–178.

Harris, K. S. (1978). Vowel duration change and its underlying physiological mechanisms. *Language and Speech, 21,* 354-361.

Harris, K. S., Tuller, B., & Kelso, J. A. S. (1986). Temporal Invariance in the production of speech. In J. S. Perkell & D. H. Klatt (Eds.), *Invariance and variability in speech processes.* Hillsdale, NJ: Lawrence Erlbaum Associates.

Hollerbach, J. (1981). An oscillator theory of handwriting. *Biological Cybernetics, 39,* 139-156.

Huggins, A. W. F. (1972). On the perception of temporal phenomena in speech. *Journal of the Acoustical Society of America, 51,* 1279-1290.

Kelso, J. A. S. (1978). Joint receptors do not provide a satisfactory basis for motor timing and positioning. *Psychological Review, 85,* 474-481.

Kelso, J. A. S. (1981). Contrasting perspectives on order and regulation in movement. In J. Long & A. Baddeley (Eds.), *Attention and performance, IX* (pp. 437-458). Hillsdale: NJ: Lawrence Erlbaum Associates.

Kelso, J. A. S., & Holt, K. G. (1980). Exploring a vibratory systems analysis of human movement production. *Journal of Neurophysiology, 43,* 1183-1196.

Kelso, J. A. S., Saltzman, E. L., & Tuller, B. (in press). The dynamical perspective on speech production: data and theory. *Journal of Phonetics.*

Kelso, J. A. S., Southard, D. L., & Goodman, D. (1979a). On the nature of human interlimb coordination. *Science, 203,* 1029-1031.

Kelso, J. A. S., Southard, D. L., & Goodman, D. (1979b). On the coordination of two-handed movements. *Journal of Experimental Psychology: Human Perception and Performance, 5,* 229-238.

Kelso, J. A. S., & Tuller, B. (1984a). Converging sources of evidence for common dynamical principles in speech and limb coordination. *American Journal of Physiology: Regulatory, Integrative, and Comparative, 246,* R928-R935.

Kelso, J. A. S., & Tuller, B. (1984b). A dynamical basis for action systems. In M. S. Gazzaniga (Ed.), *Handbook of cognitive neuroscience* (pp. 321-356). New York: Plenum.

Kelso, J. A. S., Tuller, B., & Harris, K. S. (1983). A "dynamic pattern" perspective on the control and coordination of movement. In P. MacNeilage (Ed.), *The production of speech* (pp. 138-173). New York: Springer-Verlag.

Kelso, J. A. S., Tuller, B., & Harris, K. S. (1986). A theoretical note on speech timing. In J. S. Perkell & D. H. Klatt (Eds.), *Invariance and variability in speech processes.* Hillsdale, NJ: Lawrence Erlbaum Associates.

Kelso, J. A. S., V.-Bateson, E., Saltzman, E. L., & Kay, B. (1985). A qualitative dynamic analysis of reiterant speech production: Phase portraits, kinematics, and dynamic modeling. *Journal of the Acoustical Society of America, 7,* 266-280.

Kent, R. D., & Netsell, R. (1971). Effects of stress contrasts on certain articulatory parameters. *Phonetica, 24,* 23-44.

Kozhevnikov, V. A., & Chistovich, L. A. (1966). *Rech, Artikulyatsiya, i vospriyatiye, [Speech: Articulation and perception]* (*30,* p. 543). Washington, DC: Joint Publications Research Service. (Originally published 1965)

Kugler, P. N., Kelso, J. A. S., & Turvey, M. T. (1980). On the concept of coordinative structures as dissipative structures: I. Theoretical lines of convergence. In G. E. Stelmach & J. Requin (Eds.), *Tutorials in motor behavior* (pp. 3-47). New York: North-Holland.

Kugler, P. N., Kelso, J. A. S., & Turvey, M. T. (1982). On the control and coordination of naturally developing systems. In J. A. S. Kelso & J. E. Clark (Eds.), *The development of movement control and coordination* (pp. 5-78). Chichester: Wiley.

Lehiste, I. (1970). *Suprasegmentals.* Cambridge, MA: MIT Press.

Lestienne, F. (1979). Effects of inertial load and velocity on the braking process of voluntary limb movements. *Experimental Brain Research, 35,* 407-418.

Liberman, A. M., Delattre, P. C., Gerstman, L. C., & Cooper, F. S. (1956). Tempo of frequency change as a cue for distinguishing classes of speech sounds. *Journal of Experimental Psychology, 52,* 127–137.

Lindblom, B. (1963). Spectrographic study of vowel reduction. *Journal of the Acoustical Society of America, 35,* 1773–1781.

Lindblom, B. (1983a). Economy of speech gestures. In P. F. MacNeilage (Ed.), *The production of speech* (pp. 217–245). New York: Springer-Verlag.

Lindblom, B. (in press). Phonetic universals in vowel systems. In J. Ohala (Ed.), *Experimental phonology.* New York: Academic Press.

Lindblom, B., MacNeilage, P., & Studdert-Kennedy, M. (1983). Self-organizing processes and the explanation of phonological universals. In B. Butterworth, B. Comrie, & O. Dahl (Eds.), *Universals workshop* (pp. 182–203). The Hague: Mouton.

Linville, R. (1982). *Temporal aspects of articulation: Some implications for speech motor control of stereotyped productions.* Unpublished doctoral dissertation, University of Iowa.

Lisker, L., & Abramson, A. (1964). A cross-language study of voicing in initial stops: Acoustical measurements. *Word, 20,* 384–422.

Lubker, J. (1983, October). *Comment on "Temporal invariance in the production of speech," By Harris, Tuller, and Kelso.* Paper presented at Conference on invariance and variability in speech processes, MIT, Cambridge, MA.

MacNeilage, P. F., Hanson, R., & Krones, R. (1970). Control of the jaw in relation to stress in English. *Journal of the Acoustical Society of America, 48,* 120. (Abstract)

Maxwell (1952). *Matter and motion.* New York: Dover Books. (Originally published 1877)

Mermelstein, P. (1973). Some articulatory manifestations of vowel stress. *Journal of the Acoustical Society of America, 54,* 538 (L).

Miller, J. L., & Liberman, A. M. (1979). Some effects of later-occurring information on the perception of stop consonant and semivowel. *Perception & Psychophysics, 25,* 457–465.

Munhall, K. (1985). An examination of intra-articulator relative timing. *Journal of the Acoustical Society of America, 78,* 1548–1553.

Nashner, L. M. (1977). Fixed patterns of rapid postural responses among leg muscles during stance. *Experimental Brain Research, 30,* 13–24.

Ostry, D. J., Keller, E., & Parush, A. (1983). Similarities in the control of the speech articulators and the limbs: Kinematics of tongue dorsum movement in speech. *Journal of Experimental Psychology: Human Perception and Performance, 9,* 622–636.

Pattee, H. H. (1977). Dynamic and linguistic modes of complex systems. *International Journal of Generative Systems, 3,* 259–266.

Port, R. F. (1979). The influence of tempo on stop closure duration as a cue for voicing and place. *Journal of Phonetics, 7,* 45–56.

Prigogine, I. (1984). Irreversibility and space-time structure. In W. Horsthemke & D. K. Kondepudi (Eds.), *Fluctuations and sensitivity in nonequilibrium systems* (pp. 1–11). Berlin: Springer-Verlag.

Reed, E. S. (1981). *Indirect action.* Unpublished manuscript, University of Minnesota, Center for Research in Human Learning.

Richardson, I. W., & Rosen, R. (1979). Aging and the metrics of time. *Journal of Theoretical Biology, 79,* 415–423.

Schmidt, R. A. (1982). *Motor control and learning: A behavioral emphasis.* Champaign, IL: Human Kinetics.

Shapiro, D. C., Zernicke, R. F., Gregor, R. J., & Diestel, J. D. (1981). Evidence for generalized motor programs using gait pattern analysis. *Journal of Motor Behavior, 13,* 33–47.

Shik, M. L., & Orlovskii, G. N. (1965). Coordination of the limbs during running of the dog. *Biophysics, 10,* 1148–1159.

Stone, M. (1981). Evidence for a rhythm pattern in speech production: Observations of jaw movement. *Journal of Phonetics, 9,* 109–120.

Summerfield, Q. (1975). *Information processing analyses of perceptual adjustments to source and context variables in speech.* Unpublished doctoral dissertation, Queen's University of Belfast.

Sussman, H. M., & MacNeilage, P. F. (1978). Motor unit correlates of stress: Preliminary observations. *Journal of the Acoustical Society of America, 64,* 338.

Tuller, B., Harris, K. S., & Kelso, J. A. S. (1982). Stress and rate: Differential transformations of articulation. *Journal of the Acoustical Society of America, 71,* 1534–1543.

Tuller, B., & Kelso, J. A. S. (1984). The timing of articulatory gestures: Evidence for relational invariants. *Journal of the Acoustical Society of America, 76,* 1030–1035.

Tuller, B., Kelso, J. A. S., & Harris, K. S. (1982). Interarticulator phasing as an index of temporal regularity in speech. *Journal of Experimental Psychology: Human Perception and Performance, 8,* 460–472.

Tuller, B., Kelso, J. A. S., & Harris, K. S. (1983). Further evidence for the role of relative timing in speech. *Journal of Experimental Psychology: Human Perception and Performance, 9,* 829–833.

Turvey, M. T. (1977). Preliminaries to a theory of action with reference to vision. In R. Shaw & J. Bransford (Eds.), *Perceiving, acting and knowing: Toward an ecological psychology* (pp. 211–266). Hillsdale, NJ: Lawrence Erlbaum Associates.

Turvey, M. T., & Kugler, P. N. (1984). A comment on equating information with symbol strings. *American Journal of Physiology, 246,* R925–R927.

Viviani, P., & Terzuolo, V. (1980). Space-time invariance in learned motor skills. In G. E. Stelmach & J. Requin (Eds.), *Tutorials in motor behavior* (pp. 525–536). Amsterdam: North-Holland.

9 Kinematic Patterns in Speech and Limb Movements

David J. Ostry
McGill University
J. David Cooke
University of Western Ontario

ABSTRACT

The issue of the uniqueness of the human speech system has long been a concern in psychological research. In this chapter, we have addressed an aspect of this problem by comparing findings on the motor organization of speech with the organization of voluntary movements about the elbow. We have concentrated on the kinematic regularities that accompany changes in the duration of movements. We found that the kinematic patterns for movements of the tongue dorsum were similar to those of voluntary flexion-extension movements about the elbow. In both speech and arm movements a single function described changes in movement duration. Specifically, decreases in duration were accompanied by systematic increases in the ratio of maximum velocity to movement amplitude. The existence of this single function which accommodates a wide range of changes in the duration of individual movements is consistent with the view that both in speech and limb movements, kinematic profiles are equivalent under scalar transformation.

In recent years, evidence on several aspects of the relationship between speech motor control and the control of voluntary movements of the limbs has become available. The evidence points to similarities in speech and limb systems in their inter-articulator timing patterns with changes in rate (Tuller, Kelso, & Harris, 1982), in their response to suddenly applied perturbations during movement (Folkins & Abbs, 1975), and in their basic kinematic characteristics (Ostry, Keller, & Parush, 1983). To date, the comparisons have been based on relationships between measured patterns of speech articulators and known characteristics of human limb movements. However, comparisons between speech and limb systems have yet to be combined in a single study. Because the issue of similarities as well as differences in the control of the speech articulators and the limbs is significant in determining the basic mechanisms of human motor control, it is important to carry out directly equivalent studies in the two systems.

In this chapter, we report some of our initial findings of kinematic regularities that accompany changes in duration in both limb and speech movement. Our findings are based on kinematic analyses of tongue dorsum movements in speech and of rapid flexion and extension movements about the elbow. The speech study involved the manipulation of rate, stress, vowel and consonant; the limb study examined differences in rate and movement amplitude. Although kinematic information alone is equivocal with respect to the underlying mechanisms of control, the presence of detailed kinematic similarities between speech and limb systems places significant constraints on the basic mechanisms of human movement production. Our data suggests that in both speech and limb systems, a wide range of changes in the duration of movements can be accommodated by a single function, suggesting that the nervous system produces durational changes in an equivalent fashion in both motor activities.

SPEECH METHODS

We obtained kinematic measurements of tongue dorsum movements during the production of alternately stressed consonant–vowel sequences that were rhythmical in form. The data were collected by using a computerized, pulsed ultrasound system which is described in detail elsewhere (Keller & Ostry, 1983; Ostry et al., 1983). The ultrasound transducer, which enabled the monitoring of tongue dorsum movement, was placed below the chin along the mid-line of the mandible just anterior to the hyoid bone. The transducer was positioned in an orientation that was approximately perpendicular to the Frankfort horizontal and thus to the hard palate. Final placement of the transducer was determined such that the measured distance was maximized between the position for the velar consonant k and the back vowel a and at the same time the order of back vowel heights a, o, u was preserved in the tongue dorsum measurement. Keller & Ostry (1983) report that although optimal placements differ between subjects it is possible to satisfy both criteria within about four degrees of the perpendicular to the Frankfort horizontal.

Subjects in our study produced alternately stressed consonant-vowel sequences involving velar stop consonants k and g and back vowels a and o. The sequences were produced either at a normal or a fast speech rate (Fig. 9.1). The utterances were produced in a randomized order with 35 tongue dorsum lowering movements and an equal number of tongue dorsum raising

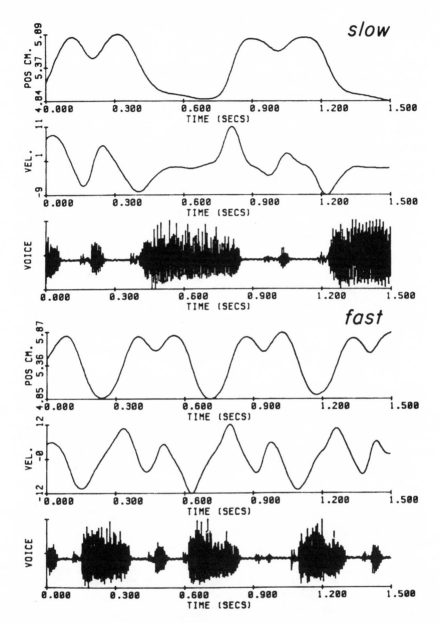

FIG. 9.1 Ultrasound record of the position and velocity of the tongue dorsum for a single subject during the production of alternately stressed consonant-vowel sequences involving the velar stop-consonant *k* and the back vowel *a*. The upper trace gives the position of the tongue dorsum over time; the numerical values indicate the distance in cm from the crystal of the ultrasound transducer to the dorsum of the tongue. The tongue is at oral closure for values at the top of the record and at the open position for the back vowel for values at the bottom. The middle panel shows the instantaneous velocity of tongue dorsum raising movements (positive values) and tongue dorsum lowering movements (negative values). The lower panel shows the corresponding raw acoustic signal. Both fast and slow speech rates are given.

225

movements obtained in each condition. Individual utterance tokens were measured to provide estimates of movement amplitude, movement maximum-velocity, and movement duration. In Fig. 9.1, examples of both fast and slow speech rates are given. In each condition, the position of the tongue dorsum over time is shown in the upper panel. The upper peaks of the position record show the tongue dorsum at oral closure for the stop consonant, while the lower values indicate the position of the tongue dorsum for the back vowel. Instantaneous velocities are shown in the middle tracing with raising velocities shown as positive values and lowering velocities as negative. A recording of the acoustic channel is given in the bottom panel. The data shown in Fig. 9.1 and the speech data described in the following sections were obtained at a 1 kHz sampling rate and then low-pass filtered using natural cubic spline functions to give a bandwidth of approximately 20 Hz (see Keller & Ostry, 1983 for a discussion of obtaining an optimal spline fit for data of this type).

ARM MOVEMENT METHODS

Kinematic measurements were obtained from movements about the right elbow, made in response to step changes in a visual target (see Thomas, Croft, & Brooks, 1976, for a detailed description of the system). Subjects were seated and held in their right hand a vertical rod attached to a manipulandum handle. The arm was supported just distal to the elbow and moved freedly about a pivot point in a horizontal plane. The target was a narrow veritical bar displayed on a video monitor placed immediately in front of the subject. A vertical cursor indicated the angular position of the arm that was being moved.

During the experiment, subjects made a series of step tracking movements that involved alternate flexion and extension movements about the elbow. The target shifted position once every three seconds, and the subject was instructed to move the handle at difference speeds in order to realign the cursor and the target within a specified time. Subjects were required to make movements of two different amplitudes (76 degrees and 39 degrees) at each of six different movement durations (200, 300, 400, 500, 700, ·and 900 msec). The trials were blocked by movement amplitude and duration; subjects produced 20 flexion and 20 extension movements for each of the 12 amplitude × movement duration combinations. In each condition a number of practice trials preceded the actual recording of kinematic data. During these trials, the experimenter gave feedback to the subject concerning the duration of the movement. Data recording began when the subject was able to consistently produce both flexion and extension movements at the specified duration. During the course of the recording trials, the subject was occasionally told to speed up or slow down in order to maintain the desired speed in each condition. The arm movement data presented here were all obtained at a 100 Hz sampling rate.

Figure 9.2 shows average records for both the 76-degree and 39-degree movements for a single subject. The upper two panels give the average angular position and velocity about the elbow for the flexion trials in the 76-degree movement condition. Average position and velocity records for the 200, 300, 400, and 500 msec durations are shown. The lower two panels give the corresponding average angular position and velocity for the 39 degree flexion movements, again for the 200, 300, 400, and 500 msec conditions. From the figure it is clear that in all conditions movements were monotonic with little terminal oscillation, even for the fastest movements.

BASIC KINEMATIC RELATIONSHIPS

Previous studies of both speech and limb movements have shown that there is a reliable correlation between movement amplitude and maximum velocity (Abbs, 1973; Cooke, 1980; Freund & Budingen, 1978; Hallett & Marsden, 1979; Kent & Moll, 1972a, 1972b; Kent & Netsell, 1971; Kozhevnikov & Chistovich, 1965; Kuehn & Moll, 1976; Ostry et al., 1983; Perkell, 1969; Stone, 1981; Sussman, MacNeilage, & Hanson, 1973). The relationship between these variables is shown here in Fig. 9.3 for the tongue dorsum lowering movements of a single subject. The figure shows a clear positive relationship between tongue dorsum movement amplitude and maximum velocity. The slope of the relationship is seen to be greater for unstressed than for stressed vowels (see also Ostry et al., 1983).

A similar relationship between movement amplitude and maximum velocity is obtained for voluntary movements about the elbow. Figure 9.4 shows this relationship for the same subject as in Fig. 9.3 for movements of two different durations. As in speech movements, the slope of the relationship varies; greater slopes are obtained for shorter duration movements. These slope changes in the arm movements are particularly instructive in the context of interpreting the slope changes observed in speech. In the speech data, the slope changes accompany differences in stress. However, as stress is confounded both with movement amplitude and duration, it is difficult to attribute the change in slope in this situation purely to stress rather than to amplitude or to duration (cf. Ostry et al., 1983).

The elbow flexion data from the present study support the view that in both systems, movement duration is the primary determinant of the slope. The slope changes for elbow flexions accompany changes in movement duration but not in movement amplitude. Thus, when amplitude and duration are varied orthogonally, it is the duration not the amplitude which produces

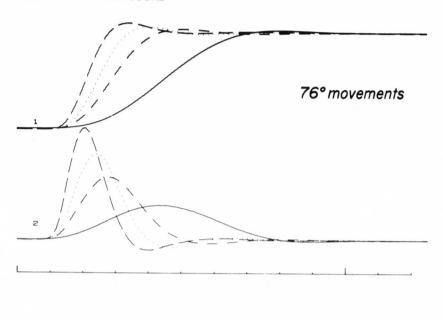

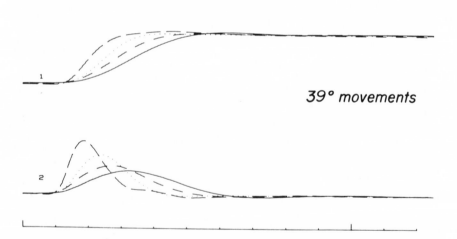

FIG. 9.2   Kinematic record of the average angular position and angular velocity about the elbow for a single subject during flexion movements of four different durations (200, 300, 400, and 500 msec). The upper panels give the average angular position (upper trace) and angular velocity (lower trace) for 76-degree movements. The four movement durations can be distinguished by the time taken to reach the final position. The 200-msec movements achieve the final position sooner than the 300-msec movements and so on. The lower panels give the comparable angular positions and angular velocities for 39-degree movements at the four different movement durations.

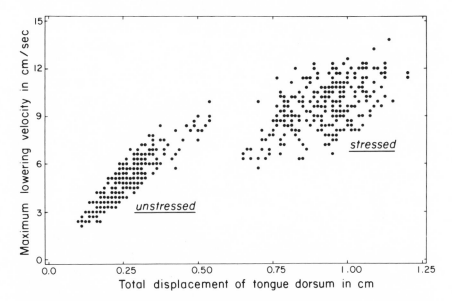

FIG. 9.3 Scattergram showing the relationship between the amplitude and maximum velocity of the tongue dorsum lowering movements during the production of alternately stressed consonant-vowel sequences. The figure shows the individual observations for all combinations of rate, vowel, consonant, and stress. The slope of the maximum-velocity/movement amplitude regression can be seen to be greater for unstressed than for stressed vowels.

changes in slope. In these arm movements, there is nothing equivalent to the stress variable in speech. Nevertheless, differences in movement duration alone are sufficient to produce changes in the arm movement slope. Although stress differences in speech may further amplify a basic durational effect, it seems safe to conclude that both in speech and arm systems, movement duration is a main factor underlying the observed differences in slope.

An understanding of the basis of the changes in slope may be provided by considering the predicted effects on movement kinematics of varying parameters of the biomechanical model of the limb. Cooke (1980) showed that if the limb is modeled by linear second order differential equations, then changes in the slope of the maximum velocity/movement amplitude relationship can be predicted on the basis of changes in static limb stiffness, the coefficient of the zero-order term in a second order system. In this model, the slope of the maximum-velocity/movement amplitude relationship varies with stiffness, greater slopes occurring as stiffness is increased. Thus, if limb and speech movements are characterized by lumped parameter second order systems in which the value of the stiffness term can be specified, then the slope changes

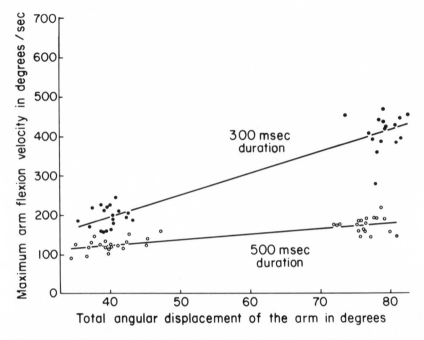

FIG. 9.4 Scattergram showing the relationship between the amplitude and maximum velocity of arm flexion movements during the production of 39-degree and 76-degree movements at two different durations. The figure shows the individual observations for all combinations of movement duration and amplitude. The subject is the same as in Fig. 9.3. The slope of the maximum-velocity/movement amplitude regression is greater for shorter duration movements, but is not affected by differences in movement amplitude.

observed here with changes in movement duration may result directly from the control of the limb's resting stiffness. Such a change could be brought about either by control of the slope of the length-tension characteristics of the limb, which is a direct measure of the limb's overall stiffness (Cooke, 1980) or through the specification of appropriate zero lengths for agonist and antagonist muscles which could likewise produce changes in the overall stiffness of the limb (Feldman, 1980).

CONTROL OF DURATION

In the data just presented, the slope of the maximum velocity/movement amplitude regression was shown to be related to movement duration. In order to examine the exact nature of this relationship and the extent to which it is similar in speech and limb systems, we plotted on a trial-by-trial basis the relationship between movement duration and the ratio of the maximum velocity to the amplitude of the movement. The ratio measure was selected for two reasons. First, its relationship to movement duration can be related to differences in movement trajectory (Nelson, 1983) and, following the argument just presented, it may also provide a trial-by-trial kinematic indicator of overall articulator stiffness.

Figure 9.5 shows, for tongue dorsum movements, the ratio of maximum velocity to movement amplitude, plotted against movement duration for all of the combinations of rate, stress, vowel and consonant that were examined in this study. Figure 9.6 gives the comparable data for the same subject for elbow flexion movements showing the individual observations for all combinations of movement amplitudes and durations. In both cases it is clear that a wide variety of changes in the duration of individual movements is readily accommodated by a single function. That is, for both articulators, the overall form of the functions is similar and in both cases all of the data lie on a single continuous function. A similar relationship observed in the kinematics of vocal fold adduction and abduction gestures (Munhall & Ostry, 1985) is consistent with the view that the nervous system produces changes in movement duration in different structures in comparable ways.

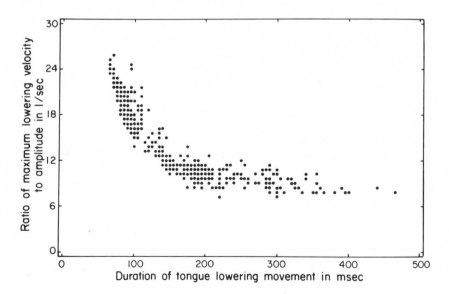

FIG. 9.5 Scattergram showing the relationship between the ratio of maximum tongue dorsum lowering velocity to movement amplitude as a function of the duration of the lowering gestures. Individual data points are again given for all combinations of rate, stress, vowel, and consonant. The data are well approximated by a single function. For this subject the value of the constant c (see text) is 1.66.

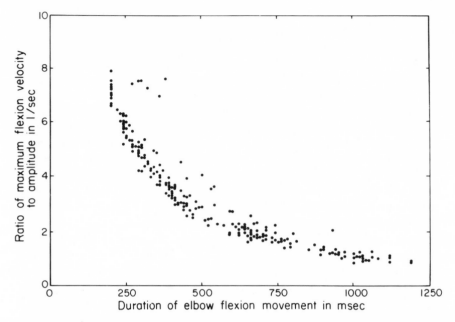

FIG. 9.6 Scattergram showing the relationship between the ratio of maximum elbow flexion velocity to movement amplitude as a function of movement duration. The individual data points for all combinations of movement duration and amplitude are given. The value of the constant c is 1.73. The subject is the same as in the previous figures.

It should be noted that the inverse character of the relationship between the maximum-velocity/movement amplitude ratio and movement duration is in itself a physical necessity. For example, when movement amplitude is held constant, velocity must increase as duration decreases. However, the particular form of the function provides important information on the articulator trajectories that are followed. Thus the specific shape of the function is by no means an uninteresting consequence of the physical law. The function provides specific information on two aspects of movement trajectories.

First, it is significant that both in speech and limb movements all of the data obtained by manipulating a variety of relevant variables lie on a single function. This is consistent with the view that kinematic patterns such as these are related by scalar transformation (Ostry & Munhall, 1985). Second, it can be shown that the particular form of the inverse relationship provides information on the actual trajectories followed. Specifically, articulator trajectories can be distinguished by quantitative differences in the coefficient of the function relating the maximum-velocity/movement amplitude ratio to movement duration (see following). Nelson (1983) has related such differences in trajectory to optimizations and tradeoffs among various performance costs and objectives.

Munhall, Ostry, and Parush (1985) have shown that trajectories of vocal fold adduction and abduction (which like the speech and limb movements of Fig. 9.5 and 9.6 can be accommodated by single functions) are equivalent under scalar transformation. That is, observations which lie along a given curve can be equated by scalar adjustments of the duration and the amplitude of a base velocity profile. Hollerbach and Flash (1982) have provided a related demonstration showing that scalar adjustment also produces an equivalence of torque profiles in multi-joint arm movements. Although subjects are clearly able to select among a range of base velocity profiles, and perhaps even alter these as the task demands warrant, evidence such as that presented here shows that both in speech and limb movements, scalar adjustment of a given base profile is a method used to achieve durational change.

In cases where movement trajectories are equivalent under scalar transformation, the relationships pictured here will be of the form:

$$\frac{V \max}{A} = \frac{c}{t} \tag{1}$$

where V max/A is the ratio of maximum velocity to movement amplitude, t is movement duration and c is a constant. It can be shown that different values of the constant c arise from different basic velocity profiles. For example, a value of $c = 2$ corresponds to movements with constant acceleration and constant deceleration; $c = 1$ corresponds to movements with instantaneous change in velocity on initiating and terminating a movement, and $c = \pi/2$ to the velocity profile associated with harmonic oscillation. Velocity profiles close to those of harmonic oscillation are obtained when either the rate of change of acceleration (jerk) is minimized ($c = 1.56$) or when the total energy expenditure is minimized ($c = 1.50$) (Nelson, 1983).

In Fig. 9.5 the best fit to the data occurs with $c = 1.66$. In Fig. 9.6 the best fit function corresponds to a value of $c = 1.73$. The average value for the vocal folds under similar conditions ranges from $c = 1.6$ to 1.8 (Munhall et al., 1985). The fact that in each case the curves relating the maximum-velocity/movement amplitude ratio to movement duration are well-fitted by a single function suggests that these different movements share a common mechanism for changing duration, perhaps involving scalar adjustments of a base movement profile. The actual value of the constant c relating the ratio and the duration measures reflects the particular velocity profile adopted for the particular task. In this study the value of the constant c is slightly different for speech and arm movements, even though the tasks are similar. The source of this difference is as yet unclear.

The selection of a particular velocity profile is to some extent under the control of the subject. Nelson (1983), for example, shows a range of velocity profiles for arm-bow movements of different speeds in violin playing. Clearly, movement duration may be altered to meet task demand by direct scalar adjustment of velocity profiles as in the present study or by altering movement trajectory. The degree to which subjects alter their base movement trajectories as opposed to applying scalar adjustments to achieve differences in movement duration and extent appears to be a fruitful area for future research.

REFERENCES

Abbs, J. H. (1973). The influence of the gamma motor system on jaw movements during speech: A theoretical framework and some preliminary observations. *Journal of Speech and Hearing Research, 16,* 175–200.

Cooke, J. D. (1980). The organization of simple skilled movements. In G. E. Stelmach & J. Requin (Eds.), *Tutorials in motor behavior* (pp. 199–212). Amsterdam: North-Holland.

Feldman, A. G. (1980). Superposition of motor programs—I. Rhythmic forearm movements in man. *Neuroscience, 5,* 81–90.

Folkins, J. W., & Abbs, J. H. (1975). Lip and jaw motor control during speech: Responses to resistive loading of the jaw. *Journal of Speech and Hearing Research, 18,* 207–220.

Freund, H.-J., & Budingen, H. J. (1978). The relationship between speed and amplitude of the fastest voluntary contractions of human arm muscles. *Experimental Brain Research, 31,* 1–12.

Hallett, M., & Marsden, C. D. (1979). Ballistic flexion movements of the human thumb. *Journal of Physiology, 294,* 33–50.

Hollerbach, J. M., & Flash, M. (1982). Dynamic interactions between limb segments during planar arm movement. *Biological Cybernetics, 44,* 67–77.

Keller, E., & Ostry, D. J. (1983). Computerized measurement of tongue dorsum movement with pulsed-echo ultrasound. *Journal of the Acoustical Society of America, 73,* 1309–1315.

Kent, R. D., & Moll, K. L. (1972a). Cinefluorographic analyses of selected lingual consonants. *Journal of Speech and Hearing Research, 15,* 453–473.

Kent, R. D., & Moll, K. L. (1972b). Tongue body articulation during vowel and diphthong gestures. *Folia Phoniatrica, 24,* 278–300.

Kent, R. D., & Netsell, R. (1971). Effects of stress contrasts on certain articulatory parameters. *Phonetica, 24,* 23–44.

Kozhevnikov, V., & Chistovich, L. (1965). *Speech: Articulation and perception* (JPRS No. 30543). Washington, DC: Joint Publications Research Service.

Kuehn, D. R., & Moll, K. L. (1976). A cineradiographic study of VC and CV articulatory velocities. *Journal of Phonetics, 4,* 303–320.

Munhall, K. G., & Ostry, D. J. (1985). Ultrasonic measurement of laryngeal kinematics. In I. R. Titze & R. C. Scherer (Eds.) *Vocal fold physiology: Biomechanics, acoustics and phonatory control* (pp. 145–162). Denver: Denver Center for the Performing Arts.

Munhall, K. G., Ostry, D. J., & Parush, A. (1985). Characteristics of velocity profiles of speech movements. *Journal of Experimental Psychology: Human Perception and Performance, 11,* 457–474.

Nelson, W. L. (1983). Physical principles for economies of skilled movements. *Biological Cybernetics, 46,* 135–147.

Ostry, D. J., & Munhall, K. G. (1985). Control of rate and duration of speech movements. *Journal of the Acoustical Society of America, 77,* 640–648.

Ostry, D. J., Keller, E., & Parush, A. (1983). Similarities in the control of the speech articulators and the limbs: Kinematics of tongue dorsum movement in speech. *Journal of Experimental Psychology: Human Perception and Performance, 9,* 622–636.

Perkell, J. (1969). *Physiology of speech production: Results and implications of a quantitative cineradiographic study.* Cambridge, MA: MIT Press.

Stone, M. (1981). Evidence for a rhythm pattern in speech production: Observations of jaw movement. *Journal of Phonetics, 9,* 109–120.

Sussman, H. M., MacNeilage, P. F., & Hanson, R. J. (1973). Labial and mandibular dynamics during the production of bilabial consonants: Preliminary observations. *Journal of Speech and Hearing Research, 16,* 397–420.

Thomas, J. S., Croft, D. A., & Brooks, V. B. (1976). A manipulandum for human motor studies. *IEEE Transactions in Biomedical Engineering, 23,* 83–84.

Tuller, B., Kelso, J. A. S., & Harris, K. S. (1982). Interarticulator phasing as an index of temporal regularity in speech. *Journal of Experimental Psychology: Human Perception and Performance, 8,* 460–472.

10 Routes and Representations in the Processing of Written Language

John C. Marshall
The Radcliffe Infirmary
Oxford, England

ABSTRACT

This chapter summarizes the nature of acquired forms of dyslexia and dysgraphia, and relates these disorders to contemporary models of reading. Postulated quasi-independent and parallel routes of processing graphemic stimuli are supported by case studies. Further, it is seen that phonological and graphemic mechanisms in reading and writing are largely independent of each other, despite the similarity between the responsible processes. The resulting functional model makes a number of specific predictions for conduction aphasia and related neurological impairments.

INTRODUCTION

The work I shall outline originated in attempts to describe the detailed symptomatology of the acquired dyslexias (Marshall & Newcombe, 1966, 1973). Once the acute stage of their illness has passed, patients who present with global alexia are rare. A patient will not typically show *no* comprehension of written material, nor, when asked to read aloud, will he or she fail to produce any response that is stimulus-related. It thus becomes important to discover precisely which words (and orthographically legal character strings) a particular patient can and cannot read; it is likewise necessary to look at the qualitative nature of the errors (paralexias) that particular patients make.

Both within and between patients one might accordingly compare the ability to read words and non-words; nouns, adjectives, verbs, and function words; morphologically simple and complex words; regularly and irregularly spelt words, and so on. Similarly, one would want to note whether the paralexic errors in reading aloud bore a visual resemblance to the stimulus (*canary* —> "carry"), an inflectional (*edit* —> "edited") or derivational (*edit* —> "edition") resemblance, a semantic resemblance (*canary* —> "parrot"), or a resemblance that could be interpreted as a 'regularization' of an exceptional correspondence between print and sound (*pint* read with a short *i* as in *hint*). Finally, it would be relevant to know whether the patient who read, for example, *great* as "greet" or *cat* as "mouse" understood the stimulus word or had alternatively understood it as the response.

Once this research program had been embarked upon, it rapidly became clear that there were radical differences between patients, and that within particular patients there were constellations of positive and negative signs that tended to cluster together. It was thus possible to construct a taxonomy of the acquired dyslexias on the basis of the psycholinguistic variables that I have summarized (Marshall & Newcombe, 1973; Patterson, 1981). The resulting classification (Newcombe & Marshall, 1981) was far more detailed than any that had previously been advanced in the clinical literature (see Friedman & Albert, 1985; Henderson, 1984), and, for a short while, it was possible to believe that a new set of neuropsychological syndromes (or symptom-complexes) had been discovered.

THE "SYNDROMES" OF ACQUIRED DYSLEXIA

The four 'syndromes' that have been investigated most thoroughly are deep dyslexia, phonological dyslexia, letter-by-letter reading, and surface dyslexia. These syndromes are now well-known and have been extensively documented in the neuropsychological literature; I shall therefore describe them only briefly here.

The most salient characteristic of deep dyslexia (Marshall & Newcombe, 1966) is the presence of above-chance rates of semantic paralexias (*close* —> "shut") when the patient is attempting to read aloud individual words (without time pressure, stimulus degradation, or context); morphological errors, both inflectional (*banned* —> "ban") and derivational (*length* —> "long") are also present, as are visually-based errors (*saucer* —> "sausage"). Function word substitutions (*for* —> "and") are found. There is a form-class hierarchy, such that concrete nouns are better read than adjectives, which are in turn better read than verbs and abstract nouns. Function words provoke especial difficulty, and even simple non-words are essentially impossible to read (*wux* —> "don't know"). No effects of orthographic regularity are found upon the accuracy of reading aloud (Newcombe & Marshall, 1984a). Reading comprehension was impaired in the first fully documented case (Marshall & Newcombe, 1966). Semantic errors were found in a word-picture pointing task (Bishop & Byng, 1984) that required no overt vocal response (Newcombe & Marshall, 1980a). Deep dyslexia is probably the "tightest" neuropsychological syndrome thus far discovered; that is, more patients who meet precisely the very restrictive, yet multi-symptom definition of the condition have been described than for any other disorder of higher cognitive functioning (Coltheart, Patterson, & Marshall, 1980).

The overt symptoms of phonological dyslexia form a proper subset of those found in deep dyslexia. The most salient features of the condition are a severe (although not usually total) inability to read non-words in the context of relatively well-preserved word-reading (Beauvois & Dérouesné, 1979; Patterson, 1982). Semantic errors are *not* found. The remaining symptomatology is extremely variable in patients who have been assigned the label phonological dyslexia. Some (but not all) patients read content words better than function words; some (but not all) read nouns better than verbs. In many patients, morphologically complex words are harder to read than simple stems, and errors tend to be inflectionally or derivationally related to the stimulus. Function word substitutions are frequently (but not inevitably) found, and when they do not occur in single-word reading they may appear in the reading of continuous text. Some visually related errors are usually seen. Comprehension of the written word, as assessed by lexical decision, synonym matching and word-picture matching is typically (but not invariably) impaired. In some patients, phonological dyslexia can be seen in the course of evolution from deep dyslexia. A more detailed description of the syndrome, and review of pertinent case reports, can be found in Sartori, Barry, and Job (1984).

As the designation suggests, letter-by-letter reading involves the sequential identification (and naming) of each letter in the presented stimulus word. Patients name, rather than sound out, the letters of words (where the orthography permits this distinction to be drawn), either out loud or sotto voce (Newcombe & Marshall, 1973). They then attempt to interpret the word on the basis of this auditory letter name sequence. In patients with intact short-term memory and intact spelling skills, reading performance may be virtually error-free (Warrington & Shallice, 1980), although painfully slow and laborious. In other cases (Newcombe & Marshall, 1973; Patterson & Kay, 1982), the whole word that is reconstructed from a correct sequence of letter-names may be a phonological paraphasia (*met* —> "M, E, T . . . meat"). Alternatively, if letter-identification (or naming) is impaired, the letter misidentification may be carried over into the whole word response (*men* —> "H, E, N . . . hen"). In 'pure' cases, neither speed nor accuracy is affected by any psycholinguistic variable other than the length (in letters) of the stimulus word. Latency of word identification is, of course, a monotonic function of word length (in letters). Stimulus words are interpreted solely on the basis of the assigned sequence of letter names (Newcombe & Marshall, 1981); when exposure duration is restricted to preclude explicit letter-naming, no comprehension of the word can be demonstrated in lexical decision or semantic classification tasks (Patterson & Kay, 1982).

In surface dyslexia (Marshall & Newcombe, 1973) the most salient dimension that affects the accuracy of reading aloud is regularity of spelling. Words that have a regular spelling, that is, whose pronunciation is derivable by general rule (*mat, praise, wheel,* for example) are read well; words whose pronunciation is irregular or exceptional (*pint, yacht, iron,* for example) are read poorly. Non-words, the pronunciation of which is, by definition, regular, can often be read as accurately as regular real words (Coltheart, 1982). In pure cases, other psycholinguistic variables have little or no effect upon accuracy. Paralexic errors to irregular words are often 'regularizations'. This will sometimes result in a real word response (e.g., *shoe* —> "show"), sometimes in a neologism (e.g., *broad* —> "brode"). In instances where the error cannot, strictly speaking, be regarded as a regularization, the false response may nonetheless incorporate a grapheme-phoneme correspondence that is appropriate to some word or set of words of the language (e.g., *bor-ough* —> "borrow", with *ough* as in *dough*). Semantic interpretation is based upon the response, not upon the stimulus. Thus if *island* is read as "izland" the patient may comment "There's no such word"; if *listen* is read with the *t* overtly pronounced, the patient may gloss the word as "That's the famous boxer" (Sonny Liston). Homophones may be read aloud correctly but nonetheless misinterpreted as the other member of the homophone pair (e.g., *billed* —> "To build up, buildings"; *oar* —> "That's the ore of metal, the raw materials"). These homophone confusions are not based solely upon overt reading, for they occur when the patient is asked to define a stimulus word prior to reading it aloud (Coltheart, 1981; Newcombe & Marshall, 1981).

The discovery of these syndromes, and their repeated confirmation in extensive single-case studies, then led investigators to inquire whether analogous constellations of impaired and preserved performance could be found in writing-to-dictation.

THE "SYNDROMES" OF ACQUIRED DYSGRAPHIA

For obvious reasons, there can be no precise analogue to pathological letter-by-letter reading for writing-to-dictation; normal writing involves (or, at least, can involve) the successive production of letters in order to form appropriate words. Yet a glance at the handwriting of many neurologically intact subjects will quickly reveal that in their normal cursive hand it is difficult or impossible to isolate an unambiguous sequence of letters; words are rather executed in a fast, fluent sweep that represents global, "holistic" properties of the word-shape. Consequent upon brain-damage, many patients (including some who have not sustained significant motor weakness) lose the ability to form freely these 'co-articulated' oscillatory patterns. Insofar as they can write at all, these patients revert to executing words as a laborious sequence of disconnected letters, often in upper case. To some extent, then, this phenomenon can be regarded as the dysgraphic equivalent of letter-by-letter reading.

The other major syndromes of reading impairment (deep, phonological, and surface dyslexia) have now all been found to have fairly exact dysgraphic equivalents.

In deep dysgraphia (Bub & Kertesz, 1982), non-words cannot be written to dictation. Concrete nouns are more accurately written than abstract nouns; verbs and function words are very poorly transcribed. Errors include semantic ("chair" —> *table*), and visual ("amount" —> *around*) paragraphias, and function word substitutions ("yours" —> *our*). In phonological dysgraphia (Shallice, 1981a), the ability to write monomorphemic content words to dictation is well-preserved in the context of a virtually complete inability to write non-words. When errors are made in writing words, many of the responses are either inflectional ("mitten" —> *mittens*) or derivational ("loveliness" —> *lovely*) paragraphias. The writing of function words is impaired relative to high-frequency content words, a pattern found for reading in many cases of phonological dyslexia.

In surface dysgraphia (Beauvois & Dérouesné, 1981; Hatfield & Patterson, 1983), the salient feature is the frequent occurrence of phonologically plausible mis-spellings (e.g., "flood" —> *flud*, "laugh" —> *laf*, and "spade" —> *spaid*). Words with a regular spelling were written more accurately than those with an irregular spelling. Homophones, when dictated in a sentential context that disambiguates them, were often transcribed as the wrong member of the pair (e.g., "sale" —> *sail*; "pain" —> *pane*). In the case of Beauvois and Dérouesné (1981), writing of nonsense syllables to dictation was well-preserved.

In short, there seems to be a good match between the primary characteristics of the principle dyslexic and dysgraphic syndromes. However, the discovery of reliable symptom-complexes is of limited interest per se. They would hold a deeper significance if the patterns of performance could be shown to cohere in a theoretically revealing fashion; they would hold a wider significance if the patterns of performance were relevant to the analysis of the routes and representations employed in normal reading and writing. It is to some problems associated with these issues that we now turn.

THE NEW DIAGRAM-MAKERS

The position advanced by Marshall and Newcombe (1973) was essentially a revival of the theoretical approach (and notational conventions) that the early diagram makers (Lichtheim, 1885) had adopted in the analysis of aphasic impairment. An account of normal reading was proposed whereby multiple routes operated, largely in parallel, to assign form, sound, and meaning to the written word. The model was expressed as a (very simple) flow diagram; boxes indicated processing stages where distinct linguistic representations are assigned to their input; arrows showed the flow of information between processing stages. It was then conjectured that the individual components of this normal functional architecture could each be independently destroyed or impaired by brain damage. The resultant performance would thus in part follow from the normal operation of the remaining intact 'boxes and arrows'; symptomatology that could not be so interpreted would be consequent upon principled restrictions or perturbations of defined processing stages.

The research program so defined (Coltheart, 1981; Newcombe & Marshall, 1981; Shallice, 1981b) has been subject to three broad classes of criticism, each, to some extent, cogent. First, it could be argued that inferences from dyslexic impairment to normal functioning are rendered invalid because overt errors may reflect (a) the consequences of widespread brain reorganization subsequent to damage; (b) the uncovering of normal, but normally unused, mechanisms after the destruction of brain-areas that usually inhibit their operation; and (c) the (sometimes "conscious") adoption of (normally unnecessary) strategies to circumvent the use of an impaired subsystem.

The possibility of quite large scale anatomical and physiological reorganization after trauma (Geschwind, 1974) cannot be denied; yet, in the absence of a specific hypothesis about the functional correlates of such changes, one can do no more than acknowledge a potential source of disinformation. The clearest disinhibition hypothesis so far proposed conjectures that semantic paralexias reflect a release of right hemispheric function from left hemisphere control (Landis, Regard, Graves, & Goodglass, 1983). If the "positive" symptoms of deep dyslexia reflected the mode of operation of (normally) latent right hemisphere mechanisms (Coltheart, 1980) the relevance of the syndrome to normal reading would be severely reduced. But, as matters stand at the moment, it is at least equally plausible to interpret semantic paralexias as pathology of the (left hemisphere) device that is responsible, in the normal case, for semantic priming (Marshall & Patterson, 1983; 1985). In general, the evidence for "right hemisphere literacy" is at best equivocal (Patterson & Besner, 1984).

By contrast, the strategy of identifying words on the basis of sequences of letter-names is clearly substitutive; the method involved is not a component of any intact reading process. But even here there is a valid inference to be drawn for normal reading; namely, that correct letter-identification is not a sufficient prerequisite for holistic word-identification.

Second, the notational conventions employed in most current theorizing are admittedly extremely crude. As Brady (1981) points out: "The box and arrows diagrams which feature in most information processing accounts of perception are highly reminiscent of the system flowcharts which used to be prepared by programmers in the early stages of developing a program" (p. 186). Such flowcharts, he continues, "have fallen into disrepute in computer science as it has been realized that they provide an impoverished representation of such a key issue as the structure of a program" (p. 186). Flowcharts, furthermore, are "wholly inadequate as a representation of process interaction" and may "unacceptably straitjacket thinking" (p. 186). One must, of course, concede the thrust of such arguments. Yet it remains true that even very elementary "box-and-arrow" diagrams have served to unify a considerable range of observations and to predict further patterns of associated and dissociated symptoms.

This latter point is important with respect to a third criticism: That the constraints upon "box-and-arrow" notation are so weak that any theory so expressed is vacuous. The force of such a critique is that, whatever new pattern of performance is found it can always be incorporated into the model by a simple (not to say simple minded) proliferation of boxes and arrows. Once again, one should probably concede the point in principle, but note that, in practice investigators do try to cover the available data with the smallest number of components and connections. And this exercise inevitably leads to a diagram that predicts new phenomena. Let us see then how the research program has developed.

THE FUNCTIONAL ARCHITECTURE OF WRITTEN LANGUAGE PROCESSING

Current models of reading (see Patterson, Marshall, & Coltheart, 1985) postulate three quasi-independent, parallel routes whereby form, meaning, and pronunciation can be assigned to the written word. One version of the standard model is shown in Fig. 10.1.

Subsequent to early Visual Analysis, an initial graphemic code is constructed (by the mechanism labelled *VGC*) which is then input to all three routes. (The extent to which words can be recognized on the basis of overall contour and transgraphemic features prior to explicit letter analysis is debatable. See Howard, 1983). This graphemic code is visual (i.e., non-phonological) but abstract (e.g., indiscriminate with respect to case). Multi-letter strings are explicitly segmented into their component letters (e.g., *cat* → C + A + T).

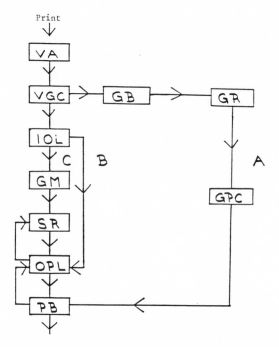

FIG. 10.1. Architecture of normal reading. VA = Visual analysis; VGC = Visual to graphemic conversion; GB = Graphemic buffer; GR = Graphemic reparsing; GPC = Graphemic to phonologic conversion; IOL = Input orthographic lexicon; GM = Graphemic morphology; SR = Semantic representations; OPL = Output phonological lexicon; PB = Phonologic buffer. A = Phonic route; B = Direct route; C = Lexico-semantic route.

THE PHONIC ROUTE

The abstract letter identities assigned by VGC are input to a short-term storage device, the Graphemic buffer. This buffer in turn provides the input for the spelling aloud procedures (not shown in Fig. 10.1) adopted by the patient with letter-by-letter reading. In normal reading, however, the flow of information is from GB to Graphemic reparsing. This latter mechanism resegments, where necessary, the letter sequence into regular graphemic "chunks." On the most restrictive definition (Coltheart, 1978), a graphemic chunk is a letter or multi-letter sequence that maps onto a single phoneme. Some words (and non-words) will not require resegmentation (i.e., *nup* $\longrightarrow$ *n* + *u* + *p*). Sequences such as *t* + *o* + *e* must, however, be reanalysed as *t* + *oe*. That is, *oe* is usually a vowel digraph with the regular pronunciation [ou]. The sequence is, of course, not a digraph in such words as *poem* or *coerce*. Such graphemic "exception" words will be misparsed by Graphemic reparsing (GR).

The output of GR is now input to Grapheme phoneme correspondence rules (GPC). Each single or multi-character grapheme is associated with the (single) phoneme that is its most regular phonological realization (e.g., *j* —> /dz/; *ea* —> /i:/). This procedure will associate an incorrect phonological code with any written word whose phonological realization is irregular. Thus, in *shoe,* the digraph *oe* will incorrectly be given the value *ou* (as in *toe*), when the exceptional pronunciation *u:* is required. The phonology of "show" will then be placed in the Phonological buffer for eventual articulation (if required); likewise the phonology of "show" (not "shoe") will be fed back into the lexical system (PB —> OPL —> SR, in Fig. 10.1).

The "core" symptomatology of "surface dyslexia" can now be interpreted as a pathology in which the lexical and direct reading routes (B and C) are (relatively) unavailable, and the patient is forced into over-reliance on extra-lexical "phonic" routines. "Pure" cases of phonological reading are, of course, rare, or non-existent (but see Bub, Cancelliere, & Kertesz, 1985). Some "sight" vocabulary is usually preserved, and in many patients there is additional damage to the phonic route itself. Partial impairment of the grapheme to phoneme conversion system will result in the selection of invalid correspondences (Marshall & Newcombe, 1973); impairment of graphemic reparsing can result in the patient pronouncing all the individual letters of a word even when they form regular digraphs and trigraphs (Newcombe & Marshall, 1985). If there is associated damage to late stages of routes B and C (i.e., post-assignment of semantic representations), the patient may regularize the pronunciation of exception words (e.g., *shoe* —> "show") but nonetheless understand the stimulus as *shoe.*

Considerations of this nature indicate that the designation surface dyslexia covers a wide range of different pathologies; "syndromes" are no more than a convenient shorthand for the core symptoms.

THE DIRECT ROUTE

The local (graphemic) and, perhaps, global features relevant to word identification feed into a component designated Input orthographic lexicon (IOL). This is the visual word recognition device (Morton, 1979) that underlies the notion of "sight" vocabulary; it contains stored representations of known words. IOL can output arbitrary codes that locate the phonological representations of known words in an Output phonological lexicon (OPL). The route from IOL to OPL can be regarded as a set of direct, unanalysed associations between visual word forms and their pronunciations.

The existence of route B is attested by the discovery of patients who succeed in reading aloud words with a regular and with an irregular spelling in the absence of significant comprehension. One of the patients described by

Warrington (1975) suffered from a progressive dementing illness that resulted in severe impairment of the semantic memory system. Initially, however, the patient showed only a very small discrepancy between her ability to read aloud regular and irregular words. The latter, *ex hypothesi*, could not be read correctly by route A ("Phonics"); as comprehension was so poor the words were apparently not read via semantic mediation. The patient thus provides evidence for route B.

Similar evidence is given by Schwartz, Saffran, and Marin (1980). Their case presented with pre-senile dementia. Despite a progressive and severe impairment of semantic knowledge (or access thereto), the patient retained, for a considerable time, the ability to read aloud single words. She could read accurately such irregular words as *tortoise, leopard, climb, both, own,* and *flood* at a time when the evidence from semantic categorization, classification and matching tasks strongly suggests that there was little or no comprehension of the meaning of the words.

THE LEXICO-SEMANTIC ROUTE

The output of the Input orthographic lexicon must also consist of a letter string that can be reanalysed into its morphological constituents. The device GM (= Graphemic morphology) performs the relevant operations and outputs a morphological code which is in turn input to the assignment of a semantic representation (SR) to the stimulus. This semantic code is then used to address an entry in OPL (= Output phonological lexicon), where an appropriate phonology is assigned for eventual articulation.

Deep dyslexia and phonological dyslexia can both be regarded as pathologies in which route C is, to a greater or lesser extent, inoperative. (On some accounts, route B would also be impaired). If there was no further pathology, there would result a condition in which all real words could be read without error and no non-words. There are no attested cases of acquired "phonological dyslexia" that are as neat as this, although Campbell and Butterworth (1985) have reported an exceptionally pure developmental case. The precise causes of the morphological errors and function word substitutions seen in deep and phonological dyslexia remain to be elucidated; the observed variability in word reading in phonological dyslexia suggests that the condition fractionates into a number of quite distinct disorders.

Similar considerations hold for "deep dyslexia." The semantic paralexias that are the cardinal feature of the condition can arise in (at least) two distinct ways. In one group of patients, semantic errors are found across tasks; they thus appear in word-picture matching (with both visual and auditory presentation) and in various semantic classification tasks that require no vocal output. In these patients, semantic paralexias would seem to reflect an instability or loss of modality-free semantic information (Newcombe & Marshall, 1980a). Yet other patients who meet the classificatory criteria for "deep dyslexia" make no semantic errors in word-picture matching (Patterson & Besner, 1984) and can often judge that their semantic errors in oral reading are wrong (Patterson, 1978). This suggests a deficit in the retrieval of appropriate phonological output rather than in the comprehension of the printed word. Once again, even the best-behaved of "syndromes" covers a variety of functionally distinct disorders. At very worst, diagrams serve to remind one that the same overt symptom may arise from loss or malfunction of different functional components.

Information-flow diagrams of normal writing have accordingly been adopted to systematize the symptomatology of the acquired dysgraphias (Ellis, 1982; Morton, 1980; Newcombe & Marshall, 1980b). Figure 10.2

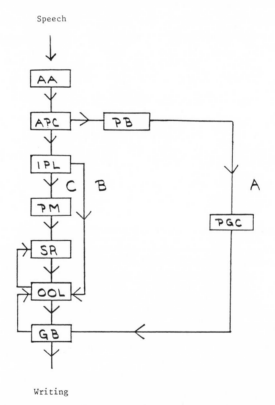

FIG. 10.2. Architecture of normal writing to dictation. AA = Auditory analysis; APC = Auditory to phonological conversion; PB = Phonologic buffer; PGC = Phonologic to graphemic conversion; IPL = Input phonological lexicon; PM = Phonological morphology; SR = Semantic representation; OOL = Oral output lexicon; GB = Graphemic buffer. A = Phonic route; B = Direct route; C = Lexico-semantic route.

represents a model of writing-to-dictation, cast in the same mould as the reading model shown in Fig. 10.1. It will be seen that with the exception of three components (the Phonological buffer, the Graphemic buffer, and the device that assigns Semantic representations), the mechanisms and routes postulated in the two models are fully disjoint. Thus grapheme-phoneme conversion rules are distinguished from phoneme-grapheme conversion rules; the phonological lexicons are divided into input and output devices, as are the orthographic lexicons. Figures 10.1 and 10.2 can accordingly be put together into one composite diagram that shares a Phonological buffer, a Graphemic buffer, and a Semantic system. A (slightly simplified) composite is shown in Fig. 10.3. The geometry of the figure has been somewhat altered in the interests of clarity and aesthetics, but it can easily be checked that topologically it is indeed the union of Fig. 10.1 and 10.2. Changes in the geometry have no effect upon the functional claims that the model represents.

It might be thought, however, that merely conjoining the models for reading aloud and writing-to-dictation would result in considerable redundancy,

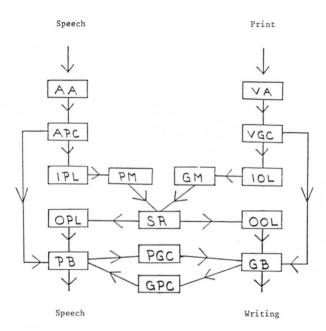

FIG. 10.3. Architecture of reading and writing. AA = Auditory analysis; APC = Auditory to phonological conversion; IPL = Input phonological lexicon; OPL = Output phonological lexicon; PB - Phonologic buffer; VA = Visual analysis; VGC = Visual to graphemic conversion; IOL = Input orthographic lexicon; OOL = Oral output lexicon; GB = Graphemic buffer; PM = Phonological morphology; GM = Graphemic morphology; SR = Semantic representations; PGC = Phonologic to graphemic conversion; GPC = Graphemic to phonologic conversion.

and that a much simplified diagram would better capture the relevant theoretical regularities. This may be so. But Fig. 10.3 and the similar diagrams in Ellis (1982); Morton (1980); and Newcombe & Marshall (1980b), which concur in postulating an (almost) total modularization of distinct reading and writing systems, do make a quite explicit prediction. With the exception of pathologies that involve common components (that cannot be bypassed), the modular model claims that: Any variety of acquired dyslexia can, in principle, co-occur in an individual patient with any (or no) variety of acquired dysgraphia (and vice-versa). This is a strong and in some ways counterintuitive prediction. Is it true?

THE RANDOM MATING MODEL

As a preliminary test of the model it is (unfortunately) necessary to revert to using gross syndrome classifications. (There are too few studies in which the reading and writing of an individual patient has been investigated in sufficient detail to fractionate the 'syndromes'). Nonetheless, it is possible to begin the appropriate collation of studies.

The three best attested acquired dyslexias (and dysgraphias) that are relevant to the conjecture are surface, phonological, and deep. The prediction is: Complete random 'mating' (assortment) between these syndromes, as shown in Table 10.1.

Table 10.1
The random mating model for co-occurrences between the acquired dyslexias and dysgraphias

Dyslexia		Dysgraphia
	a) Surface	0
1:	b) Phonological	0
	c) Deep	0
	a) Surface	Surface
2:	b) Phonological	Surface
	c) Deep	Surface
	a) Phonological	Phonological
3:	b) Surface	Phonological
	c) Deep	Phonological
	a) Deep	Deep
4:	b) Surface	Deep
	c) Phonological	Deep
	a) 0	Surface
5:	b) 0	Phonological
	c) 0	Deep

The relevant empirical question is now: How many of the fifteen predicted pairings shown in Table 10.1 are actually attested?

There is no shortage in the published literature of the homomorphic pairings 2a, 3a, and 4a. Thus surface dyslexia is known to co-exist with surface dysgraphia in patient A.D. of Deloche, Andreewsky, and Desai (1982), and patient A.B. of Coltheart, Masterson, Byng, Prior, and Riddoch (1983). The closeness of fit between reading and writing can be clearly seen in a recent patient of our own, M.S. (Newcombe & Marshall, 1985):

tale	—>	[taelij]
whip	—>	[wahip]
feat	—>	[fijaet]
suit	—>	[su:it]
whom	—>	[waham]
goes	—>	[go-es]

READING ALOUD (M.S.)

"click"	—>	KLIK
"woman"	—>	WUMUN
"guess"	—>	GES
"busy"	—>	BIZE
"room"	—>	REWM
"iron"	—>	IUN

WRITING TO DICTATION (M.S.)

Phonological dyslexia can co-exist with phonological dysgraphia, as in patient P.R. of Shallice (1981a). P.R. has a mild phonological dyslexia with impaired non-word reading in the context of a severe phonological dysgraphia. Errors are frequently derivational and/or structurally similar to the correct response; mixed structural and semantic errors are also found:

"loveliness"	—>	LOVELY
"truth"	—>	TRUE
"defect"	—>	DEFECTION
"custom"	—>	CUSTARD
"anxiety"	—>	ANGUISH
"salad"	—>	CELERY

WRITING TO DICTATION (P.R.)

If one is prepared to diagnose phonological dysgraphia when writing is very seriously impaired, then case A.M. of Patterson (1982) is also homomorphic: derivational and structurally-similar errors appear in both reading and writing.

Deep dyslexia co-occurs with deep dysgraphia in the two patients of Saffran, Schwartz, and Marin (1976); in patient J.F.M. of Assal, Buttet, and Jolivet (1981); and in our original deep dyslexic, G.R. (Marshall & Newcombe, 1966). G.R. produces copious semantic errors in both tasks, viz:

truth	—>	"honest"
kill	—>	"murder"
ancient	—>	"historic"
bill	—>	"receipt"
foreign	—>	"overseas"
glory	—>	"hero"

READING ALOUD (G.R.)

"cake"	—>	BUN
"star"	—>	MOON
"page"	—>	READ
"plane"	—>	SHIP
"read"	—>	BOOK
"nephew"	—>	UNCLE

WRITING TO DICTATION (G.R.)

Heteromorphic cases are somewhat harder to find. The most convincing pub-lished case is R.G. (Beauvois & Dérouesné, 1979, 1981). R.G. has surface dysgraphia in the context of phonological dyslexia. There is a severe reading deficit for reading non-words, while in writing to dictation non-words are well coped with and numerous phonologically plausible errors are made:

"rameau"	—>	RAMO
"souk"	—>	SOUC
"photo"	—>	FAUTO
"eglise"	—>	AIGLISE
"copeau"	—>	COPOT
"pigeon"	—>	PIJON

WRITING TO DICTATION (R.G.)

It is possible that Case 1 of Sevush, Roeltgen, Campanella, and Heilman (1983) shows phonological dysgraphia in the context of surface dyslexia. The patient is reported as making "occasional word substitutions typical of 'pho-nologic agraphia' ", whilst in reading aloud there is a 'regularity effect' on percentage correct and some regularizations in the error pattern.

A further heteromorphic case has been reported by Newcombe and Marshall (1984b). M.C.H. presented with surface dyslexia in the context of deep dysgraphia. She is better at reading aloud regularly than irregularly spelt words, and her errors include regularizations and other phonologic miscorrespondences typical of surface dyslexia.

sew	—>	"sue"
heir	—>	"here"
broad	—>	"brode"
bear	—>	"beer"
knob	—>	"kenob"
chaos	—>	"chose"

READING ALOUD (M.C.H.)

Homophone confusions were also in evidence when the patient was asked to define written words (*eye* —> "I think"). By contrast there was no regularity effect in writing-to-dictation. Semantic paragraphias (some misspelled) were, however, found.

"book"	—>	READING
"tree"	—>	PLANTS
"cousin"	—>	SISTER
"bagpipe"	—>	PUMP
"star"	—>	BRIGH
"pencil"	—>	WRITEING

WRITING TO DICTATION (M.C.H.)

The first case of preserved (single-word) reading or writing we have located with a central dysgraphia or dyslexia in the other task is case J.C. II of Bub and Kertesz (1982). In this patient, deep dysgraphia co-occurs with intact single-word reading (although the oral reading of sentences "was markedly telegraphic").

"time"	—>	CLOCK
"yacht"	—>	BOAT
"give"	—>	TAKE
"our"	—>	MY
"blom"	—>	FLOWER
"lobigner"	—>	OYSTER

WRITING TO DICTATION (J.C.II)

Bub (this volume) has presented a further case (C.H.) of preserved reading, but now in the context of phonological dysgraphia.

Although the number of filled cells in the random assortment model is far from complete, the discovery of some heteromorphic pairings does suggest that the overlap between the reading and writing systems may be quite small. Extensive and systematic search would be required in order to try and fill in all cells of the random assortment model. If this enterprise succeeds, our confidence in the theory would be greatly strengthened. If a long-term search fails, three options are open:

1. Continue to support the model (and assume that patients who complete the cells will eventually be discovered);

2. Recast the functional model in order to account for the pattern of filled and empty cells (and then see what further independent predictions arise from the revised theory);

3. Continue to support the model *qua* functional theory, and assume that an anatomico-physiological account can be provided for the missing cells.

It would be unwise to dismiss this last option out of hand. We might accordingly draw the moral that the new diagram-makers should pay more attention to the geometry of their models and cast aside the article of faith that topology is all.

CODA AND BONUS?

It could still be claimed, with some justification, that even if all the cells in Table 10.1 were to be filled, the result would be merely a classificatory description. True, yet the union of Fig. 10.1 and 10.2 has resulted in an unexpected bonus. Consultation of Fig. 10.3 reveals the existence of a route for auditory repetition that is, in the relevant central components, identical with the (impaired) routes that are implicated in deep and phonological dyslexia and dysgraphia.

Figure 10.3 thus predicts the existence of repetition disorders (conduction aphasias) in which the psycholinguistic symptomatology is identical to that seen in the corresponding pathologies of transcoding. No 'price' is paid for this prediction; no additional "boxes and arrows" need to be drawn. Better still, the prediction appears to be true.

Michel (1979) has described a patient in whom the syntactic hierarchy for oral repetition of single words paralleled that seen in deep dyslexia. Concrete nouns and adjectives were repeated with greater success than verbs, adverbs and abstract nouns. The patient (M.R.) would rarely attempt to repeat pronouns, prepositions, conjunctions or articles, and the repetition of nonsense syllables was quite impossible. Semantic errors were frequent; on some sessions with concrete nouns, semantic paraphasias were made on over 50% of the trials.

"buffet"	$\rightarrow$	"divan"
"mendiant"	$\rightarrow$	"clochard"
"noyau"	$\rightarrow$	"pêche"
"mer"	$\rightarrow$	"vacances"
"chaussure"	$\rightarrow$	"soulier"
"rapide"	$\rightarrow$	"maintenant"

IMMEDIATE ORAL REPETITION (M.R.)

It can be seen, from Fig. 10.3, that in order to "force" oral repetition into this semantic route there must be a functional impairment of the route from APC (Auditory phonological conversion) to PB (The Phonologic buffer). This route also feeds PGC (Phoneme to Grapheme conversion). If this route is unavailable, it follows that the patient *must* also manifest deep dysgraphia. The prediction is upheld.

"crabe"	$\rightarrow$	*homard*
"auto"	$\rightarrow$	*voiture*
"biche"	$\rightarrow$	*gazelle*
"chaussure"	$\rightarrow$	*soulier*
"couleur"	$\rightarrow$	*drapeau*
"buffet"	$\rightarrow$	*chaise*

WRITING TO DICTATION (M.R.)

The model does not require that oral reading should be impaired in this patient. And the patient could indeed read aloud quite well, with fair, albeit not perfect, comprehension. Semantic errors were never found when the patient read aloud and fair reading of nonsense syllables was possible. The same constellation of deep dysgraphia and semantic errors in the immediate repetition of single words is also found in the previously mentioned case of M.C.H. (Newcombe & Marshall, 1984b).

Auditory repetition parallel to the more restricted conditions of phonological dyslexia and dysgraphia has also been found. Bub (this volume) reports that M.V. shows very poor non-word repetition in the context of relatively well-preserved word repetition. Although monomorphemic real words were well-repeated, multi-morphemic words gave rise to errors of substitution, addition and deletion of inflectional and derivational morphology.

I conclude, then, that simple diagrams should not yet be dispensed with as a means of systematizing some basic observations of cognitive neuropsychology. The informed reader will, however, have noticed that the intact single-word and non-word repetition of G.R. (Marshall & Newcombe, 1966) and J.C. II (Bub & Kertesz, 1982) is a severe embarrassment to the model outlined in Fig. 10.3. The diagram predicts that all patients with deep dysgraphia will also manifest 'deep dysrepetonia', the condition shown by M.R. (Michel, 1979) and M.C.H. (Newcombe & Marshall, 1984b). G.R. and J.C. II most emphatically do not! Figure 10.3 thus incorporates an empirical claim (i.e., is falsifiable) and must be modified in the light of evidence. The theoretical issue which then arises is: Can Fig. 10.3 be modified without cost (that is, without the addition of further boxes and arrows)? Or is it rather the case that there is even more modularization of the reading, writing, and auditory repetition systems than Fig. 10.3 already countenances?

REFERENCES

Assal, G., Buttet, J., & Jolivet, R. (1981). Dissociations in aphasia: A case report. *Brain and Language, 13,* 223–240.
Beauvois, M. F., & Dérouesné, J. (1979). Phonological alexia: Three dissociations. *Journal of Neurology, Neurosurgery and Psychiatry, 42,* 1115–1124.
Beauvois, M. F., & Dérouesné, J. (1981). Lexical or orthographic agraphia. *Brain, 104,* 21–49.
Bishop, D., & Byng, S. (1984). Assessing semantic comprehension: Methodological considerations, and a new test. *Cognitive Neuropsychology, 1,* 233–244.
Brady, M. (1981). Toward a computational theory of early visual processing in reading. *Visible Language, 15,* 183–214.
Bub, D., Cancelliere, A., & Kertesz, A. (1985). Whole-word and analytic translation of spelling to sound in a non-semantic reader. In K. E. Patterson, J. C. Marshall, & M. Coltheart (Eds.), *Surface dyslexia: Neuropsychological and cognitive analyses of phonological reading* (pp. 14–34). London: Lawrence Erlbaum Associates.
Bub, D. & Kertesz, A. (1982). Deep agraphia. *Brain and Language, 17,* 146–165.

Campbell, R., & Butterworth, B. (1985). Phonological dyslexia and dysgraphia in a highly literate subject: A developmental case with associated deficits of phonemic processing and awareness. *Quarterly Journal of Experimental Psychology, 37A,* 435–475.

Coltheart, M. (1978). Lexical access in simple reading tasks. In G. Underwood (Ed.), *Strategies of information processing* (pp. 151–216). London: Academic Press.

Coltheart, M. (1980). Deep dyslexia: A right-hemisphere hypothesis. In M. Coltheart, K. Patterson, & J. C. Marshall (Eds.), *Deep dyslexia* (pp. 326–380). London: Routledge & Kegan Paul.

Coltheart, M. (1981). Disorders of reading and their implications for models of normal reading. *Visible Language, 15,* 245–286.

Coltheart, M. (1982). The psycholinguistic analysis of acquired dyslexias: Some illustrations. *Philosophical Transactions of the Royal Society of London, B298,* 151–164.

Coltheart, M., Masterson, J., Byng, S., Prior, M., & Riddoch, J. (1983). Surface dyslexia. *Quarterly Journal of Experimental Psychology, 35,* 469–496.

Coltheart, M., Patterson, K., & Marshall, J. C., (Eds.). (1980). *Deep dyslexia.* London: Routledge & Kegan Paul.

Deloche, G., Andreewsky, E., & Desai, M. (1982): Surface dyslexia: A case report and some theoretical implications for reading models. *Brain and Language, 15,* 12–31.

Ellis, A. W. (1982). Spelling and writing (and reading and speaking). In A. W. Ellis (Ed.), *Normality and pathology in cognitive functions* (pp. 113–146). London: Academic Press.

Friedman, R. B., & Albert, M. (1985). Alexia. In K. M. Heilman & E. Valenstein (Eds.), *Clinical Neuropsychology,* (2nd ed., pp. 49–74). New York: Oxford University Press.

Geschwind, N. (1974). Late changes in the nervous system: An overview. In D. Stein & J. Rosen (Eds.), *Plasticity and recovery of function in the central nervous system* (pp. 467–508). New York: Academic Press.

Hatfield, F. M., & Patterson, K. E. (1983). Phonological spelling. *Quarterly Journal of Experimental Psychology, 35A,* 451–468.

Henderson, V. W. (1984). Jules Déjerine and the third alexia. *Archives of Neurology, 41,* 430–432.

Howard, D. (1983). *Reading without letters?* Paper delivered to the Venice Conference on The Cognitive Neuropsychology of Language.

Landis, T., Regard, M., Graves, R., & Goodglass, H. (1983). Semantic paralexia: A release of right hemisphere function from left hemisphere control? *Neuropsychologia, 21,* 359–364.

Lichtheim, L. (1885). On aphasia. *Brain, 7,* 433–484.

Marshall, J. C., & Newcombe, F. (1966). Syntactic and semantic errors in paralexia. *Neuropsychologia, 4,* 169–176.

Marshall, J. C., & Newcombe, F. (1973). Patterns of paralexia: A psycholinguistic approach. *Journal of Psycholinguistic Research, 2,* 175–199.

Marshall, J. C., & Patterson, K. E. (1983). Semantic paralexia and the wrong hemisphere: A note on Landis, Regard, Graves and Goodglass (1983). *Neuropsychologia, 21,* 425–427.

Marshall, J. C., & Patterson, K. E. (1985). Left is still left for semantic paralexias: A reply to Jones and Martin (1985). *Neuropsychologia, 23,* 689–690.

Michel, F. (1979). Préservation du langage écrit malgré un déficit majeur du langage oral (A propos d'un cas clinique). *Lyon Médical, 241,* 141–149.

Morton, J. (1979). Word recognition. In J. Morton & J. C. Marshall (Eds.), *Psycholinguistics series* (Vol. 2, pp. 107–156). London: Elek.

Morton, J. (1980). The logogen model and orthographic structure. In U. Frith (Ed.), *Cognitive processes in spelling* (pp. 117–133). London: Academic Press.

Newcombe, F., & Marshall, J. C. (1973). Stages in recovery from dyslexia following a left cerebral abscess. *Cortex, 9,* 329–332.

Newcombe, F., & Marshall, J. C. (1980a). Response monitoring and response blocking in deep dyslexia. In M. Coltheart, K. Patterson, & J. C. Marshall (Eds.), *Deep dyslexia* (pp. 160–175). London: Routledge & Kegan Paul.

Newcombe, F., & Marshall, J. C. (1980b). Transcoding and lexical stabilization in deep dyslexia. In M. Coltheart, K. Patterson, & J. C. Marshall (Eds.), *Deep dyslexia* (pp. 176–188). London: Routledge & Kegan Paul.

Newcombe, F., & Marshall, J. C. (1981). On psycholinguistic classifications of the acquired dyslexias. *Bulletin of the Orton Society, 31,* 29–46.

Newcombe, F., & Marshall, J. C. (1984a). Varieties of acquired dyslexia: A linguistic approach. *Seminars in neurology, 4,* 181–195.

Newcombe, F., & Marshall, J. C. (1984b). Task- and modality-specific aphasias. In F. C. Rose (Ed.), *Progress in aphasiology (Advances in neurology)* (Vol. 42, pp. 139–144). New York: Raven Press.

Newcombe, F., & Marshall, J. C. (1985). Reading and writing by letter-sounds. In K. E. Patterson, J. C. Marshall, & M. Coltheart (Eds.), *Surface dyslexia: Neuropsychological and cognitive analyses of phonological reading* (pp. 35–51). London: Lawrence Erlbaum Associates.

Patterson, K. E. (1978). Phonemic dyslexia: Errors of meaning and the meaning of errors. *Quarterly Journal of Experimental Psychology, 30,* 587–601.

Patterson, K. E. (1981). Neuropsychological approaches to the study of reading. *British Journal of Psychology, 72,* 151–174.

Patterson, K. E. (1982). The relation between reading and phonological coding: Further neuropsychological evidence. In A. W. Ellis (Ed.), *Normality and pathology in cognitive functions* (pp. 77–111). London: Academic Press.

Patterson, K. E., & Besner, D. (1984). Is the right hemisphere literate? *Cognitive Neuropsychology, 1,* 315–341.

Patterson, K. E., & Kay, J. (1982). Letter-by-letter reading: Psychological descriptions of a neurological syndrome. *Quarterly Journal of Experimental Psychology, 34A,* 411–442.

Patterson, K. E., Marshall, J. C., & Coltheart, M., (Eds.). (1985). *Surface dyslexia: Neuropsychological and cognitive analyses of phonological reading.* London: Lawrence Erlbaum Associates.

Saffran, E. M., Schwartz, M. F., & Marin, O. S. M. (1976). Semantic mechanisms in paralexia. *Brain and Language, 3,* 255–265.

Sartori, G., Barry, C., & Job, R. (1984). Phonological dyslexia: A review. In R. N. Malatesha & H. A. Whitaker (Eds.), *Dyslexia: A global issue* (pp. 339–356). The Hague: Martinus Nijhoff.

Schwartz, M. F., Saffran, E. M., & Marin, O. S. M. (1980). Fractionating the reading process in dementia: Evidence for word-specific print-to-sound associations. In M. Coltheart, K. Patterson, & J. C. Marshall (Eds.), *Deep dyslexia* (pp. 259–269). London: Routledge & Kegan Paul.

Sevush, S., Roeltgen, D. P., Campanella, D. J., & Heilman, K. M. (1983). Preserved oral reading in Wernicke's aphasia. *Neurology, 33,* 916–920.

Shallice, T. (1981a). Phonological agraphia and the lexical route in writing. *Brain, 104,* 413–429.

Shallice, T. (1981b). Neurological impairment of cognitive processes. *British Medical Bulletin, 37,* 187–192.

Warrington, E. K. (1975). The selective impairment of semantic memory. *Quarterly Journal of Experimental Psychology, 27,* 635–657.

Warrington, E. K., & Shallice T. (1980). Word-form dyslexia. *Brain, 103,* 99–112.

11 Speech Perception and Modularity: Evidence from Aphasia

Sheila E. Blumstein
Department of Linguistics
Brown University

ABSTRACT

In this chapter, we attempt to explore the modularity hypothesis particularly with respect to the speech processing system. Results from the study of aphasia suggest that the speech processing system operates in terms of a specialized vocabulary and set of operations tied specifically to language processing. This vocabulary involves the transformation of a continuous acoustic signal into discrete phonetic segments and ultimately into phonetic features. Further, the speech processing system seems to be separate from general auditory processing mechanisms and in this sense forms a sub-module of the language system. Nevertheless, the speech processing system seems to be interactive rather than autonomous with respect to the language module. That is, speech perception deficits do not seem to occur independent of deficits in higher levels of language and further, these deficits seem to be tied directly to and interact with deficits in lexical access.

Recent theories of language processing have suggested that language is modular. That is, it is suggested that the processing of language turns on mechanisms that are specialized for language and that are, in essence, apart from those mechanisms subserving other higher cortical functions. More importantly, the claim that language is modular requires that the language system be comprised of a specialized working vocabulary or set of primitives and a highly constrained set of operations dictated by theoretical principles inherent to language. There are a number of versions of a modular theory of language. Perhaps the strongest and most constrained are those of Fodor (1983), Garrett (1980), and Forster (1979), who hypothesize that language consists of submodules or autonomous subsystems, each with its own vocabulary and each with a restricted domain of analysis and processing. These sub-modules include lexical, syntactic, semantic, and message levels.

The major focus of research on the modularity issue has centered on the autonomy of the lexical processor (Swinney, 1982, but cf. Tyler & Marslen-Wilson, 1982), and the nature of the syntactic processor or parser (cf. Forster, 1979; Tannenhaus, Carlson, & Seidenburg, 1985; Frazier & Fodor, 1978). What has not been explicitly addressed within the modular framework is the nature of the phonological/phonetic processor. Surely, it is the case that the processing of the sound system of language requires a separate vocabulary from that of syntax, and the rules of phonology form a specialized sub-set of operations independent of higher levels of language processing. And yet, although the phonological rules of language are clearly specialized and internalized by the speaker-hearer, the question arises if there is a phonological level of representation that is "independent" of these other modules.

Phonological rules have as one of their primary functions specifying a possible word or meaningful unit in the language, i.e., it has its primary force with respect to the lexicon. Nonwords in a language are either phonological accidental gaps, i.e., words not found in the lexicon although phonologically allowable, e.g. *blik,* or they violate the phonological rules specifying what a possible word in the language may be, e.g. *bnik.* Therefore, it is probably the case that the specification of the phonological properties of the word (or minimal form-meaning unit) are not realized as a separate component independent of the lexicon, but rather form an inherent part of the lexicon. Nevertheless, the interpretation of the phonological form of lexical entries still is required for both speech production and language comprehension. Presumably, the 'vocabulary' of these forms as well as the rules for converting abstract phonological forms into articulatory commands in speech production and the rules for converting the acoustic waveform into a discrete phonological representation in speech perception requires specialized processing. It is the goal of this chapter to explore the nature of the phonological component with respect to the speech perception system.

The study of aphasia provides a potentially important source of information for such study, as it provides a window into the operating/organizing characteristics of the language system. In particular, it may be possible to answer a number of fundamental questions concerning the modularity of language including;

1. Is language modular? That is, can the language processing system be impaired independent of other cognitive systems;

2. If language is modular, is it functionally autonomous? That is, are the sub-modules functionally independent or do they interact with each other at all levels of language processing;

3. If there are separate modules, what is the nature of the vocabulary and processing operation for each module?; and

4. How are these modules organized for normal language processing?

With respect to the nature of the phonological component, the study of aphasia can help determine:

1. The nature of the vocabulary used in the phonological representation of language;

2. The nature of the processing operations, i.e., how the system converts a continuous acoustic waveform into discrete phonological properties;

3. The extent to which speech processing is modular, in the sense that it is independent of non-language auditory processing;

4. The extent to which speech processing is autonomous, in the sense that speech/phonetic processing is independent of other linguistic modules.

It is to these questions that we turn in the remainder of this chapter.

NATURE OF THE VOCABULARY IN THE PHONOLOGICAL REPRESENTATION OF LANGUAGE

The auditory perception of a word requires some type of transformation of the physical signal into a representation for lexical access. One critical question is the nature of this representation. It is perfectly possible that the representation of a word is stored as a wholistic auditory pattern (cf. Klatt, 1980). And yet, it has been generally hypothesized that the lexical representation of words is defined in terms of segments, i.e., individual sound units corresponding to phonemes and, more particularly, in terms of phonetic features defining these segments. Phonetic features are, in theory, the 'vocabulary' of lexical representation. They correspond to minimal articulatory/acoustic attributes which occur together to uniquely define a particular segment in the language inventory. For example, the segment /d/ is a consonant in contrast to a vowel, [+consonantal]; it is made with a complete closure in the mouth in contrast to a production with a different release characteristic, [+stop]; the closure is at the alveolar ridge in contrast to at the lips or velum, [+alveolar]; the vocal cords are vibrating in the vicinity of the stop release in contrast to beginning vibration some time after the release, [+voiced].

Evidence from aphasia is generally consistent with the view that lexical items are stored in terms of phonetic features. Luria (1966, 1970) was probably the first to hypothesize that auditory language comprehension deficits in aphasia might be attributable to impairments in the perception of sound contrasts. Luria hypothesized that Wernicke's aphasics, in particular, had a loss of "phonemic hearing", i.e., they are unable to perceive the underlying features comprising the sounds of speech such that they misperceive words that are phonologically similar. For example, given an array of pictures including a bee, a key, or the letter T, Wernicke's aphasics have difficulty pointing to the appropriate picture corresponding to the auditorily presented word.

We investigated in more detail the extent to which Wernicke's aphasics in particular, and aphasic patients in general, show deficits in auditory discrimination of stimuli varying in terms of their phonological features (Blumstein, Baker, & Goodglass, 1977). The discriminations required were divided among the distinctive feature values of place of articulation, voicing, and voice and place. The English stop consonants [p t k b d g] were used as the critical target contrasts. Both one and two syllable words were constructed contrasting equally in initial and final position for single syllables and in initial and medial position for the two syllable stimuli.

Results showed that aphasic patients made more errors on non-words than real word stimuli. Nevertheless, the phonological patterns of breakdown were similar across both types of stimuli. In particular patients made more errors in discriminating stimuli distinguished by one distinctive feature than by more than one distinctive feature, and comparing the single feature contrasts, place of articulation was more difficult than voicing contrasts. Thus, it is clearly the case that phonetic features comprise a critical dimension in the descriptive vocabulary of the phonological representation of language.

It is also worth noting that bundles of features define segmental properties of speech, and it is clear that segments also seem to be a critical part of the vocabulary of phonological representation. In the study just described (Blumstein, Baker, & Goodglass, 1977), discrimination pairs were also presented in which either the order of the constituent phonemes varied—for example, *mane* versus *name*, *task* versus *tax*; or the constituent phonemes of the unstressed syllable of a two syllable stimulus varied—for example, *tránsport* versus *tránsfer*, *descríbe* versus *prescríbe*. Patients clearly had difficulty discriminating these stimulus pairs, with about equally impaired performance in phoneme discrimination and syllable discrimination, and milder impairments in phoneme order discrimination. Clearly, then, aphasic patients show deficits reflecting not only the nature of the phonetic features comprising words, but also in segmental organization as well. Such findings are consistent with data from speech production in both normals and aphasics implicating not only phonetic features but also phonetic segments as critical units in the underlying representation of lexical items (Blumstein, 1973; Shattuck-Hufnagel, 1975).

THE NATURE OF PHONETIC PROCESSING

That phonetic features may be part of the vocabulary of lexical representation says nothing about how the perceptual system converts a continuous speech signal into the more abstract phonetic feature representation. Research in normal speech perception has as yet not provided a clear picture of this process. Nevertheless, it has been shown that listeners convert a continuous acoustic waveform into discrete segments, and further, that they show a very particular sensitivity to the acoustic parameters inherent in the stimuli. In particular, a continuum of stimuli may be generated in which the endpoint stimuli contain acoustic parameters appropriate to two different phonetic categories (ex. [da] and [ta]), and the remaining stimuli vary systematically between these parameters along a particular acoustic dimension. Listeners perceive this continuum of stimuli categorically. That is, when asked to label the stimuli, they divide the range into two separate categories with a fairly discrete change in the perception of the category at a particular stimulus along the continuum. When asked to discriminate the stimuli, they discriminate at a high degree of accuracy only those stimuli which they label as two different phonetic categories. Those stimuli labelled in terms of the same phonetic category are discriminated only slightly better than chance. This particular relation between labelling and discrimination has been called categorical perception (Liberman, Cooper, Shankweiler, & Studdert-Kennedy, 1967), and it has been shown to be a critical attribute for processing of those acoustic dimensions relating in particular to consonant perception.

The question with respect to aphasia is whether the deficits in speech perception relating to phonetic features and phonetic segments described earlier reflect impairments in the processing of those acoustic dimensions contributing to the phonetic representation of language. Investigations of categorical perception of speech in aphasia would help address this question. In addition, it provides a means of exploring the perception of the phonetic categories of speech independent of higher levels of language processing such as word meaning. As we see, however, the pattern of results obtained even in the perception of nonsense syllables implicates the importance of the relation between sound and meaning in speech perception deficits in aphasia.

Several studies have been conducted exploring categorical perception in aphasia (Basso, Casati, & Vignolo, 1977; Blumstein, Cooper, Zurif, & Caramazza, 1977; Blumstein, Tartter, Nigro, & Statlender, 1984). These studies have focused on two phonetic dimensions—voicing and place of articulation. For voicing, the acoustic dimension varied was voice-onset time, defined as the timing relation between the release of the consonant and the onset of vocal cord vibration, and the synthetic speech continuum varied between the exemplar stimuli [da] and [ta]. For place of articulation, two dimensions were varied. In one set of stimuli, the formant transitions varied in frequencies passing through the ranges known to be appropriate for the consonants [b d g] followed by steady-state formant frequencies appropriate to the vowel [a]. The second set of stimuli was identical to the first, except that a 5 ms noise burst appropriate to each place of articulation was appended to the transitions, thus producing a continuum varying in both formant transitions and burst onset. Using two stimulus continua for place of articulation, one with transitions only and the other with burst and transitions, allowed us to determine whether the presence of an additional acoustic cue, known to be important for place of articulation (Stevens & Blumstein, 1978), would enhance either labeling or discrimination ability.

The results of these studies are fairly straightforward. Three patterns of results emerged which cut across types of aphasia. Figure 11.1 shows these patterns for the perception of VOT (Blumstein, Cooper, Zurif, & Caramazza, 1977). In the first pattern, subjects could both label and discriminate the test stimuli. In this case, the slope of the obtained functions and the locus of the

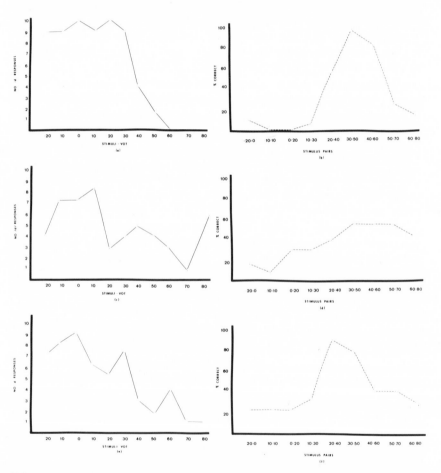

FIG.11.1. Labeling (a,c,e) and discrimination (b,d,f) performance on a voice-onset time continuum by three aphasic patients. Reprinted with permission from *Neuropsychologia, 15,* S. E. Blumstein, W. E. Cooper, E. B. Zurif, and A. Caramazza, *The Production and Perception of Voice-Onset Time in Aphasia,* 1977, Pergamon Press, Ltd.

phonetic boundaries were similar to those found for normals. In the second, they could neither label nor discriminate the test stimuli and the obtained functions showed no particular pattern. In the third, there was a dissociation between the ability to label and discriminate the stimuli. In particular, subjects showed a spared ability to discriminate the stimuli in the face of a complete failure to systematically identify the stimuli. Further, the obtained discrimination functions were similar in both shape and cross-over boundaries to those of normals. Figure 11.2 shows discrimination functions for the two place of articulation continua for normal controls and for those aphasic patients who could discriminate but not label the test stimuli. The similarity in the obtained functions between the two groups for the transition

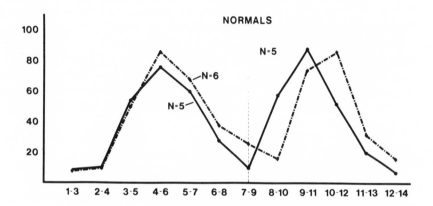

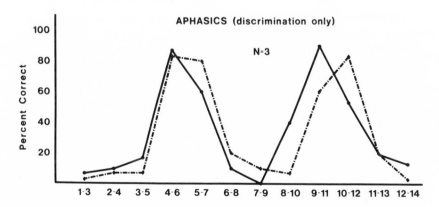

FIG.11.2. Discrimination of place of articulation in normals and aphasics. The solid line represents the burst plus transition stimuli and the dotted line represents the transition-only stimuli. Reprinted with permission from *Brain and Language*, 1984, *22*, p. 136.

only stimuli (represented by the dotted lines) and the burst plus transition stimuli (represented by the solid lines) is clearly shown. What is interesting is that the dissociation between labeling and discrimination ability found in the place of articulation study was not affected by the number and type of acoustic cues in the test continuum. Thus, a subject either succeeded or failed to label or discriminate the stimuli. If he succeeded, he would be able to do so for both stimulus continua, and if he failed, he would be unable to do so for either stimulus continuum.

The fact that no perceptual shifts were obtained for the discrimination and labeling functions compared to normals and that the discrimination functions remained stable even in those patients who could not label the stimuli underscores the stability of the categorical perception phenomenon in the face of brain-damage to the language areas. Further, these results are consistent with the view that the ability to discriminate categories of speech underlies the ability to use them linguistically for labeling (cf. Blumstein, Cooper, Zurif, & Caramazza, 1977; Eimas, Siqueland, Jusczyk, & Vigorito, 1971). Perhaps more importantly, the dissociation between labeling and discrimination suggests that the basis of the speech perception deficit in aphasic patients does not turn on a speech perception deficit per se, but rather on the stability of the link between the phonological representation and its label. To label a stimulus requires an ability to maintain a stable phonological representation for a particular lexical item—and it is this relation which seems to be compromised in a large number of aphasic patients.

MODULARITY OF SPEECH PROCESSING

The hypothesis that speech processing is modular would be supported if it could be shown that processing of the sounds of speech is independent or distinct from processing of other auditory nonlanguage stimuli. It is obviously the case that the auditory system processes both speech and non-speech by transforming air pressure waves into mechanical and ultimately electrical events that activate the brain. However, several researchers have suggested that speech is "special" in that it requires specialized mechanisms tuned to extract those properties of speech used in language communication (Liberman et al., 1967; Stevens & Blumstein, 1981). Let us explore how the study of aphasia may bear on this issue.

One important observation that provides at least, at first cut, support for the modularity of speech is the distinction between two syndromes—auditory agnosia and aphasia proper. In auditory agnosia, the patient shows a selective impairment in the recognition of nonverbal sounds and noises—so that he is unable to appropriately categorize environmental sounds as dogs barking, horns honking, or bells ringing, and he often fails to discriminate these sounds as well (Vignolo, 1969). In contrast, patients with speech perception deficits in aphasia generally are able to recognize non-verbal auditory stimuli, while displaying the types of speech perception deficits described earlier.

Nevertheless, although the distinction between verbal and non-verbal stimuli seems to be instantiated differently by the brain, the acoustic structure of the verbal and non-verbal stimuli is quite different. A stronger test of the claim of the modularity of speech is to determine whether generalized auditory mechanisms underlie the processing of speech sounds and, thus whether deficits in speech processing reflect deficits in auditory processing. This issue can be studied in two ways. In the first, manipulations may be made of acoustic dimensions which may not affect the phonetic percept but that may in principle enhance general auditory processing. The question to be answered is whether such auditory manipulations "improve" speech processing. Another way this question may be studied is to compare the processing of a speech signal to its auditory analogue, i.e., a nonspeech auditory signal that shares certain critical acoustic dimensions with a particular speech stimulus. Both methodologies have been recently applied to aphasia, although many more detailed studies will be required before the modularity of speech hypothesis can be fully explored.

As shown earlier, perception of place of articulation contrasts in aphasia is particularly impaired. The question arises why this dimension seems to be so vulnerable in aphasia. One possibility has to do with the acoustic properties inherent in place of articulation contrasts. In particular, acoustic properties for place of articulation seem to reside in the rapid spectral changes over a short time domain spanning about 25 ms (Stevens & Blumstein, 1978; 1981). Tallal (Tallal & Newcombe, 1978; Tallal & Piercy, 1975) has hypothesized that the basis for impairments in processing place of articulation lies in the rapidity with which such spectral changes need to be resolved. In work with language-disabled children as well as adult aphasics, she suggested that increasing the duration of the formant transitions to provide, as it were, more time to resolve these spectral changes might improve place of articulation discrimination. Although she showed significant improvement in perception for language-disabled children, her results with aphasics were less clearcut, as they showed only a nonsignificant improvement in perception when transition length was increased (Tallal & Newcombe, 1978). We decided to pursue this question in more detail by exploring both discrimination and labeling for place of articulation in stimuli containing formant transitions varying in duration. Stimuli included exemplar [da] and [ga] stimuli with or without bursts and containing F2 and F3 formant transitions of either 45, 65, or 85 ms duration.

Results can be summarized as follows. Neither labeling nor discrimination performance was improved as a consequence of lengthening formant transitions. In fact, subjects' labeling performance was significantly worse with the longest (85) ms transition length compared to either the 45 or 65 ms transition length conditions. Thus, there is no evidence that enhancement of an auditory dimension that still maintains the phonetic quality of a speech stimulus improves the perception of that stimulus. In this case, time or duration was the critical variable, and it failed to provide improved performance for the perception of place of articulation.

As just indicated, the distinction among place of articulation contrasts in stop consonants turns on the spectral properties of the signal in the vicinity of the stop release. It is the case that the differences in the burst frequency and the frequency and direction of the formant transitions contribute to these different spectral characteristics. In particular, for [da] versus [ga] the F3 formant transitions are falling in the former and rising in the latter, and the burst frequency excites F4 in the former case and F3 in the latter case. Given these differences, we attempted to determine if a non-speech analogue to the [da ga] stimuli would show similar perceptual performance to that of the speech stimuli. In particular, if it is the case that auditory processing underlies speech processing, then perceptual performance of speech and non-speech analogues should be correlated. If a subject can discriminate the non-speech stimuli, he should be able to discriminate the speech stimuli; if he is unable to discriminate the non-speech stimuli, he should be unable to discriminate the speech stimuli. Dissociations in performance would suggest that the underlying basis for the processing of the two types of stimuli is different or at least is not directly related. Figure 11.3 shows the results of discrimination performance on a set of speech stimuli contrasting [da] and [ga] and a comparable set of non-speech stimuli. As the Figure shows, the ability to perform both tasks is not necessarily related. In general, patients perform better on the speech discrimination task than the non-speech task, although two patients (a Wernicke and an anomic) performed better on the non-speech than speech stimuli. More importantly, of the 5 subjects who could not meet criterion on the non-speech task (i.e., could not perform better than chance on a pre-test containing exemplars of the stimulus contrasts), 4 were able to perform the speech discrimination task, and two performed at a very high level (8.8 and 9.4 out of 10). Thus, there is a dissociation in performance between the perception of speech and non-speech stimuli, with the ability to discriminate speech stimuli independent of the ability to discriminate non-speech sounds.

In sum, the results of these two studies are consistent with the view that speech processing is modular. That is, although speech processing clearly requires processing mechanisms of the auditory system, the nature of this processing seems to be distinct from generalized auditory processing. In this sense, processing of speech does indeed seem to be "special" (Liberman, Cooper, Shankweiler, & Studdert-Kennedy, 1967).

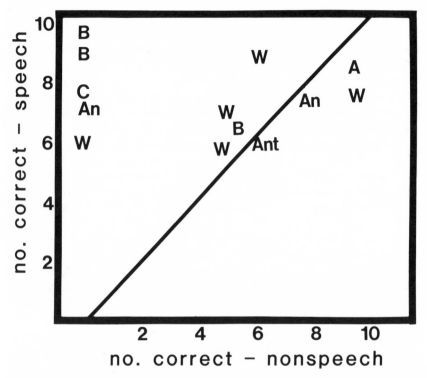

FIG.11.3. Discrimination performance (out of 10) of aphasic patients (B = Broca, C = Conduction, W = Wernicke, A = Anomic, Ant = Anterior) on speech stimuli and non-speech analogues.

THE AUTONOMY OF THE SPEECH PROCESSOR

Although it is clearly the case that the speech perception system must inform higher levels of language processing including lexical access and syntactic parsing, it is less clear whether the operation of this system is in some sense independent of these other levels of processing. For a system to be functionally autonomous, it must operate only on input from lower level systems, and it, in principle, can not be affected by other modules that are downstream from it (cf. Fodor, 1983; Forster, 1979). Thus, although the speech processing system may affect other sub-modules of language, if it is autonomous, its processing should not be affected by lexical, syntactic, or semantic factors. If speech processing were affected by these higher levels, then the speech processor would be interactive rather than autonomous (cf. Marslen-Wilson &

Tyler, 1980). In an interactive system, the operating characteristics of the speech system would not operate solely on information internal to it. Such information would include the vocabulary and operating characteristics of the speech processing system such as the transformation of the acoustic signal to a phonetic representation and the phonological rules of the language system. Rather, an interactive speech system would be influenced by the vocabulary of other submodules of language including the lexical status of a word, the semantic properties of that word, its grammatical function, and so on.

Results from aphasia provide some evidence that suggest that the speech processing system is interactive rather than autonomous with respect to the language module. This evidence comes from a number of studies that have attempted to explore the basis of auditory language comprehension deficits in aphasia and the extent to which speech perception problems contribute to such deficits.

Perhaps the weakest form of evidence supporting an interactive view of speech processing is that among the aphasia syndromes, there are none that seem to reflect a selective problem in speech processing. It has been shown that even Wernicke's aphasics who seem to have an impairment in phonemic hearing are no more impaired in phonemic discrimination tasks than are mixed anterior or global aphasics. Moreover, their performance on these tasks is better than other groups despite the fact that the Wernicke's aphasics display the poorest auditory language comprehension ability (Blumstein, Baker, & Goodglass, 1977). In fact, results from a large number of studies have shown a poor correlation between speech perception abilities and auditory language comprehension (Basso et al., 1977; Jauhainen & Nuutila, 1977; Miceli, Gainotti, Caltagirone, & Masullo, 1980; Lesser, 1978). These results not only suggest that the basis for auditory comprehension deficits can not be due to selective impairments in speech processing, but also show that all aphasic patients regardless of clinical syndrome and degree of language comprehension impairment show some deficit in speech processing. Perhaps the only aphasic syndrome for which there is some small suggestion that the deficit is selective with respect to speech is pure word deafness. However, this syndrome is very rare, it is often accompanied by more general auditory perceptual deficits, and it usually occurs with bilateral lesions or deep unilateral lesions cutting callosal fibers to the opposite hemisphere (Hecaen & Albert, 1978).

Nevertheless, the failure to show selective speech deficits does not in itself indicate that the speech processing system is not an autonomous sub-system. What is more problematic for the autonomous hypothesis are the results discussed earlier in this chapter showing that (a) aphasic patients' discrimination ability is affected by the lexical status of the stimulus pairs (Blumstein, Baker, & Goodglass, 1977); and (b) aphasic patients seem to display particular difficulty in speech perception tasks when the task requires them to use the sounds of speech linguistically, i.e. to relate sound and meaning. With respect to the first point, the fact that aphasic patients' ability to discriminate sound contrasts varies as a function of whether the test stimuli are real words or nonsense syllables suggests that the speech perception system is not operating independent of meaning. That is, the lexical status of a phonological form is affecting perception, not just the phonological properties inherent in that form. With respect to the second point, the fact that aphasic patients display deficits in speech processing especially when they must provide a speech sound with a linguistic label suggests again that the processing of the vocabulary of the phonological system is functionally related and inextricably tied to sound-meaning correspondences.

Two studies have explicitly explored the relation between phonological factors and lexical access with respect to aphasia. In the first study, Baker, Blumstein, and Goodglass, (1981) found an interaction between phonological and semantic factors in lexical access. In this study, they devised a series of tasks designed to increase systematically the demands for semantic processing of auditorily presented words. In all tasks, the same set of test words was used. These words were monosyllabic names of picturable objects, and the words themselves varied in terms of the phonological distance of the correct response from the test foils including voice, place, and voice plus place. In the first task, subjects were required to make an auditory discrimination (same–different) on the set of words (e.g., *pear-bear*). The second task was an auditory–visual discrimination task in which subjects heard an auditorily presented word, e.g., *pear,* and were required to determine if the visually presented picture of the words was the same (e.g., *pear*) or different (e.g., *bear*). In the third task, subjects were also presented with an auditorily presented word (e.g., *pear*) but they had to choose the visually correct match out of a set of four pictures including the correct match (e.g., *pear*), a phonologically related real word (e.g., *bear*), a semantically related word to the target word (e.g., *grapes*), or a semantically related word to the phonologically similar foil (e.g., *wolf*).

Results showed that for both Wernicke's and Broca's aphasics, when semantic demands increased, phonological discrimination suffered. That is, subjects made increasing numbers of errors from tasks 1–3, and within each task, they made more errors with words separated by the feature place, then the feature voice, and fewest with the features voice and place. When phonological discrimination was more difficult, semantic processing suffered. That is, while semantically based errors outnumbered phonologically based errors in the third task, the degree to which such errors were made varied as a function of the phonological contrasts in the stimulus array. Thus, more semantically based errors were made with words in which the test array included place contrasts than voice contrasts and fewest errors occurred with voice/place contrasts. Although Wernicke's aphasics were more impaired than

Broca's aphasics at all levels, their performance was disproportionately impaired as semantic mediation was introduced.

It is important to note that the pattern of results obtained indicates that both Broca's and especially the Wernicke's aphasic deficit is neither purely a low-level speech processing deficit, nor is it purely a semantic coding deficit. Rather, the deficit seems to lie in the relation between the phonological structure of a word and its meaning. That phonological structure plays a critical role can be seen in the results of the second and third tasks. In both tasks, a significant feature effect was obtained, despite the fact that the subject was presented with a single auditory stimulus followed by a visual stimulus. The phonological contrast giving rise to the feature effect then was dictated by the relation between the auditory stimulus and the visual choice presented to the subject. Presumably, the contrast was created in the arousal of the names of the items in the visual display or to the creation of a phonological representation of the visual stimuli. That is, in the second task, in order for a subject to show a feature effect for voicing given the auditory stimulus "bear", he would have had to encode the picture of "pear" phonologically to make his decision. If the subject were doing this task on a purely semantic basis, i.e. encoding the phonological shape of "bear" into a semantic representation and comparing it to the picture "pear", no feature effect would have been found. Similar reasoning applies to the significant feature effect found in the third task.

In a more recent study with normals, Milberg, Blumstein, and Dworetzky (1984) also found that phonological factors affected semantic facilitation in a lexical decision task. However, unlike the study of Baker et al. (1981) which varied the phonological properties of real words, they showed effects of the phonological similarity of non-words on the semantic facilitation of real words. In particular, they presented normal subjects with auditorily presented word-pairs for lexical decision on the second word (target). They systematically varied the first word (prime) in the following ways: in one condition, the prime was semantically related to the target (*cat-dog*); in the second, the prime was a nonword which was phonologically one feature from the semantically related prime (*gat-dog*); in the third, the prime was a nonword which was several phonetic features from the semantically related prime (*wat-dog*); and in the fourth, the control condition, the prime was a real word semantically and phonologically unrelated to the target (*table-dog*). Results, presented in Fig. 11.4 showed a linear relationship between phonetic distance and lexical decision facilitation. That is, subjects showed the shortest reaction time to semantically related words, followed in increasing order by nonwords related by one feature, nonwords related by more than one feature, and semantically unrelated real words. These results suggest that in normals, phonological factors do interact with lexical access, and perhaps more importantly even nonwords at some level of processing access the lexi-

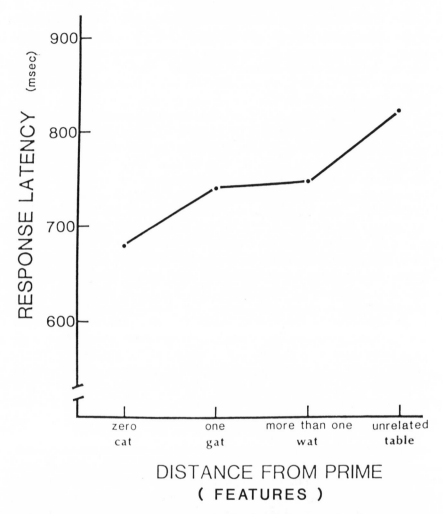

FIG.11.4.   Response latency to real word targets preceded by a semantically related real word prime (zero), a non-word distinguished from the semantically related word by one phonetic feature or more than one phonetic feature, and a semantically unrelated real word.

con. This access seems to be a function of the phonological distance of a non-word from a possible real word in the language. Although the results with normals clearly support the view that phonological factors do in fact influence semantic mediation in lexical access, it is instructive to explore the performance of aphasic patients on such tasks. It is possible that aphasics may show patterns of dissociation not found in normals, patterns which may provide clues as to the autonomy or lack of autonomy of the lexical access system from phonological processing. Earlier studies have shown that aphasic patients do show semantic facilitation in a lexical decision task (Blumstein, Milberg, & Schrier, 1982; Milberg & Blumstein, 1981). The question to pursue then is whether such facilitation is affected by phonological factors, as seems to be the case in normals.

To date, 12 aphasic patients have been tested, representing a number of diagnostic groups including Broca's, Wernicke's, anomic, conduction, transcortical motor, and global aphasics. Two patterns of results have emerged. These are shown in Fig. 11.5. It is important to note that the two groups behave similarly on the baseline condition (unrelated real words) and on the semantically related condition (zero). Thus, both groups show, as reported in earlier studies, semantic facilitation in a lexical decision task. However, their performance differed with respect to the phonologically related non-word primes. In one pattern (II), representing the performance of seven patients, the aphasics show phonological facilitation in that they are faster in making a lexical decision when a non-word prime (i.e., *gat* or *wat*) phonologically related to a semantically related real word prime (*cat*) precedes the target (*dog*). However, unlike normals, they do not show the linear relation based on phonetic distance. These results suggest that these patients have a fragile and impaired phonetic system in which even non-words which have a large phonetic distance from possible words still access the lexicon. The consequence of such an impairment could be that a large number of entries in the lexicon would be presumably activated without the 'filtering' effect provided by a normally functioning speech perception system. This impairment could influence importantly lexical-semantic access, because there is in effect a reduced threshold for activation of lexical items in the language.

This first pattern of results is consistent with the view that the speech processing system may indeed be autonomous, since any phonological form which is a possible word activates the lexicon. However, the second pattern of results suggests that there is indeed a complex interaction of phonological representation and lexical access. In particular, for this second group of patients, access to the lexicon crucially hinges on whether the auditorily presented phonological form directly represents a possible lexical item. That is, the perceptual input is processed by the language processing system *only in so far as* it has lexical status. Let us review these findings.

In the second pattern (I), representing the performance of 5 subjects, the phonological form of the nonword prime has *no* effect on the lexical decision for a real-word. In fact, reaction time to the target words preceded by non-words is at least as slow (if not slower) than the semantically unrelated prime. These results indicate that as long as a stimulus is a nonword, no facilitation will occur for a real word relative to the unrelated word baseline. Thus, for the speech processing system of these aphasics, the auditory input must match the stored phonological representation of a word in the lexicon.

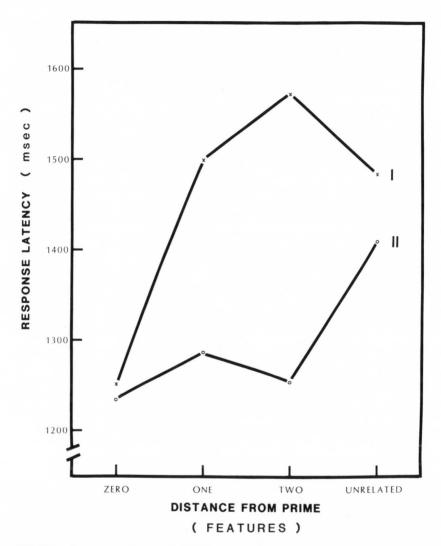

FIG.11.5. Response latency of two groups of aphasic patients to real word targets preceded by a semantically related word prime (zero), a non-word distinguished by one phonetic feature from the semantically related prime (one) or more than one phonetic feature (two), and a semantically unrelated real word (unrelated).

If it does not, the lexicon is not addressable. Such results indicate that these aphasics have a speech processing deficit specifically related to lexical access. In particular, they can only access the lexicon with a good exemplar of the phonological representation of that word. Unlike the perceptual system of normals which actively processes noisy inputs and "normalizes" them with respect to possible real word entries, the aphasics have a much more limited access to their lexical system. Such limited access could well affect comprehension of words and ultimately of sentences. More importantly, it indicates that the phonological system is not independent of the lexical access system.

ACKNOWLEDGMENTS

This research was supported in part by Grant NS 06209 to the Boston University School of Medicine, and Grant NS 22282 to Brown University.

REFERENCES

Baker, E., Blumstein, S. E., & Goodglass, H. (1981). Interaction between phonological and semantic factors in auditory comprehension. *Neuropsychologia, 19*, 1–16.
Basso, A., Casati, G., & Vignolo, L. A. (1977). Phonemic identification defects in aphasia. *Cortex, 13*, 84–95.
Blumstein, S. E. (1973). *A phonological investigation of aphasic speech*. The Hague: Mouton.
Blumstein, S. E., Baker, E., & Goodglass, H. (1977). Phonological factors in auditory comprehension in aphasia. *Neuropsychologia, 15*, 19–30.
Blumstein, S. E., Cooper, W.E., Zurif, E., & Caramazza, A. (1977). The perception and production of voice-onset time in aphasia. *Neuropsychologia, 15*, 371–383.
Blumstein, S. E., Milberg, W., & Schrier, R. (1982). Semantic processing in aphasia: Evidence from an auditory lexical decision task. *Brain and Language, 17*, 301–315.
Blumstein, S. E., Tartter, V. C., Nigro, G., & Statlender, S. (1984). Acoustic cues for the perception of place of articulation in aphasia. *Brain and Language, 22*, 128–149.
Eimas, P. D., Siqueland, E. R., Jusczyk, P., & Vigorito, J. (1971). Speech perception in infants. *Science, 171*, 303–306.
Fodor, J. (1983). *The modularity of mind*. Cambridge, MA: Bradford.
Forster, K. I. (1979). Levels of processing and the structure of the language processor. In W. E. Cooper & E. C. T. Walker (Eds.), *Sentence processing* (pp. 27–85). New York: Wiley.
Frazier, L., & Fodor, J. D. (1978). The sausage machine: A new two-stage parsing model. *Cognition, 6*, 291–325.
Garrett, M. (1980). Levels of sentence production. In B. Butterworth (Ed.), *Language production* (pp. 177–221). New York: Academic Press.
Hecaen, H., & Albert, M. (1978). *Human neuropsychology*. New York: Wiley.
Jauhiainen, T., & Nuutila, A. (1977). Auditory perception of speech and speech sounds in recent and recovered cases of aphasia. *Brain and Language, 4*, 572–579.
Klatt, D. (1980). Speech perception: A model of acoustic-phonetic analysis and lexical access. In R. A. Cole (Ed.), *Perception and production of fluent speech* (pp. 243–288). Hillsdale: Lawrence Erlbaum Associates.
Lesser, R. (1978). *Linguistic investigations of aphasia*. London: Arnold.
Liberman, A. M., Cooper, F. S., Shankweiler, D. P., & Studdert-Kennedy, M. (1967). Perception of the speech code. *Psychological Review, 74*, 431–461.
Luria, A. R. (1966). *Higher cortical functions in man*. New York: Basic Books.
Marslen-Wilson, W. D., & Tyler, L. K. (1980). The temporal structure of spoken language understanding. *Cognition, 8*, 1–71.
Miceli, G., Gainotti, G., Caltagirone, C., & Masullo, C. (1980). Some aspects of phonological impairment in aphasia. *Brain and Language, 11*, 159–169.

Milberg, W., Blumstein, S. E., & Dworetzky, B. (1984). *Phonological factors in semantic facilitation: Evidence from auditory lexical decision tasks.* Manuscript submitted for publication.

Shattuck-Hufnagel, S. (1975). *Speech errors and sentence production.* Unpublished doctoral dissertation, Massachusetts Institute of Technology.

Stevens, K. N., & Blumstein, S. E. (1978). Invariant cues for place of articulation in stop consonants. *Journal of the Acoustical Society of America, 64,* 1358-1368.

Stevens, K. N., & Blumstein, S. E. (1981). The search for invariant acoustic correlates of phonetic features. In P. D. Eimas, & J. L. Miller (Eds.), *Perspectives in the study of speech* (pp. 1-38). Hillsdale: Lawrence Erlbaum Associates.

Swinney, D. (1982). The structure and time-course of information interaction during speech comprehension, lexical segmentation, access, and interpretation. In J. Mehler, E. Walker, & M. Garrett (Eds.), *Perspectives on mental representations* (pp. 151-167). Hillsdale: Lawrence Erlbaum Associates.

Tallal, P., & Newcombe, F. (1978). Impairment of auditory perception and language comprehension in dysphasia. *Brain and Language, 5,* 13-24.

Tallal, P., & Piercy, M. (1975). Developmental aphasia: The perception of brief vowels and extended stop consonants. *Neuropsychologia, 13,* 69-74.

Tannenhaus, M., Carlson, G. N., & Seidenberg, M. S. (1985). Do listeners compute linguistic representations. In P. Dowty, L. Kartunnen, & A. Zwicky (Eds.), *Natural language parsing: Psychological, computational, and theoretical perspectives* (pp. 359-408). Cambridge: Cambridge University Press.

Tyler, L. K. & Marslen-Wilson, W. D. (1982). Speech comprehension processes. In J. Mehler, E. Walker, & M. Garrett (Eds.), *Perspectives on mental representation* (pp. 359-408). Hillsdale: Lawrence Erlbaum Associates.

Vignolo, L. (1969). Auditory agnosia: A review and report of recent evidence. In A. L. Benton (Ed.), *Contributions to clinical neuropsychology* (pp. 172-208). Chicago: Aldine.

12

The Neurofunctional Modularity of Cognitive Skills: Evidence from Japanese Alexia and Polyglot Aphasia

Michel Paradis
Department of Linguistics
McGill University

ABSTRACT

Evidence from double dissociations between aspects of reading and writing in Japanese dyslexic and dysgraphic patients, as well as between the various languages of polyglot aphasic patients, is interpreted as supportive of the hypothesis that cognitive processing is fractionable into subcomponents, themselves fractionable into sub-subcomponent modules. The demonstrated double-dissociative inhibition of various aspects of language processing is taken as evidence of their neurofunctional modularity. More specifically, it is argued that the faculty of language fractions into as many vertical subsystems as there are languages represented in the patient's brain, that within each language subsystem reading and writing are isolable modular subsubsystems, and that there are as many such modular subsubsystems as there are orthographies involved.

One of the fundamental questions that concern the neuropsychologist of language is whether language processing goes through a sequential (horizontal) series of processes common to all cognitive skills (e.g., perception, memory, reasoning), or whether language is represented in the brain as a vertical system independent of other cognitive functions. It will be argued that neuropsychological evidence from Japanese dyslexia and dysgraphia as well as from polyglot aphasia points to the organization of cognitive skills into independent (though interactive) neurofunctional modular systems, not dependent on a number of common basic processes that would underlie all cognitive functions.

For the purpose of this chapter, a module is defined as an isolable unit with a specific purpose, functioning as a component of a larger unit. The evidence which will be presented is interpreted as indicative of a neurofunctional organization of cognitive skills into vertical systems of horizontal modules. A vertical system roughly corresponds to a faculty, or capacity, or a specific cognitive domain (e.g., language). A vertical functional system may fraction into equally vertical modular subsystems (e.g., various languages). A neurofunctional system may thus be considered as a modular neurosystem comprising two or more modular subsystems, themselves fractionable into subcomponent functional modules. The criterion for neurofunctional modularity is the demonstration of double dissociation between cognitive skills or between two components of a cognitive skill. These dissociations are generally observed subsequent to focal brain injury. Following Caramazza (1984) it will be assumed that at least in some cases (if not in all cases) there is a transparent relation between pathological performance and normal cognition. However, the model need not make any anatomical claims. It is described in terms of neuro-*functional* systems, and selective inhibition of a particular component function is taken as evidence of its existence as an independent neural functional unit. Several subsystems may be considered part of a larger system (or several modules as part of a subsystem) when it can be demonstrated that they are often inhibited together as a whole. Nor is the model committed to the claim that different systems of modules are subserved by faculty-specific underlying mechanisms of a nature different from that of the basic neural principles underlying any other neural modular system. The model only implies that certain neural circuits are (possibly—but not necessarily—exclusively) devoted to a particular cognitive skill. Those circuits may be constituted of the same basic elements functioning in accordance with the same basic laws of neural activity as any other circuit. Indeed it would be surprising if the various cognitive skills did not make use of similar basic neurofunctional principles. Basic elements (biochemical properties, neurons) and basic functional mechanisms (organization of systems of neurons, biochemical reactions) will be assumed to be uniform across cognitive domains.

EVIDENCE FROM JAPANESE DYSLEXIA AND DYSGRAPHIA

Let us turn to the evidence. The data culled from the Japanese literature since the beginning of the century and reported in Paradis, Hagiwara and Hildebrandt (1985) reveal a number of double dissociations in the reading and writing performance of Japanese brain damaged patients. The Japanese writing system combines syllabic and ideographic characters: two sets of syllabic characters (*hiragana* and *katakana,* collectively known as *kana*), and one set of ideographic characters (*kanji*). *Katakana* is used to transcribe foreign words, and also to signal emphasis (in a way similar to the use of italics in English print), *hiragana* is used to write grammatical morphemes (derivational suffixes, case markers, inflections, postpositions, etc.). There is a one-to-one correspondence between each *kana* and the syllable it represents, as well as between each Japanese syllable and the *kana* that represents it, with only 5 minor context-dependent exceptions: The syllables [o] and [ɛ] are represented by the character for [u] and [i] respectively, when they occur as the second of a geminate vowel in some words; the topic marker [wa] is spelled [ha] and the directional marker [ɛ] is spelled [hɛ]; a character of the same shape as the *kana* for [tsu] but of smaller size is used to represent the second of any geminate consonant. The character for [jo], but of smaller size, indicates the palatalization of the previous character.

Thus overall, the *kana* script represents a very regular set of grapheme-syllable correspondences.

On the other hand, each *kanji* generally stands for a morpheme. It has two or more pronunciations which are not systematically related to the shape of the character. Each lexical morpheme is represented by a different character (even when homophonous, which is often the case). So on the one hand we have a system totally phonologically based (and, like the phonemes of alphabetical scripts, *kana* are basically without meaning, except of course in the case of monosyllabic words, just as in English some letter names correspond to words: bee, tea, pea, eye) and on the other hand a system of characters arbitrary with respect to pronunciation but generally representative of a meaning. The two scripts are systematically combined in normal writing since, as we have seen, *kanji* are used to represent lexical morphemes and *kana* to represent grammatical (bound or free) morphemes, and a sentence necessarily includes both (for further details, see Paradis et al., 1985).

Kanji can be compared to digits in the English or French numeral system in that there is no systematic (analytic) correspondence between sound and grapheme; that is, there is nothing in their shape indicative of their pronunciation, nor is each shape always pronounced in the same way, depending on context: 3 [θri:] but [θərti] in the context of the sequence 32; 2 [tu:] but [twɛnti] in the sequence 25 and [tuhʌndrəd] in the sequence 264; or even more clearly in French 2 [dø] but [vɛ̃t] in the sequence 27. The French system even contains an analog to *jukuji-kun,* in which the pronunciation of a compound *kanji* is independent of the pronunciation of each individual character in any of its usual readings: 7 [sɛt] and 2 [dø] are pronounced [swasãtduz]. 7 never stands for [swasãt] nor 2 for [duz]. A digit is thus somewhat analogous to a single character *kanji*, a two or three digit number to a multicharacter or compound *kanji* with a *jukuji-kun* pronunciation.

Various types of dissociations between the ability to read (and/or write) and comprehend words in *kana* and *kanji* have been observed among

Japanese brain damaged patients. A review of the Japanese literature since the beginning of the century (Paradis et al., 1985) reveals patients able to read aloud and comprehend *kanji* but unable to read aloud and comprehend words written with *kana* characters, as well as patients able to read aloud and understand words written with *kana* but not *kanji*. This double dissociation points to the independence of *kana* and *kanji* as functional systems, since either one is capable of selective impairment and of selective preservation. As with other languages, there is also a double dissociation between the ability to read and the ability to write, leading to alexia without agraphia and agraphia without alexia, thus establishing reading and writing as two separate neurofunctional systems. The same kinds of dissociation as in reading are evidenced in the selective ability to write *kana* or *kanji*. Some patients are able to write *kanji* but not *kana* while some patients are able to write *kana* but not *kanji*.

The independence of the reading and writing systems from each other, as well as of the *kana* and *kanji* subsystems from each other within each system, is further demonstrated by cases of better reading *kanji* than *kana* in the context of better writing *kana* than *kanji*, as well as the reverse, namely, better reading *kana* than *kanji* in the context of better writing *kanji* than *kana*. Thus so far, four independent neurofunctional systems, each susceptible of double dissociation in addition to selective impairment and selective preservation are clearly documented: *kanji* reading, *kana* reading, *kanji* writing, *kana* writing.

In reading, a further double dissociation obtains between the ability to read words out loud and the ability to comprehend their meaning, independently for *kana* and for *kanji*. One patient was able to understand words spelled in *kana* better than he could read them aloud, some could read aloud words written in *kana* without comprehension. The same dissociation was observed with *kanji*: some patients could read *kanji* aloud without comprehending them, some could comprehend *kanji* without being able to read them aloud. Some patients were able to read *kanji* aloud better than words spelled in *kana*, others were able to read aloud words in *kana* better than in *kanji*. Some patients are reported to have been able to comprehend *kanji* better than words spelled with *kana* but at the same time they could read aloud *kana* better than *kanji*.

Hence, *kanji* reading and *kana* reading rely on different neurofunctional systems; *kanji* writing and *kana* writing are likewise subserved by separate systems. *Kanji* reading and *kanji* writing are further neurofunctionally differentiated as well as *kana* reading and *kana* writing. It is not just that reading is different from writing, simply because each function relies on different peripheral mechanisms, since *kana* reading and *kanji* writing can be selectively impaired in the same person, and each system can be selectively impaired or selectively operative for only one script. Each function (reading, writing) for each script (*kana, kanji*) can thus be regarded as an independent neurofunctional system.

Reading may be considered a vertical neurofunctional system which in Japanese fractionates into a *kanji* and a *kana* subsystem. The same fractionation is evidenced in bilinguals between different writing systems (Roman/ Cyrillic alphabet; English alphabetic/Chinese ideographic; etc.). Further fractionation of the *kana* system in Japanese into a *hiragana* and a *katakana* subsystem is suggested by a dissociation in writing reported by Ohta and Koyabu (1970).

EXTENSION TO ALL WRITING SYSTEMS

Different orthographies allow different strategies and hence different kinds of impairment. The type of possible errors in reading and/or writing is constrained by what can go wrong in the system. Dyslexic (and dysgraphic) symptoms are necessarily a function of the logical possibilities inherent in the impaired system. For instance, if a feature of the system is absolutely regular, there is no possibility of error by over-generalization; if there is only one type of script (as in most languages) there is only one system for reading (though here again, numerals may—and indeed do—show differential impairment). An orthographic system with no grapheme-phoneme correspondence rules (say, a totally ideographic system) could not lead to the acquisition of a grapheme-phoneme correspondence module. A fortiori, an individual who never learned to read, obviously does not possess a neurofunctional reading system and is not susceptible to pure alexia (or, for that matter, to any other form of dyslexia).

Thus, it is reasonable to assume that whenever a particular strategy is appropriate to perform a given cognitive skill, given the structure of the symbolic system involved, a neurofunctional module or series of consecutive and/or parallel modules will develop.

Within this framework, each box in the diagram of John Marshall's (1982a) reading model qualifies as a (horizontal) neurofunctional module, each capable of being selectively impaired or of remaining selectively operative, yielding the various patterns of dyslexia reported in the literature. Each route available to the normal reader is seen as a (vertical) subsystem within the (vertical) system of reading (and, *mutatis mutandis,* for the writing system, inasmuch as each module exhibits a double dissociation with respect to its reading analogue).

Because Japanese has not one, but two, systems of orthography, one may expect two separate vertical neurofunctional subsystems, one for each type of script. Because each system contains some exceptions, each route postulated for English readers by Marshall (1982a) should be available for each script in Japanese, and cases of surface and deep dyslexia have indeed been described in Japanese patients, for each type of script. More sophisticated classes of stimuli should also allow to identify cases of phonological dyslexia as well as direct written-word-to-oral-word dyslexia in both scripts (Paradis et al., 1985).

Inasmuch as numerous cases of alexia without agraphia (Ajax, 1967, 1977; Beauvois & Dérouesné, 1979; Caplan & Hedley-Whyte, 1974; Cohen et al., 1976; Donoso, Santander, & Santos, 1980; Greenblatt, 1973; Judd, Gardner, & Geschwind, 1983; Johansson & Fahlgren, 1979; Karanth, 1981; Mani, Fine, & Mayberry, 1981; Michel et al., 1979; Reinvang, 1975; Sroka, Solsi & Bornstein, 1973; Turgman, Goldhammer, & Braham, 1979; Vincent et al., 1977), of agraphia without alexia (Auerback & Alexander, 1981; Dubois, Hécaen, & Marcie, 1969; Fau et al., 1976, Laine & Marttila, 1981; Valenstein, & Heilman, 1979), and more recently cases of double dissociation between phonological dyslexia and surface dysgraphia (Beauvois & Dérouesné, 1981), and between surface dyslexia and phonological dysgraphia (Roeltgen, Sevush, & Heilman, 1983) have been documented, reading and writing may be considered to be represented as independent systems, each subserved by its own neurofunctional substrate. Besides, cases of pure acquired alexia and pure acquired agraphia (i.e., without aphasia), as well as cases of aphasia without alexia (Heilman et al., 1979) and aphasia without agraphia (Michel et al., 1979), reflect the independence of reading and writing from the spoken language system.

EVIDENCE FROM APHASIA IN BILINGUALS AND THE CASE FOR NEUROFUNCTIONAL INHIBITION

The literature on aphasia in bilinguals and polyglots over the past 150 years (Paradis, 1983) has provided us with sufficient evidence to conclude that two languages in the same brain are neurofunctionally isolable (Paradis, 1980). As many as 37 cases of selective loss of one of the patient's languages have been reported; an additional 11 manifested a clearly differential pattern of recovery, one of their languages being much less impaired than the other; in 16 cases one language did not become available until the other had been maximally restored; 12 cases have been reported to exhibit reciprocal antagonism, namely, the language first recovered would regress as a second language became available again and improved (Paradis, 1977). It has been repeatedly argued that it is not necessary to involve (gross anatomical) differential localization to account for these phenomena, and that selective temporary or permanent inhibition of the neural substrate underlying each language is a more economical explanation (Paradis, 1977, 1980, 1983; Pitres, 1895). The case in favour of inhibition over differential localization is made even stronger by the recovery pattern of patients exhibiting alternate antagonism (Paradis, Goldblum, & Abidi, 1982). Because each language is alternately accessible while the other is not, its unavailability cannot be explained by the selective destruction of the neural substrate of one of the languages.

Recently a case of selective aphasia in a trilingual patient was observed (Paradis & Goldblum, in press). After surgical removal of a parasitic cyst in the right rolandic area, a 27-year-old male right-handed patient exhibited obvious language deficits in one of his three languages with no measurable deficits in the other two. He spoke Gujarati, Malagasy, and French before his operation. Gujarati was the language of his parents and relatives, and was spoken daily with them and with other members of the Indian Community of Madagascar. Malagasy was used daily with the local population. All of the patient's schooling was in French, the only language in which he was literate. He used French daily at work.

Postoperatively, the patient showed no deficits in French. However, after his family had complained that he had difficulties in Gujarati, he was tested in Gujarati and Malagasy. Malagasy did not reveal any measurable impairment. There were, however, noticeable deficits in Gujarati. The patient stuttered considerably, had a significantly depressed verbal fluency score (6 as opposed to 33 in French) and exhibited severe difficulties in naming as well as with our version of the token test (using real objects instead of tokens). Spontaneous speech was seriously hampered by his stuttering (which was totally absent in his other two languages).

Until then it was believed to be theoretically impossible to suffer aphasia in one language without some aphasia in the other. Freud wrote in 1891 "It never happens that an organic lesion causes an impairment affecting the mother tongue and not a later acquired language." Hemphill (1976) went one step further and states: "all languages are invariably affected."

The patient was seen again the following year in Montreal where he had gone to visit a relative. His performance on the French battery was comparable to his earlier pre- and post-operative performance in Paris, showing no measurable deficits. His Gujarati had been recovered over an eight-month period following his operation. However at the same time, his Malagasy had begun to deteriorate and when he was tested in November 1982 in Montreal, his Malagasy was laborious, anomic, and dyssyntactic.

In other words, the patient had undergone an antagonistic recovery, thus reinforcing the notion of selective inhibition and disinhibition operating over extended periods of time, and confirming the assumption that each language is stored as a separate neurofunctional system.

Likewise, because a given pattern of dissociation in Japanese patients may shift to a dissociation in the opposite direction over the recovery period, in a way reminiscent of the antagonistic recovery of some polyglot aphasic patients, it is reasonable to assume that each writing subsystem is independently susceptible to selective inhibition and disinhibition. This is additional evidence in support of the neurofunctional modularity hypothesis in that whatever can be selectively inhibited can reasonably be assumed to constitute a neurofunctional system, or subsystem, or component module.

In cases of differential, selective, successive and antagonistic recoveries, one language as a whole is clearly selectively impaired. We may therefore presume that each language (qua *langue*) consistutes a subsystem of the faculty of language (qua *langue*). The faculty of language itself as a whole is capable of pathological dissolution, as evidenced by cases of parallel recovery, and hence may be assumed to be subserved by one neurofunctional macrosystem. In other words, language (qua *langage*) constitutes a specific cognitive domain (as opposed to other cognitive domains, such as gnosis), fractionable into subsystems (various languages). Each language undergoes similar types of processes (though independently) as opposed to the types of processes used in other systems (e.g., object recognition).

Recently (Paradis, 1984), the point was made that not only are the two languages of a bilingual neurofunctionally distinct, but so is the ability to translate in each direction. Four independent (though obviously interconnected) systems have been shown to be involved in the performance of the cognitive task of interpretation (i.e., oral translation on demand): the system underlying the source language, that underlying the target language, and that underlying the connections between the source language and the target language, plus a fourth, underlying connections subserving translation in the opposite direction, when source and target languages are reversed.

Whereas differences in performance between oral comprehension and oral production could be accounted for by a single underlying system with different thresholds of activation (comprehension being easier than expression), translation from L_a to L_b and from L_b to L_a have been shown to be independent neurofunctional systems capable of double dissociation, as well as being independent with respect to which language is available for spontaneous expression, or indeed whether neither is available for use.

Systems underlying translation from L_a to L_b and L_b to L_a can be selectively inhibited so that translation is possible in any one direction and not in the other, irrespective of the availability of the source language or of the target language for spontaneous use (Paradis et al., 1982). In addition, translation can be impossible in both directions while both languages are available (Goldstein, 1948; Paradis et al., 1982 Case 1) or possible even though neither language is available for spontaneous use (Veyrac, 1931).

MODULAR ORGANIZATION OF THE BRAIN

Independently, the modular organization of cortical connections (Goldman-

Rakic, 1982), as well as the modular organization of the brain as a whole into relatively small units (Mountcastle, 1978) has been demonstrated. Local neural circuits of large numbers of cells linked together by a complex intramodular connectivity form multicellular modular units (Mountcastle, 1978). It is certainly not unreasonable to suppose that there exists a systematic connection between neurofunctional modules and neuroanatomical modules. Indeed, on the basis of evidence from rCBF studies in human subjects and from 2-deoxyglucose experiments in the non human primates, Goldman-Rakic (1982) argues that neuroanatomical modules may constitute a functional unit of brain activity, that neuronal explanations of higher order cognitive processes—including language—need to take account of the brain's predisposition to split its afferent and efferent connections into units (p. 470), that the segregated organization of connections may be important for information processing in general, and language processing in particular (ibid.). She insists on the fact that modular organization characterizes the fiber systems of association cortex as well as those of sensory systems. Similarly, Mountcastle (1978) considers that there is now general agreement that cytoarchitecturally different regions, together with their own unique set of extrinsic connections (i.e., patterns of thalamic, cortico-cortical, interhemispheric and long descending connections) subserve distinctive functions.

With respect to the localization of neural substrates underlying spoken language, reading and writing, we have not yet reached such a level of precision. Electrical stimulation techniques used on bilingual brains (Ojemann & Whitaker, 1978; Rapport, Tan, & Whitaker, 1983) are probably what comes closest to deliminating areas of cortex involves in language functions, but the method does not allow to isolate the various inextricably interwoven patterns of neural circuits subserving each language within the vast anatomical area that a square centimeter of stimulation represents. On the other hand, at a gross anatomical level, the correlation between site of lesion and type of dissociation between reading and/or writing *kana* and *kanji* points to a greater involvement of the left temporal area for *kana* processing, and of the left parieto-occipital area for *kanji* processing (see Paradis, Hagiwara, & Hildebrandt, 1985, Fig. 4.1-4.4). It seems equally appropriate to hypothesize that oral reading involves cortex in the traditional language area proper, whereas reading comprehension depends more crucially on cortex in the left parieto-occipital area (see Fig. 4.5 in Paradis et al., 1985).

Similar correlations have also been reported between site of lesion (temporal vs. occipito-parietal) and ability to read ideographic versus alphabetic script (Lyman, Kwan, & Chao, 1938), and between ability to write French (with a many-to-one correspondence between phoneme and grapheme) and Russian (with a one-to-one such correspondence) in the context of a preserved ability to read both languages, each language having a one-to-one correspondence between grapheme and phoneme (Luria, 1960).

SUMMARY AND CONCLUSIONS

In summary, the various dissociations in reading and writing displayed by Japanese patients and analyzed in Paradis et al. (1985) demonstrate the existence, at least in some individuals, of a functionally independent connection between graphic shape and sound, graphic shape and meaning, and meaning and sound, for each type of script, thus confirming the functional independence of neural subsystems in the processing of Japanese reading and writing. These data are interpreted as supporting Caramazza's (1984) basic assumption that cognitive processing is fractionable into processing components, that these components are fractionable into subcomponents, themselves fractionable into sub-subcomponent modules. This leads us to what Marshall (1982b) has termed *a mosaic model of the brain-mind in which functional modules map fairly directly onto discrete, punctuate but large anatomical modules.* Indeed some specific deficits have been shown to be consistently correlated with lesions in areas of the temporal lobes, others with lesions in the parieto-occipital region.

The evidence from polyglot aphasia indicates that language subdivides into as many neurofunctional subsystems as there are languages represented in a speaker-hearer's brain; languages themselves subdivide into various subsystems, most conspicuously reading and writing as differentiated from each other and from spoken language, which itself, of course, further subdivides, as attested by the various dissociation in aphasia reported over the past 50 years.

Modules, subsystems and systems (each with its own internal structure, mode of functioning and purpose) are presumed to be interconnected (and interactive in the normal course of events) but capable of functioning independently. Through their interconnections, activation of elements in one system can activate elements in another. Their autonomy is attested by selective impairment and selective preservation. A double dissociation between two subsystems or two modules is interpreted as evidence of their mutual independence. A module is defined as a horizontal processing component in a vertical system (or subsystem). It can be further assumed that the various neurofunctional modules are subserved by the same neural properties, the same basic organization of brain structure and the same neurophysiological processes. Thus learning language would make use of the same basic principles as learning anything else, except that it would recruit neurons in areas specific to the kinds of tasks required (partly depending on the modalities of acquisition, e.g., spoken language vs. sign language).

But what is most important is that (a) double dissociations in behavior do occur and are well-documented between languages of polyglot aphasics, between performance in either language and translation ability, as well as between the directions of translation, thus establishing each language (as well as translation in each direction) as a neurofunctional system; and that (b) double dissociations also occur and are well-documented between the reading of *kana* and the reading of *kanji*, the writing of *kana* and the writing of *kanji*, the reading and the writing of *kana*, the reading and the writing of *kanji*, oral reading and reading comprehension for *kana*, oral reading and reading comprehension for *kanji*, oral reading for *kana* and reading comprehension for *kanji* as well as oral reading for *kanji* and reading comprehension for *kana*.

If we are committed to the belief that cognitive behavior is an emergent property of systems of neurons (see Bunge, 1980), that in any event verbal behavior is anchored in the brain and derives from an underlying neural substrate, and that damage to, or inhibition of, the neural substrate results in behavior alteration, we are led to the conclusion that each language of the bilingual speaker-hearer is subserved by a distinct neurofunctional system, that the Japanese writing system is represented as a collection of neurofunctional subsystems, and that each subsystem further fractionates into a series of neurofunctional modules.

REFERENCES

Ajax, E. T. (1967). Dyslexia without dysgraphia. *Archives of Neurology, 17*, 645–652.

Ajax, E. T. (1977). Alexia without agraphia and the inferior splenium. *Neurology, 27*, 685–688.

Auerback, S. H., & Alexander, M. P. (1981). Pure agraphia and unilateral optic ataxia associated with left superior parietal lobule lesion. *Journal of Neurology, Neurosurgery and Psychiatry, 44*, 430–432.

Beauvois, M. F., & Dérouesné, J. (1979). Phonological alexia: Three dissociations. *Journal of Neurology, Neurosurgery and Psychiatry, 42*, 1115–1124.

Beauvois, M. F., & Dérouesné, J. (1981). Lexical or orthographic agraphia. *Brain, 104*, 21–49.

Bunge, M. (1980). *The mind-body problem, a psychobiological approach.* Oxford: Pergamon Press.

Caramazza, A. (1984). The logic of neuropsychological research and the problem of patient classification in aphasia. *Brain and Language, 21*, 9–20.

Caplan, L. R., & Hedley-Whyte, T. (1974). Cuing and memory dysfunction in alexia without agraphia. *Brain, 97*, 251–262.

Cohen, D. N., Salanga, V. D., Hully, W., Steinberg, M. C., & Hardy, R. (1976). Alexia without agraphia, *Neurology, 26*, 455–459.

Donoso, A., Santander, M., & Santos, G. (1980). Alexia without agraphia. Anatomoclinical analysis of a case. *Neurocirurgia, 38*, 29–37.

Dubois, J., Hécaen, H., Marcie P. (1969). L'agraphie "pure". *Neuropsychologia, 7*, 271–286.

Fau, R., Groslambert, R., Bertholet, M., Jeantet, M., & Demange, A. M. (1976). Directional agraphia with mirror writing. *Lyon Médical, 235*, 401–405.

Goldman-Rakic, P. S. (1982). Organization of frontal association cortex in normal and experimentally brain-injured primates. In M. A. Arbib, D. Caplan, & J. C. Marshall (Eds.), *Neural models of language processes* (pp. 460–484). New York: Academic Press.

Goldstein, K. (1948). *Language and language disturbances.* New York: Grune & Stratton.

Greenblatt, S. H. (1973). Alexia without agraphia or hemianopsia. *Brain, 96*, 307–316.

Heilman, K. M., Rotlui, L., Campanella, D., & Wolfson, S. (1979). Wernicke's and Global aphasia without alexia. *Archives of Neurology, 36,* 129–133.

Hemphill, R. E. (1976). Polyglot aphasia and polyglot hallucinations. In S. Krauss (Ed.), *Encyclopedic handbook of medical psychology* (pp. 398–400). London: Butterworth.

Johansson, T., & Fahlgren, H. (1979). Alexia without agraphia: Lateral and medial infarction of the occipital lobe. *Neurology, 29,* 390–393.

Judd, T., Gardner, H., & Geschwind, N. (1983). Alexia without agraphia in a composer. *Brain, 106,* 435–457.

Karanth, P. (1981). Pure alexia in a Kannada-English bilingual. *Cortex, 17,* 187–197.

Laine, T., & Marttila, R. J. (1981). Pure agraphia: A case study. *Neuropsychologia, 19,* 311–316.

Luria, A. R. (1960). Differences between disturbance of speech and writing in Russian and French. *International Journal of Slavic Linguistics and Poetry, 3,* 13–22.

Lyman, R., Kwan, S. T., & Chao, W. H. (1938). Left occipito-parietal brain tumor with observations on alexia and agraphia in Chinese and English. *Chinese Medical Journal, 54,* 491–516.

Mani, S. S., Fine, E. J., & Mayberry, A. (1981). Alexia without agraphia. Localization of the lesion of computerized tomography. *Computerized Tomography, 5,* 95–97.

Marshall, J. C. (1982a, March). *Taxonomies of dyslexia.* Lecture presented at the Montreal Neurological Institute.

Marshall, J. C. (1982b). What is a symptom-complex? In M. A. Arbib, D. Caplan, & J. C. Marshall (Eds.), *Neural models of language processes* (pp. 389–409). New York: Academic Press.

Michel, R., Schott, B., Boucher, M., & Kopp, N. (1979). Anatomical and clinical correlation in a case of alexia without agraphia. *Revue neurologique, 135,* 347–364.

Mountcastle, V. B. (1978). An organizing principle for cerebral function: the unit module and the distribution system. In G. M. Edelman & V. B. Mountcastle, *The mindful brain* (pp. 7–50). Cambridge: MIT Press.

Ohta, Y., & Koyabu, S. (1970). A clinical study on constructional agraphia in Japanese. *Psychiatria et Neurologia Japonica, 12,* 959–964.

Ojemann, G., & Whitaker, H. A. (1978). The bilingual brain. *Archives of Neurology, 35,* 409–412.

Paradis, M. (1977). Bilingualism and aphasia. In H. A. Whitaker & H. Whitaker (Eds.), *Studies in neurolinguistics* (Vol. 3, pp. 65–121). New York: Academic Press.

Paradis, M. (1980). Contributions of neurolinguistics to the theory of bilingualism. In R. K. Herbert (Ed.), *Applications of linguistic theory in the human sciences* (pp. 180–211). East Lansing: Michigan State University.

Paradis, M. (Ed.) (1983). *Readings on Aphasia in Bilinguals and Polyglots.* Montreal: Didier.

Paradis, M. (1984). Aphasie et traduction. *META, 29,* 57–67.

Paradis, M., & Goldblum, M. C. (in press). Selective crossed aphasia followed by reciprocal antagonism in a trilingual patient. *Journal of Neurolinguistics.*

Paradis, M., Goldblum, M. C., & Abidi, R. (1982). Alternate antagonism with paradoxical translation behavior in two bilingual patients. *Brain and Language, 15,* 55–69.

Paradis, M., Hagiwara, H., & Hildebrandt, N. (1985). *Neurolinguistic aspects of the Japanese writing system.* New York: Academic Press.

Pitres, A. (1895). Etude sur l'aphasie chez les polyglottes. *Revue de Médecine, 15,* 873–899.

Rapport, R. L., Tan, C. C., & Whitaker, H. A. (1983). Language function and dysfunction among Chinese- and English-speaking polyglots: Cortical stimulation, Wada testing, and clinical studies. *Brain and Language, 18,* 342–366.

Reinvang, I. R. (1975). Alexia without agraphia. A patient with rare aphasic symptoms. *T. Norske Laegeforen, 95,* 34–36.

Roeltgen, D. P., Sevush, S., & Heilman, K. M. (1983). Phonological agraphia: Writing by the lexical-semantic route. *Neurology, 33,* 755–765.

Sroka, H., Solsi, P., & Bornstein, B. (1973). Alexia without agraphia with complete recovery. *Confinia neurologica, 35,* 167176.

Turgman, J., Goldhammer, Y., & Braham, J. (1979). Alexia without agraphia, due to brain tumor: A reversible syndrome. *Annals of Neurology, 6,* 265–268.

Valenstein, E., & Heilman, K. M. (1979). Apraxic agraphia with neglect-induced paragraphia. *Archives of Neurology, 36,* 506–508.

Veyrac, G.-J. (1931). *Etude de l'aphasie chez les sujets polyglottes.* Thèse pour le doctorat en médecine, Université de Paris.

Vincent, F. M., Sadowsky, C. H., Saunders, R. L., & Reeves, A. G. (1977). Alexia without agraphia, hemianopia or color-naming deficit: A disconnection syndrome. *Neurology, 27,* 689–691.

Author Index

Subject Index